S0-BRX-528

Crocheting
FOR
DUMMIES®
2ND EDITION

by Karen Manthey, Susan Brittain, and Julie Armstrong Holetz

WILEY

Wiley Publishing, Inc.

Crocheting For Dummies®, 2nd Edition

Published by
Wiley Publishing, Inc.
111 River St.
Hoboken, NJ 07030-5774
www.wiley.com

Copyright © 2010 by Wiley Publishing, Inc., Indianapolis, Indiana

Published simultaneously in Canada

No part of this publication may be reproduced, stored in a retrieval system or transmitted in any form or by any means, electronic, mechanical, photocopying, recording, scanning or otherwise, except as permitted under Sections 107 or 108 of the 1976 United States Copyright Act, without either the prior written permission of the Publisher, or authorization through payment of the appropriate per-copy fee to the Copyright Clearance Center, 222 Rosewood Drive, Danvers, MA 01923, (978) 750-8400, fax (978) 646-8600. Requests to the Publisher for permission should be addressed to the Permissions Department, John Wiley & Sons, Inc., 111 River Street, Hoboken, NJ 07030, (201) 748-6011, fax (201) 748-6008, or online at http://www.wiley.com/go/permissions.

Trademarks: Wiley, the Wiley Publishing logo, For Dummies, the Dummies Man logo, A Reference for the Rest of Us!, The Dummies Way, Dummies Daily, The Fun and Easy Way, Dummies.com, Making Everything Easier, and related trade dress are trademarks or registered trademarks of John Wiley & Sons, Inc. and/or its affiliates in the United States and other countries, and may not be used without written permission. All other trademarks are the property of their respective owners. Wiley Publishing, Inc., is not associated with any product or vendor mentioned in this book.

LIMIT OF LIABILITY/DISCLAIMER OF WARRANTY: THE PUBLISHER AND THE AUTHOR MAKE NO REPRESENTATIONS OR WARRANTIES WITH RESPECT TO THE ACCURACY OR COMPLETENESS OF THE CONTENTS OF THIS WORK AND SPECIFICALLY DISCLAIM ALL WARRANTIES, INCLUDING WITHOUT LIMITATION WARRANTIES OF FITNESS FOR A PARTICULAR PURPOSE. NO WARRANTY MAY BE CREATED OR EXTENDED BY SALES OR PROMOTIONAL MATERIALS. THE ADVICE AND STRATEGIES CONTAINED HEREIN MAY NOT BE SUITABLE FOR EVERY SITUATION. THIS WORK IS SOLD WITH THE UNDERSTANDING THAT THE PUBLISHER IS NOT ENGAGED IN RENDERING LEGAL, ACCOUNTING, OR OTHER PROFESSIONAL SERVICES. IF PROFESSIONAL ASSISTANCE IS REQUIRED, THE SERVICES OF A COMPETENT PROFESSIONAL PERSON SHOULD BE SOUGHT. NEITHER THE PUBLISHER NOR THE AUTHOR SHALL BE LIABLE FOR DAMAGES ARISING HEREFROM. THE FACT THAT AN ORGANIZATION OR WEBSITE IS REFERRED TO IN THIS WORK AS A CITATION AND/OR A POTENTIAL SOURCE OF FURTHER INFORMATION DOES NOT MEAN THAT THE AUTHOR OR THE PUBLISHER ENDORSES THE INFORMATION THE ORGANIZATION OR WEBSITE MAY PROVIDE OR RECOMMENDATIONS IT MAY MAKE. FURTHER, READERS SHOULD BE AWARE THAT INTERNET WEBSITES LISTED IN THIS WORK MAY HAVE CHANGED OR DISAPPEARED BETWEEN WHEN THIS WORK WAS WRITTEN AND WHEN IT IS READ.

For general information on our other products and services, please contact our Customer Care Department within the U.S. at 877-762-2974, outside the U.S. at 317-572-3993, or fax 317-572-4002.

For technical support, please visit www.wiley.com/techsupport.

Wiley also publishes its books in a variety of electronic formats. Some content that appears in print may not be available in electronic books.

Library of Congress Control Number: 2010920653

ISBN: 978-0-470-53645-2

Manufactured in the United States of America

10 9 8 7 6 5

WILEY

About the Authors

Karen Manthey discovered her passion for crochet during the 1970s while she was working as a graphic artist. In 1984, her training in art and understanding of crochet led her to a job illustrating the magazine *Crochet Fantasy*. Her task was to create the intricate crochet diagrams that accompany many of today's patterns. She soon moved on to become editor of the magazine, all the while continuing to do the illustrations and frequently designing projects for publication. After 20 years of working in an office, Karen now works from home, devoting her time to freelance technical editing and crochet diagrams for numerous books, magazines, yarn companies, and designers.

Susan Brittain's fascination with crochet began very early, around 4 or 5 years of age. She would watch her grandmother, who had lost her sight in midlife, spend hours crocheting beautiful afghans for friends and family, counting the stitches with her fingers. By the age of 8, Susan was crocheting her own projects, starting with simple patterns such as scarves and moving on to afghans, toys, and sweaters. Although her creative streak has led her to learn many different crafts, crochet has been a steady thread throughout. Susan combined work with pleasure as assistant editor for *Crochet Fantasy* magazine for a little more than two years, contributing as a designer as well. After moving west with her family, she continues to crochet and design pieces for various yarn companies.

Julie Armstrong Holetz was a child of the '70s — flower power, bell bottoms, macramé, and crochet. Taking what she learned from her mom, Julie's first crochet projects were simple squares that made perfect blankets for her dolls. Throughout her life, Julie has experimented with other arts and crafts, but she always returns to the meditative comfort of crochet. In 2005, Julie started her own business working as a freelance writer, editor, and designer in the craft industry. She has designed patterns for several popular books and magazines and serves as a freelance technical editor for prominent craft book publishers and magazines such as *Interweave Crochet, Knitscene,* Potter Craft, and Interweave Press. Julie lives, plays, and crochets on the eastside of Seattle with her husband and two children.

Dedication

To Karen's husband, Darryl Manthey, for teaching her the meaning of perseverance, and to her daughter, Tanya Manthey, for her patience and her sense of humor, which have kept her mother going through this project and everything else.

To Susan's husband, Paul Brittain, for his love, support, and understanding, and to her daughter, Angela, for putting up with the mess and the crazy schedule, and for waiting until I finished "just one more row."

To Julie's mom, Traudl Foster, for encouraging her to be fearless in the face of creativity, and to her daughter, Ally Holetz, for helping her pick colors when there were so many to choose from.

Authors' Acknowledgments

We would like to thank Mike Lewis, our acquisitions editor, who was always there to put us on the right track, providing encouragement and support when we needed it.

Special thanks to Georgette Beatty, our project editor, whose keen insights and suggestions made our book the best it could be.

Thank you to Jennifer Tebbe, our copy editor, and Judith Obee, our technical reviewer, for carefully reviewing our work.

Thanks also to Rachel Russ and Sylvia Hager at Blue Sky Alpacas, Peggy Wells at Brown Sheep Co., Margery Winter at Berroco, Inc., Cilene Martins-Castro at DMC Corporation, Jeanne Duncan at Fiesta Yarns, and Jean Dunbabin at Cascade Yarns for generously providing yarns for the projects featured in this book.

Thank you to Alicia South, art coordinator, for her stylish perspective, and to Matt Bowen, photographer, for his beautiful photography.

Thanks to Swati Gunale, Mallory King, Jacqueline Porter, and Madeline Jakowczyk, the models who helped make our crochet come to life, and to Lukas and Jodie Gogis for the use of their beautiful home where several of the photographs were taken.

From Karen

Special thanks go to my husband, Darryl, for his encouragement, patience, love, and support. Also, thanks to my daughter, Tanya, for putting up with the mess, the late (and less-than-perfect) meals, as well as my lack of attention and focus. I couldn't have done it without you both.

Additional thanks go to Susan, my original partner in this project, for her optimistic approach to life. Thanks for giving me the courage to face this challenge and not letting me give up before we even began.

And finally, thanks to Julie for bringing her excellent sense of style and creativity to this second edition of *Crocheting For Dummies*.

From Susan

Special thanks go out, first and foremost, to my husband, Paul, for his unfailing support (once again) throughout the whole writing process. Without his encouragement and support, this book may never have come to be.

Thanks also to my daughter, Angela, who constantly urged me to "keep going and get it done" and gave me the time I needed to pull all the new material together.

Thanks again to Karen for her expertise, for making sure the work came in on time, and for catching the slips that I missed.

Finally, thanks to Julie for her hard work and for providing a fresh new look to the patterns and introducing a "greener" way to crochet.

From Julie

I am so thankful for my husband, Steve, who is always patient and supportive, especially when deadlines loom. The whole family thanks him for stepping in when I threatened to make burritos for the fourth night in a row.

Special thanks go to my children, Thad and Ally, who banded together when I had to write and couldn't play.

Thanks also to Karen for her thoughtful insight on the technical aspects of crochet stitches and illustrations. I am envious of her talent.

I am very grateful to Megan Granholm, who deftly crocheted a few of the project samples, making my deadlines easier to achieve.

And finally, many thanks to Sue for her guidance, support, and expertise — all of which helped make the project flow smoothly and on time.

Publisher's Acknowledgments

We're proud of this book; please send us your comments at http://dummies.custhelp.com. For other comments, please contact our Customer Care Department within the U.S. at 877-762-2974, outside the U.S. at 317-572-3993, or fax 317-572-4002.

Some of the people who helped bring this book to market include the following:

Acquisitions, Editorial, and Media Development

Senior Project Editor: Georgette Beatty
(Previous Edition: Laura B. Peterson, Christina Guthrie, Kelly Ewing, Marcia L. Johnson)

Acquisitions Editor: Michael Lewis

Copy Editor: Jennifer Tebbe
(Previous Edition: Kristin DeMint, Esmeralda St. Clair)

Assistant Editor: Erin Calligan Mooney

Editorial Program Coordinator: Joe Niesen

Technical Editor: Judith Obee

Editorial Manager: Michelle Hacker

Editorial Assistant: Jennette ElNaggar

Art Coordinator: Alicia B. South

Cover Photo: Color Photography by Matt Bowen

Cartoons: Rich Tennant
(www.the5thwave.com)

Composition Services

Project Coordinator: Katherine Crocker

Layout and Graphics: Timothy C. Detrick, Joyce Haughey, Nikki Gately, Melissa K. Jester, Mark Pinto, Christine Williams

Special Art: Color Photography by Matt Bowen

Proofreaders: Melissa Cossell, Betty Kish

Indexer: Christine Karpeles

Publishing and Editorial for Consumer Dummies

    Diane Graves Steele, Vice President and Publisher, Consumer Dummies

    Kristin Ferguson-Wagstaffe, Product Development Director, Consumer Dummies

    Ensley Eikenburg, Associate Publisher, Travel

    Kelly Regan, Editorial Director, Travel

Publishing for Technology Dummies

    Andy Cummings, Vice President and Publisher, Dummies Technology/General User

Composition Services

    Debbie Stailey, Director of Composition Services

GARY PUBLIC LIBRARY

Contents at a Glance

Introduction 1

Part I: Crochet 101 5

Chapter 1: Hooking into a Life of Crochet 7
Chapter 2: Tools of the Trade 15
Chapter 3: Creating Consistency with Gauge 33
Chapter 4: Decoding Crochet Patterns 41

Part II: Basic Stitches and Techniques 57

Chapter 5: Focusing on Fundamental Stitches 59
Chapter 6: Long, Longer, Longest: Several Common Crochet Stitches 89
Chapter 7: Shaping Up and Slimming Down: Increasing and
Decreasing Stitches 117
Chapter 8: I've Been Here Before: Crocheting in Circles 131
Chapter 9: Crocheting in Technicolor 155

Part III: Advanced Stitches and Techniques 169

Chapter 10: Fancy Stitches That Steal the Show 171
Chapter 11: Creating Texture in Unexpected Ways 187
Chapter 12: Like Knitting with a Hook: Tunisian Crochet 209
Chapter 13: Filet and Mesh Crochet: Creating a New Style 231
Chapter 14: Building on Your Skills with Motifs 255

Part IV: Putting It All Together 269

Chapter 15: Connecting the Parts: Joining Seams 271
Chapter 16: Design 101: Crocheting Your First Sweater 291
Chapter 17: Finishing Functionally: Borders, Buttons, and Pockets 307
Chapter 18: It's All in the Details: Embellishing Crochet 329
Chapter 19: Neatness Counts: Fixing, Blocking, and Caring for Your Work 335

Part V: The Part of Tens 349

Chapter 20: Ten Ways to Do Good with Crochet 351
Chapter 21: Ten Variations on Crochet 361

Appendix: Sources and Resources 369

Index 373

3 9222 03182 0025

GARY PUBLIC LIBRARY

Table of Contents

Introduction 1

About This Book...1
Conventions Used in This Book...2
What You're Not to Read..2
Foolish Assumptions..2
How This Book Is Organized 3
    Part I: Crochet 101 3
    Part II: Basic Stitches and Techniques.........................3
    Part III: Advanced Stitches and Techniques.................3
    Part IV: Putting It All Together 3
    Part V: The Part of Tens 4
Icons Used in This Book 4
Where to Go from Here...4

Part 1: Crochet 101 5

Chapter 1: Hooking into a Life of Crochet 7

Starting with Crochet Fundamentals 8
    Gathering all of your tools..8
    Adjusting tension..9
    Crocheting from a pattern 9
Mastering Basic Crochet Techniques 10
    Practice makes perfect...10
    Shape up..10
    Round and round you go 10
    Color it in 11
Adding New Stitches and Techniques to Your Crochet Repertoire 11
    Having fun with new stitches 11
    Creating funky fabrics 11
    Being square (and other shapes too).......................12
Finishing Your Work: Taking Pride in What You've Made 12
    Putting the pieces together 12
    Tending to the final details 12
    Taking care of your crochet masterpieces................13
Making Your Crochet Experience a Good One Overall....13

Chapter 2: Tools of the Trade 15

The One Tool You Can't Do Without: A Crochet Hook......15
    Surveying the anatomy of a crochet hook................15
    Looking at the make and size of hooks 17

Figuring Out Yarn Features and Functions 20
   Sizing up yarn weights 20
   Checking out the different types of yarn 22
   Sorting out yarn packaging...24
   Deciphering yarn labels 25
   Matching your yarn to your project..27
Tool Time: Other Tools of the Trade..29
   Gathering basic tools 29
   Treating yourself to little luxuries 31

Chapter 3: Creating Consistency with Gauge **33**
Understanding Why You Should Bother with Gauge................................33
Working a Gauge Swatch 34
   Making your swatch the right size..35
   Blocking your swatch 36
   Measuring stitches and rows 36
   Measuring stitches and rounds..37
   Over- or undershooting the mark...38
Flying Solo: Establishing Your Own Gauge..39

Chapter 4: Decoding Crochet Patterns **41**
Breaking Down the Sections of a Crochet Pattern 41
Figuring Out Written Instructions 43
   Keeping it short with abbreviations...43
   Working terms and phrases 46
   Pondering parentheses 46
   Bracing yourself for brackets...47
   Interpreting special symbols in written patterns 48
   Repeating rows and rounds..49
Not Just a Pretty Picture: Stitch Symbols and Diagrams........................50
   Cracking the International Crochet Symbols code.........................51
   Following a stitch diagram...52

Part II: Basic Stitches and Techniques **57**

Chapter 5: Focusing on Fundamental Stitches **59**
In the Beginning: Preparing to Crochet 59
   Determining the correct hand for hooking....................................59
   Getting a grip on the hook and yarn..60
   Working a slipknot...63
   Wrapping the yarn over the hook...65
Tied Up in Stitches: The Three Basics..66
   The (almost) universal starter: Chain stitch.................................66
   The utility stitch: Slip stitch 70
   The old standby: Single crochet...72

Foundation Stitches: The Chain and the First Row All in One 74
Your first foundation single crochet 75
Your second foundation single crochet and beyond 76
Taking Things to the Next Level: Row Two 78
Turning your work 78
Climbing to new heights with turning chains 79
Starting the next row 80
The Anatomy of a Stitch 82
All's Well That Ends Well: Fastening Off 83
Cutting the yarn 83
Weaving in the end 84
Luxurious Washcloth Projects 84
Simple Luxurious Washcloth project 84
Luxurious Washcloth with Border project 85
Baby washcloth 88

**Chapter 6: Long, Longer, Longest: Several Common
Crochet Stitches** **89**
Doing a Double Crochet 90
First things first: Row 1 90
Turning around and beginning again: Row 2 92
Trying Your Hand at the Triple Crochet 94
Starting with Row 1 94
Moving on to Row 2 96
Diving into Double Triple Crochet 97
First things first: Row 1 97
Turning around and beginning again: Row 2 99
Hooking a Half Double Crochet 100
Starting with Row 1 101
Moving on to Row 2 102
Creating Even More Height Variation with Extended Stitches 104
Extended single crochet 104
Extended double crochet 107
Running on Empty: Joining a New Ball of Yarn 109
Joining at the end of a row 110
Joining in the middle of a row 111
Sassy Scarf Project 112
Materials and vital statistics 112
Directions 113
Finishing 115

**Chapter 7: Shaping Up and Slimming Down: Increasing
and Decreasing Stitches** **117**
Making It Grow: Increasing Stitches 118
Increasing anywhere with single crochet 118
Increasing with double crochet at the beginning of a row 119
Increasing with double crochet in the middle or end
of a row 120

Diminishing Results: Decreasing Stitches 121
    Decreasing with single crochet 121
    Decreasing with double crochet 123
    Decreasing with slip stitches at the start of a row 125
    Decreasing by skipping stitches 126
    Decreasing by stopping and turning before you reach
        the end of a row 126
Simple Ripple Blanket Project 127
    Materials and vital statistics 127
    Directions 128
    Optional directions for different sizes 130

Chapter 8: I've Been Here Before: Crocheting in Circles 131

Lord of the Center Rings 131
    Joining chain stitches into a ring 132
    Working stitches in the chain stitch 134
    Working stitches in an adjustable ring 136
Uniting Your Ring 138
    Single crochet 138
    Double crochet and other stitches 139
Adding Rounds 139
    The second round of single crochet 140
    The second round of double crochet 140
Another Option: Spiraling Up and Up 142
    Working in a spiral 142
    Ending the spiral 143
Adding Another Dimension 143
    Starting to add dimension 143
    Deciding how to wrap up your work 144
Bucket Hat Project 145
    Materials and vital statistics 146
    Directions 146
Amigurumi Pup Project 149
    Materials and vital statistics 149
    Directions 149
    Assembly 154

Chapter 9: Crocheting in Technicolor 155

Bringing Designs to Life: Joining Colors 155
    Changing color at the beginning (or end) 156
    Changing color midstream 157
Hitching a Ride: Carrying the Yarn 158
    Carrying on the wrong side 158
    Working over a carried strand 159
    Carrying on the right side 160
    Carrying up the side 161

Demystifying Color Codes and Charts......................................162
    Abbreviating color names in patterns 162
    Charting color change...163
Crafty Math: Understanding the Fibonacci Sequence 164
Mod Pillow Project 165
    Materials and vital statistics 166
    Directions...166
    Finishing..168

Part III: Advanced Stitches and Techniques 169

Chapter 10: Fancy Stitches That Steal the Show 171

Spicing Things Up with Pattern Stitches 171
    Showing the V: The V-stitch 172
    Seeing XXXs: The crossed double crochet stitch......172
    Spreading out: The shell stitch 173
    Grouping multiple like stitches: The cluster stitch.....174
    Getting decorative: The picot stitch..........................175
    Working backward: The reverse single crochet stitch.................176
Moving into the Third Dimension with Texture Stitches.......177
    Gently bumping along: The bobble stitch 178
    Not a magic dragon: The puff stitch 179
    Forget the butter: The popcorn stitch 180
    Feeling loopy: The loop stitch 182
Elegant All-Season Wrap Project 183
    Materials and vital statistics 183
    Directions...184
    Finishing..186

Chapter 11: Creating Texture in Unexpected Ways...............187

Switching Up Your Stitch Placement 187
    Working into the top and other loops........................188
    Stitching up the sides...189
Bucking Tradition and Working Stitches in Spaces and
  Other Interesting Places...190
    Squeezing into spaces 190
    Going around the middle with post stitches...............191
    Solidifying fabric with linked stitches 195
    Spiking into previous rows 198
When Shrinking Is A-Okay: Felting Your Crocheted Projects 200
    Felting by machine..201
    Felting by hand...201
Textured Scarf Project 202
    Materials and vital statistics 202
    Directions...202
    Finishing..203

Basketweave Scarf Project 203
Materials and vital statistics 204
Directions...204
Felted Shoulder Bag Project..205
Materials and vital statistics 205
Directions...206
Finishing..208

Chapter 12: Like Knitting with a Hook: Tunisian Crochet.........209

Taking a Look at Tunisian Crochet Tools....................210
Creating the Tunisian Simple Stitch...........................211
Starting with a foundation row 212
Continuing to the second row and beyond 213
Binding off..214
Shaping the Tunisian Simple Stitch.............................215
Increasing in Tunisian simple stitch................215
Decreasing in Tunisian simple stitch 216
Varying Your Tunisian Crochet 217
Tunisian knit stitch...217
Tunisian purl stitch 219
Coloring Your Tunisian Crochet..................................221
Crocheting with more than one color.............221
Cross-stitching on top of Tunisian crochet....224
Absorbent Hand Towel Project 227
Materials and vital statistics 227
Directions...228
Finishing..229

Chapter 13: Filet and Mesh Crochet: Creating a New Style.......231

Filet Crochet for Newbies...232
Breaking down filet crochet stitches...............232
Following a chart..232
Chaining the foundation....................................234
Creating spaces..234
Building blocks...236
Combining spaces and blocks............................237
Diving into Deeper Waters: Shaping Your Filet Crochet Design............238
Increasing spaces and blocks............................238
Decreasing spaces and blocks 244
Spacin' Out with Lacets and Bars................................246
Getting fancy with lacets...................................246
Bridging the gap with bars 247
Making Mesh, the Simplest Lace 248
Butterfly Runner Project...250
Materials and vital statistics 250
Directions...250
Optional directions for corner variation 251
Finishing..252

String Market Bag Project...252
    Materials and vital statistics 252
    Directions...253

Chapter 14: Building on Your Skills with Motifs 255

Granny's a Square: Cornering Your Rounds 255
    The first round 256
    The second round..256
    The third round and beyond 257
Don't Be Square: Motifs of Different Shapes 258
    The lacy hexagon motif...258
    The flat flower motif 260
    The layered flower motif 261
Raindrop Earrings Project...264
    Materials and vital statistics 264
    Directions...265
    Finishing...265
    Assembly..265
Flower Power Project..266
    Materials and vital statistics 266
    Directions...266
    Finishing...268

Part IV: Putting It All Together 269

Chapter 15: Connecting the Parts: Joining Seams. 271

Sewing Pieces Together..272
    Whipping up the whipstitch for shorter stitches 272
    Saving the blanket stitch for taller stitches................................274
    Creating invisible seams with the mattress stitch 275
    Fashioning sturdy seams with the backstitch.............................278
Crocheting Pieces Together...280
    Joining with a slip stitch seam 281
    Joining with single crochet...283
    Joining with a row of stitches..284
    Joining on the last row or round...286
Granny Square Cuff Project...288
    Materials and vital statistics 288
    Directions...289
    Finishing...290
    Assembly..290

Chapter 16: Design 101: Crocheting Your First Sweater 291

Choosing Stitches and Yarn for Your Sweater...............................292
    Making the right pattern choice 292
    Finding the right yarn..293

Selecting a Super Sweater Style..294
    Baring your arms: Sleeveless sweaters..............................294
    Going the classic route: Pullovers.....................................295
    Buttoning up: Cardigans..296
    Getting visually interesting: Motifs and vertical rows.........297
Sizing Up the Sweater Situation...298
    Understanding sweater pattern sizes.................................298
    Figuring out fit...299
    Customizing your pattern..300
Simple Sweater Project...301
    Materials and vital statistics..302
    Directions...302
    Assembly..306
    Finishing...306

Chapter 17: Finishing Functionally: Borders, Buttons, and Pockets...307
Adding Trims: Edgings, Borders, and Collars.............................307
    Outlining your designs with edging....................................308
    Bordering your masterpieces with ribbing..........................308
    Gracing your neck with a common collar............................312
Holding Things Together: Buttonholes, Ties, and Drawstrings.....313
    Making room for buttons: Buttonholes...............................313
    Keeping your clothes on (or just spicing them up):
        Ties and drawstrings..318
Purely Pockets...319
    Patch pockets: Tacked onto the front................................319
    Slashed pockets: Slotted in the front................................320
    Inseam pockets: Positioned at your sides
        for ultimate convenience...320
Girl's Versatile Camisole Project...321
    Materials and vital statistics..321
    Directions...322
    Assembly..326
    Finishing...326

Chapter 18: It's All in the Details: Embellishing Crochet.........329
Hanging Off the Edge: Fringe and Tassels.................................329
    Tying a piece together with fringe.....................................330
    Tacking on tassels..331
Adding Special Touches with Buttons and Embroidery................333
    Attaching unique buttons..333
    Easing into elegant embroidery..334

Chapter 19: Neatness Counts: Fixing, Blocking, and Caring for Your Work 335

    Troubleshooting Mistakes as You Crochet...........................335
        You're struggling to fit your hook into the stitches 336
        The edges of the fabric are shrinking................................336
        The edges of the fabric are getting wider............................337
        The foundation edge is tighter than the rest of the fabric 337
        The corners are curled...338
    Blocking Your Way into Perfect Shape 338
        The essential tools..339
        Wet blocking...340
        Spray blocking..341
        Heat blocking...342
        Blocking with starch...343
    Shaping Three-Dimensional Designs with Household Items.............345
    From This Day Forward: Caring for Your Work.......................346
        Scrub-a-dub-dub: Washing your work.............................346
        Rest in peace, dear sweater: Storing your work 347

Part V: The Part of Tens 349

Chapter 20: Ten Ways to Do Good with Crochet...................351

    Share Your Passion with a Crochet Basket............................351
    Host a Stash Swap Party for Friends 351
    Teach Someone How to Crochet 352
    Donate Crochet Supplies to Community Groups 352
    Crochet for a Cause...352
    Buy Local Yarn...353
    Use Eco-Friendly Fibers and Natural-Colored Yarn 353
    Crochet Green Items for Your Home 354
    Recycle Old Fabric with a Crocheted Rag Rug 354
        Materials and vital statistics 355
        Directions..355
    Save the Planet One Crocheted Bag at a Time........................357
        Materials and vital statistics 357
        Directions..358

Chapter 21: Ten Variations on Crochet........................361

    Irish Crochet 361
    Free-Form Crochet..362
    Surface Crochet 363
    Tapestry Crochet..364
    Broomstick Lace..364

Hairpin Lace 365
Double-Ended Crochet 366
Crocheting on Fabric.. 366
Bead Crochet.. 367
Wire Crochet 368

Appendix: Sources and Resources.................................. 369

Yarn Sources 369
Crochet Magazines 370
Online Crochet Communities.. 371
The Crochet Guild of America 371

Index 373

Introduction

· ·

*N*o longer is crocheting considered something your grandmother did while sitting on the porch in her rocking chair. Crocheted designs are everywhere, from the racks in your favorite clothing store to fashion catalogs — even to the runways in Paris and Milan. Celebrities have started crocheting, and the craft even shows up in movies and television shows. The reasons for this comeback are many, and we hope that by reading this book you discover some of those reasons and begin to enjoy a lifelong affair with crochet.

Even though crochet is a time-honored craft, that doesn't mean it's behind the times. Advances in technology have made yarns softer and more colorful, with wonderful new textures appearing every time you turn around. No longer are crocheters limited to solid or variegated colors; yarn is now hand painted and space dyed. Although worsted-weight yarn is still a staple in every crocheter's yarn cache, so many varieties of weights and textures are available today that we're at a loss as to how to categorize them all.

You're never too old or too young to discover crochet. The skills that you master, the benefits that you receive, and the beautiful heirlooms that you create can last a lifetime and, ideally, be passed on to future generations.

About This Book

Crocheting For Dummies, 2nd Edition, gives first-time crocheters hands-on experience with new skills and serves as a reference tool for those who already have some basic crochet know-how. We kick off the book by taking you step by step through the process of gathering your materials, crocheting your first stitches, and finishing off a piece of crocheted fabric. If that sounds somewhat overwhelming, relax. We include detailed written instructions and easy-to-follow illustrations throughout this book.

Each part of *Crocheting For Dummies,* 2nd Edition, contains chapters full of information relevant to each other, with successive parts adding more building blocks to your crochet knowledge. If you already have some crochet experience and are looking to refine and expand your techniques, then the later chapters are for you. There we include more advanced stitches and techniques, along with many tips to guide you. Finally, each part contains several projects that allow you to practice your newfound skills on fun and useful designs while feeling a sense of accomplishment for a job well done.

Conventions Used in This Book

We use the following conventions throughout the book to make the world of crochet easier for you to dive into:

- ✔ New terms appear in *italics* and are closely followed by an easy-to-understand definition.

- ✔ **Bold** text highlights the action parts of numbered steps.

- ✔ Web addresses appear in `monofont`. (Some URLs may have broken across multiple lines as we laid out this book, but rest assured we haven't added any spaces or hyphens. Just type in the address as you see it.)

- ✔ When we first introduce a new stitch or technique, we include its abbreviation in parentheses to help you become familiar with the shorthand used in crochet patterns. We also include the abbreviation the first time a stitch is mentioned in a set of numbered steps.

- ✔ The specific part of an illustration that relates to the step you're working on is shaded dark gray. For example, if you're inserting your hook into a certain stitch, that stitch is shaded so you can see exactly where to go.

What You're Not to Read

We hope, of course, that you read every word in this book, but if you're short on time, don't worry — feel free to skip sidebars (the shaded gray boxes throughout the chapters). They contain interesting information, but they're not crucial to your understanding of crochet.

Foolish Assumptions

How does that saying about assuming something go? Well, never mind about that. We explain each step as clearly and concisely as possible, so you don't need any prior experience to understand the concepts introduced in this book.

We are assuming, however, that by picking up this book, you have a desire to master the art of crochet. Beyond that, all we ask is that you give it your best shot and don't give up.

How This Book Is Organized

Crocheting For Dummies, 2nd Edition, is divided into five parts, with a total of 21 chapters and one appendix. Each part focuses on a different aspect of crochet. Here's a rundown of what each part contains.

Part I: Crochet 101

Part I tells you all about the craft of crochet and the many benefits you can derive from it. It describes the tools you need to get started and how to wade through the abundance of materials on the market. This part also explains what gauge is (and why it's so important) and decodes crochet abbreviations and instructions so you can follow them with ease.

Part II: Basic Stitches and Techniques

Here's where we really start getting down to the nuts and bolts of crochet. Part II offers fully illustrated, step-by-step instructions on creating the basic stitches upon which almost all crochet is based. It also opens the door to several basic techniques, such as increasing and decreasing to shape your work, crocheting in the round, and working with more than one color at once.

Part III: Advanced Stitches and Techniques

Part III introduces you to the many ways you can combine the basic stitches to create a variety of common stitch patterns. Here you discover how to create multiple textures by working in different places within a stitch and how to magically transform your project from loose and flimsy to sturdy and solid. Finally, you encounter three new techniques that are well worth exploring: Tunisian crochet, filet crochet, and motifs.

Part IV: Putting It All Together

Sometimes you may need to crochet a project in separate sections rather than one whole piece. Part IV to the rescue! It introduces you to the basics of sweater construction with projects that include a pullover sweater and a simple camisole. It also shows you the various methods for joining pieces of crocheted fabric to create a whole. And not only do you discover how to add special touches, embellishments, and final details but you also find out how to turn your slightly rumpled pieces into smooth and shapely designs.

Part V: The Part of Tens

Part V includes a list of ten activities that allow you to share your talent and passion for crochet with others. And because seeing the many ways you can vary crochet is a kick, we include a list of ten variations for you to check out. Last, but certainly not least, following this part is an appendix of sources and resources that you'll find handy as you continue your crocheting journey.

Icons Used in This Book

 This icon highlights important points. You should remember them and apply them when dealing with the skills shown.

 This icon clues you in to some tips of the trade that more experienced crocheters have discovered over time.

 When you see this icon, read carefully. It marks potential pitfalls and helps you steer clear of frustrating and time-consuming mistakes.

Where to Go from Here

Now that the introductions are over, it's time to begin. The fun part is that where you start is entirely up to you! *Crocheting For Dummies,* 2nd Edition, is written so you can start reading whatever section best fits your skill level.

- ✔ If you're an absolute beginner, we suggest starting with Part I. It has all the essential information that you need to begin crocheting.

- ✔ If you already have some experience with the basics and want to expand your knowledge, then look ahead to the chapters on more advanced stitches and techniques. Whenever we feel that you should know something that was covered in a previous chapter, we refer you to that chapter.

- ✔ If you used to crochet and are coming back to it (sometimes life just gets too busy for fun stuff like this), skim through the chapters to reacquaint yourself with the techniques. The stitches themselves haven't changed, but the materials have, and you may come across some useful info.

Part I
Crochet 101

The 5th Wave

By Rich Tennant

"That one? That's your P-100 industrial hook, used mostly for crocheting chain-link fences, mesh grill tops, that sort of thing."

In this part . . .

This part unlocks the deep, dark mystery of crochet and sets you on a journey to discover a whole new skill and a lifetime of crocheting pleasure. Here, we introduce you to the tools and materials you need to begin crocheting. And if you've ever tried to read a crochet pattern and wondered, "What does all this gibberish mean?" wonder no more; we introduce you to the terminology, abbreviations, and symbolic language of crochet in the following pages. We also explain the importance of gauge and how it affects everything you crochet. By the end of this part, you'll be ready to start playing with some basic crochet skills.

Chapter 1

Hooking into a Life of Crochet

In This Chapter

▶ Beginning with the basics of crochet

▶ Surveying fundamental techniques

▶ Expanding your selection of stitches and techniques

▶ Wrapping up your projects and sharing tips for a lifetime of happy crocheting

Crochet has numerous beneficial qualities. Here are just a few of them:

✔ The soothing rhythm of creating stitches can calm even the most frazzled nerves. If you're one of those people who can't stand to be idle, crochet is a wonderful way to let your body get a bit of rest and not feel like you're wasting time. If your family is always clamoring for you to sit down and watch a TV show or a special movie at night, go ahead, but bring along your hook and yarn.

✔ Crochet is also a wonderful take-along project. You can crochet on family road trips as well as on trains and planes (although you'll have to use plastic hooks when crocheting on public transportation these days).

✔ According to psychological studies that have been done on the benefits of crochet, the focus needed to create something takes your mind off the bazillion little things hollering for your attention and gives your brain some much-needed downtime.

✔ Crochet also serves as an outlet for your creativity and provides a sense of satisfaction when you complete your design and can look at it and say, "I created this myself."

✔ Crochet has physical benefits as well. People suffering from various forms of arthritis have used it as a form of physical therapy. The constant movement required helps keep the hands limber and the joints from stiffening up.

We hope that at least one of these reasons is enough to set you on the path to practicing this enjoyable craft. To find out more about crochet, take a look at the basics we present in this chapter.

Starting with Crochet Fundamentals

If you're like most people these days, finding the time to figure out something new can be a challenge. With crochet, you can pick it up when you have some time, put it down when you don't, or take it with you on the run. There's no mess to clean up and nothing to babysit. And you can easily find hooks and yarn at your local discount or craft store, as well as at the many specialty yarn stores that have cropped up in many towns. Basically, you don't need to wait to start crocheting while you special order some obscure item.

In the following sections, we introduce you to the fundamentals of crochet: the tools you need, how to measure gauge, and how to decipher crochet patterns. These fundamentals are what you need to know to successfully start your new crochet hobby.

Gathering all of your tools

One of the greatest things about crochet is that you don't need to invest in tons of fancy materials or create a new room in your house to store a bunch of equipment. All you need to get started are a couple hooks, preferably from different manufacturers so you can find a style you're comfortable with, and a skein of yarn. You probably have the other stuff that you need, such as a pair of scissors, a bag to keep all of your supplies in, and a comfy place to sit, at home already.

Chapter 2 gives you the skinny on the various types of hooks and yarns, as well as some of the other crochet gadgets available. As with any new undertaking, understanding the basics about the materials that you're working with is essential.

If you bought this book ten minutes ago and are already at the yarn shop, you probably just want to get a cheap hook and some yarn so you can start practicing stitches right away. Here's what you need to get started (for less than $5):

✔ **A size H-8 U.S. (5 mm) crochet hook:** This size hook is comfortable to work with, and the size of stitch it creates is easy to see.

✔ **A light, solid-colored, worsted-weight yarn, preferably made of acrylic or wool fibers:** Acrylic and wool yarns are great for practicing with because they're inexpensive, and light-colored yarn is best initially because you may have a hard time seeing your stitches if the yarn you're working with is too dark or multicolored.

Gibberish anyone?

A while back, we had an experience that shows just how funny crochet instructions can look when you're not familiar with the terminology. A young girl was leafing through a crochet magazine looking at the pictures, or so we thought. When we started paying attention to the noises she was making, we laughed so hard our sides split. The girl was reading the instructions phonetically (*ch 3, dc in next sc, sc in next dc,* see what we mean?). Try this with one of the patterns at the ends of the chapters, and you'll see what we mean. Crochet abbreviations really can look like a bunch of gibberish. Don't worry, though; they're actually pretty simple to decipher, as you find out in Chapter 4.

Adjusting tension

Making sure that your finished projects end up being the correct size is important. After all, who needs a doily the size of a coaster or an afghan that can double as a slipcover for a sectional couch?

By using some simple math and working a gauge swatch (see Chapter 3), you ensure that your stitches are the right size and tension for your design. So don't skip over the stuff at the beginning of the pattern directions; checking your materials and gauge keeps you out of trouble.

Crocheting from a pattern

Even crocheters with years of experience work from patterns, so knowing how to read them is important. Chapter 4 tells you what the abbreviations and symbols in patterns mean and how to decipher the instructions. To ease you into the language of crochet, we provide an explanation immediately after each line of instruction, although we urge you to take a stab at reading the "normal" instructions because that's how all crochet publications present them.

To help you get used to all the abbreviations and symbols, we include them in parentheses every time we introduce a new stitch or technique (which we fully explain in plain English, by the way). The first project patterns at the ends of the chapters either partially or completely explain the directions in plain English, but by Chapter 8 we provide the directions solely in Crochetese. (Never fear; you can always flip back to Chapter 4 if you don't remember something.)

Mastering Basic Crochet Techniques

Aside from figuring out the basic stitches, you need to understand a few fundamental techniques: adding and subtracting stitches, changing colors, and working in a circle. All of these techniques are really quite easy, and mastering them can help you create fabulous designs. We give you a brief introduction to these basic techniques, as well as the importance of practicing them, in the next sections.

Practice makes perfect

You don't learn to walk or ride a bike in a day, so don't expect to become a crochet pro in just 24 hours. Getting good at crochet takes practice, but probably not as much as you may think. Start with the basic chain stitch (described in Chapter 5) and practice until you're comfortable with the motions your hands must make. Then move on to another stitch. Each successive stitch, which we walk you through step-by-step in Chapters 5 and 6, builds on another, so try not to skip any of them, at least in the beginning. We don't want you to get frustrated and throw your work down. Believe us, in no time at all, you'll be moving right along.

The majority of *Crocheting For Dummies,* 2nd Edition, presents techniques from a right-hander's point of view, but we don't forget you lefties. All the information contained in this book (and there's plenty of it!) applies to you as well. In Chapter 5, we get you started on the basics by illustrating steps from both the left- and right-handed perspectives. There we also give you a few tips to help you work your way through the rest of the book from a left-handed perspective.

Shape up

After you have the basic stitches down, it's time to break away from the straight lines and give your projects some curves. Check out Chapter 7 to see just how easy it is to shape your projects by adding and subtracting stitches. Don't worry; the math is simple, and so are the techniques.

Round and round you go

Because crochet stitches are so easily manipulated, you can go where other forms of needlework can't, such as in circles. Although the first few chapters have you going back and forth in rows, Chapter 8 throws open the door to the world of crocheting in the round. All sorts of great projects — think doilies, afghans, and sweaters — are worked in rounds. This basic variation is easy, so don't be afraid to try the projects in this book that are worked in rounds.

Color it in

Crochet is by no means monochromatic. Yes, you've seen homes with white doilies scattered on every surface or the hat and scarf sets made in a single, dull color. But just wait until you walk into your local craft store or yarn shop. Your senses may just be assaulted by the multitude of colors and textures now available.

 Changing colors and carrying colors are variables you can take into consideration to turn a ho-hum design into a work of art (and Chapter 9 shows you how to do just that).

Adding New Stitches and Techniques to Your Crochet Repertoire

When you've mastered the basics, then you're ready to move on to even more fun stuff — new techniques and stitch combinations that add up to some creative works of art, as explained in the following sections.

 Many so-called specialty stitches (see Chapter 10) are nothing more than the combination of a couple different basic stitches, just with a new name. So don't be intimidated if a new technique or stitch seems too complex. Broken down, it's nothing more than the basics you already know.

Having fun with new stitches

You can do many amazing things with your crochet hook. Who says you have to work stitches in only one place? Because crochet is just a bunch of interlocking loops, you can stick your hook in myriad places to create stitches that are flat or textured, square or round — the variety is nearly endless. Chapter 11 has more on working your yarn in different spots. It also includes a fun technique called felting, which takes your project from loose and flimsy to solid and durable.

Creating funky fabrics

Two types of crochet that create unique fabrics are Tunisian crochet (see Chapter 12) and filet crochet (see Chapter 13). You work them by using very specific stitch placements and by following a chart. Both of these techniques are easy to master, and the designs you create with them make you look like you've been crocheting for years.

Being square (and other shapes too)

Crochet doesn't need to just go back and forth; you can create lots of cool shapes with your hook. The granny square is one of the most popular motifs in the crochet stitch library, but many more motifs exist in all shapes and sizes. Make just one for a decoration or join them together for a blanket, wrap, or pillow. The possibilities are endless! Head to Chapter 14 for all the details.

Finishing Your Work: Taking Pride in What You've Made

More goes into finishing your work than simply weaving in that last end of yarn. You may need to sew pieces together, add a pretty border, or tack on a tassel. After all that handling, often your new creations look a bit misshapen, so you need to do some blocking or shaping to pretty 'em up. And although you may not have spent a fortune on materials, we bet you probably don't want to ruin that new sweater on the first wash. The next sections give you a preview of what all can go into finishing your masterpieces.

Putting the pieces together

Many crochet designs are composed of several pieces that you need to put together to form the whole. Chapter 15 walks you through the various methods for joining fabric, whether you sew pieces together with a yarn needle and yarn or you use your hook and crochet the separate pieces together. And because sweaters are such popular items to crochet, Chapter 16 deconstructs the specific pieces that make up a sweater.

Tending to the final details

When you're finished crocheting, you want to make sure your piece looks its best. Does it need any special finishing touches? What about some pockets? Or maybe a fringe? Chapters 17 and 18 give you the scoop on adding these and more.

You may need to block or starch (refer to Chapter 19) your work to get it into shape. Blocking is a simple process that requires water, a little heat, or some starch to help coax your design into place. Don't leave out this step! The pattern's instructions may not mention blocking, but if your piece looks a little off, it could probably use a little blocking to whip it into shape.

Taking care of your crochet masterpieces

Now that you have this wonderful new creation, whether it's wearable or a home décor item, you want to take certain measures to ensure it stands the test of time. If you care for it properly (as explained in Chapter 19), you can pass down your crocheted work for generations to come.

Making Your Crochet Experience a Good One Overall

You'll inevitably experience highs and lows while you work to master crochet. Because we want your highs to be more plentiful than your lows, we're sharing a few tips that will help make your journey to crochet mastery a happier one:

- ✔ **Hold the hook and yarn the way that feels the most natural and comfortable to you.** We illustrate the most common ways in Chapter 5, but you may feel better using a different method.

- ✔ **Always read the stitch descriptions at the beginning of each pattern.** Different publications may use different names for stitches. Crochet isn't standardized, so you may encounter names you don't recognize. The pattern's stitch descriptions should clear up any confusion.

- ✔ **Check to see whether you're working from a British or an American pattern before you begin.** Patterns published in Great Britain and Australia, as well as some patterns published in Canada, use different terminology for even the basic stitches. For example, they call the American single crochet a *double crochet* and the American double crochet a *treble crochet.* You can end up crocheting something completely different from what you intended if you don't know what type of terminology you're working with. (Flip to Chapter 4 for a list of U.S. to UK conversions.)

- ✔ **Pick a place to work where you have few distractions.** As when mastering any new skill, being able to focus is important.

- ✔ **Practice each new stitch or technique by working a swatch.** Crochet stitches often build on each other, so make sure you're comfortable with one stitch before moving on to the next one. And don't throw away your swatches — they can come in handy when you need something on which to practice making borders or buttonholes.

- ✔ **Put your hook and yarn down and come back later if you start to feel frustrated with a new stitch.** Sometimes a little distance can clear up a previously difficult section.

✔ **Find an experienced crocheter to help explain a new technique that you're having a hard time with.** If you don't know anyone who crochets, try your local yarn shop. You can usually find someone there who's well versed in the craft and more than happy to help you.

✔ **Mark the pages of the books that you feel are most important or helpful to you.** This way you can easily find the references you're looking for.

Chapter 2

Tools of the Trade

In This Chapter

▶ Getting to know your new best friend — the crochet hook

▶ Discovering the many characteristics of yarn

▶ Understanding how to decode yarn labels

▶ Reviewing other helpful crochet tools

As with any new project that you decide to undertake, you first have to figure out what tools and materials you need to get the job done. For crocheting, your needs are pretty simple. Grab a hook and some yarn, find a comfortable seat, and you're ready to go.

In this chapter, we introduce you to the different types of crochet hooks and when to use them, show you your yarn options and how to choose the right one for your project, and help you read a yarn label. We also include lists of other tools that aren't necessary all the time but can be useful when you're crocheting different types of designs.

The One Tool You Can't Do Without: A Crochet Hook

A crochet hook is the single most important tool you use when crocheting. The next sections tell you everything you need to know about one, including why it's shaped the way it is, the function of each part, and the purpose of different hook materials.

Surveying the anatomy of a crochet hook

Even though you may think a crochet hook is nothing more than a straight stick with a hook on one end, it actually has five distinct and necessary parts, which you can see in Figure 2-1.

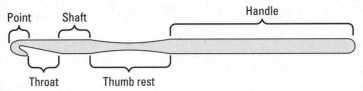

Figure 2-1:
The five
parts of a
crochet
hook.

Each part of a crochet hook performs a specific function.

- **Point:** You insert the point of the hook into previously made stitches. It must be sharp enough to slide easily through the stitches, yet blunt enough so that it doesn't split the yarn or stab your finger.

- **Throat:** The throat does the actual hooking of the yarn and pulls it through a stitch. It must be large enough to grab the yarn size that you're working with but small enough to prevent the previous loop from sliding off.

- **Shaft:** The shaft holds the loops that you're working with, and its diameter, for the most part, determines the size of your stitches.

- **Thumb rest:** The thumb rest helps keep the hook positioned in the right direction. Without it, the hook can twist in the wrong direction, and you can find yourself gripping the hook too tightly — leaving you with hooker's cramp! (You'll know what this is as soon as you feel the pain in the palm of your hand and your fingers.) The thumb rest should be sandwiched between your thumb and middle finger when you hold the hook, letting you easily rotate the hook as you work each stitch.

- **Handle:** The handle is used for balance or leverage. In the under-the-hook method of holding the hook (see Chapter 5), the handle helps keep the hook steady and well balanced. In the over-the-hook method of holding it, the handle is held against the heel or palm of your hand and provides the leverage needed to maneuver the hook properly.

Different brands of crochet hooks have slightly different shapes. Some have sharp points, whereas others have more rounded points. Some have distinct, flat, cutout throats, whereas others have smoother, rounded throats. Nowadays, most of the standard-size and steel hooks have thumb rests, although the largest of the standard hooks don't. (See the next section for the lowdown on the different types of hooks.) Take some time to experiment with a couple different brands of crochet hooks to find the one that you're most comfortable handling. You'll be glad you did.

Looking at the make and size of hooks

Crochet hooks may come in a seemingly endless array of sizes and materials, but all of them actually fall into two main categories:

- **Standard hooks** are typically made of aluminum or plastic (and sometimes wood); you normally use them when working with the larger sizes of yarn, such as sport weight, worsted weight, and those that are even thicker. (We describe different yarn weights later in this chapter.) Standard hooks measure about 6 inches in length and vary in thickness from 2.5 millimeters to 19 millimeters.

  Plastic crochet hooks can bend or break with heavy use, so we recommend using aluminum hooks for the standard sizes simply because they literally last forever — provided they don't disappear.

- **Steel hooks,** which are the smallest of all crochet hooks, are used for crocheting with thread and fine yarns. They're made of — wait for it — steel, and they measure about 5 inches in length and run from 0.75 millimeters to 3.5 millimeters wide.

In crochet, you work each stitch until only one loop remains on the hook, so you don't need a lot of space to hold loops (for the exception to the rule, check out the Tunisian stitch in Chapter 12). Therefore, the hooks are a convenient length, unlike the needles in our sister craft — knitting.

The size of a crochet hook refers to the thickness of the hook, which in turn determines the size of the stitches it creates. The photo in Figure 2-2 gives you an idea of the size variation in hooks. You can expect to run across three different systems for marking hook sizes:

- U.S. (American), which uses a letter/number combo
- Continental (metric), which uses millimeters
- UK (English), which uses numbers

For standard hooks using the U.S. or metric system, the higher the number or further the letter is in the alphabet, the larger the hook. For example, a D-3 U.S. hook is smaller than a K-10½ U.S. hook. For steel hooks, which use only a number designation, the opposite holds true. The higher the number, the smaller the hook. Fortunately, you don't need to worry about keeping the different systems straight because hooks are usually labeled with both the U.S. letter/number designation as well as the numeric metric designation.

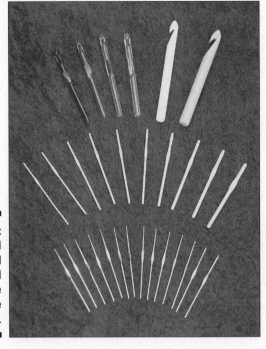

Figure 2-2:
Standard
and steel
hooks and
the range
of available
sizes.

Table 2-1 is a conversion chart showing the most commonly used sizes of both steel and standard hooks. (*Note:* Throughout this book, we refer to U.S. hook sizes as well as metric sizes.)

Table 2-1	Common Crochet Hook Sizes	
Steel Crochet Hooks		
U.S. (American)	*Continental (Metric)*	*UK (English)*
2	2.25 mm	1½
4	2 mm	2½
6	1.8 mm	3½
7	1.65 mm	4
8	1.5 mm	4½
9	1.4 mm	5
10	1.3 mm	5½

Standard Crochet Hooks		
U.S. (American)	**Continental (Metric)**	**UK (English)**
B-1	2.25 mm	13
C-2	2.75 mm	11
D-3	3.25 mm	10
E-4	3.5 mm	9
F-5	3.75 mm	-
G-6	4 or 4.25 mm	8
7	4.5 mm	7
H-8	5 mm	6
I-9	5.5 mm	5
J-10	6 mm	4
K-10½	6.5 mm	3

When shopping for crochet hooks, don't be afraid to try out lots of different brands and sizes. Hooks are inexpensive, and having extras of the most common sizes doesn't hurt. Even after you've found the style that you're comfortable with, hang on to other hooks you've collected as backups. You never know when you're going to lose your favorite hook and urgently need a replacement!

Ten handy household uses for crochet hooks

If you thought that crochet hooks were just for crocheting, guess again. Here are some additional interesting uses for them:

✔ Pull a yarn snag to the inside of a sweater.

✔ Reweave a dropped stitch while knitting.

✔ Pull a drawstring through its casing.

✔ Fix a tangled necklace.

✔ Rescue a ring you dropped down the drain.

✔ Pull hair through the holes of the cap when highlighting your hair.

✔ Weave a potholder by using a loom.

✔ Weave anything through anything.

✔ Stake up a plant.

✔ Spear the last olive at the bottom of the jar.

Figuring Out Yarn Features and Functions

First things first: Forget about that scratchy, bulky yarn your grandmother used. The variety of yarn available today is astounding, to say the least. You can find everything from the basic solid-color acrylic yarns and silky-soft wool blends to long, fringy eyelash yarn and sequined yarn. In addition to going over yarn weights, styles, and materials, the sections that follow show you what to do with yarn packaging and labels and how to choose the right yarn for your projects.

Sizing up yarn weights

Yarn *weight* or *size* refers to the general thickness of a yarn and can range from very thin to superthick. You can describe the weight of a yarn in numerous ways, but the majority of yarn companies tend to adhere to several common weight descriptions. The following list, although not all-inclusive, outlines the most common sizes of yarn in order from the thinnest to the thickest strands (check out Figure 2-3 to see how the different weights compare visually):

- **Lace weight:** Lace weight yarns include *crochet thread* and tend to be very thin yarns commonly used for doilies, filet crochet, and shawls.

- **Fingering weight:** Also known as *sock* or *baby weight,* this thin yarn is generally used to make lightweight garments, baby items, and designs with an open and lacy pattern.

- **Sport weight:** This medium-weight yarn is great for many different types of patterns, including sweaters, baby blankets, scarves, and shawls.

- **Double Knitting (DK) weight:** Sometimes referred to as *light worsted,* this yarn is slightly thicker than sport weight and can be used in the same patterns, but the resulting fabric is somewhat heavier.

- **Worsted weight:** Worsted weight is probably the most commonly used size of yarn and also the most readily available. It's great for afghans, sweaters, scarves, hats, slippers, and toys.

- **Chunky weight:** This yarn is sometimes referred to as *heavy worsted* or *bulky* weight. It's thicker than worsted weight and is used for afghans, jackets, and rugs.

- **Super bulky weight:** This yarn is a very thick, warm yarn and is generally used to make jackets, afghans, rugs, and heavy outdoor sweaters.

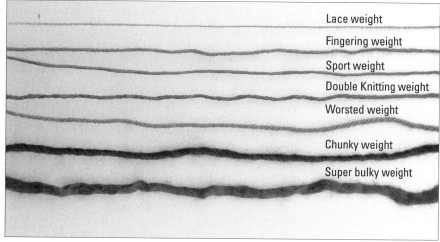

Lace weight

Fingering weight

Sport weight

Double Knitting weight

Worsted weight

Chunky weight

Super bulky weight

Figure 2-3:
A
comparison
of yarn
weights.

In an attempt to provide a universally accepted classification of sizes, the Craft Yarn Council of America has developed the Standard Yarn Weight System, offering yarn weight symbols that represent the categories of yarn along with their common gauge ranges and recommended hook sizes. Many yarn manufacturers include the yarn weight symbols on the label to help you find suitable yarn substitutions. Figure 2-4 shows the symbols for lace, super fine, fine, light, medium, bulky, and super bulky weights (from 0 to 6).

Figure 2-4:
The
Standard
Yarn Weight
System.

Yarn Weight, Symbol, & Category Names	0 LACE	1 SUPER FINE	2 FINE	3 LIGHT	4 MEDIUM	5 BULKY	6 SUPER BULKY
Type of Yarns in Category	Fingering 10-count crochet thread	Sock, Fingering, Baby	Sport, Baby	Double Knitting, Light Worsted	Worsted, Afghan, Aran	Chunky, Craft, Rug	Bulky, Roving

Source: Craft Yarn Council of America's www.YarnStandards.com

REMEMBER

Even though the different thicknesses of yarns are named by weight, as in worsted weight or sport weight, the size (diameter) of the yarn is actually what that name is referring to. The terms *size* and *weight* are interchangeable when referring to the thickness of a yarn.

Checking out the different types of yarn

Yarns are made up of a wide variety of materials, ranging from natural fibers like wools, cottons, and silks to synthetics such as acrylic, rayon, and nylon. You can also find pretty much any combination or blend of these materials. We give you an overview of the different types of yarn in the following sections.

When choosing yarn for a project, take into consideration how you'll use the piece. If you're making a baby blanket, choose a yarn that can stand up to repeated washings. If you're making a tablecloth or bedspread that'll some-day be an heirloom piece, invest in good-quality cotton that can withstand the test of time without falling apart. For a warm sweater, you can't beat wool for durability and warmth. (Head to the later section "Matching your yarn to your project" for some additional tips on making an informed decision when picking out your yarn.)

Wool

Of all the natural fibers used to make yarn, wool is the most popular choice to work with when you're creating a piece that you want to endure for years to come. Wool is resilient (which helps the stitches retain their shape), soft, easy to work with, and relatively lightweight. It comes in many different sizes, from fingering weight to bulky. You can crochet with wool to make everything from beautiful, warm-weather sweaters to cozy, wintertime pullovers, hats, scarves, mittens, socks, and afghans. Wool is fairly low maintenance as well, but be careful to read a particular yarn's label for specific washing instructions.

Although most wool comes from various breeds of sheep, you can obtain luxu-rious wool yarns from other animals as well. Fuzzy mohair and cashmere come from goats, and delicate, fluffy, Angora yarn comes from the Angora rabbit.

If you're allergic to wool, don't despair. Look for a synthetic instead. Many new synthetics mimic the real stuff so well that if you don't spill your secret, no one will know.

Silk

Spun from the cocoon of the silkworm, silk yarn has a smooth, often shiny finish. It's lightweight and absorbent, making it a perfect choice for warm-weather garments. Silk is often combined with cotton or wool to increase its elasticity and durability.

Cotton

Once used mainly to make doilies, bedspreads, and tablecloths, cotton has become a versatile yarn. It comes in a wide range of sizes, from very fine threads to worsted-weight yarn. Garments made from cotton yarn are wash-able, durable, and have that great cotton comfort. Cotton yarn is also a good choice for home décor items such as place mats, potholders, and curtains.

Synthetics

Synthetic yarn is produced from man-made fibers such as acrylic, rayon, nylon, and polyester. Designed to look like the natural-fiber yarns, synthetic yarns are readily available in a wide range of sizes, colors, and textures and are generally less expensive than their natural counterparts. These yarns, especially those made from acrylic, are good for afghans and baby blankets because they require little care. (However, you should still be sure to check the label for washing instructions.) Synthetic yarns are quite often used in combination with natural fibers, which gives you even more new textures, colors, and qualities of yarn to crochet with.

Novelty yarns

Novelty yarns are fun and funky and make your pieces interesting without requiring complicated stitch patterns. From soft, fringy eyelash yarn and velvety chenille to bumpy bouclé, glittering metallics, and slinky ribbon, these yarns can add a fresh, fashionable look to any piece you create.

Organic yarns, fair trade fibers, and sustainably sourced fibers

Ecologically friendly yarns are a growing trend in the yarn world as crafters work to lessen their hobbies' impact on the environment. Among the yarns found in this category are organic, fair trade, and sustainably sourced yarns. *Organic yarns* come from companies that make their products without the use of man-made chemicals, so plants and animals are raised without synthetic pesticides or fertilizer. *Fair trade fibers* come from companies who work to improve labor conditions for their farmers and workers. *Sustainably sourced yarns* have been produced with minimal impact on the earth, meaning the fiber is cultivated without excess waste of or damage to the earth's resources.

Some major yarn brands and local yarn shops have added eco-friendly yarns to their line, but these still tend to be more expensive than other yarns. However, as more crafters support those brands that make a conscious effort to produce earth-friendly fibers, the more abundant and cheaper those fibers will become.

Other materials

If you're feeling adventurous, you can crochet with any material that resembles a string. Throw caution to the wind and use fine, colored wire and hemp to crochet cool jewelry, nylon cord to whip up waterproof bags and outdoor seat cushions, and even embroidery floss and sewing thread to create appliqués and accents. Check out Chapter 20 for ideas on how to crochet with cut-up strips of fabric or plastic grocery bags (gives a whole new meaning to "reduce, reuse, recycle," huh?).

Sorting out yarn packaging

Yarn is commonly packaged (or *put up*) in three different ways: as a skein, a ball, or a hank. You can crochet with balls and skeins of yarn as you buy them. Hanks, however, require a bit of preparation.

- ✔ **Ball:** If your ball of yarn is wound around a cardboard center, just grab the end on the outside of the ball, and you're ready to go. If the ball has an open center, your best bet is to find the end of the yarn from inside the ball. Using the inside end keeps the ball from rolling around the floor or becoming a new toy for your cat.

- ✔ **Skein:** The most common form of packaging, a *skein* is an oblong, machine-wound bundle of yarn. You start crocheting with the inside end. Sometimes it's already pulled to the outside for you. In that case, just give it a tug, and it'll pull out smoothly and evenly. If the yarn end isn't visible at either end of the skein, reach into the small indentation on either end of the skein and pull out a few strands; you'll find the end buried inside there. Sometimes the label has an arrow pointing to the correct end of the skein to pull from, but more often than not, you have to guess. If the first end doesn't work, try the other end; it has to be in there somewhere! Working from the inside of the skein keeps the yarn tangle free.

- ✔ **Hank:** A *hank* is a large circle of yarn twisted into a figure-eight shape. Trying to work from a hank soon results in a tangled mess and plenty of frustration, so you need to first wind it into a ball. Unfold and then untwist the hank so that it's a circle of yarn. Place the large circle of yarn over a chair back or your knees, or have someone hold it with out-stretched arms. Find the outside end of the yarn and *loosely* wind it into a ball.

To wind a ball of yarn the inexpensive way, start by laying the outside end of the hank across three or four of your fingers. With the other hand, wrap the yarn loosely around those fingers about 20 times. Remove the wrapped yarn all at once, rotate it 90 degrees, and lay it across the same three or four fingers of your hand. Wrap the yarn loosely around those fingers about 20 times. Remove the yarn from your hand, pinching it to keep it from unraveling, and rotate it 90 degrees. Continue to lay the yarn across your hand, wrap about 20 times (more or less is fine), remove, and rotate. As you go, you'll notice that the yarn begins to form a ball. After you make a ball, continue to wrap in one direction several times; then rotate the ball and continue wrapping until all of the yarn is in ball form.

Winding a ball too tightly can stretch your yarn, and you definitely don't want that. Stretched-out yarn may spring back into shape when your work is finished, and you may have to hand down your size-12 sweater to your size-10 daughter.

Deciphering yarn labels

Yarn labels contain a lot of valuable information that you need to take note of to make sure your project turns out right. Check out the label in Figure 2-5 and the following list for the lowdown on label info.

Figure 2-5: Identifying key information on a yarn label.

Yarn labels include most, if not all, of the following information:

- ✔ **Article number (1):** Some manufacturers assign a number to each different type of yarn they produce for identification purposes. This number comes in handy when you're ordering yarn directly from the manufacturer or another mail-order source.

- ✔ **Brand name (2):** A yarn company may manufacture several different types or *brands* of yarn.

- ✔ **Care instructions (3):** As with any item that needs to be cleaned, yarn has specific care instructions. Some yarns require little care; you simply throw them in the washer and dryer. Other yarns need some TLC and should be handwashed and laid flat to dry. Still others should be sent to the dry cleaner. Be sure that the care instructions will work well for your finished work, or else your creation may end up on the top shelf of the closet! Many manufacturers use the International Fabric Care Symbols shown here. For more information on these symbols, see Chapter 19.

  If you mix more than one type of yarn in a project, the care requirements should be similar. Otherwise you may end up with a stretched (or shrunken) section after you launder your piece the first time.

- ✔ **Color name and number (4):** Yarn colors are identified in two different ways: by name and/or number.

- ✔ **Company name and logo (5):** This is the name of the company that manufactures the yarn. Sometimes contact information, such as address, telephone number, and Web site, is included as well.

✔ **Dye lot number (6):** The *dye lot* number identifies yarns that are dyed in the same batch. Although companies strive to match the colors as closely as possible, slight variations exist from lot to lot. Even if skeins of different dye lots look the same when you hold them together, you may end up with a distinct color difference in your finished project.

To ensure an even color throughout your work, buy enough yarn from the same dye lot to complete your entire project. If you have to go back and buy more at a later date, chances are you won't be able to find yarn from the same dye lot.

If you do end up with skeins of the same color but different dye lots, here's a trick to make the color variation less noticeable. If you have equal numbers of skeins in each dye lot, crochet two rows with a skein of one dye lot, and then crochet the next two rows with a skein from the second dye lot. Continue to switch skeins of each dye lot after every two rows to end up with a subtle striped pattern. If you only have one skein that has a different dye lot than the remaining skeins, you can still do the same thing, but you'll want to work in the odd dye lot less frequently depending on how many skeins you have to work with.

✔ **Gauge (7):** Gauge is a measurement that helps you keep your crochet stitches consistent. It's the number of stitches and rows in a given measurement that you should get with a particular yarn by using the recommended hook size for that yarn. If the label only gives a knitting gauge, you can use this gauge as a guide because crochet hook sizes correspond to knitting needle sizes. Flip to Chapter 3 for more on gauge.

✔ **Manufacturer's address (8):** Sometimes the manufacturer's address is listed separately from the name, and it can come in handy if you have questions about the yarn or are having trouble locating a retail store that sells the product.

✔ **Ply (9):** *Ply* refers to the number of smaller strands twisted together to form the larger single strand of yarn. This number can be deceptive, though, because a fine yarn can be a 3- or 4-ply yarn, whereas a bulky yarn can be just 2 ply. Worsted-weight yarns are generally 4 ply, but some cotton yarns can be made up of 8 or more strands. The ply may be included on the label along with the size or weight of the yarn; for example, 4-ply worsted-weight yarn or 2-ply bulky-weight yarn.

✔ **Recommended hook size (10):** Sometimes the label suggests a certain hook size so you can work to the proper gauge for a specific yarn size. The recommended hook size is a good place to start, although you may find that you need to use a smaller- or larger-size hook, depending on how you work your stitches and how loose you want them to be. You can achieve a lacy texture by using a much larger hook than recommended. On the other hand, if you want a tight, stiff fabric (like for a tapestry bag), you should use a smaller hook than the one the label calls for.

✔ **Weight (11):** This number reflects the actual weight of the whole skein, ball, or hank of yarn, as opposed to the weight (size) of the yarn strand. The weight is usually quoted in ounces and/or grams.

✔ **Yardage (12):** The yardage is the length of the yarn (in yards or meters) that's in the ball or skein. This information is important because you don't want to get partway through your project and then realize that you don't have enough yarn.

✔ **Yarn content (13):** Yarn content is the stuff your yarn is made of — wool or acrylic, cotton or silk, a blend of two or more fibers, or one of the many other fibers available.

Matching your yarn to your project

When selecting yarn you must always take your project's design, pattern, color, and texture into consideration. Certain patterns work better with simple yarns and solid colors; others can showcase more exotic yarns. The following sections offer advice for properly matching your yarn to your project.

Working with color and texture

A wide array of wonderfully colored yarns is available today, from bright, jewel-toned solids to hand-painted, variegated yarns. If your pattern is simple, try a multicolored yarn. Using colorful yarns allows you to create a beautiful work of art without having to work a more complex stitch pattern.

If you've chosen a design with fancier stitches, stick to a more basic yarn. A smooth, solid-color yarn adds definition to your stitches and allows them to stand out. ***Remember:*** You want your fancy stitch work to be seen! Today's vibrant, solid yarn colors are available in both matte and shiny finishes. Both finishes work equally well, so choose the one you like best.

Working with novelty yarns (think eyelash yarn or fun fur) can be tricky because seeing the stitches as you're crocheting is sometimes difficult. Don't let this downside put you off; instead, plan to take more time and effort to work up your creation. When first working with novelty yarns, try using them as an accent to your piece in borders, edgings, and collars until you get used to them. This way, if you make a mistake, at least you won't have to take your whole design apart. Besides, these novelty yarns can be overwhelming when used in excess.

The more intricate your stitch design is, the simpler your yarn should be. The more interesting the yarn is, the simpler the pattern should be.

Choosing natural or man-made fibers

When picking out your yarn, think about what your design will be used for. Soft wools and shimmery silks work beautifully for winter sweaters and dressy tops. High-quality cotton produces a wonderful summer cardigan or an heirloom doily, bedspread, or tablecloth. Natural fibers cost a little more and require more TLC than man-made fibers, but they hold up well over a long period of time.

If you're making baby items or large designs, such as afghans, opt for a good-quality synthetic yarn, such as acrylic. Made to mimic the natural fibers, synthetic yarns come in a wide range of sizes and colors and can be smooth and soft to the touch. They're also easy to care for. In most cases, they can be thrown in the washer and dryer and still stand up well to the wear and tear of everyday use. Synthetic yarns are usually cheaper than their natural counterparts, which is a good thing when you're creating a design that uses a lot of yarn.

Substituting yarns

If you have your heart set on making the design exactly as you see it in the pattern picture, use the yarn listed in the pattern materials list. But if that gorgeous afghan is made in shades of pink and your décor is blue, don't be afraid to change the color scheme. Or if your budget doesn't accommodate the high-priced wool called for in that sweater design, look for a comparable synthetic or a less-expensive wool blend.

If you're substituting for more than just color, however, make sure that the yarn you choose is the same size or weight and can accommodate the same gauge. (See Chapter 3 for details on gauge.) For example, if the pattern calls for a worsted-weight yarn, make sure you get another worsted-weight yarn. If you choose a bulky yarn instead, you'll end up with a design that's considerably larger than planned. If you're making something wearable, substitutions can cause disastrous results.

Another important consideration when substituting yarns is total yardage. If the pattern calls for five skeins of a sport-weight yarn that has 400 yards to each skein for a total of 2,000 yards, make sure you purchase enough of whatever sport-weight yarn you choose so that you have a total of 2,000 yards.

The manufacturer's gauge on the yarn label can help when you want to substitute one yarn for another. Just compare the gauge listed on the yarn label with the pattern gauge to determine the correct-size yarn to swap. We explain how to decipher a yarn label earlier in this chapter.

Creating your own yarn combinations

For even more variety, work with two or three different strands of yarn held together as one to create a unique blend of colors or textures. You can use two or more strands of the same weight of yarn to produce an extremely thick fabric (this is what those really big hooks are made for).

If you want to use several strands in a pattern that calls for only one, make sure the yarns you put together equal the same weight yarn that the pattern calls for. For example, if a design calls for a worsted-weight yarn, you can use two or three strands of a fingering-weight yarn because that would approximately equal a worsted weight. If you're unable to come up with the correct weight, be sure to make a gauge swatch and adjust your hook size to achieve the proper gauge (see Chapter 3 for help).

Note: Working with more than one strand of yarn at a time can be tricky. Watch out for all those extra loops of yarn that you'll encounter.

Tool Time: Other Tools of the Trade

Although your crochet hook and yarn are your primary tools when crocheting, several other items can come in handy. Some of these tools are necessary; others, though not essential, are just nice to have.

You probably want to have a safe place to keep all of this neat new stuff you have. Most craft stores carry a variety of cases that you can use to store all of your crochet supplies. Consider storing smaller items in a small zippered case and placing it in a larger case or carrying bag along with your yarn.

Gathering basic tools

Several basic tools make crocheting easier. Some of our favorites include those in Figure 2-6. The following list describes each one, moving counterclockwise from the scissors:

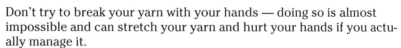

✔ **Scissors:** Small scissors with a sharp point work best. They're more manageable than large scissors, and you're less likely to snip at the wrong place. Craft and fabric stores carry a variety of scissors, and many come with carrying cases or are collapsible.

Don't try to break your yarn with your hands — doing so is almost impossible and can stretch your yarn and hurt your hands if you actually manage it.

✔ **Ruler and tape measure:** These tools are necessary when measuring for gauge (see Chapter 3) and for measuring your work in progress. Try to find a ruler and tape measure that feature both standard and metric measurements.

✔ **Rustproof straight pins:** These pins are absolutely necessary when pinning down a project that you're going to *block* (meaning shape; see Chapter 19). After putting so much time into your project, it'd be a shame to ruin it by failing to use rustproof pins and ending up with reddish-brown spots throughout your creation.

✔ **Safety pins:** Safety pins have a gazillion uses, such as marking a spot in your work that you ripped out, holding two pieces together while sewing a seam, keeping track of increases and decreases, and marking the right side of your work.

The safety pins without coils are the best. They slip in and out of your stitches easily, and the yarn doesn't catch on them.

✔ **Removable stitch markers:** You can find a variety of stitch markers at your local yarn or craft store; however, you need to make sure you buy the kind that can be used with crochet. Knitting stitch markers are closed rings, but crochet stitch markers are removable. Be sure to look for markers that have a split; they're often referred to as *split stitch markers*.

Although removable stitch markers aren't absolutely essential, having some type of marker comes in handy when you have to mark the end of a specific row or a certain stitch within the row where you're going to work an increase or decrease. In a pinch, a piece of contrasting colored yarn, a safety pin, or a bobby pin works just as well.

✔ **Yarn bobbins:** These are usually plastic, and you use them to wrap different colors of yarn on when you're working a multicolored piece. (See Chapter 9 for pointers on working with more than one color of yarn.)

✔ **Yarn and tapestry needles:** Yarn and tapestry needles have larger eyes than regular sewing needles to accommodate yarn. Yarn needles have a blunt point, which slips through the stitches without splitting the yarn. Tapestry needles are a bit smaller in diameter, have a sharper point, and are generally used when working with cotton thread. You use these needles often for weaving in ends, sewing motifs, or sewing seams.

Yarn needles come in steel or plastic styles. Our preference is the steel variety because the plastic ones tend to bend and break over time.

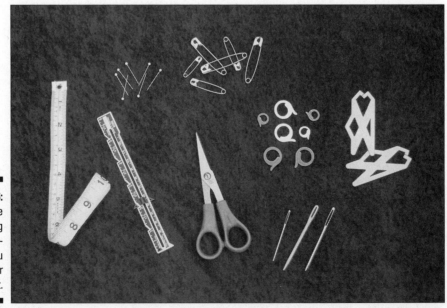

Figure 2-6: More crocheting paraphernalia that you may need or want.

Don't forget to keep a pad of paper and a pencil on hand. Keeping notes while you work is a must if you make any changes to a pattern or are designing your own piece. Even if you think you'll remember the changes you made, write them down. The simplest, smallest stitch change can slip from your mind far faster than you may expect.

Treating yourself to little luxuries

The basic tools in the preceding section ensure that your crochet experience is more successful, but you can also invest in a few little luxuries that'll make it more fun. Here are a few tools that aren't absolutely necessary but can be a treat to have:

- **Hook roll:** After you've amassed a fair number of crochet hooks, you may want a case to help keep them organized. A hook roll has individual pockets for the hooks that make it easier to find the exact hook you need. Simply place the hooks in the pockets and roll up the case. You can purchase a hook roll for $10 to $20 at your local yarn shop or online.

- **Yarn ball winder:** A yarn ball winder can set you back about $40, but it makes winding yarn into balls much faster. Just secure one tail end of a hank or skein to the ball winder and turn the handle until all of the yarn has been wound into a neat little cake. This process takes just a couple minutes, and you end up with a string that's ready to go from the center.

- **Swift:** Instead of relying on a friend or chair back to hold your yarn while you wind it into a ball, why not turn to a swift? Most swifts look a little like a rotating wooden umbrella. Simply unfold the hank, place it on the swift, and start winding. You can use a swift on its own or with a yarn ball winder. Either way, the cost of a swift ranges from $50 to $70.

Chapter 3

Creating Consistency with Gauge

. . . .

In This Chapter

▶ Recognizing the value of gauge

▶ Whipping up a properly sized gauge swatch

▶ Setting gauge all on your own

. . . .

Making sure your stitches are consistently the right size is very important when crocheting, particularly when you're whipping up clothing. (Otherwise, your sweater may be lopsided, or your scarf may morph into a table runner.) In order to get the shape and size you want, you must check the gauge provided in the pattern. *Gauge* is simply the ratio of a given number of stitches or rows to inches (or some other unit of measurement), such as seven stitches per inch or four rows per inch. You use this ratio to keep your stitches consistent and the size of your design on track. Working to the proper gauge ensures not only that the project you make is neat and attractive but also that the amount of yarn the pattern specifies is sufficient to complete the project.

This chapter shows you how to test your gauge by crocheting a *gauge swatch* (or *sample*) and how to adjust your gauge to equal the one that the pattern requires. We also explain how to set your own gauge (if that's what you want to do).

Understanding Why You Should Bother with Gauge

Although you can certainly start a project without first checking your gauge, crocheting a gauge swatch so you can get a feel for the right ratio of stitches to inches is really important. If your gauge is off by even a little bit, your finished design may be off by several inches. If you don't bother to check your gauge, you may spend beaucoup bucks on materials and many hours, days, or weeks crocheting only to find that the sweater you made is a perfect fit for the neighbor's Chihuahua.

When you're making a design from a published pattern, the pattern almost always recommends a gauge for you to follow. The pattern designer determines this gauge by taking into account the recommended yarn and hook size, the type of stitches used in the pattern, and the desired result.

Look for the recommended gauge at the beginning of the pattern instructions. (A subtle hint to check your gauge first thing!) Although garment patterns usually mention both a stitch and a row gauge, the stitch gauge is the most important one to match. It determines the width of each piece of the design, which, when you sew the front and back together, adds up to the finished bust measurement.

For example, say you're making a sweater and the required gauge is 8 stitches = 2 inches, and you want a finished bust measurement of 40 inches (or 20 inches across the back). The pattern may call for 80 stitches across the back (80 stitches ÷ 8 stitches × 2 inches = 20 inches). If your gauge measures 7 stitches = 2 inches, then working 80 stitches ÷ 7 stitches × 2 inches = 22 inches. Your sweater back would therefore measure 22 inches, and the finished bust would measure 44 inches! See how having your gauge off by just 1 stitch can make your garment a much different size than what you intended? In this case, the finished sweater would be 4 whole inches larger than intended.

Many sweater patterns allow for your row gauge being off a little by telling you to work to the desired length in inches, regardless of how many rows it takes you to get there. However, if your stitch gauge is off, your sweater may be too wide or too narrow, and that's something you can't adjust without tearing out all of your hard work and at least some of your hair.

Note: The yarn manufacturer may also recommend a particular gauge on the yarn label. This gauge may be quite different from the one in your pattern, but that's okay. Sometimes, the pattern designer wants to create a looser or tighter stitch pattern than the standard that the yarn manufacturer set. Follow the pattern gauge to get the same results as the pictured project.

Working a Gauge Swatch

Working a gauge swatch may seem like a waste of valuable crocheting time, but it's worth the effort. In addition to making sure your stitches and rows are the same size as the pattern's (which ensures a perfect-fitting garment), a gauge swatch lets you practice any new stitches found in the pattern *and* become familiar with the yarn you're using. In the next sections, we explain how to create and block a swatch of the right size, how to measure stitches in relation to rows and rounds, and how to correct your gauge with additional swatches.

Making your swatch the right size

Different types of patterns call for different types of gauges. A simple pattern that uses just one stitch, like a single crochet stitch, states the gauge as a certain number of stitches and rows per a given number of inches. However, some patterns have a set of several different stitches that repeats across the row. In this case, the pattern states the gauge as one entire stitch repeat per a given number of inches.

Work the stitches for your gauge swatch according to the instructions in the pattern. However, you probably want to make it bigger than what the instructions specify in order to get an accurate measurement.

Crocheters tend to crochet tighter at the beginning and end of rows than in the body of their work. So multiply the inches indicated in the stitch gauge by the inches indicated in the row gauge to figure out how big to make your swatch. For example, if the gauge calls for 7 stitches = 2 inches and 8 rows = 2 inches, make your swatch at least 4 inches square. That way you can measure in the center of the swatch and get an accurate measurement of your normal pace. If you're working a gauge that has a repeated set of stitches, you may need to make it bigger than 4 inches square.

Note: The swatches pictured in this chapter are made up of two colors so you can better identify the center stitches, but you can just use a single color when working your own gauge swatches.

Putting swatches to good use

Although you may feel a little impatient when you have to spend your time crocheting a gauge swatch, you can make that time and effort seem less painful if you find a use for all of those practice swatches. Following are a few ideas:

- Use them as coasters.

- Make a swatch large enough to use as a doll blanket.

- Sew several swatches together to form a pillow front or wall hanging sampler.

- Sew many swatches together to make a patchwork afghan.

- Keep a scrapbook of your swatches to inspire future projects.

- Practice edgings and borders on the sides of your swatches.

- Use lacy cotton swatches as appliqués on sweatshirts or jeans.

Blocking your swatch

To get an accurate measurement of your stitches, you have to treat your swatch just as you plan to treat your finished project. Check to see whether your pattern requires you to block your final design. *Blocking* is a process that evens out the stitches and gets the final piece into the right shape. It usually involves getting the piece wet, whether you submerge it in a tub of water or just steam it, and then shaping the piece by hand into the correct measurements and allowing it to dry. After blocking your gauge swatch, you can measure your true gauge, therefore accurately predicting whether your finished design will be true to form. (See Chapter 19 to find out how to block your work.)

Blocking your gauge swatch is especially important if you're working with natural fibers, such as wool and cotton.

Measuring stitches and rows

After you make (and possibly block) a gauge swatch with the materials and hook size that the pattern recommends, measure the stitches and rows in your swatch to determine whether you have too many, too few, or just the right number for the given gauge.

Measuring a swatch of single crochet

The following swatches show you how to correctly measure gauge in a fabric made up of single crochet stitches (see Chapter 5 for instructions on single crochet). Figure 3-1a shows that you have 7 stitches in 2 inches. Figure 3-1b shows that 8 rows of single crochet = 2 inches.

Figure 3-1:
Measuring gauge for a single-stitch pattern.

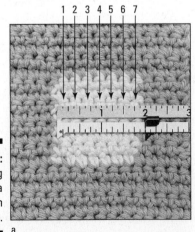
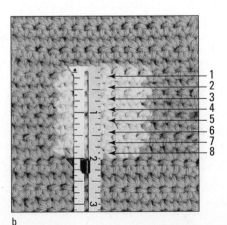

a

b

Measuring a swatch made with a repeating pattern

Figure 3-2 shows you how to measure crocheted fabric that uses different stitches, worked in rows.

- ✔ When measuring a stitch gauge in a swatch that has a repeating pattern of combination stitches, be sure to include the total repeat in your measurement. Figure 3-2a points out each shell for the repeating shell pattern; the width of 2 shells is 3¼ inches.

- ✔ When measuring a row gauge, always measure the rows from the base of one row to the base of another row above it. If you measure to the top of a row, your gauge will be off because the base of the row lies in the valley of the previous row. Figure 3-2b points out each shell for the repeating pattern and shows that 4 rows in the shell pattern is equal to 2¼ inches high.

Figure 3-2:
Measuring gauge over a repeating pattern of stitches.

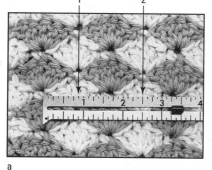

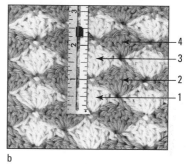

When working with a pattern such as the one in Figure 3-2, the gauge usually includes one or more repeats of the pattern, so you need to make a swatch that's at least 2 inches wider and taller than the number of inches indicated in the stitch gauge. For example, if the stitch gauge = 3¼ inches, you need to work a swatch at least 5¼ inches wide to get an accurate gauge. The row gauge for a pattern that has a 2-row repeat, such as this one, should be a multiple of 2 rows (2, 4, or 6 rows) to reflect how the pattern will work up in length. For example, the gauge for this pattern is 4 rows = 2¼ inches. For an accurate row gauge, work a swatch at least 6 rows deep, or approximately 3½ inches.

Measuring stitches and rounds

If you're working a *round* (stitches crocheted in a circle rather than rows; see Chapter 8 for details), such as with a doily, you figure out the gauge by measuring the diameter of the swatch after you've made a certain number of rounds. The pattern usually states how many rounds to make for the swatch; look for verbiage along the lines of "First X rounds = X inches." Figure 3-3a shows 3 rounds of double crochet stitches that equal 3½ inches in diameter. Figure 3-3b shows the first 2 rounds of a hexagon motif that equal 3 inches in diameter across the widest point.

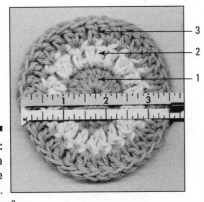

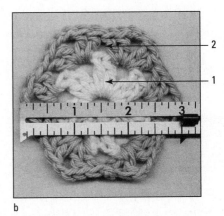

Figure 3-3: Measuring a stitch gauge in rounds.

a

b

If you're crocheting with cotton thread in rounds (or rows, for that matter), you can usually use a smaller gauge swatch than when you crochet with yarn, but you take the measurements the same way no matter what material or hook size you're using.

Over- or undershooting the mark

If your gauge is different from the one the pattern specifies, you can correct it by changing hook sizes and making another swatch.

- ✔ If you have more stitches than the pattern calls for, your work is too tight, and you should make another swatch with a larger hook.

- ✔ If you have fewer stitches than the pattern calls for, you're working too loosely, and you need to use a smaller hook to achieve the desired result. Figure 3-4 shows what a swatch looks like if you crochet too loosely (or if you use too large a hook) for a desired stitch gauge of 6 stitches in 2 inches. Notice how the white center section exceeds the required 2-inch gauge.

In either situation, keep adjusting hook sizes and working swatches until you get the right gauge.

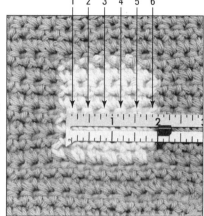

Figure 3-4:
What
happens
when you
crochet too
loosely.

Everyone crochets a little differently. After you get to know your own crochet
style (whether you tend to crochet tightly or loosely), you may be able to
choose the proper hook size even before making the first swatch for a pattern.
Changing hook size is the best way to compensate for your individual style of
crochet. If you consciously try to tighten or loosen up your stitches to achieve
the proper gauge, you invariably return to your natural style as you go along
and then wind up with the wrong gauge.

If you don't work on a project for several days or weeks or months, be sure to
recheck your gauge before continuing with the project. Time away can affect
your gauge, which varies depending on your stress level and other outside factors. You may need to adjust your hook size to maintain the original gauge.

Flying Solo: Establishing
Your Own Gauge

After you get the hang of crocheting, you may want to try designing your own
sweaters, scarves, and afghans. Suppose you have a stitch pattern in mind and
you want to figure out how many stitches to work to create the size that you
need — in other words, you want to set the right gauge for your project. The
following steps make it easy:

1. **Work a swatch of the pattern using the desired materials.**

2. **Change hook sizes as needed until the swatch has the look and feel
   you want.**

3. **Measure how many stitches your swatch has per inch (or several inches).**

For example, if your gauge measures 7 stitches = 2 inches and you want to make a sweater that measures 36 inches around, or 18 inches across the back, cross multiply to calculate the correct number of stitches (x) you need to begin the back. Remember cross multiplication from elementary school? In order to find x, you first multiply 7 by 18. Then you divide that answer by 2. So in this case you have $7 \times 18 = 126$ and $126 \div 2 = 63$ stitches. Working 63 stitches produces a back width of 18 inches.

Never skip over the gauge stage when you create your own crochet master-pieces. The gauge swatch is a necessary tool for creating a useful and beautiful work of art.

Chapter 4

Decoding Crochet Patterns

. . . .

In This Chapter

▶ Getting familiar with the various sections in crochet patterns

▶ Reading written pattern instructions

▶ Recognizing stitch symbols and diagrams as instructions

. . . .

Sometimes you may work thousands of stitches for one crochet project. If crochet instructions were all written out, stitch by stitch by stitch without any abbreviations or shortcuts, one pattern would fill an entire book. Fortunately, crochet instructions have their own special abbreviations and a form of shorthand that simplify the written directions, saving space and a lot of tedious reading time.

Some patterns also use the International Crochet Symbols (see Figure 4-1 later in this chapter) to create pictorial diagrams of a crocheted design. You may find these diagrams easier to follow than the text when dealing with intricate patterns.

After you get a handle on the abbreviations and symbols of crochet design, reading a crochet pattern is a cinch. In this chapter, we help you decipher the unique language of crochet instructions.

Note: If you're reading this book in order, note that the stitches are explained in order of complexity. If you want to know right away what a double crochet or popcorn stitch is, head to the table of contents or the index to find the related chapter.

Breaking Down the Sections of a Crochet Pattern

Most crochet patterns found in magazines or books have several different sections that you must be familiar with if you want to concentrate on crocheting your masterpiece rather than deciphering the instructions for it. The following

list introduces the most common pattern sections (some patterns will have more; others will have fewer):

- ✔ **Level of experience:** Most patterns give you a general idea of the complexity of the pattern and whether it's suitable for a beginner, advanced beginner, intermediate crocheter, or advanced crocheter. Don't automatically shy away from a supposedly advanced pattern, though. Take a look at it before deciding that it's too complex for your ability.

- ✔ **Materials:** The materials section lists everything you need to complete the project, specifically

  - **Yarn:** The yarn section of the materials list tells you all you need to know to get the right yarn for the project: the brand name, the specific yarn name, the fiber composition of the yarn, the size of the yarn (such as sport weight or worsted weight), the weight and yardage of each skein, and how many skeins (or hanks or balls) you need. (See Chapter 2 for the full scoop on yarn and how to read those pesky labels.)

  - **Hook:** The next item in the list is the size crochet hook (or hooks) you need.

  - **Additional materials:** The materials list also includes any additional materials you need, such as a yarn needle, sewing thread, buttons, or beads.

- ✔ **Size information:** This part tells you the finished dimensions of the project. If you're making a garment, this part gives you the size ranges (check out Chapter 16 for details on sweater sizing). It may also include a *schematic,* which is a diagram showing the dimensions of each piece used to make up the finished design.

- ✔ **Gauge:** The pattern gives the gauge for a design, each and every time. Always work to the specified gauge so you wind up with the right size design. (Check out Chapter 3 for information on gauge.)

- ✔ **Stitches:** Most patterns list the stitches used and give directions for any advanced stitches or techniques.

- ✔ **Crocheting directions:** The bulk of the pattern is the step-by-step instructions for crocheting the design. They may be written out row by row (or round by round), or they may include a pictorial diagram as well. If you're supposed to crochet the project in several pieces, the pattern gives instructions for each piece. If keeping track of the right and wrong sides of a project is important for a certain pattern, the instructions designate which row is which. For example, if the first row of the work is the right side, the instructions for the first row appear like this: Row 1 (RS). All subsequent odd-numbered rows are then considered right side, and even-numbered rows are considered wrong side. (See the later sections "Figuring Out Written Instructions" and "Not Just a Pretty Picture: Symbols and Diagrams" for the nitty-gritty details of reading directions.)

✔ **Assembly:** If a design is made in several pieces, this section shows you how to put it all together.

✔ **Finishing:** Here's where you add the final details, which can be as simple as sewing on buttons or as complex as adding borders and collars. If an item needs to be blocked, you find the specifics on that task here (refer to Chapter 19 for more on blocking).

Figuring Out Written Instructions

Written instructions are, by far, the most common way to present a crochet pattern. The various abbreviations and symbols — and combinations of the two — may seem like a foreign language to you in the beginning. That's okay. Consider the following sections your Crochet Dictionary. They explain each of the parts used in written instructions and how they all fit together.

Keeping it short with abbreviations

Most crochet stitches have shortened names or abbreviations. For example, instead of saying *double crochet stitch* throughout a pattern, the instructions abbreviate this stitch as *dc*. As we introduce terms and stitches throughout this book, we also give you their abbreviations to help you become familiar with the shorthand. Table 4-1 lists the most common abbreviations (they include stitches and other pertinent information).

Table 4-1	Common Crochet Abbreviations
Abbreviation	*Spelled-Out Term*
approx	approximately
beg	begin(ning)
bet	between
blp	back loop only
BP	back post
CC	contrast color
ch	chain
dc	double crochet
dec	decrease(s)(d)(ing)
dtr	double triple crochet

(continued)

Table 4-1 *(continued)*

Abbreviation	Spelled-Out Term
flp	front loop only
foll	follow(ing)
FP	front post
hdc	half double crochet
inc	increase(s)(d)(ing)
MC	main color
patt	pattern
rem	remaining
rep	repeat
rib	ribbing
rnd(s)	round(s)
RS	right side
sc	single crochet
sl st	slip stitch
st(s)	stitch(es)
tog	together
tr	triple crochet
WS	wrong side
yo	yarn over the hook

Crochet abbreviations don't have periods after them in order to keep the instructions as clutter free as possible. If you do come across a period that isn't at the end of the sentence or action, it's probably attached to an abbreviation that's easily confused with another word. For instance, you may see *inches* abbreviated as *in.* to avoid confusion with *in* the word.

One other notation that you see quite frequently in pattern instructions is the hyphen. Instructions commonly use the hyphen when referring to a chain loop; the hyphen denotes the number of chains you work to create a particular loop. For example, a *ch-5 loop* is a loop made up of five chain stitches. Don't confuse this instruction, however, with *ch 5*, which instructs you to make a chain of five chain stitches in a row.

Some patterns combine several basic stitches into a more complex stitch. For example, five double crochet stitches worked in the same stitch are collectively known as a *shell* because the result resembles the shape of a clamshell. Besides having their own names, these special stitches may also have their own abbreviations. (Chapter 10 defines many of these combination stitches and gives you their abbreviations.)

Special stitches aren't standardized and may have different definitions in each pattern that you encounter. For example, one pattern may define a shell as five double crochet stitches, but another pattern may define it as only three double crochet stitches. Before diving into a new project, be sure to check the beginning of the pattern's instructions for the definition of each special stitch.

Distinguishing between American and British crochet terminology

Just as hook sizes differ depending on where you live (as explained in Chapter 2), the crochet terminology used in the United States is different than that used in the United Kingdom and Australia. For example, what's called a single crochet in the United States is called a double crochet in the United Kingdom.

No one is entirely sure how this different crochet terminology came about, but one theory is that the UK terms refer to the number of loops you have on the hook after you draw a loop through the next stitch and that the U.S. terms refer to the number of times you move the hook to complete the stitch. For example, after you've drawn the yarn through the stitch in the previous row, you have two loops on your hook, or a *double* loop, hence the United Kingdom's *double crochet*. To complete the stitch, you only have to draw the yarn through both loops on the hook once, which is a *single* movement, hence the United States' *single crochet*.

Following is a breakdown of what certain stitches are called in the United States and what they go by in the United Kingdom:

U.S. Stitch Name	*UK Stitch Name*
Single crochet (sc)	Double crochet (dc)
Double crochet (dc)	Treble (tr)
Half double crochet (hdc)	Half treble (htr)
Triple crochet (trc)	Double treble (dtr)
Slip stitch (sl st)	single crochet (sc)

The bottom line: Unless a pattern comes from the United Kingdom or Australia, or it specifically states that it's using UK terminology, go ahead and assume it's written using the U.S. crochet terms we explain in this book.

Working terms and phrases

Crochet patterns often contain jargon that isn't abbreviated, such as the following terms that explain where and how to work stitches:

- **Loop:** A *loop* is three or more chain stitches worked in a row. To work in a loop, insert your hook into the hole underneath the loop, not in any one stitch, and then complete the stitch indicated.

- **Space:** Usually, a *space* refers to the space created by working one or more chain stitches in between other stitches. To work in the space, insert your hook into the hole underneath the chain stitches and complete the stitch indicated.

- **Work across:** Crochet the designated stitch or stitches across the whole length of the row.

- **Work around:** When working in rounds, crochet the same stitch or stitch pattern repeatedly until you come back to the starting point.

- **Work across (or around) to within last 2 sts:** Crochet the designated stitches until you have two stitches left to work in at the end of the row or round; the instructions tell you what to do in the last two stitches.

Pondering parentheses

Instead of detailing each and every stitch or action involved in a row or round, instruction writers use parentheses to designate a repeated set of actions and stitches or to sum up a row. Here's a list of the different reasons instruction writers use these handy little arcs:

- **To isolate a set of two or more stitches that you work all in one stitch:** For example, you may find something like

    (2 dc, ch 2, 2 dc) in next sc

    This notation means that in the next single crochet stitch, you want to crochet two double crochet stitches, chain two, and then work two more double crochet stitches.

- **To enclose a set of stitches that you repeat a number of times in succession:** For example:

    (dc in next 3 sts, ch 2, skip next 2 sts) twice

    In plain English, this notation means that you work a double crochet stitch in each of the next three stitches, chain two, skip the next two stitches, and then repeat that by working a double crochet stitch in each of the next three stitches, chaining two, and skipping the next two stitches again.

✔ **To sum up a completed row or round:** If you see (16 dc) at the end of the instructions for a row, you should have 16 double crochet stitches in that row. Likewise, (8 loops) means you've completed eight loops, and (4 ch-3 loops made) means you've made four loops that are each three chain stitches long.

✔ **To distinguish different sizes in a garment pattern:** If a garment pattern is written for three sizes, it includes separate instructions for the two larger sizes in parentheses. For example:

> dc in each of next 10 (12, 14) sts

So you work 10 double crochet stitches if you're going for the small size, 12 double crochet stitches for medium, and 14 double crochet stitches for large.

To make a pattern with multiple sizes listed easier to follow, you may want to highlight, underline, or circle the numbers that pertain to your desired size throughout the pattern.

Bracing yourself for brackets

Crochet instructions use brackets in the following ways:

✔ **Some patterns use brackets interchangeably with parentheses to isolate repeated phrases of stitches.** They may also appear as a set or phrase within another set of brackets or parentheses. For example:

> (2 dc, ch 5, sl st in fifth ch from hook forming a ring, [4 sc, ch 3, 4 sc] in ring just made, 2 dc) in next ch-2 space

In other words, start by working two double crochet stitches in the chain-2 space. Next, chain five stitches and slip stitch in the fifth chain from the hook to form a ring. Then work four single crochet stitches, chain three, and work four single crochet stitches again in the ring you just formed. Finally, complete the operation by working two more double crochet stitches in the same chain-2 space you started out in.

✔ **Patterns use brackets within parentheses to sum up the number of stitches for different sizes.** So to sum up the number of stitches in each size, a numeric phrase at the end of a row in a sweater pattern might say

> (72 [76, 80] sts)

This notation means that when you reach the end of the row, you've worked a total of 72 stitches for a small-size sweater, 76 for a medium, and 80 for a large.

Interpreting special symbols in written patterns

Patterns use symbols such as bullets (•), asterisks (*), plus signs (+), and crosses (†) in instructions to show the repetition of a series of crochet stitches. Bullets and asterisks are the most common symbols, but the symbol you see in a particular pattern really depends on the preference of the publication. This book uses only asterisks.

In the sections that follow, we describe the use of symbols in written patterns. You most often see just one symbol or two symbols used.

Using one symbol

Some patterns use only one symbol at the beginning of a phrase and then direct you to repeat from that symbol a designated number of times. Here's an example of what we mean:

> * Dc in each of the next 3 sts, ch 2, skip next 2 sts; rep from * 5 times.

In this example, you work all the information after the asterisk once and then repeat the same series of steps five more times for a total of six times in all.

You may also see asterisks marking both the beginning and end of a repeated phrase. The instructions may reference this repeat again if the phrase within the asterisks is used at a different section of the row or round. Check out this example:

> Ch 3, * dc in each of next 3 dc, ch 2, skip next 2 sts *; rep from * to * once, dc in each of next 6 sts, ch 2, skip next 2 sts; rep from * to * twice, dc in each of last 4 dc.

Just to make sure you're interpreting Crochetese properly, check out the following plain-English translation of the preceding example and see whether it jives with your understanding of the abbreviated instructions:

1. **Chain 3.**

2. **Double crochet stitch in each of the next 3 double crochet stitches, chain 2, and skip the next 2 stitches.**

3. **Repeat Step 2.**

4. **Double crochet stitch in each of the next 6 stitches, chain 2, and skip the next 2 stitches.**

5. **Repeat Step 2 twice.**

6. **Double crochet stitch in each of the last 4 double crochet stitches.**

Using two sets of symbols

In more complicated patterns, you may see two sets of symbols, such as single asterisks (*) and double asterisks (**), to designate two different repeats in the same row or round.

> * Dc in dc, ch 2, skip next 2 sts *; rep from * to * 3 times, ** dc in next dc, 2 dc in next space **; rep from ** to ** 3 times.

In plain English, this notation means you need to

1. **Double crochet stitch in the double crochet stitch, chain 2, and then skip the next 2 stitches.**

2. **Repeat Step 1 three times.**

3. **Double crochet stitch in the next double crochet stitch and then work 2 double crochet stitches in the following space.**

4. **Repeat Step 3 three times.**

On the other hand, you may find the single asterisk phrase within the double asterisk phrase, denoting a repeated phrase within the larger set of repeated instructions. See for yourself in this example:

> ** 5 dc in loop, ch 2, skip next 2 dc, * dc in next dc, ch 2, skip next 2 dc *; rep from * to * 5 times **; rep from ** to ** 3 times.

In this case, you work the ** to ** phrase a total of 4 times to go around the entire piece, but within that phrase is another * to * phrase that you work a total of 6 times within each ** to ** repeat.

Confused? Here's the rundown in plain English:

1. **Work 5 double crochet stitches in the loop, chain 2, and then skip the next 2 double crochet stitches.**

2. **Work 1 double crochet stitch into the next double crochet stitch, chain 2, and then skip the next 2 double crochet stitches.**

3. **Repeat Step 2 five times, which brings you to the next loop.**

4. **Repeat Steps 1 through 3 three times.**

Repeating rows and rounds

Sometimes a pattern includes several identical rows or rounds. To save space, the instructions may group these rows together and write out the directions only once, as follows:

> **Rows 2–7:** Ch 1, sc in each sc across, *turn.*

This notation means you chain one, single crochet stitch into each single crochet stitch across the row, and then turn to complete one row. However, you work this row of single crochet consecutively for Rows 2 through 7 (for a total of six rows).

If you're to repeat two (or more) different rows in the same order, you'll see the first two rows written out and then the subsequent rows written as a repeat, as follows:

Row 2: Ch 1, sc in each st across, *turn.*

Row 3: Ch 3 (turning ch for dc), dc in each sc across, *turn.*

Rows 4–9: Rep Rows 2–3 (3 times).

So for Row 2, you chain one, single crochet in each stitch across the row, and then turn your work. For Row 3, you chain three, double crochet into each single crochet stitch across the row, and turn. Then you go back and work Row 2 again and then Row 3, repeating Row 2 and Row 3 consecutively until you've worked them a total of four times each.

Not Just a Pretty Picture: Stitch Symbols and Diagrams

Some pattern books and crochet magazines give you a pictorial description of the pattern design — a picture that may or may not have written directions alongside it. These *stitch diagrams* are like a road map of the pattern, laying out each individual stitch in relation to the others so you get the forest and the trees at once.

The advantages of stitch diagrams are numerous:

✔ You can see the number and placement of the stitches at a glance.

✔ You can observe what the design should look like so that if your creation doesn't resemble the diagram, you can easily identify your mistake.

✔ You can highlight or outline the repeated pattern in each row or round to make it easy to follow.

✔ You can mark where you leave off when you put your work down so you know where to begin the next time you crochet.

The beauty of stitch diagrams is that anyone can read them, regardless of what language he or she speaks. That's why the individual stitch symbols that make up the diagrams are called *International Crochet Symbols.* So, if you come across a terrific pattern in a Japanese book, you can make it from the diagram. Although these symbols and diagrams may look like hieroglyphics to you now, you'll be reading them as naturally as you read this sentence after reviewing the following sections.

Cracking the International Crochet Symbols code

Although they're called International Crochet Symbols, the symbols for crochet stitches aren't universally accepted yet, which means you may find slight variations in different publications. Nonetheless, we compiled a list of standard symbols (see Figure 4-1) that we use consistently throughout this book; these are the symbols for the most common crochet stitches. We include the symbols for more advanced stitches in their respective chapters.

Each symbol roughly resembles the shape and proportions of the stitch that it represents. The number of tick marks drawn diagonally across the middle of the symbols indicates the number of times that you yarn over at the beginning of the stitch. For example, the double crochet has one tick mark (yarn over once), the triple crochet has two tick marks (yarn over twice), and so on.

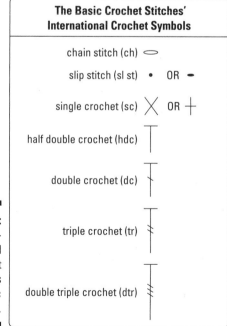

Figure 4-1:
The International Crochet Symbols for basic stitches.

Following a stitch diagram

The preceding section introduces you to the individual stitch symbols and what they look like. In this section, we combine all the symbols to create a stitch diagram like you'd see in a pattern. Then we deconstruct the diagram for you in plain English.

Getting a grip on stitch diagram fundamentals

Here's a quick rundown of the basics you should know before you read a stitch diagram:

- ✔ Each row or round in a diagram is numbered so that you know where to begin — Row 1.

- ✔ On a pattern done in rounds, the numeral in the center of the beginning ring indicates the number of chain stitches in the center ring.

- ✔ Because most crochet instructions are repetitive and most publications have limited space, a diagram may show a repeated set of stitches just a few times. But those few repeats are all you need to crochet the entire piece.

- ✔ When working in rows, the right-side row number is placed on the right-hand side of the diagram, which means you work from the right side to the left side. On wrong-side rows, the number is on the left-hand side, so you follow the diagram from left to right.

- ✔ When working in rounds, you read the diagram counterclockwise, without turning between rows unless the instructions specifically tell you to do so.

- ✔ Stitch diagrams are generally laid out from the right-handed crocheter's point of view, but a left-handed crocheter can read them just as well if he or she reverses the direction of the pattern and works from left to right rather than right to left. To work in rounds, a lefty still follows the pattern counterclockwise, but he or she works the piece clockwise, thus reversing the direction of the pattern.

- ✔ Because crochet is somewhat three-dimensional, the two-dimensional stitch diagram has some limitations. So if a pattern also has written instructions, you want to check those out as well.

Translating a stitch diagram into written instructions

Now it's time to try your hand at reading an actual stitch diagram. The one in Figure 4-2 is for a lacy pattern that you work in rows. (To try out a stitch diagram for a design in rounds, head to Chapter 8.) Notice that this particular stitch diagram doesn't look complete. Because this pattern is worked in identical rows consisting of repeated sets of stitches (the eight-stitch repeat in each row is shaded), the diagram shows only a few rows to save space. *Remember:* The pattern will always tell you how many rows to make to get the exact result it shows.

If you want to go your own way and make a piece wider, narrower, longer, or shorter than the pattern specifies — for example, a runner that's 12 inches wide or a tablecloth that's 52 inches wide — just add more sets of repeats to each row and add more rows.

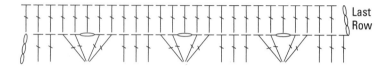

Last
Row

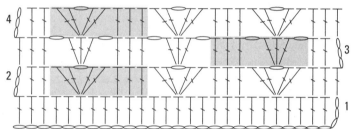

Figure 4-2: Stitch diagram of a repeated lacy-row pattern.

To begin this design, you make a foundation chain (represented by the row of oval chain stitch symbols at the bottom of Figure 4-2) that's about the width you want, making sure it's a multiple of eight stitches (to allow for the repeat). Then you chain two more for the end of the row plus three more for the turning chain for the first double crochet of Row 1. For example, you could start with 21 chain stitches ($2 \times 8 + 2 + 3 = 21$) or 85 chain stitches ($10 \times 8 + 2 + 3 = 85$). Figure 4-2 starts with 29 chain stitches ($3 \times 8 + 2 + 3 = 29$).

The following steps take you from Row 1 to the last row. The Crochetese appears first, but it's followed by the plain-English translation so you can see how the written instructions correspond to the visual diagram. Figure 4-3 shows you what the piece should look like when you're done.

1. **Row 1: Dc in fourth ch from hook, dc in each ch across, *turn*.**

   Double crochet stitch in the fourth chain from the hook, double crochet in each chain going across, and then turn.

2. **Row 2: Ch 3 (turning ch for first dc), dc in each of next 2 dc, * skip next 2 dc (2 dc, ch 1, 2 dc) in next dc, skip next 2 dc, dc in each of next 3 dc *; rep from * to * across, ending with last dc of last rep in top of turning ch, *turn*.**

For Row 2, chain 3 to make the turning chain for the first double crochet stitch and double crochet in each of the next 2 double crochet stitches. For the repeated part of this row (the instructions that are shown between the asterisks), skip the next 2 double crochet stitches, work 2 double crochet stitches into the next double crochet, chain 1, work 2 more double crochet stitches in the same double crochet, skip the next 2 double crochet stitches, and then work 1 double crochet in each of the next 3 double crochet stitches. Repeat this section until you reach the end of the row, ending with a double crochet in the top of the previous row's turning chain. Turn your work.

3. **Row 3: Ch 3 (turning ch for first dc), dc in each of next 2 dc, * ch 1, skip next 2 dc, 3 dc in next ch-1 sp, ch 1, skip next 2 dc, dc in each of next 3 dc *; rep from * to * across, ending with last dc of last rep in top of turning ch, *turn*.**

To complete Row 3, chain 3 for your turning chain and then work 1 double crochet stitch in each of the next 2 double crochet stitches. For the repeated part of this row (the instructions that are shown between the asterisks), chain 1, skip the next 2 double crochet stitches, work 3 double crochet stitches in the next chain-1 space, chain 1, skip the next 2 double crochet stitches, and then work 1 double crochet stitch in each of the next 3 double crochet stitches. Repeat this section until you reach the end of the row, ending with a double crochet in the top of the previous row's turning chain. Turn your work.

4. **Row 4: Ch 3 (turning ch for first dc), dc in each of next 2 dc, * skip next 2 sts, (2 dc, ch 1, 2 dc) in next dc, skip next 2 sts, dc in each of next 3 dc *; rep from * to * across, ending with last dc of last rep in top of turning ch, *turn*.**

To complete Row 4, chain 3 for your turning chain and then work 1 double crochet stitch into each of the next 2 double crochet stitches. For the repeated part of this row (the instructions shown between the asterisks), skip the next chain-1 space and the next double crochet stitch, work 2 double crochet stitches, chain 1, work 2 more double crochet stitches into the next double crochet stitch, skip the next double crochet stitch and the next chain-1 space, and then work 1 double crochet stitch into each of the next 3 double crochet stitches. Repeat this section until you reach the end of the row, ending with a double crochet in the top of the previous row's turning chain. Turn your work.

5. **Rep Rows 3–4 for desired length.**

Repeat Row 3 and then repeat Row 4, alternating these 2 rows until your piece is as long as you want it to be.

6. **Last Row: Ch 3 (turning ch for first dc), dc in each st and space across, ending with dc in top of turning ch. Fasten off.**

   Begin the last row from the right side, chain 3 for your turning chain, and then work 1 double crochet stitch in each double crochet stitch and each chain-1 space across the entire row. You should have the same number of double crochet stitches in this row as you have in Row 1. Fasten off your work.

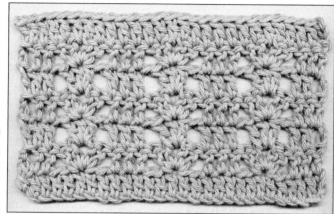

Figure 4-3:
A swatch
of lacy-row
pattern.

Part II
Basic Stitches and Techniques

The 5th Wave   By Rich Tennant

"Crocheting has a language all its own. You go down the pike, lasso the yarn, allemande right, rabbit comes up the hole, then do-si-so back to the starting gate."

In this part . . .

This part gets down to the nitty-gritty techniques you need for crocheting. We unravel the mysteries of the basic stitches that you need to start making beautiful and useful crocheted projects. We also delve into the subjects of increasing and decreasing, crocheting in circles, and working with more than one color of yarn.

To help demonstrate these new topics, we provide several projects that you'll be crocheting in no time flat. To get you used to reading crochet patterns, the projects start out with both the Crochetese and the plain-English translations. By the end of the part, however, we eliminate the translations. (*Note:* If you're ever not entirely comfortable reading the instructions in Crochetese, you can always refer to Chapter 4 for help deciphering the abbreviations.)

Chapter 5

Focusing on Fundamental Stitches

In This Chapter

▶ Getting a grip on crochet preparation

▶ Keeping you in (three) stitches and deciphering the parts of a complete stitch

▶ Creating the foundation and turning your work around

▶ Fastening off your yarn

▶ Pampering yourself with soft, luxurious washcloths

When you think about it, crochet is nothing more than a series of loops made with a hook and some yarn, worked row on row or round after round. Piece o' cake! This chapter takes you through the basics of getting your loops right: from picking up your hook and holding your yarn to completing your first rows of stitches. It also includes diagrams and instructions for both lefties and righties.

In the Beginning: Preparing to Crochet

Before you even attempt your first stitch, you need to get some basic skills under your belt. The following sections explain which hand you should crochet with and show you how to hold the hook and yarn and how to get the yarn on the hook with slipknots and yarn overs.

Determining the correct hand for hooking

The "right" hand for holding your crochet hook isn't necessarily the one on your right side. Your *dominant hand* — the one you write with, eat with, and do just about everything else with — is the hand you should hold your hook in. This is the hand that does most of the action; your other hand guides the yarn and holds the work you've already completed.

All the information in this book deals with techniques from a right-hander's point of view, but it applies to you lefties as well. Don't get discouraged. Your motions are exactly the same. If the instruction says right, think left; if it says left, think right. In order to make sure you get off on the right foot (or should we say left foot?), however, the beginning crochet techniques in this chapter include diagrams for both hands. See the nearby sidebar, "For southpaws only," for some additional techniques to help you through the rest of this book.

Getting a grip on the hook and yarn

Even though you crochet with only one hook, both hands are busy the whole time. Your dominant hand holds the hook, and your other hand holds the yarn. We explain how in the next sections.

Holding the hook

Holding your crochet hook is pretty simple. You just need to get the correct grip on it. If your hand isn't comfortable, it can cramp up, resulting in uneven stitches. Crocheting should be relaxing, not a continuous fight with the hook and yarn. Experiment with the two following positions to see which one feels more comfortable for you. Both are common ways of holding the crochet hook that work just fine — for lefties *or* righties:

 ✔ **Over-the-hook position:** Place your dominant hand over the hook with the handle resting against your palm and your thumb and middle finger grasping the thumb rest (see Figure 5-1).

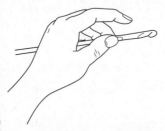

Figure 5-1:
The over-the-hook position for lefties and righties.

 ✔ **Under-the-hook position:** Hold the hook as you would a pencil with the thumb rest between your forefinger and thumb (see Figure 5-2).

Figure 5-2:
The under-
the-hook
position for
lefties and
righties.

Holding the yarn

After you decide how you want to hold the hook, you're ready for the yarn. Your *yarn hand* — the hand not holding your hook — has an important job: Not only does it feed the yarn to your crochet hook but it also controls the tension of the yarn.

Right-handed crocheters wrap the yarn over their left hand; left-handed crocheters wrap the yarn over their right hand. Figure 5-3 shows you what yarn wrapped around your hand should look like. (It may look like it, but your fingers really don't have to be contortionists to get into position.)

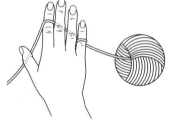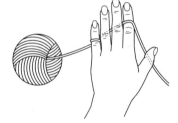

Figure 5-3:
Wrapping
the yarn
over your
yarn hand.

The following steps offer one common method for wrapping the yarn around your hand:

1. **Starting from underneath your hand, bring the yarn up between your little finger and ring finger.**

2. **Wrap the yarn around your little finger to form a loop.**

3. **Draw the yarn under your ring finger and middle finger.**

4. **Bring the yarn up to the top of your hand between your middle finger and forefinger.**

5. **Finally, lay the yarn over your forefinger and under your thumb.**

For southpaws only

If thinking left rather than right just isn't concrete enough for you, use the following tips to help you work your way through a crochet pattern from the opposite perspective:

- **Replace the word *right* with *left* in pattern instructions.** If you're planning to crochet with your left hand, look over the pattern, cross out the word *right,* and replace it with the word *left.* This troubleshooting step can be especially helpful when you're doing "right front" and "left front" shaping on a sweater.

- **Rely on a mirror image.** If you're a picture person who relies on illustrations to help you understand a concept, hold the pictures in this book up to a mirror to view them as they should be for lefties. Doing so may be a bit awkward, but a quick view from the correct angle may help you visualize better. A makeup mirror that has a base and can sit on the open page works well and leaves your hands free to follow the image in the mirror.

- **Trace your way to success.** If you want a more permanent illustration, or if the mirror trick just doesn't cut it for you, trace the diagrams and illustrations on a piece of tracing paper and then flip the paper over. Doing so gives you the view from the left-hand side. (Want a more high-tech approach? If you have a scanner and a photo software application on your computer, scan the diagrams and illustrations and flip them horizontally.)

- **Try to crochet the right-handed way.** If you're brand-new to the craft and somewhat ambidextrous, you can try crocheting right-handed. You may be surprised that your hands do just what you tell them, thereby avoiding the extra work of having to translate the instructions.

To keep the yarn in place, grasp the end of the yarn between your middle finger and thumb. You can control the yarn tension by raising or lowering your forefinger, so practice wrapping and rewrapping the yarn around your yarn hand. If you ever feel that your working yarn is too loose or too tight, stop and rewrap to get the proper tension. (Don't worry. This motion soon becomes an ingrained habit.)

Note: Other methods of wrapping the yarn around your hand exist. If you prefer, you can just wrap the yarn around your forefinger twice, or you can weave the yarn through all of your fingers except your little finger. Regardless of the method you choose, the goal should be to allow the yarn to flow smoothly and evenly through your fingers so you can apply just the right amount of tension.

When you first start working with yarn, use a light, solid-color, worsted-weight yarn (see Chapter 2 for the basics on yarn). This type of yarn allows you to see your stitches more clearly and manipulate the yarn more easily. Textured or variegated yarn takes a little more babying.

From this point on, the diagrams in this chapter aren't marked "lefty" or "righty." But here's a clue: The left diagrams in the figures are for lefties, and the right diagrams are for righties.

Working a slipknot

To get started on any crocheted piece, you first have to *join,* or attach, the yarn to the hook with a slipknot. The standard slipknot is really simple. Just follow these steps:

1. **Beginning about 6 inches from the end of the yarn, make a loop that looks somewhat like a pretzel.**

   Refer to the pretzel-shaped loop on the hook in Figure 5-4.

2. **Insert your hook through the center of the loop and draw the working end of the yarn through.**

   Refer to the shaded section of the pretzel-shaped loop in Figure 5-4.

Figure 5-4:
Pulling the yarn through the loop.

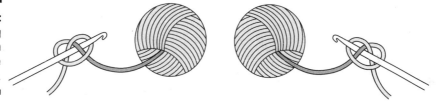

3. **Pull gently on both ends of the yarn to tighten the loop around the hook (see Figure 5-5).**

   Pulling on the tail end alone tightens the knot below the hook, and pulling on the working end adjusts the loop around the hook.

Figure 5-5:
Tightening the loop around the hook.

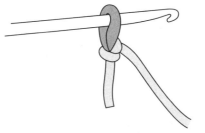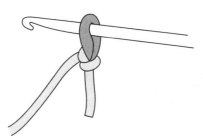

A good slipknot should slide easily up and down the hook's shaft, but it shouldn't be so loose that it slides off over the end of the hook. If your knot is too loose, gently pull on the working end of the yarn to snug it up. Also, because you have to pull your hook back through to make your first stitch, your slipknot shouldn't be too tight either. If it is too tight, simply tug on the loop to loosen it, leaving some space below the hook where the yarn for the next stitch will pass through.

If pulling on the working end of the yarn doesn't tighten your slipknot on the hook but yanking on the tail end does, you made your slipknot backwards. Simply remove the loop from the hook, tug on both ends to release the knot, and try again.

Now that you have the yarn on the hook, you're ready to begin making stitches. Make sure your hands are in the proper position, holding the slipknot with your yarn hand. If you're using the over-the-hook method for holding the hook (with your forefinger on top of the hook, your thumb underneath, and the shaft resting against your palm), see Figure 5-6 for the proper position of both hands.

Figure 5-6:
Proper position of both hands for the over-the-hook position.

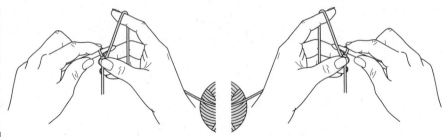

If you're more comfortable with the under-the hook position (where you're holding the hook similar to the way you'd hold a pen or pencil), refer to Figure 5-7 for a visual of the proper positioning.

Figure 5-7:
Proper position of both hands for the under-the-hook position.

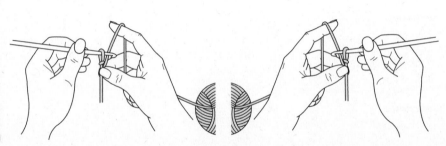

Wrapping the yarn over the hook

Wrapping the yarn over the hook, called a *yarn over* (abbreviated *yo*), is the most basic step to any crochet stitch. Sometimes you yarn over before you insert the hook into the next stitch, sometimes after, and sometimes you yarn over two or more times. The location and number of yarn overs really depends on the stitch.

Yarning over is very simple, but you have to do it right. Otherwise you won't be able to draw the yarn smoothly through the stitch. Practice the yarn over motion until you're comfortable with it. To yarn over correctly, follow these steps:

1. **Make a slipknot.**

2. **Slide the slipknot onto the hook's shaft.**

3. **With your yarn hand, hold the tail of the slipknot between your thumb and middle finger.**

4. **Using the forefinger of your yarn hand, bring the yarn up behind the hook.**

5. **Lay the yarn over the hook's shaft, positioned between the slipknot and the throat of the hook, as shown in Figure 5-8.**

Figure 5-8:
What a finished yarn over looks like when done correctly.

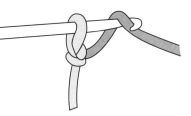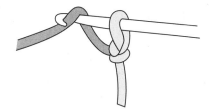

Always try to keep the loops on the hook loose enough so they slide easily on the hook.

If you try to wrap the yarn over your hook from front to back (see Figure 5-9), rather than from back to front, crocheting is more difficult, and you end up with twisted, tangled stitches.

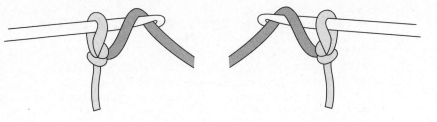

Figure 5-9:
An incorrect
yarn over.

Tied Up in Stitches: The Three Basics

Three basic stitches are used most often in crochet: the chain stitch, the slip stitch, and the single crochet. The next sections walk you through how to create these simple stitches.

The first few stitches you make are often the hardest because you don't have much material to grasp onto with your yarn hand. Be patient; we promise it gets easier.

The (almost) universal starter: Chain stitch

The *chain stitch* (abbreviated *ch*) is the basis for all crochet. Almost every pattern begins with a chain stitch. If you're working in rows, your first row is a series of chain stitches, which (not surprisingly) is called a *foundation chain.* When you're ready to start a new row, guess what? You use the chain stitch! Sometimes you work just a few chain stitches and join them together to create a ring, which you use when working in rounds (see Chapter 8 for more about rounds).

In the following sections, we explain how to make the chain stitch and provide pointers on a few basic techniques, such as controlling the tension of your yarn, distinguishing the right side of the fabric from the wrong side, counting stitches, and working other stitches into chain stitches.

Creating your first chain stitch

Here's how to create your first chain stitch:

1. **Make a slipknot.**

   See the earlier "Working a slipknot" section for instructions.

2. **Slide the slipknot onto the hook's shaft.**

3. **With the forefinger of your yarn hand, yarn over the hook (yo) from back to front while holding the tail of the slipknot between the thumb and middle finger of your yarn hand.**

4. **Slide the yarn from the yarn over onto the throat of the hook.**

5. **With your hook hand, rotate the hook toward you so the throat faces the slipknot.**

6. **With gentle pressure upward on the hook, pull the hook (which is carrying the wrapped strand of yarn) through the loop on your hook, as shown in Figure 5-10.**

   You now have 1 complete chain stitch (ch) and 1 loop remaining on your hook.

Figure 5-10:
Making a
chain stitch.

Repeat Steps 3 through 6 until you feel comfortable with this motion.

Whenever you're drawing the hook through a loop or stitch, rotate it so the throat faces slightly downward and apply gentle pressure upward on the hook so it doesn't catch on any other loops of yarn. Pulling the hook away from the knot opens up the loop on the hook slightly and helps to provide space for the new yarn to go through the loop.

Controlling your yarn tension

Each chain stitch should be the same size as the one before it, which means that you're keeping your yarn tension even for all of your stitches. (See Figure 5-11.) If your stitches aren't the same size, don't get frustrated. The chain stitch takes practice, but pretty soon, you'll find yourself moving right along.

Try these tips for fixing tight and loose chain stitches:

✔ If you find that your stitches are very tight and it's difficult to draw the hook through the stitch, try relaxing your hands. You're probably pulling too tightly on the yarn as you're drawing it through.

✔ If you find that your stitches are too loose, shorten up the distance between your yarn hand and hook hand, and lift the forefinger of your yarn hand, thereby creating more tension.

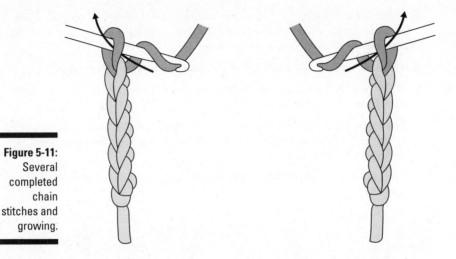

Figure 5-11:
Several
completed
chain
stitches and
growing.

As your chain gets longer and your hands get farther apart, you may have trouble controlling your work. Just let go of the bottom of your chain and, with the thumb and middle finger of your yarn hand, grab onto the chain closer to the hook, as Figure 5-12 shows. Holding the chain closer to the hook keeps your work stationary so you can control your stitches and maintain even tension. As your work gets longer, keep readjusting so you're always holding your completed work relatively close to the hook. (*Note:* This bit of advice applies to all of your work as you're crocheting, not just chains. In fact, you'll probably find that you do it without even thinking about it after a while.)

Figure 5-12:
Hold
completed
chain
stitches
closer to
the hook to
control your
work.

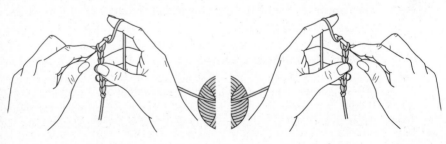

Telling right from wrong

Each stitch has a *right side* (front) and a *wrong side* (back). The right side of the chain is smooth, and you can see each stitch clearly. The wrong side has a small bumpy loop on each stitch. Figure 5-13 shows both the right and wrong sides of a chain.

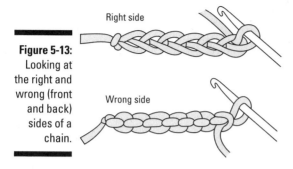

Figure 5-13:
Looking at
the right and
wrong (front
and back)
sides of a
chain.

Right side

Wrong side

When you're talking about the right or wrong side of a piece of crocheted fabric, the first row of stitches (not counting the foundation chain) is generally considered the right side. You can always distinguish which side of the fabric you're looking at by locating the tail of the foundation chain. If it's on your left (that is, if you're right-handed), then the right side is facing you; if it's on the right, then the wrong side is toward you. (The reverse is true for lefties.)

Counting stitches

Knowing what to count as a stitch is important when figuring out whether you've crocheted enough chain stitches for your foundation chain. Fortunately, it's quite easy. The loop on your hook doesn't count as a stitch. The first stitch is the one directly below your hook, and you begin counting from there, continuing down the chain until you reach the last chain stitch before the slipknot, which you don't count either. For example, Figure 5-14, in the next section, shows a chain of six chain stitches.

Working other stitches into chain stitches

To work your next row of stitches into the chain stitches, you have to know where to insert your hook. If you look at an individual stitch, you see that it consists of three separate loops or strands of yarn: two strands that create the V on the right side, which are called the *top 2 loops,* and a third that creates the bump on the wrong side. You can insert your hook anywhere in the stitch and start stitching, but you get the best results like this: With the right side of the chain facing you, insert your hook between the top loops and under the back bump loop, catching the loops on your hook (as shown in Figure 5-14). Working in the chain stitches like this gives you a neat base without any loose loops hanging down. (See the later "The Anatomy of a Stitch" section for more about top loops and the other parts of a complete crochet stitch.)

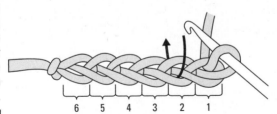

Figure 5-14:
Knowing where to insert your hook in the foundation chain.

The utility stitch: Slip stitch

The *slip stitch* (abbreviated *sl st*) is the flattest (or smallest) of all the crochet stitches, and only the chain stitch is easier to make. Although you can use it to crochet a fabric, the slip stitch is really more of a utility stitch. Here are a few of its uses:

- ✔ **Making a seam:** Slip stitching is good for joining pieces of crocheted fabric. Because the slip stitch is relatively flat, it doesn't create a bulky seam. (See Chapter 15 for more on joining pieces of crochet.)

- ✔ **Shaping your work:** If you have to travel from one point to another to shape a crocheted item, such as for armholes in a garment, and you don't want to fasten off your yarn and rejoin it, the slip stitch is ideal because it's so flat it's almost invisible.

- ✔ **Joining a new ball of yarn:** When you have to join your yarn in a new place, whether for shaping purposes or to change colors (see Chapter 9), you use the slip stitch to attach it.

- ✔ **Creating a ring:** If you're working in rounds (like for a doily), the slip stitch joins one end of the chain to the other to create a ring. (We explain how to work in rounds in Chapter 8.)

- ✔ **Finishing the edges of your work:** Used as a final row or round on a design, the slip stitch creates a nice, neat border.

- ✔ **Embellishing crocheted fabric:** You can slip stitch across the surface of a piece of crocheted fabric to create the look of embroidery. (Chapter 18 gives you lots of embellishment ideas.)

- ✔ **Forming combination stitches:** You can combine the slip stitch with other stitches to form fancy-schmancy stitches. For example, you can combine the chain stitch with the slip stitch to form a *picot* stitch. (For more on combination stitches, see Chapter 10.)

The following steps show you how to make a slip stitch that forms a ring:

1. **Make a chain that's 6 chain stitches (ch 6) long.**

2. **Insert the hook into the first chain stitch you made.**

   This is the stitch that's farthest from your hook, as shown in Figure 5-15.

Figure 5-15:
Inserting
the hook
into the first
chain stitch
made.

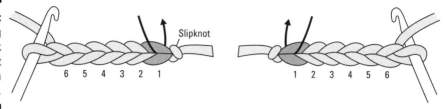

3. **With your yarn hand, yarn over (yo) by wrapping the yarn from back to front over the hook; with your hook hand, rotate the throat of the hook toward you.**

4. **While applying gentle pressure upward, draw the hook with the wrapped yarn back through the stitch and then through the loop on the hook in one motion (see Figure 5-16).**

Figure 5-16:
Wrapping
the yarn
over the
hook (yo)
and pulling
it through
the loops.

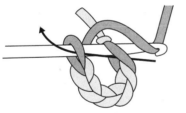 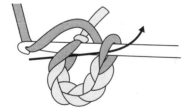

One slip stitch (sl st) is complete, and 1 loop remains on your hook. See Figure 5-17.

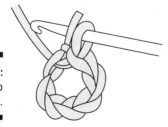

Figure 5-17:
Finishing up
a slip stitch.

The slip stitch forming a ring is all we show here, but no matter where you work the stitch, you always do it the same way.

The old standby: Single crochet

The *single crochet* (abbreviated *sc*) is the most fundamental of all stitches. A compact stitch, it creates a tight, dense fabric. You use this stitch over and over again, alone or in combination with other stitches. In the following sections, we explain how to make your first single crochet and complete a full row.

Creating your first single crochet

To begin your first row of single crochet:

1. **Make a foundation chain by doing 17 chain stitches (ch 17).**

2. **With the right side of the foundation chain facing you and your yarn hand holding the foundation chain, insert the hook from front to back into the second chain from the hook. (See Figure 5-18.)**

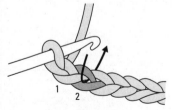

Figure 5-18: Inserting the hook into the second chain stitch from the hook.

3. **With your yarn hand, yarn over (yo) by wrapping the yarn from back to front over the hook.**

4. **Rotate the throat of the hook toward you with your hook hand.**

5. **Pull the hook with the wrapped yarn through the stitch, as Figure 5-19 shows.**

   You should have 2 loops on your hook.

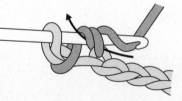
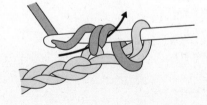

Figure 5-19: Drawing the yarn through the stitch.

6. **With your yarn hand, yarn over again and then rotate the throat of the hook toward you with your hook hand.**

7. **Draw the hook with the wrapped yarn through both loops on the hook, as shown in Figure 5-20.**

   One single crochet (sc) is complete, and 1 loop remains on your hook.

Figure 5-20:
Pull the yarn gently through both loops on the hook.

Continuing your first row of single crochet

Here's how to work the next single crochet stitch and continue the row:

1. **Insert your hook from front to back into the next chain stitch (ch), as shown in Figure 5-21.**

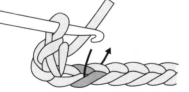
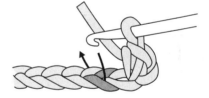

Figure 5-21:
Inserting the hook into the next chain stitch.

2. **Repeat Steps 3 through 7 from the first single crochet stitch instructions in the preceding section to complete the second stitch.**

3. **Work 1 single crochet stitch (sc) in each chain stitch across the foundation chain.**

   You should have 16 single crochet stitches, or 1 row of single crochet, as in Figure 5-22.

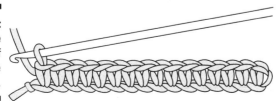

Figure 5-22:
A complete row of single crochet.

If you're wondering what happened to your 17th chain stitch, remember that you worked your first single crochet into the second chain from the hook. The skipped chain stitch is considered a turning chain that brings you up to the level needed to work your first stitch of the new row (see the "Climbing to new heights with turning chains" section, later in this chapter, for more on this topic).

Working stitches into the foundation chain isn't easy. Even experienced crocheters can have a tough time with this technique. But after the first few rows, you have more fabric to hold on to, which makes inserting your hook much easier.

Foundation Stitches: The Chain and the First Row All in One

Sometimes a pattern may direct you to use foundation stitches rather than a foundation chain made up of chain stitches. *Foundation stitches* are a nifty way to make the foundation chain and first row of stitches all at the same time. Easily adapted to any stitch, like the single crochet that we describe earlier in this chapter, each foundation stitch is made up of two parts: the foundation chain (which is at the base) and one standard stitch.

Foundation stitches have a few advantages over the standard foundation chain. They're generally

- Easier to keep track of, especially when you're working a long foundation row

- Good at keeping the tension of the foundation chain and first row even and consistent

- More elastic than standard foundation chains, making them especially suitable for garments

- Handy for making multiple increases at the ends of a row (see Chapter 7 for the scoop on increases)

You can work any stitch as a foundation stitch, but to keep it simple, we show you how to work several foundation single crochet (abbreviated *fsc*) in the following sections. **Remember:** Each *foundation single crochet* is a blend of one foundation chain stitch and one single crochet.

To make taller foundation stitches, you need to add a chain stitch to the beginning of the first row and make the required yarn overs as for the regular stitch. For example, to make a foundation double crochet (abbreviated *fdc*), begin with three chains and yarn over the hook before beginning the first stitch. Make the foundation chain as you would for the foundation single crochet and then work the loops off two at a time as you would a normal double crochet stitch (Chapter 6 has more on double crochet).

Your first foundation single crochet

Follow these steps to create your first foundation single crochet:

1. **Begin with 2 chain stitches (ch 2).**

   Refer to the earlier "The (almost) universal starter: Chain stitch" section for guidance on forming this stitch.

2. **Insert the hook from front to back into the chain farthest from the hook.**

3. **Yarn over (yo) by wrapping the yarn from back to front over the hook and pull the yarn through the chain stitch. See Figure 5-23.**

   You should have 2 loops on the hook.

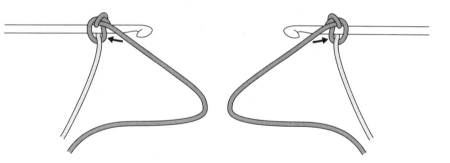

Figure 5-23:
Pulling
your yarn
through a
chain stitch.

4. **Yarn over the hook and pull the yarn through the first loop (the one closest to the hook end) on the hook.**

   Well done! You've just completed the foundation chain portion (shown in Figure 5-24) of your first foundation single crochet stitch (fsc).

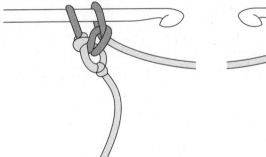

Figure 5-24:
Finishing the
foundation
chain
portion.

5. **Yarn over the hook and pull the yarn through both loops on the hook.**

   This completes the single crochet (sc) portion (shown in Figure 5-25) of your first foundation single crochet stitch.

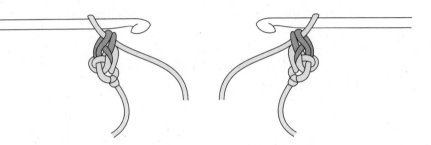

Figure 5-25:
Finishing
the single
crochet
portion.

Your second foundation single crochet and beyond

After you make your first foundation single crochet, follow these steps to create your second one:

1. **Insert the hook from front to back into the chain stitch (ch) made at the base of the previous stitch (see Figure 5-26).**

2. **Yarn over (yo) by wrapping the yarn from back to front over the hook and pull the yarn through the chain stitch.**

   You should have 2 loops on the hook (see Figure 5-27).

3. **Yarn over the hook and pull the yarn through the first loop on the hook (the one hanging out closer to the hook end).**

   This completes the foundation chain portion (shown in Figure 5-28) of your second foundation single crochet stitch (fsc).

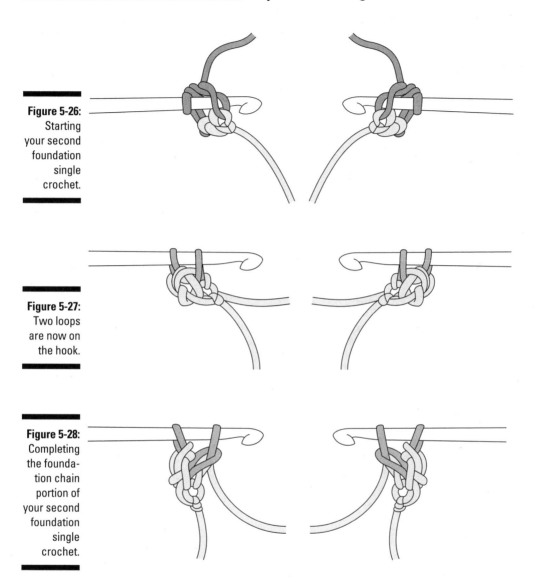

Figure 5-26: Starting your second foundation single crochet.

Figure 5-27: Two loops are now on the hook.

Figure 5-28: Completing the foundation chain portion of your second foundation single crochet.

4. **Yarn over the hook and pull the yarn through both loops on the hook.**

   Tada! You've now completed the single crochet (sc) portion (shown in Figure 5-29) of your second foundation single crochet stitch.

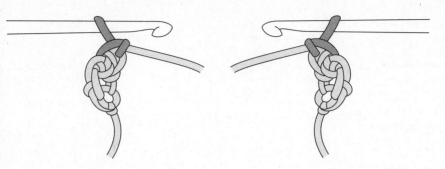

Figure 5-29:
Completing
the single
crochet
portion of
your second
foundation
single
crochet.

Repeat Steps 1 through 4 for each foundation single crochet you need in a particular pattern.

Taking Things to the Next Level: Row Two

If you read the earlier section on the single crochet stitch and followed the steps, you now have a complete row of single crochet, and you're probably thinking, "Now what?" The answer's simple: You turn around and work back the same way you came. The following sections show you how to turn your work around so that the tops of the stitches in the previous row are in the proper position, which way to turn, and how to begin that first stitch of the new row.

Turning your work

To turn your work around so you can start a new row of stitches, keep the last loop on your hook and simply take the completed work, which should be positioned under your hook hand, and turn it toward you until the work is positioned under your yarn hand (see Figure 5-30). This way, you hold the work between the middle finger and thumb of your yarn hand, your yarn is positioned behind your work, and the hook is in place to work the beginning stitches of the next row.

Keep in mind that each time you turn your work to crochet back across the previous row, a different side of the piece will be facing you. If the first row is designated as the right side of the piece, then when you turn to work the second row, the wrong side is facing you. The third row again has the right side facing you, and so on. (See the earlier "Telling right from wrong" section for a refresher on what the right and wrong sides of a piece look like.)

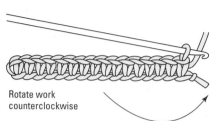
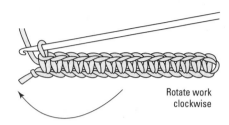

Figure 5-30:
Turning your work in order to crochet back across the row.

Rotate work counterclockwise

Rotate work clockwise

Climbing to new heights with turning chains

After you turn your piece around, you're ready to crochet the *turning chain,* the one or more chain stitches that you make after you've turned your work and are about to begin your next row. The purpose of the turning chain is to bring your yarn to the height necessary in order to work the first stitch of your next row or round.

The number of chain stitches you make in the turning chain depends on what the next stitch in the row is, because some stitches are taller than others. Figure 5-31 shows the height differences of several turning chains used for successively taller stitches. (See Chapter 6 for more info on taller stitches.)

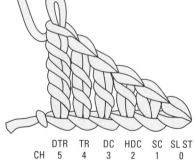
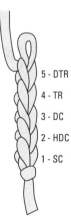

Figure 5-31:
A comparison of turning chain heights.

	DTR	TR	DC	HDC	SC	SL ST
CH	5	4	3	2	1	0

5 - DTR
4 - TR
3 - DC
2 - HDC
1 - SC

Table 5-1 lists the number of chain stitches you need for several frequently used stitches.

Table 5-1 How Many Chain Stitches Make a Turning Chain?	
Stitch Name	*Number of Turning Chains Needed*
Slip stitch (sl st)	0
Single crochet (sc)	1
Half double crochet (hdc)	2
Double crochet (dc)	3
Triple crochet (tr)	4
Double triple crochet (dtr)	5

The turning chain almost always counts as the first stitch of the next row, except for the single crochet. (The single crochet turning chain isn't wide enough to substitute for the first single crochet of the row and creates a rough edge to your rows. Working a single crochet stitch in the first stitch of the row fills out each row on the end.)

Starting the next row

Going back and forth and back and forth may not get you places in real life, but it sure does when you're crocheting in rows. The following steps show you how to make your turning chain and begin a new row of single crochet, so grab your completed row of 16 single crochet stitches from the earlier single crochet section:

1. **Turn your work to prepare for the next row.**

2. **Make 1 chain stitch (ch 1).**

   This is your turning chain for single crochet (sc).

3. **Insert your hook from front to back underneath the top 2 loops of the first stitch, as shown in Figure 5-32.**

Figure 5-32: Inserting the hook under the top 2 loops of the first stitch.

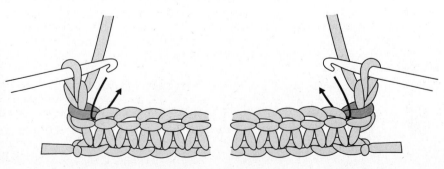

4. **Yarn over (yo) by wrapping the yarn from back to front over the hook.**

5. **Draw your yarn through the stitch, as shown in Figure 5-33.**

Figure 5-33: Drawing the yarn through the stitch.

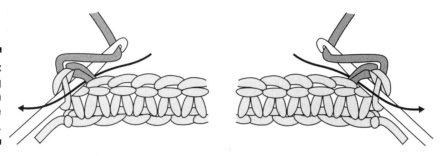

6. **Yarn over again by wrapping the yarn from back to front over the hook.**

7. **Draw your yarn through the 2 loops on the hook.**

   Now you have 1 single crochet in the second row completed, and 1 loop remains on the hook. (See Figure 5-34.)

Figure 5-34: A new row with one complete single crochet.

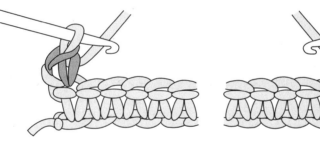

To complete the row, work one single crochet stitch in each single crochet stitch from the previous row and continue doing so all the way to the end. You work the stitches exactly the same way as when you're working them into the foundation chain; you just place your hook in the top of a stitch from a previous row instead. Make sure to count your stitches when you get to the end of the row. You should have exactly the same number of stitches in the second row as in the first (in this case, 16).

Some patterns like to change things up and may tell you to insert your hook in a different place in the previous row. But if no specific instructions are given, always work the stitches in each subsequent row under the top 2 loops of the stitch in the previous row. This is the best way to create a smooth, even fabric.

Working a practice swatch helps you figure out new stitches and start making them like a pro. Use worsted-weight yarn (it's easiest to work with) and a size H-8 U.S. (5 mm) hook (see Chapter 2 for more on yarn weights and hook sizes) to make a foundation chain that's approximately 4 inches long and then chain 1 for your turning chain. Work as many rows of single crochet as you need to until you feel comfortable with the new stitch and your stitches have a smooth, even look.

The Anatomy of a Stitch

After you're comfortable holding the hook and the yarn and making a few basic stitches, you're ready to explore the anatomy of a stitch in more detail so you know where to put the hook for stitches we cover in the rest of this book. Fortunately, a stitch's anatomy isn't nearly as complicated as that of the frog you dissected in high school.

The following list breaks down each part of a stitch (you can check out Figure 5-35 for the visual):

- **Top 2 loops:** The two loops you see at the top of the stitch.
- **Front loop:** The top loop closest to you.
- **Front-most loop:** The loop found at the front of a stitch, just below the front loop. This loop is found in stitches with at least one extra yarn over, like the half double crochet or double crochet. (See Chapter 6 for an introduction to these stitches.)
- **Back loop:** The top loop farthest from you or behind the front loop.
- **Back-most loop:** The loop found at the back of a stitch just below the back loop. This loop is found in stitches with at least one extra yarn over, like the half double crochet or double crochet.
- **Base:** The two loops at the bottom of the stitch. The base of a new stitch is the top of the stitch below it.

  The base is the most stable part of a stitch to work into when working a border or sewing pieces together.

- **Post:** The body of the stitch, located between the top 2 loops and the base. It varies in height depending on the stitch and is also referred to as the *stem*. When it's located at the end of a row and you're working into it when adding a border or edging, the post is also considered the side of the stitch.

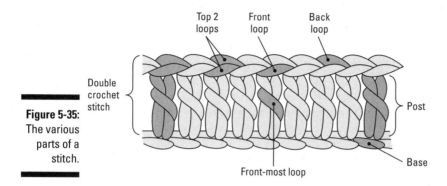

Figure 5-35:
The various parts of a stitch.

Top 2 loops

Front loop

Back loop

Double crochet stitch

Post

Base

Front-most loop

All's Well That Ends Well: Fastening Off

Sooner or later, you're going to come to the end of your design and need to *fasten off* (cut) the yarn. Or maybe you're working with different colors and need to fasten off one color to join the new color (see Chapter 9 for more on switching colors). The next sections show you how and where to cut the yarn and what to do with the leftover tail.

Cutting the yarn

To fasten off your yarn, cut it about 6 inches from the hook. (See the next section to find out why you leave this much yarn.) Using your hook, draw the cut end of the yarn through the last remaining loop on your hook, as shown in Figure 5-36. Pull gently on the tail of yarn to snug up the end. This action keeps your work from coming apart without you having to make large, unsightly knots.

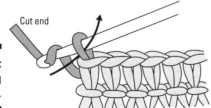

Cut end

Figure 5-36:
Fastening off.

Weaving in the end

Weaving in the leftover tail through a few stitches ensures that your yarn ends are secured and hidden, resulting in a neatly finished appearance. To do this, thread the remaining yarn tail onto a yarn needle (which we introduce in Chapter 2). Being careful not to split the yarn of the stitches, weave the 6-inch tail of yarn through four or five stitches — kind of in a zigzag pattern. To really make the end secure, go back the way you came, weaving the end backward through those same few stitches. When finished, cut the yarn about ¼ inch from the fabric and gently pull the fabric. The end disappears like magic, and your work is secure.

The stitches you weave your ends through depend on the position of the tail end.

- ✔ If your end comes out at the top or bottom of the piece, simply weave it back and forth under the top loops of the stitches along the same row.

- ✔ If your end emerges along the side of the fabric, weave it vertically, either up or down, through the stitches found along the same edge.

Always check to make sure your woven ends aren't visible from the right side of the work. If you find that one is, simply pull it through the fabric to the wrong side.

Luxurious Washcloth Projects

The following projects let you practice your newfound basic skills while creating luxuriously soft and absorbent washcloths that are suitable for yourself or as gifts for friends. Check out both projects in the color section.

Simple Luxurious Washcloth project

The yarn used in this project is a lofty, organic, worsted-weight cotton that grows softer with each wash and is easy to find in an array of natural or bright colors. Feel free to use the given color (shown in the color section) or choose your own to match your style. One skein contains enough yarn to make two cloths.

Materials and vital statistics

- ✔ **Yarn:** Blue Sky Alpacas "Organic Cotton" worsted-weight yarn (100% organic cotton), (3.5 oz. [100 g], 150 yds [137 m] each skein): 1 skein of #80 Bone

Note: If you can't find the Blue Sky Alpacas cotton, a suitable substitution is Lion Brand "Nature's Choice Organic Cotton."

✔ **Hook:** Standard crochet hook size I-9 U.S. (5.5 mm) or size needed to obtain gauge

✔ **Large-eyed yarn needle**

✔ **Measurements:** 10 in. x 10 in. square

✔ **Gauge:** 14 sts and 16 rows in sc = 4 in.

✔ **Stitches used:** Chain stitch (ch), single crochet (sc)

Directions

The following directions are written in plain English, not Crochetese, to help walk you through your first project. Refer to the chain stitch section and single crochet section earlier in this chapter for details on each stitch.

1. **Create your foundation chain by working 36 chain stitches in a row (ch 36).**

2. **To complete Row 1, work 1 single crochet stitch (sc) in the second chain from the hook and then work 1 single crochet stitch in each chain across the row.**

   You should have 35 complete single crochet stitches.

3. **Turn your work and then chain 1 for the single crochet turning chain to prepare for the next row.**

4. **To complete the next row, work 1 single crochet stitch in each single crochet stitch across the row.**

   You should have 35 complete single crochet stitches in this row.

5. **Repeat Steps 3 and 4 until you have 40 rows on your work.**

6. **Fasten off your yarn and weave in the loose ends using the yarn needle.**

Luxurious Washcloth with Border project

This project, a simple adaptation of the previous washcloth, takes your skills to the next level with the addition of a bright and colorful border. Working on this project requires a few additional techniques, such as adding a new yarn color (see Chapter 9) and working into the sides of the rows (refer to Chapter 11). The yarn we recommend is soft and comes in a variety of beautiful colors.

Materials and vital statistics

- ✔ **Yarn:** Blue Sky Alpacas "Organic Cotton" worsted-weight yarn (100% organic cotton), (3.5 oz. [100 g], 150 yds [137 m] each skein): 1 skein of #80 Bone (A)

  Blue Sky Alpacas "Dyed Cotton" worsted-weight yarn (100% organic cotton), (3.5 oz. [100 g], 150 yds [137 m] each skein): 1 skein each of

  - #601 Poppy (B for the small washcloth shown in the color insert)
  - #634 Periwinkle (B for the large washcloth shown in the color insert)

  Note: The pattern calls for only one color to be used in the border, but both colors are shown in the color section. Choose whichever color you prefer for your border, or choose another one to suit your décor.

  Note: If you can't find the Blue Sky Alpacas cotton, a suitable substitution is Lion Brand "Nature's Choice Organic Cotton."

- ✔ **Hook:** Standard crochet hook size I-9 U.S. (5.5 mm) or size needed to obtain gauge

- ✔ **Large-eyed yarn needle**

- ✔ **Measurements:** 10 in. x 10 in. square

- ✔ **Gauge:** 14 sts and 16 rows in sc = 4 in.

- ✔ **Stitches used:** Chain stitch (ch), single crochet (sc), slip stitch (sl st)

Directions

As in the preceding project, the following directions are written in plain English rather than Crochetese to help walk you through each step. Refer to the chain stitch, slip stitch, and single crochet sections earlier in this chapter for details on each stitch. Figure 5-37 shows the stitch diagram for this washcloth.

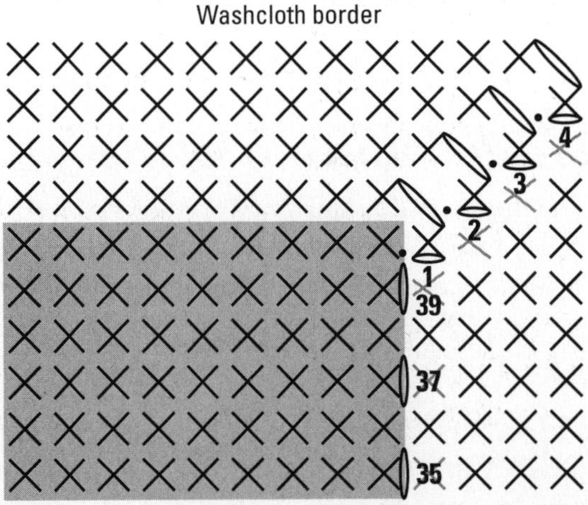

Washcloth border

Figure 5-37: The stitch diagram for the Luxurious Washcloth with Border project.

To make the washcloth's body, follow these steps:

1. **With A, create your foundation chain by working 29 chain stitches in a row (ch 29).**

2. **To complete Row 1, work 1 single crochet stitch (sc) in the second chain from the hook and then work 1 single crochet stitch in each chain across the row.**

   You should have 28 complete single crochet stitches.

3. **Turn your work and then chain 1 for the single crochet turning chain to prepare for the next row.**

4. **To complete the next row, work 1 single crochet stitch in each single crochet stitch across the row.**

   You should have 28 complete single crochet stitches in this row.

5. **Repeat Steps 3 and 4 until you have 32 rows on your work.**

6. **Fasten off your yarn and weave in the loose ends using the yarn needle.**

After you finish crocheting the washcloth's body, follow these steps to start the border:

1. **Insert your hook in the last stitch of the last row you worked and draw B through so you have 1 loop on the hook.**

   See Chapter 9 for information on how to join a new color.

2. **Make a corner by working 1 chain (ch 1) and then work 1 single crochet (sc), 1 chain, and 1 more single crochet all in the same stitch.**

3. **Working across the side edge of the washcloth, work 1 single crochet in each row-end stitch across to the last row-end stitch.**

4. **Make a corner by working 1 single crochet, 1 chain, and 1 more single crochet all in the last row-end stitch.**

   You should have 33 single crochet stitches between the 2 chain spaces.

5. **Working across the foundation edge, work 1 single crochet stitch in each chain stitch across to the last chain.**

6. **Work 1 single crochet, 1 chain, and 1 more single crochet all in the last chain stitch of the foundation edge.**

7. **Repeat Steps 3 and 4 once.**

8. **Work 1 single crochet stitch in the next stitch and in each stitch across until you reach the first single crochet of the border.**

9. **Work 1 slip stitch (sl st) in the first single crochet stitch to join.**

To continue Round 2 of the border:

1. **Continuing in the same direction, and without turning the piece, work 1 slip stitch (sl st) into the chain space.**

2. **Work 1 single crochet (sc), 1 chain (ch), and 1 more single crochet all in the same chain space.**

3. **Work 1 single crochet in the next single crochet and in each single crochet across to the chain space at the next corner.**

   There should be 33 single crochets between the 2 chain spaces.

4. **Work 1 single crochet, 1 chain, and 1 more single crochet all in the corner chain space.**

5. **Repeat Steps 3 and 4 twice.**

6. **Work 1 single crochet in the next single crochet and in each single crochet across to the first single crochet stitch of Round 2.**

7. **Work 1 slip stitch in the first single crochet stitch to join.**

8. **Repeat Round 2 twice more before fastening off the yarn and weaving in the loose ends.**

Baby washcloth

The two washcloth patterns provided earlier in this chapter make a generously portioned washcloth, but you can easily adjust the size to create a smaller washcloth or one that's perfect for a baby. All you need to do is work half the number of chains for either the basic washcloth or the washcloth with a border.

The washcloth with the orange border featured in the color section measures 5 inches square. To create one that's similar, make 15 chains and then work back and forth on 14 single crochets for 15 rows. Next, work the border as instructed in the preceding section.

Chapter 6

Long, Longer, Longest: Several Common Crochet Stitches

In This Chapter

▶ Creating four of the most common crochet stitches

▶ Extending a couple basic stitches

▶ Discovering two ways to join a new ball of yarn

▶ Crocheting your first scarf

*T*he beauty of crochet is that you can create so many patterns and textures by combining just three basic motions:

✔ Yarning over the hook

✔ Inserting your hook

✔ Drawing your yarn through

The first three stitches in this chapter — the double crochet, the triple crochet, and the double triple crochet — are each made a step taller than the one before with one extra yarn over. How simple is that? The fourth stitch, the half double crochet, is slightly different but makes sense after you master the other stitches in this chapter. We also throw in a couple extra stitches that are simple, extended variations on some basics. Each of the stitches presented in this chapter produces a slightly different textured fabric. When you combine them, the variety of possible patterns is endless!

Of course, now that you're making so many stitches, you're going to run out of yarn, so this chapter also shows you how to join a new skein without any unsightly lumps, bumps, or knots. You can put your newfound skills to use in the Sassy Scarf project at the end of this chapter. It's a beautiful design that you'll be proud to show off.

Doing a Double Crochet

The *double crochet* (abbreviated *dc*) is one of the most common crochet stitches and is about twice as tall as a single crochet, which debuts in Chapter 5. A fabric made of all double crochet stitches is fairly solid, but not stiff, and is great for sweaters, shawls, afghans, place mats, or any number of other home décor items. You can also combine the double crochet stitch with other stitches to produce many interesting patterns and textures. The next sections show you how to create the first two rows of the double crochet stitch.

First things first: Row 1

The following steps set you up to work your first double crochet stitch (see Chapter 5 for a refresher on foundation chains and turning chains):

1. **Make a foundation chain by doing 15 chain stitches (ch 15).**

2. **Chain 3 more stitches for the turning chain.**

   The double crochet turning chain makes your edges even with the height of the new row and is counted as a double crochet stitch (dc).

Most pattern books combine the steps for making a foundation chain and turning chain into one by telling you to chain a total of 18.

Now you're ready for your first double crochet.

1. **Yarn over the hook (yo).**

   Always yarn over from back to front when any of the taller stitches call for it.

2. **Insert your hook between the 2 front loops and under the back bump loop of the fourth chain (ch) from the hook.**

   Figure 6-1a provides the visual for this step. Refer to Chapter 5 for details on working into chain stitches.

Figure 6-1:
Beginning a
double
crochet
stitch.

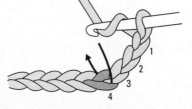

a

b

3. **Yarn over the hook.**

4. **Gently pull the wrapped hook through the center of the chain stitch, carrying the wrapped yarn through the stitch.**

   You should now have 3 loops on your hook, as shown in Figure 6-1b.

5. **Yarn over the hook.**

6. **Draw your yarn through the first 2 loops on your hook, like in Figure 6-2a.**

Figure 6-2:
Drawing
your yarn
through the
loops.

a   b

7. **Yarn over the hook.**

8. **Draw your yarn through the last 2 loops on the hook, as in Figure 6-2b.**

   One double crochet stitch (dc) is now complete. You should have 1 loop remaining on your hook.

To finish your first row of double crochet, work one double crochet stitch in each successive chain stitch across the foundation chain, beginning in the next chain of the foundation chain, as shown in Figure 6-3a. You should have 16 double crochet stitches in Row 1 (counting the turning chain as the first double crochet). Take a look at Figure 6-3b to see what the end of the first row of double crochet looks like.

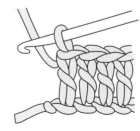

Figure 6-3:
Finishing the
first row of
double
crochet.

a   b

Turning around and beginning again: Row 2

To work the second row of double crochet, follow these steps:

1. **Turn your work so that the back side is facing you.**

   Chapter 5 explains how to turn your work correctly.

2. **Chain 3 (ch 3) to create the turning chain.**

3. **Yarn over the hook (yo).**

4. **Skipping the first stitch of the row directly below the turning chain, insert your hook into the next stitch.**

   Skipping the first stitch on taller stitches, such as the double crochet, keeps the edges even and straight. Figure 6-4a illustrates the right place to insert your hook, and Figure 6-4b shows the wrong one.

Figure 6-4:
Correctly (and incorrectly) inserting the hook for the first stitch of Row 2.

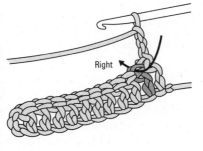 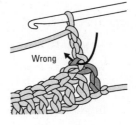

Right   Wrong

a   b

5. **Repeat Steps 3 through 8 from the preceding section in each of the next 14 double crochet stitches (dc).**

   Be sure to yarn over before inserting your hook into each stitch.

6. **Work 1 double crochet in the top chain of the previous row's turning chain, as shown in Figure 6-5.**

   You should have 16 double crochet stitches in Row 2 (counting the turning chain as 1 double crochet).

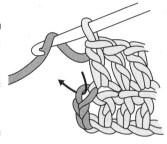

Figure 6-5:
Inserting the hook in the top chain of the turning chain.

Repeat these steps for each additional row of double crochet until you feel comfortable working this stitch. Figure 6-6 shows you how rows of double crochet look as a fabric.

Figure 6-6:
Several rows of double crochet.

Don't work a stitch into the first stitch of the row after the turning chain. Doing so produces an extra stitch, and if you continue to add a stitch in each row, your design grows ever wider as it gets longer and longer. Also, don't forget to put a double crochet into the top of the turning chain when you get to the end of a row. If you do, you'll lose a stitch, and continuing to drop a stitch per row makes your design narrower and narrower as it grows longer and longer. Be sure to count your stitches frequently to make sure you haven't inadvertently gained (or lost) any along the way.

Sometimes, especially when you're working with bulky yarn or a larger-than-usual hook, the turning chain on a double crochet row leaves a gap at the beginning of the row. To get a neater edge, try chaining two rather than three stitches for the turning chain.

Trying Your Hand at the Triple Crochet

The *triple crochet* (abbreviated *tr*), also called a *treble crochet* in many publications, is slightly longer than the double crochet. This stitch creates longer openings between the stitches and therefore produces a very loose fabric. For example, if you make a sweater with triple crochet, you'll want to wear a blouse under it or else risk revealing too much. However, the triple crochet is usually combined with other stitches in order to create pattern variety and produce interesting textures and fancier stitches. The following sections break down how to crochet your first two rows of triple crochet.

Starting with Row 1

Follow these steps so you're ready to make your first row of triple crochet (and, if necessary, check out Chapter 5 to refresh your memory on chains):

1. **Make a foundation chain by doing 15 chain stitches (ch 15).**

2. **Chain 4 more stitches for the turning chain.**

If a particular pattern tells you to start Row 1 of triple crochet by chaining 19, don't be surprised. It has merely combined the steps for making a foundation chain and turning chain into one.

To begin your first triple crochet stitch:

1. **Yarn over the hook (yo) 2 times.**

   Don't forget to yarn over from back to front.

2. **Insert your hook into the fifth chain (ch) from the hook, as shown in Figure 6-7a.**

3. **Yarn over the hook.**

4. **Gently pull the wrapped hook through the center of the chain stitch, carrying the wrapped yarn through the stitch.**

   You should have 4 loops on your hook, like in Figure 6-7b.

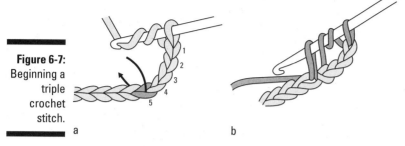

Figure 6-7:
Beginning a triple crochet stitch.

a   b

5. **Yarn over the hook.**

6. **Draw your yarn through the first 2 loops on your hook, as in Figure 6-8a.**

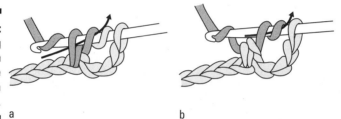

Figure 6-8:
Drawing the yarn through the loops on your hook.

a   b

7. **Yarn over the hook.**

8. **Draw your yarn through the next 2 loops on your hook.**

    See Figure 6-8b for the visual.

9. **Yarn over the hook.**

10. **Draw your yarn through the last 2 loops on your hook.**

    Figure 6-9a illustrates Step 10, and Figure 6-9b depicts a finished triple crochet stitch (tr) with 1 loop remaining on the hook.

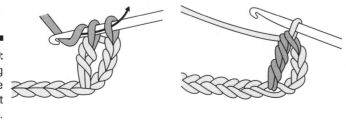

Figure 6-9:
Completing a triple crochet stitch.

a   b

To finish the row, yarn over twice and insert your hook into the next chain of the foundation chain, just like in Figure 6-10a. Work one triple crochet in each successive chain across the foundation chain. You should have 16 triple crochet stitches in Row 1 (counting the turning chain as 1 triple crochet). Figure 6-10b shows the end of the first triple crochet row.

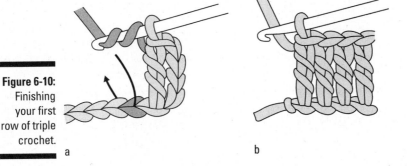

Figure 6-10: Finishing your first row of triple crochet.

a   b

Moving on to Row 2

To begin your second row of triple crochet, follow these steps:

1. **Turn your work.**

   Refer to Chapter 5 for help properly turning your work.

2. **Chain 4 (ch 4) for the turning chain.**

3. **Yarn over the hook (yo) 2 times.**

4. **Skipping the first stitch of the row directly below the turning chain, insert your hook into the next stitch.**

   Figure 6-11 depicts the right spot to insert your hook.

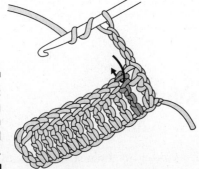

Figure 6-11: Inserting your hook in the second stitch.

5. **Repeat Steps 3 through 10 from the preceding section in each of the next 14 triple crochet stitches (tr).**

   Be sure to yarn over twice before inserting your hook in each stitch.

6. **Work 1 triple crochet in the top chain of the previous row's turning chain.**

   When you count the turning chain as 1 triple crochet, you should have 16 triple crochet stitches in Row 2.

Repeat these six steps for each additional row of triple crochet. Continue working rows of triple crochet until you feel comfortable with this stitch. To see how rows of triple crochet look as a fabric, check out Figure 6-12.

Figure 6-12: Several rows of triple crochet.

Diving into Double Triple Crochet

The *double triple crochet* (abbreviated *dtr*) is even taller than a triple crochet. As a fabric, it's loose and holey and commonly used in lacy designs, particularly doilies and other fine cotton crochet patterns. The following sections will have you stitching your first two rows of double triple crochet in no time.

First things first: Row 1

Before you begin a double triple crochet stitch:

1. **Make a foundation chain by working 15 chain stitches (ch 15).**

2. **Chain 5 more stitches for the turning chain.**

   Check out Chapter 5 for the lowdown on chains.

Most patterns combine these two steps and have you chain 20 to start, so don't be thrown off if you see that somewhere.

To complete your first double triple crochet stitch, perform the following seven steps:

1. **Yarn over the hook (yo) 3 times.**

   Always yarn over from back to front. Otherwise, you'll get frustrated when the yarn you're drawing through the stitch falls off the hook.

   If you're using the over-the-hook position to hold the hook, press the yarn-over loops to the hook with your index finger to prevent the chain from coiling around the hook.

2. **Insert the hook into the sixth chain (ch) from the hook, as shown in Figure 6-13a.**

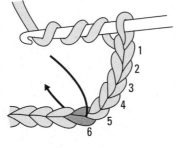 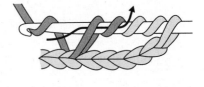

Figure 6-13:
Inserting
your hook
into the
sixth chain
from the
hook.

a   b

3. **Yarn over the hook.**

4. **Gently pull the wrapped hook through the center of the chain stitch, carrying the wrapped yarn through the stitch.**

   You should now have 5 loops on your hook (see Figure 6-13b).

5. **Yarn over the hook.**

6. **Draw your yarn through the first 2 loops on your hook.**

   You should have 4 loops remaining.

7. **Repeat Steps 5 and 6 three more times until you have only 1 loop left on the hook.**

   Congratulations! Your first double triple crochet stitch (dtr) is now complete.

To finish the row, begin a new double triple crochet stitch in the next chain of your foundation chain, as indicated in Figure 6-14a. Work one double triple crochet in each successive chain across the foundation chain, taking care to yarn over three times before inserting the hook in each chain. When you finish the row, you should have 16 double triple crochet stitches in Row 1 (counting the turning chain as 1 double triple crochet). Figure 6-14b illustrates what the end of the first row of double triple crochet looks like.

 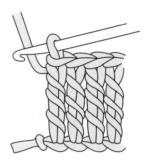

Figure 6-14: Finishing the first row of double triple crochet.

a   b

Turning around and beginning again: Row 2

To work the second row of double triple crochet, follow these steps:

1. **Turn your work.**

   Chapter 5 explains how to turn your work correctly.

2. **Chain 5 (ch 5) for the turning chain.**

3. **Yarn over the hook (yo) 3 times.**

4. **Skipping the first stitch of the row directly below the turning chain, insert your hook into the next stitch.**

5. **Repeat Steps 3 through 7 in the preceding section in each of the next 14 double triple crochet stitches (dtr).**

   Be sure to yarn over 3 times before inserting your hook in each stitch.

6. **Work 1 double triple crochet stitch in the top chain of the previous row's turning chain.**

   You should have 16 double triple crochet stitches in Row 2 (counting the turning chain as 1 double triple crochet).

Making your stitches even longer

Each additional yarn over that you make at the beginning of a stitch adds length to the completed stitch. So if you continue to add yarn overs, you produce longer and longer stitches. Here's a breakdown of the yarn overs involved in several different stitches (note that the stitch names may vary in different publications):

- **Single crochet (sc):** No yarn over

- **Double crochet (dc):** Yarn over 1 time

- **Triple crochet (tr):** Yarn over 2 times

- **Double triple crochet (dtr):** Yarn over 3 times

- **Triple triple crochet (trtr):** Yarn over 4 times

- **Double triple triple crochet (dtrtr):** Yarn over 5 times

- **Quadruple triple triple crochet (quad):** Yarn over 6 times

The longer stitches are used infrequently, but they do exist. Theoretically, you can continue to make longer and longer stitches indefinitely, as long as your hook can hold all the loops.

Repeat these six steps for each additional row of double triple crochet, continuing until you feel comfortable with this stitch. Figure 6-15 shows you how rows of double triple crochet look as a fabric.

Figure 6-15: Several rows of double triple crochet.

Hooking a Half Double Crochet

The *half double crochet* (abbreviated *hdc*) is kind of an oddball stitch, and you make it differently from all the other stitches that appear earlier in this chapter. It falls in between a single crochet and a double crochet in height, but instead of working off two loops at a time, you draw the yarn through three loops on the hook. This action produces a fairly tight fabric similar to one made with a single crochet stitch. You can see how to make the first two rows of half double crochet in the next sections.

Starting with Row 1

Follow these steps to get started:

1. **Make a foundation chain with 15 chain stitches (ch 15).**
2. **Chain 2 more for the turning chain.**

   Check out Chapter 5 for the scoop on chains.

Most pattern books combine the steps for making a foundation chain and turning chain into one by telling you to chain a total of 17.

To create your first half double crochet stitch:

1. **Yarn over the hook (yo).**

   Don't forget to yarn over from back to front.

2. **Insert your hook into the third chain (ch) from the hook, as shown in Figure 6-16a.**

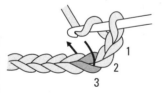 

Figure 6-16:
Beginning a
half double
crochet.

a   b

3. **Yarn over the hook.**
4. **Gently pull the wrapped hook through the center of the chain stitch, carrying the wrapped yarn through the stitch.**

   You should have 3 loops on your hook, just like in Figure 6-16b.

5. **Yarn over the hook.**
6. **Draw your yarn through all 3 loops on your hook.**

   Figure 6-17a depicts Step 6, and Figure 6-17b shows a completed half double crochet stitch (hdc).

To complete a full row of half double crochet stitches, begin in the next chain of the foundation chain, as indicated in Figure 6-18a. Work one half double crochet stitch in each successive chain across the foundation chain. When you count the turning chain as 1 half double crochet stitch, you should have 16 half double crochets at the end of Row 1. Figure 6-18b shows the end of the first half double crochet row.

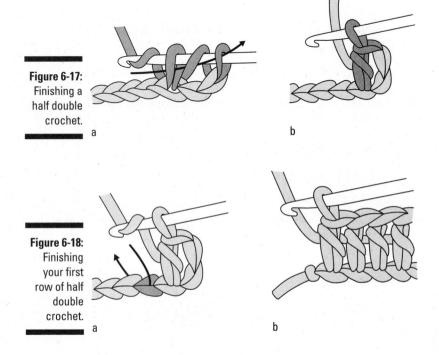

Figure 6-17: Finishing a half double crochet.

a   b

Figure 6-18: Finishing your first row of half double crochet.

a   b

Moving on to Row 2

Here's how to begin the second row of half double crochet:

1. **Turn your work.**

   Refer to Chapter 5 for help properly turning your work.

2. **Chain 2 (ch 2) for the turning chain.**

3. **Yarn over the hook (yo).**

4. **Skipping the first stitch of the row directly below the turning chain, insert your hook into the next stitch, as in Figure 6-19.**

5. **Repeat Steps 3 through 6 from the preceding section in each of the next 14 half double crochet stitches (hdc).**

   Be sure to yarn over before inserting your hook into each stitch.

6. **Work 1 half double crochet in the top chain of the previous row's turning chain.**

   You should have 16 half double crochet stitches in Row 2 if you count the turning chain as 1 half double crochet.

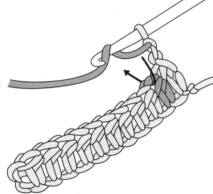

Figure 6-19:
Working a
half double
crochet into
the second
stitch.

Repeat these steps for each additional row of half double crochet and continue working rows of half double crochet until you feel comfortable with this stitch. To see how rows of half double crochet look as a fabric, check out Figure 6-20.

Figure 6-20:
Several
rows of half
double
crochet.

Creating Even More Height Variation with Extended Stitches

Occasionally a pattern may direct you to make *extended crochet stitches*, which are a little taller than the regular version of the same stitch. They also provide variation in texture with a slightly improved drape, meaning a fabric made of extended stitches is softer and less dense than one made with standard stitches.

You can adapt any stitch into an extended stitch. How? Instead of adding a yarn over to the beginning of the stitch, like the taller stitches described earlier in this chapter, extended stitches include a chain stitch in the middle of the stitch to give a little extra lift.

In the following sections, we show you how to work two common extended stitches — the extended single crochet and the extended double crochet.

An extended stitch is usually abbreviated by adding an *E* before the standard abbreviation. So the abbreviation for extended double crochet, for example, is Edc.

Extended single crochet

The *extended single crochet* (abbreviated *Esc*) is a simple variation on the standard single crochet (abbreviated *sc*), which we describe in Chapter 5. Follow these steps to start:

1. **Create a foundation chain by working 15 chain stitches (ch 15).**

2. **Chain 1 more for the turning chain.**

Now you're ready to begin your first extended single crochet stitch.

1. **Insert your hook into the second chain (ch) from the hook.**

2. **Yarn over the hook (yo).**

   Move from back to front, never front to back.

3. **Gently pull the wrapped hook through the center of the chain stitch, carrying the wrapped yarn through the stitch (as shown in Figure 6-21).**

   Now you should have 2 loops on your hook.

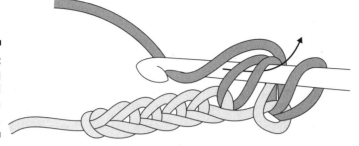

Figure 6-21:
Beginning
an extended
single
crochet.

4. **Yarn over the hook.**

5. **Work a chain stitch by drawing the hook, with the wrapped yarn, through the first loop on the hook**

   Refer to Figure 6-22a for the visual.

6. **Yarn over the hook.**

7. **Draw the yarn through both loops on the hook, as shown in Figure 6-22b.**

   Well done! Your first extended single crochet stitch (Esc) is now complete.

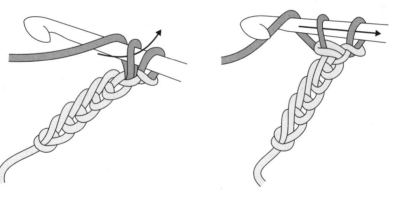

Figure 6-22:
Finishing an
extended
single
crochet.

a   b

To work the next extended single crochet stitch and continue the row:

1. **Insert your hook into the next chain stitch (ch), yarn over the hook (yo), and pull the yarn through the chain stitch.**

   You should have 2 loops on the hook.

2. **Repeat Steps 4 through 7 from the preceding instructions to complete the second extended single crochet stitch (Esc).**

3. **Work 1 extended single crochet stitch in each chain stitch across the foundation chain by repeating Steps 1 and 2.**

   You should have 15 extended single crochet stitches in the row. Figure 6-23 shows you what a completed row of extended single crochet looks like.

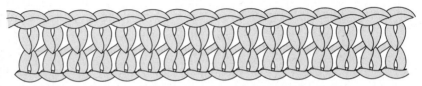

Figure 6-23: One row of completed extended single crochet.

For the next row, simply turn your work and make one chain for the turning chain. Begin the first extended single crochet in the first stitch from the previous row.

Figure 6-24 shows how rows of extended single crochet look as a fabric.

Figure 6-24: Several rows of extended single crochet.

Extended double crochet

The *extended double crochet* (abbreviated *Edc*) is a variation on the standard double crochet stitch (abbreviated *dc*) that we describe earlier in this chapter. To get started:

1. **Make a foundation chain by working 15 chain stitches (ch 15).**
2. **Chain 3 more stitches for the turning chain.**

To create your first extended double crochet stitch, follow these steps:

1. **Yarn over the hook (yo).**

   Always yarn over from back to front.

2. **Insert your hook into the fourth chain (ch) from the hook.**

   Refer to Figure 6-1a earlier in this chapter for the proper positioning.

3. **Yarn over the hook.**

4. **Gently pull the wrapped hook through the center of the chain stitch, carrying the wrapped yarn through the stitch.**

   You should now have 3 loops on your hook. (Refer to Figure 6-1b earlier in this chapter for the visual of this step.)

5. **Yarn over the hook.**

6. **Work a chain stitch by drawing the yarn through the first loop on the hook, as in Figure 6-25.**

Figure 6-25:
Making a chain stitch for your extended double crochet.

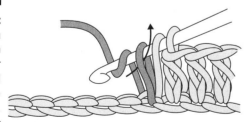

7. **Yarn over the hook.**

8. **Draw the yarn through the first 2 loops on your hook, like in Figure 6-26a.**

9. **Yarn over the hook.**

10. **Draw the yarn through the last 2 loops on the hook, as shown in Figure 6-26b.**

One extended double crochet stitch (Edc) is now complete, and you should have 1 loop remaining on your hook.

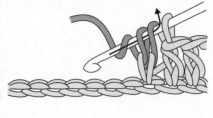

Figure 6-26:
Finishing an extended double crochet stitch.

a   b

To work your next extended double crochet and continue the row:

1. **Yarn over the hook (yo) and insert your hook into the next chain stitch (ch).**

2. **Yarn over and pull the yarn through the chain stitch.**

   You should have 3 loops on the hook.

3. **Repeat Steps 5 through 10 from the preceding instructions to complete the second extended double crochet stitch (Edc).**

4. **Work 1 extended double crochet stitch in each chain stitch across the foundation chain by repeating Steps 1 through 3.**

   When you count the turning chain as the first extended double crochet, you should have 16 extended double crochet stitches in Row 1. Figure 6-27 shows the end of the first extended double crochet row.

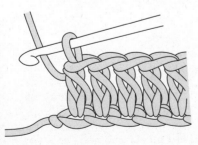

Figure 6-27:
Finishing the first row of extended double crochet.

To begin the next row of extended double crochet, turn your piece and make three chains for the turning chain. Skipping the first stitch, work your first extended double crochet stitch into the next stitch on the previous row and follow Steps 1 through 3 of the preceding instructions. Take a look at Figure 6-28 to see what rows of extended double crochet look like as a fabric.

A crocheting constant: Stitch width

Crochet stitches vary in either length or height, never width. That's because all stitches are the same width when worked properly with the same yarn and hook. Whether you're making a row of 16 chain stitches or fancy three-dimensional stitches, the width of your piece should be the same. After you complete the stitch and have one loop remaining on your hook, the top of the stitch is still the same width as all the other stitches because the size of hook you're using determines the size of both that last loop and the width of the stitch.

Figure 6-28: Several rows of extended double crochet.

Running on Empty: Joining a New Ball of Yarn

Every ball or skein has a limited amount of yarn on it, so sooner or later you're going to run out of yarn in the middle of a project. Joining a new ball or skein of yarn correctly is as important to the appearance of your work as the actual stitches. You may find the process awkward at first, but you'll be an old hand at it in no time. You can join a new ball of yarn in any stitch of a row, but making the transition at the end of a row creates a neater appearance. We describe both methods in the sections that follow.

Don't give in to the temptation to just tie the beginning end of the new ball to the tail end of the first ball. This sloppy method produces an unsightly knot in your work.

Joining at the end of a row

The following steps use a swatch of fabric made with double crochet stitches, so if you haven't already made a swatch, refer to the "Doing a Double Crochet" section, earlier in this chapter, to get ready. After you've completed a few rows, follow these steps to join new yarn at the end of a row:

1. **Double crochet (dc) across the row, stopping before the last stitch of the row.**

2. **Work the last double crochet to the point where only 2 loops are left on the hook.**

3. **Wrap the cut end of the new yarn around the hook, from back to front.**

   The *working end* of the yarn (the end that's attached to the ball or skein) should be the end closest to you.

4. **Draw the new yarn through the 2 loops on your hook.**

   Figure 6-29 illustrates how to perform this step. Note that you should have 2 strands of yarn hanging down.

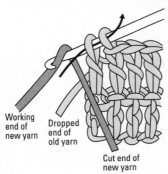

Figure 6-29: Drawing new yarn through both loops on your hook.

Working end of new yarn

Dropped end of old yarn

Cut end of new yarn

5. **Tug on the dropped end of the old yarn at the base of the double crochet to tighten up the stitch.**

   The remaining tail of the old yarn is the *tail end.* It goes into hiding when you weave it into the fabric later on.

Joining in the middle of a row

Sometimes you have no choice but to join new yarn in the middle of a row, such as when you shape necklines or armholes in a garment. To join a new ball or skein in such cases, work as follows:

1. **Make a slipknot on the end of the new ball of yarn.**

   See Chapter 5 for details on making a slipknot.

2. **Insert your hook into the stitch where you want to join in the new yarn.**

3. **Place the new yarn's slipknot on the hook.**

4. **Draw the slipknot through the stitch, as shown in Figure 6-30.**

   One loop is now on your hook, and you're ready to begin crocheting the new row.

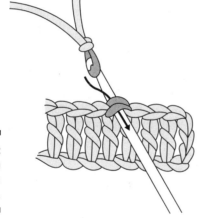

Figure 6-30:
Joining yarn
with a
slipknot.

You can weave the ends of the yarn in later with a yarn needle, but we recommend working over the strands while crocheting the next row in order to save time. To work over the strands, lay them down over the tops of the stitches in the current row; then when you work your stitches, the strands are captured in the bases of your stitches. Cut off any excess yarn after you've covered a few inches.

Weaving in yarn ends is a tedious, thankless job — and one you should avoid whenever you can. Some projects allow you to leave ends dangling off to the side to be incorporated into fringe. You can also leave ends dangling on the side if they can be sewn into a seam later on. Border stitches are also good for covering your ends. (For more information about crocheting borders, see Chapter 17.) However you go about avoiding weaving in your yarn ends, just don't try to cover too many strands in one area, or else you'll create a messy lump along the edge of your project.

Sassy Scarf Project

A scarf is a quick, easy, and versatile project that showcases your new skills. The pattern in this section incorporates the first four stitches introduced in this chapter and gives you the opportunity to practice each of them while creating a great fashion accessory.

You work this scarf lengthwise, progressing from rows of short stitches to rows of long and longer stitches before working back down again. Don't be intimidated by the number of stitches you need in each row. If you can count, you're good to go. Counting stitches, whether as you go or when you reach the end of a row, is as much a part of crocheting as the stitches themselves.

Feel free to let your creative impulses run wild. We give you the list of materials you need to make this scarf as it's shown in the color section, but you can choose your own color or color combination using any worsted-weight yarn. You can even add rows to make the scarf wider. Have fun and feel confident in your abilities to make this scarf your very own!

Materials and vital statistics

- **Yarn:** Caron International "Country" worsted-weight yarn (75% microdenier acrylic/25% merino wool), (3 oz. [85 g], 185 yds [170 m] each skein): 3 skeins of #0014 Deep Purple

- **Hook:** Crochet hook size H-8 U.S. (5 mm) or size needed to obtain gauge

- **Large-eyed yarn needle**

- **Measurements:** 8 in. wide x 68½ in. long

- **Gauge:** 7 sts = 2 in.; 4 rows in patt = 2 in.

- **Stitches used:** Chain stitch (ch), single crochet (sc), half double crochet (hdc), double crochet (dc), triple crochet (tr), double triple crochet (dtr)

Directions

The following instructions are written in crochet-pattern lingo with plain English following each step. If you don't recall how to make the various stitches, refer to the specific directions for each in this chapter and in Chapter 5.

Figure 6-31 shows a reduced sample of the scarf pattern as a stitch diagram to give you the opportunity to try reading diagrams. (Flip to Chapter 4 to refresh your memory on the different abbreviations and symbols.) Happy crocheting!

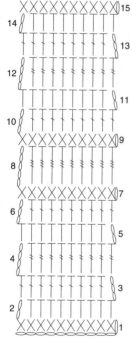

Figure 6-31: The stitch diagram of the Sassy Scarf project.

1. **Foundation chain: Ch 241.**

   Create your foundation chain by working 241 chain stitches in a row.

2. **Row 1: Sc in second ch from hook, sc in each ch across (240 sc), *turn*.**

   To complete Row 1, work 1 single crochet stitch in the second chain from the hook, work 1 single crochet stitch in each chain stitch across the row, and then turn your work.

3. **Row 2: Ch 2 (counts as first hdc), hdc in each st across (240 hdc),** *turn.*

   To complete Row 2, chain 2 for your turning chain, skip the stitch directly below the turning chain, work 1 half double crochet stitch in each stitch across the row, and then turn your work.

4. **Row 3: Ch 3 (counts as first dc), dc in each st across (240 dc),** *turn.*

   To complete Row 3, chain 3 for your turning chain, skip the stitch directly below the turning chain, work 1 double crochet stitch in each stitch across the row, and then turn your work.

5. **Row 4: Ch 4 (counts as first tr), tr in each st across (240 tr),** *turn.*

   To complete Row 4, chain 4 for your turning chain, skip the stitch directly below the turning chain, work 1 triple crochet stitch in each stitch across the row, and then turn your work.

6. **Row 5: Ch 2 (counts as first hdc), hdc in each st across (240 hdc),** *turn.*

   To complete Row 5, chain 2 for your turning chain, skip the stitch directly below the turning chain, work 1 half double crochet stitch in each stitch across the row, and then turn your work.

7. **Row 6: Ch 3 (counts as first dc), dc in each st across (240 dc),** *turn.*

   To complete Row 6, chain 3 for your turning chain, skip the stitch directly below the turning chain, work 1 double crochet stitch in each stitch across the row, and then turn your work.

8. **Row 7: Ch 1, sc in each st across (240 sc),** *turn.*

   To complete Row 7, chain 1 for your turning chain, work 1 single crochet stitch in each stitch across the row, and then turn your work.

9. **Row 8: Ch 5 (counts as first dtr), dtr in each st across (240 dtr),** *turn.*

   To complete Row 8, chain 5 for your turning chain, skip the stitch directly below the turning chain, work 1 double triple crochet stitch in each stitch across the row, and then turn your work.

10. **Row 9: Ch 1, sc in each st across (240 sc),** *turn.*

    To complete Row 9, chain 1 for your turning chain, work 1 single crochet stitch in each stitch across the row, and then turn your work.

11. **Row 10: Ch 3 (counts as first dc), dc in each st across (240 dc),** *turn.*

    To complete Row 10, chain 3 for your turning chain, skip the stitch directly below the turning chain, work 1 double crochet stitch in each stitch across the row, and then turn your work.

12. **Row 11: Ch 2 (counts as first hdc), hdc in each st across (240 hdc),** *turn.*

    To complete Row 11, chain 2 for your turning chain, skip the stitch directly below the turning chain, work 1 half double crochet stitch in each stitch across the row, and then turn your work.

13. **Row 12: Ch 4 (counts as first tr), tr in each st across (240 tr), *turn*.**

    To complete Row 12, chain 4 for your turning chain, skip the stitch directly below the turning chain, work 1 triple crochet stitch in each stitch across the row, and then turn your work.

14. **Row 13: Ch 3 (counts as first dc), dc in each st across (240 dc), *turn*.**

    To complete Row 13, chain 3 for your turning chain, skip the stitch directly below the turning chain, work 1 double crochet stitch in each stitch across the row, and then turn your work.

15. **Row 14: Ch 2 (counts as first hdc), hdc in each st across (240 hdc), *turn*.**

    To complete Row 14, chain 2 for your turning chain, skip the stitch directly below the turning chain, work 1 half double crochet stitch in each stitch across the row, and then turn your work.

16. **Row 15: Ch 1, sc in each st across (240 sc). Fasten off.**

    To complete Row 15, chain 1 for your turning chain, work 1 single crochet stitch in each stitch across the row, and then fasten off your yarn.

Finishing

After you finish the body of the scarf, it's time to add the finishing details — a little dose of fringe. To add fringe to your scarf, cut your yarn into 12-inch lengths. Using two lengths of yarn for each fringe, single knot one fringe in each stitch across each short edge of the scarf. For more about fringes, check out Chapter 18.

Chapter 7

Shaping Up and Slimming Down: Increasing and Decreasing Stitches

. . . .

In This Chapter

▶ Adding some width and shape to your design with increases

▶ Tapering your crocheted creation with decreases

▶ Making a fun, colorful throw

. . . .

*C*rocheting would be pretty boring if all you could make were squares and rectangles. Sure, you could make armloads of scarves or afghans, but you probably want to branch out and create some shape. In this chapter, we show you how to widen and narrow your designs by simply adding or taking away a few stitches.

Note: This chapter shows you how to increase and decrease with single crochet stitches (see Chapter 5) or double crochet stitches (see Chapter 6), but you work increases and decreases with other stitches exactly the same way. Most patterns explain how to work the increases and decreases necessary for that particular design, so be sure to read all the pattern instructions before beginning.

When increasing or decreasing stitches, always count your stitches to make sure you have the correct number on your work.

Making It Grow: Increasing Stitches

Increasing stitches (abbreviated *inc*) is just what it sounds like: You add stitches to a row so that it has more stitches than the previous one in order to broaden the shape of your design. Depending on the type of design you're making, you can increase stitches anywhere in the row — at the beginning, end, or middle; in every other stitch; or any place where you want the shaping to occur. If you're working from a pattern, it'll always tell you exactly where to place your extra stitches. No guesswork necessary!

Adding a stitch at the beginning or end of a row is a common way to increase stitches while working in rows. This method creates a smooth, tapered edge to your piece. Adding stitches to the middle of a row makes the shaping more subtle, allowing your piece to bend or angle out from the center, as with many shawl patterns.

Regardless of where the increase occurs, you usually make it by working two or more stitches into one stitch. Most stitches, no matter how tall they are, have the same steps for working an increase in the middle or end of a row. Working an increase at the beginning of a row of single crochet, however, is a little different than with the taller stitches.

In the following sections, we show you how to increase with single crochet and double crochet at the beginning of a row. Keep in mind that increases at the beginning of a row for stitches taller than single crochet are worked in the same way as the double crochet, counting their own specific turning chain as the first stitch of the increase (flip to Chapter 5 for more on turning chains).

If you're working in rounds, increasing usually occurs in each successive round to accommodate the larger circumference of the design. See Chapter 8 for more on working in rounds.

Increasing anywhere with single crochet

Because the turning chain in a single crochet row doesn't count as a stitch, increasing one single crochet at the beginning of a row is the same as doing it in the middle or at the end of a row. Wherever you want to increase one single crochet (the pattern will tell you where to do this), just work two single crochet stitches in the designated stitch, like in Figure 7-1a. Figure 7-1b illustrates a completed single crochet increase, and Figure 7-1c shows the stitch symbol you'd see in a diagram.

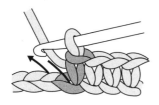 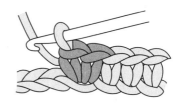

a   b

Figure 7-1:
Increasing
with single
crochet.

c

Increasing with double crochet at the beginning of a row

If the pattern calls for an increase in stitches at the beginning of a row and you're working with stitches taller than single crochet, adding stitches to the beginning of a row is a little different than adding them in the middle or at the end. The main difference is that taller stitches require a turning chain at the beginning of a row. To figure out how to add one double crochet stitch at the beginning of a row, make a swatch of double crochet stitches and then follow these steps:

1. **Chain 3 (ch 3).**

   This is the same number of chains required for a double crochet turning chain, which counts as the first stitch.

2. **Work your next double crochet stitch (dc) into the first stitch of the row.**

   The first stitch of the row is the stitch directly below the turning chain, the one that you usually skip — see Figure 7-2a. Check out the completed stitch in Figure 7-2b and its symbol as you'd see it in pictorial crochet diagrams in Figure 7-2c. *Note:* The stitch you make in this step is the increase stitch.

3. **Finish the rest of the row as you normally would, working 1 double crochet stitch in each stitch across the row.**

   To double-check your work, count your stitches (including the turning chain). You should have 1 more stitch in this row than you have in the previous row.

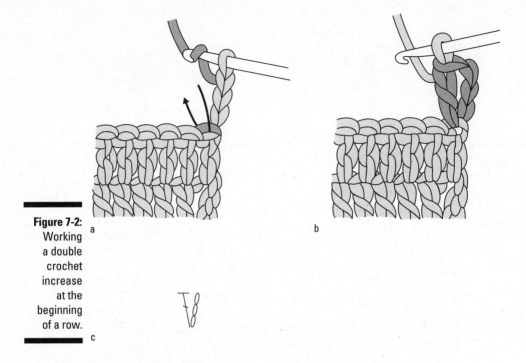

Figure 7-2:
Working
a double
crochet
increase
at the
beginning
of a row.

a

b

c

Increasing with double crochet in the middle or end of a row

Sometimes a pattern may call for an increase at the end of a row or while you're working your way across a row. Basically, you work an increase in the middle or at the end of a row the same way you work an increase at the beginning of a row, except you don't have to worry about the turning chain. See what we mean in the following instructions:

1. **Work across your row until you get to the designated increase stitch or the last stitch of the row.**

2. **Work 2 double crochet stitches (dc) into the designated stitch.**

   Figure 7-3a illustrates how to perform Step 2, and Figure 7-3b shows a completed increase in the middle of a row. Figure 7-3c is the symbol for a double crochet increase in the middle or end of a row as you'd see it in pictorial crochet diagrams.

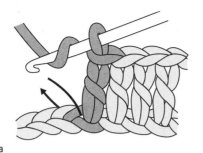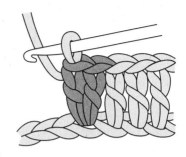

Figure 7-3:
Working
a double
crochet
increase in
the middle
of a row.

a

b

c

Diminishing Results: Decreasing Stitches

When you want to shape your design so that it gets smaller, you need to decrease your stitches. You can *decrease* a stitch (abbreviated *dec*), which is really just subtracting a stitch, in the same places that you increase stitches — at the beginning or end of a row or somewhere in the middle. Decreasing takes a few more steps, but it's really just as simple as increasing. In the following sections, we describe several useful methods for decreasing stitches.

Decreasing with single crochet

When a single crochet decrease is called for, the pattern will typically tell you where the decrease(s) should be made. You decrease single crochet stitches in the middle or end of a row by turning two separate stitches into one, which is a two-step process. But because of these two steps, you have to think ahead and start the first part one stitch before the actual decrease is designated in your pattern.

To begin the two-part process of turning two single crochet stitches into one, start the first single crochet as you normally would.

1. **Insert your hook into the first stitch of the decrease.**

2. **Yarn over the hook (yo).**

3. Draw the yarn through the stitch.

You should have 2 loops remaining on your hook.

With the two loops still on your hook, begin the second part of the decrease by working the second single crochet.

1. Insert your hook into the next stitch, as shown in Figure 7-4.

2. Yarn over the hook (yo).

Figure 7-4:
Beginning
the second
part of
a single
crochet
decrease.

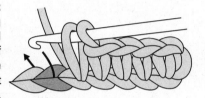

3. Draw the yarn through the stitch.

You should now have 3 loops on your hook.

4. Yarn over.

5. Draw the yarn through all 3 loops on your hook, just like in Figure 7-5a.

Figure 7-5b shows 1 complete single crochet decrease, and Figure 7-5c denotes the stitch symbol for this action.

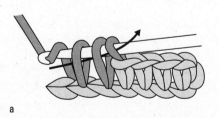
a

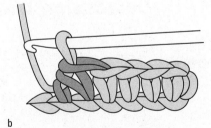
b

Figure 7-5:
Finishing
a single
crochet
decrease.

c

Decreasing with double crochet

The double crochet decrease can be used in the middle of a row or round or at the beginning or end of a row or round (the pattern you're working with should tell you exactly where). It's almost identical to the single crochet decrease described in the preceding section except it has one more step.

Begin the first part of the decrease by starting the first double crochet as you would for a normal double crochet stitch.

1. **Yarn over the hook (yo).**

2. **Insert your hook into the next stitch.**

3. **Yarn over.**

4. **Draw the yarn through the stitch.**

   You should have 3 loops on the hook.

5. **Yarn over.**

6. **Draw the yarn through the first 2 loops on your hook.**

   As you can see from Figure 7-6, 2 loops remain on the hook.

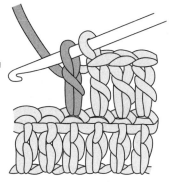

Figure 7-6:
Completing the first part of a double crochet decrease.

In the second part of the decrease, you work the second double crochet stitch and join it with the first to complete the decrease. (***Note:*** At this point, your first stitch is actually a *half-closed stitch,* in other words, one that has been partially completed.) With the two loops still on your hook, start to work the second double crochet stitch as you would a regular stitch.

1. **Yarn over the hook (yo).**

2. **Insert your hook into the next stitch, as shown in Figure 7-7.**

3. **Yarn over.**

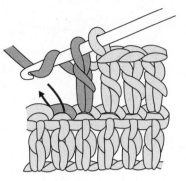

Figure 7-7:
Beginning the second part of a double crochet decrease.

4. **Draw the yarn through the stitch.**

   You should now have 4 loops on your hook.

5. **Yarn over.**

6. **Draw the yarn through the first 2 loops on your hook.**

   Three loops should still be on your hook.

7. **Yarn over.**

8. **Draw the yarn through all 3 loops on your hook, like in Figure 7-8a.**

   If you look at the tops of the stitches in Figure 7-8b, you see only 1 stitch across the top of the 2 underlying stitches. This is 1 complete double crochet decrease. Figure 7-8c introduces you to the stitch symbol for this particular decrease.

If you want to decrease at the very beginning of a row and you're working with a stitch that requires a turning chain (in other words, a double crochet stitch or anything taller), you work the decrease a little differently than one in the middle or at the end of a row. Make your turning chain a stitch shorter than you normally would (for example, chain 2 rather than 3 for a double crochet) and then continue across the row as normal. When you work the next row, don't work a stitch in the shortened turning chain. This process takes care of the decrease and leaves a smooth edge.

To avoid this kind of a decrease at the beginning of a double crochet row, a pattern may place a decrease in the second and third stitch rather than in the first two stitches. The opposite end of the row would then have the decrease placed one stitch in from the end to be symmetrical with the beginning of the row. This way you continue to work the turning chain and last stitch like usual and the decrease still falls toward the beginning and end of the row.

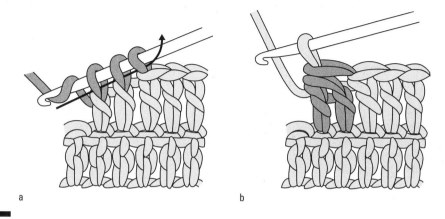

a   b

Figure 7-8:
Finishing
a double
crochet
decrease.

c

Decreasing with slip stitches at the start of a row

One handy method for decreasing at the beginning of a row is to slip stitch across the number of stitches that you want to decrease. You use this method when you need to decrease more than just one or two stitches, typically for shaping the armholes or neck edges in a garment. The resulting look is a squared-off corner.

To find out exactly how decreasing with slip stitches works, take a swatch of double crochet stitches and work the following steps to decrease three stitches at the beginning of a row:

1. **Work 1 slip stitch (sl st) in each of the first 4 stitches.**

   Head to Chapter 5 for instructions on working a slip stitch.

2. **Chain 3 (ch 3) for the turning chain, which also counts as the first double crochet stitch (dc).**

3. **Skip the stitch under the turning chain and then work a double crochet in the next stitch.**

4. **Continue to work a double crochet in each stitch across the row.**

   Figure 7-9 shows you how this decrease should look.

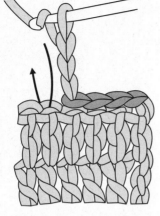

Figure 7-9:
Decreasing
three double
crochet
stitches
with slip
stitches.

Decreasing by skipping stitches

Skipping stitches is an easy way to decrease stitches in a row. It's an especially good tactic when you're shaping armholes or necklines, but you can actually decrease by skipping stitches anywhere in the row — at the beginning, middle, or end. You can skip any number of stitches, but the more you skip, the larger the gap created by the skipped stitches will be. That's why decreasing by skipping stitches works best when you're dealing with single crochet stitches.

To decrease by skipping stitches, simply work to the stitch the pattern tells you to decrease. Then skip the designated stitch, working the stitch before and after it as usual.

Decreasing by stopping and turning before you reach the end of a row

An alternate method of decreasing stitches at the end of a row is to just stop before you get to the last stitch. This technique, which can be used with any stitch, gives you a rather squared-off look and is quite often used when shaping garments. Here's how to perform this pretty simple decreasing tactic:

1. **Work across the row until you have the number of stitches that your work requires.**

2. **Stop crocheting and turn your work, leaving the remaining stitches on the current row unworked.**

   Refer to Chapter 5 for instructions on properly turning your work.

3. **Make your turning chain and then work back across the previous row in the same manner as if you'd crocheted all the way to the end.**

Figure 7-10 shows this decrease after you've turned your work.

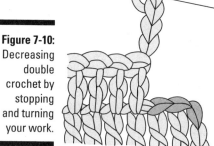

Figure 7-10: Decreasing double crochet by stopping and turning your work.

Simple Ripple Blanket Project

Practice your new shaping skills with this fun, colorful blanket, which you can check out in the color section. The larger size is perfect for a twin size bed, or even as a cozy throw to brighten up your couch, but you can easily change the size by using the optional instructions we provide. The gentle waves in the pattern are shaped by alternating an even number of increase stitches with decrease stitches so you always end each row with the same number of stitches.

The easy-care acrylic yarn used to make this blanket comes in a wide variety of colors, so feel free to play with the number of colors and the size of each color block. You can even change up the brand of yarn if you want to. Just make sure that the yarn you buy is the same size and weight as the yarn noted in the pattern (see Chapter 2 for more on yarn substitution) and that you can come up with the right gauge. (Find out all about gauge in Chapter 3.)

Materials and vital statistics

▶ **Yarn:** Coats & Clark Red Heart "Super Saver" worsted-weight yarn (100% acrylic), Article #E300 (7 oz. [198 g], 364 yds [333 m] each skein): 2 skeins each of

- #624 Tea Leaf (green) (A)
- #724 Baby Pink (pink) (B)

- #360 Café (brown) (C)
- #381 Light Blue (blue) (D)
- #579 Pale Plum (purple) (E)
- #316 Soft White (white) (F)

✔ **Hook:** Crochet hook size I-9 U.S. (5.5 mm) or size needed to obtain gauge

✔ **Large-eyed yarn needle**

✔ **Measurements:** 40 in. wide x 60 in. long

✔ **Gauge:** 14 sts and 8 rows = 4 in. in wave patt

Note: For the gauge swatch, make 31 chain stitches. Work Rows 2 through 10 all in the same color. Then place your ruler straight across the width of your swatch and count the stitches across 4 inches of 1 row, following the wave pattern. Count each increase as 2 double crochet and each decrease as 1 double crochet.

✔ **Stitches used:** Chain stitch (ch), double crochet (dc), **Dec 1 dc:** * (Yo, insert hook in next st, yo, draw yarn through st, yo, draw yarn through first 2 loops on hook) twice, yo, draw yarn through 3 loops on hook *.

Directions

We give you the directions for the following project as you'd see them in the real world of crochet, complete with abbreviations, followed by the plain-English format. (We also provide the blanket's stitch diagram in Figure 7-11.) Feel free to follow whichever set of instructions you're most comfortable with (and check out Chapter 4 to brush up on the abbreviations). Your design will turn out super no matter which format you follow.

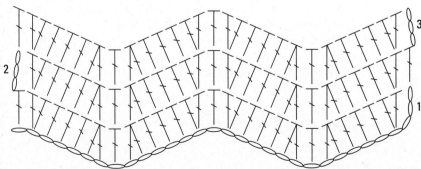

Figure 7-11: The stitch diagram for the Simple Ripple Blanket.

1. **Foundation chain: With A, ch 143.**

   Create your foundation chain by working 143 chain stitches with green.

2. **Row 1: Skip first 3 ch from hook (counts as first dc), * 2 dc in next ch (inc made), dc in each of next 3 ch, dec 1 dc over next 2 ch, dc in next ch, dec 1 dc over next 2 ch, dc in each of next 3 ch, 2 dc in next ch, dc in next ch *; rep from * to * 9 more times across, *turn* — 141 dc.**

   To complete Row 1, skip the first 3 chain stitches from the hook (the 3 skipped stitches are the turning chain and count as your first double crochet stitch), * work 2 double crochet in the next chain, work 1 double crochet in each of the next 3 chain stitches, decrease 1 double crochet by working a decrease over the next 2 chain stitches, work 1 double crochet in the next chain, decrease 1 double crochet over the next 2 chain stitches, work 1 double crochet in each of the next 3 chain stitches, work 2 double crochet in the next chain, work 1 double crochet in the next chain *; repeat the instructions from * to * 9 more times and then turn your work. You'll have 141 double crochet stitches.

3. **Rows 2–3: Ch 3 (counts as first dc), * 2 dc in next dc, dc in each of next 3 dc, dec 1 dc over next 2 dc, dc in next dc, dec 1 dc over next 2 dc, dc in each of next 3 dc, 2 dc in next dc, dc in next dc *; rep from * to * across, *turn*.**

   To complete Row 2, chain 3 for your turning chain (which counts as the first double crochet), * work 2 double crochet in the next double crochet, work 1 double crochet in each of the next 3 double crochet stitches, decrease 1 double crochet over the next 2 double crochet stitches, work 1 double crochet in the next double crochet, decrease 1 double crochet over the next 2 double crochet stitches, work 1 double crochet in each of the next 3 double crochet stitches, work 2 double crochet in the next double crochet, work 1 double crochet in the next double crochet *; repeat the instructions from * to * across the row and then turn your work. Work Row 3 the same way as Row 2.

4. **Row 4: Rep Row 2 across until 1 st remains. In the last st, work the first part of the dc, with A, until 2 loops remain on the hook, join B and complete the dc as usual, *turn*.**

   To complete Row 4, repeat Row 2 across the row to the last stitch. Work 1 double crochet in the last stitch until 2 loops remain on the hook. Drop green, yarn over with pink, draw through the last 2 loops on the hook, and then turn. (See Chapter 9 to find out how to change colors.)

5. **Rows 5–7: With B, rep Row 2.**

   To complete Rows 5 through 7, work as for Row 2 using pink rather than green.

6. **Row 8: Rep Row 2 across until 1 st remains. In the last st, work the first part of the dc, with B, until 2 loops remain on the hook, join C and complete the dc as usual, *turn*.**

   To complete Row 8, repeat Row 2 across the row to the last stitch. Work 1 double crochet in the last stitch until 2 loops remain on the hook. Drop pink, yarn over with brown, and draw through the last 2 loops on the hook; then turn.

7. **Rows 9–20: Rep Rows 5–8 for D and E and then rep Rows 5–8 for F until 1 st remains on the last row. In the last st, work the first part of the dc, with F, until 2 loops remain on the hook, join A and complete the dc as usual, *turn*.**

   To complete Rows 9 through 20, work Rows 5 through 8 for blue, then purple, then white until 1 stitch remains. Work 1 double crochet, with white, in the last stitch until 2 loops remain on the hook. Drop white, yarn over with green, draw through the last 2 loops on the hook, and then turn.

8. **Work in est patt working 4 rows each in the following color sequence: A, B, C, D, E, F until blanket measures 60 in. and each color has been worked a total of 5 times. Don't turn on the last row. Fasten off. Weave in loose ends.**

   Continue to work Rows 5 through 8, working 4 rows each in the following color order: green, pink, brown, blue, purple, white. Work until the blanket is about 60 inches long and each color block has been worked a total of 5 times. On the last row, don't turn. Fasten off instead and weave in loose ends with your yarn needle.

Optional directions for different sizes

To lengthen or shorten the blanket, simply adjust the number of rows you work until it's the desired size. To change the width of the blanket, add or subtract 10 chains from the first step for every 3 inches of width, and then follow the pattern adjusting how many times you repeat the stitch pattern in Step 2 (10 chains = 1 repeat).

Chapter 8

I've Been Here Before: Crocheting in Circles

In This Chapter

▶ Creating and joining a center ring

▶ Adding additional rounds to your ring

▶ Spiraling to avoid visible seams

▶ Giving your work dimension

▶ Crocheting the perfect hat and a playful pup

Who says that going in circles doesn't get you anywhere? Obviously that person has never crocheted! Whether you want to make a stylish hat to wear throughout the year or a cute stuffed toy to give to your niece for her birthday, you need to be able to crochet a circle by working in rounds.

Crocheting rounds is no more difficult than working rows. Instead of working back and forth, you work around in a circle, increasing the number of stitches you work in each round to accommodate the growing circumference. This chapter shows you three common methods for creating a center ring, which is the basis for all rounds, and how to work rounds of stitches off of it. We also describe how to work in a spiral and make three-dimensional shapes.

Practice your new skills on the cute Bucket Hat project at the end of this chapter. Then, after you've mastered working in rounds, try your hand at our Amigurumi Pup project, a little stuffed dog guaranteed to warm your heart.

Lord of the Center Rings

To begin a design that you work in rounds, you must first create a center ring. The *center ring* is the foundation for all crocheted designs that are worked in rounds — just like the foundation chain you use when working in rows (see Chapter 5). The three most frequently used methods for creating a center ring are as follows:

- ✔ Working chain stitches into a ring
- ✔ Working a round of stitches into one chain stitch
- ✔ Working stitches into an adjustable loop of yarn

The following sections show you these three methods, when you want to use each, and how to end a round and be in the proper position to start the next round.

Joining chain stitches into a ring

The most common method for creating a center ring is to make a chain and close it into a ring with a slip stitch. (See Chapter 5 for the how-to on making chain stitches and slip stitches.) Use this method when your first round is made up of a fairly large number of stitches and you need the room in which to fit them, or if the design calls for an obvious hole in the center of the piece.

The next sections explain how to create the center ring and work your first round off of that ring.

Making a center ring

The following steps show you how to create a simple center ring of six chain stitches:

1. **Chain 6 (ch 6).**

2. **Insert your hook from front to back into the first chain stitch you made, as shown in Figure 8-1, in order to form a ring.**

Figure 8-1:
Making the
center ring
chain.

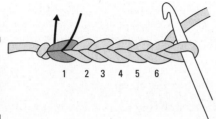

1   2   3   4   5   6

3. **Yarn over your hook (yo).**

4. **Draw the yarn through the stitch and through the loop on your hook, like in Figure 8-2a.**

   Your center ring is now complete. It should look like the one in Figure 8-2b.

Figure 8-2: Completing the center ring.

a   b

The number of stitches in the beginning chain determines the size of the hole that the center ring creates, as well as how many stitches you can work into the center ring. Make sure the ring is large enough to accommodate the number of stitches you'll be working in it. On the other hand, make sure it's not so long that you have a big loose hole in the center. *Note:* When you're working a pattern, it tells you how many chain stitches you need for the proper-size center ring.

Working the first round

After you make the center ring, you're ready to crochet your first round. Just as when you're beginning a new row, you first need to determine the number of turning chain stitches necessary in order to bring your hook up to the proper level for the next round of stitches. (The number of turning chains you need depends on the stitch you're about to work; Chapter 5 has a chart that shows how many turning chain stitches the basic crochet stitches require.)

Now here's the really easy part about working with a center ring: Instead of inserting your hook into the actual stitches of the center ring, just go through the center hole! The following steps show you how to work single crochet stitches into the center ring:

1. **Chain 1 (ch 1) to make the turning chain for single crochet (sc).**

2. **Insert your hook into the center ring so that the hook end is behind the ring. (See Figure 8-3a.)**

Figure 8-3:
Working a
single
crochet into
the center
ring.

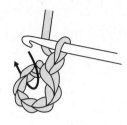 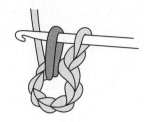

a   b

3. **Yarn over the hook (yo).**

4. **Draw the yarn through the center ring to the front of the ring. (Refer to Figure 8-3b.)**

5. **Yarn over the hook.**

6. **Draw the yarn through the 2 loops on your hook.**

   Your first completed single crochet stitch should look like the one in Figure 8-4a, where the arrow shows how you must insert the hook for the next stitch.

Figure 8-4:
Working
a round of
single
crochet.

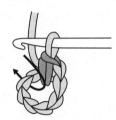 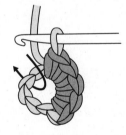

a   b

Continue to work single crochet stitches into the ring until you can't fit anymore (see Figure 8-4b for the visual). You may fit in more stitches than you expect because the center ring will stretch somewhat.

Working stitches in the chain stitch

The second most common method for creating a center ring is to work all the stitches for the first round in one chain stitch. You generally use this method when the design calls for a small hole in the center of the pattern or almost no hole at all.

To start a center ring this way, chain one stitch (this is what you work the stitches in) plus the number of stitches required for the turning chain, depending on which particular stitch you work in the first round. (See Chapter 5 for a list of the most common turning chain lengths.)

Follow these steps to work your first round of double crochet stitches into a chain stitch. *Note:* We chose the double crochet as our starting stitch, but the process works the same whichever stitch you choose to start with.

1. **Chain 1 (ch 1).**

2. **Chain 3 more for the double crochet stitch's (dc) turning chain.**

3. **Yarn over the hook (yo).**

4. **Insert your hook into the fourth chain from the hook, as shown in Figure 8-5.**

   This is the first chain stitch you made; it becomes your center ring chain stitch.

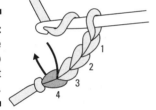

Figure 8-5: Inserting the hook into your first chain stitch.

5. **Work 1 complete double crochet stitch in the center ring chain stitch.**

   Do this by yarning over, drawing the yarn through the center ring chain stitch, yarning over, drawing the yarn through the first 2 loops on the hook, yarning over, and drawing the yarn through the first 2 loops on the hook. (See Chapter 6 for more on how to make a double crochet stitch.)

6. **Continue working double crochet stitches in the same center ring chain stitch until you're comfortable with the process.**

   For the next stitch, yarn over, insert your hook into the center ring chain stitch, and complete the stitch as you would a regular double crochet. Figure 8-6a shows you how to begin the third stitch, and Figure 8-6b shows a growing number of completed stitches.

   The turning chain for double crochet stitches worked in the round always counts as the first stitch.

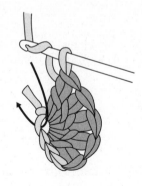

Figure 8-6:
Making your first round of double crochet in the center ring chain stitch.

a   b

Working stitches in an adjustable ring

The third most common method for creating a center ring is to work your first round of stitches into an adjustable ring. An adjustable ring allows you to make any number of stitches in the first round of a circle because the beginning loop can slide open or closed as needed. After you've made your adjustable ring, work the first round of stitches into the center and then pull the tail end until the center is closed. Use this method when you want the hole at the center of a project to be completely closed.

You can work an adjustable ring with any stitch; just remember to work the required number of turning chains before working your first stitch into the ring (see Chapter 5 for a refresher on turning chains). Follow these steps to work one round of single crochet into the center of an adjustable ring:

1. **Leaving a 2-inch tail, make a loop by crossing the working end of the yarn over the tail end and pinching the loop where the ends cross with the thumb and index finger of your nondominant hand.**

   The *working end* is the one attached to the ball of yarn. Figure 8-7a shows what this step looks like.

2. **Insert your hook through the center of the ring.**

3. **Yarn over (yo) with the working end of the yarn and draw the yarn through the ring as shown in Figure 8-7b.**

   You now have 1 loop on your hook.

4. **Chain 1 (ch 1).**

   This is the turning chain for a single crochet (sc).

5. **Insert the hook through the center of the ring, yarn over, and draw up a loop (see Figure 8-8a).**

   You now have 2 loops on your hook.

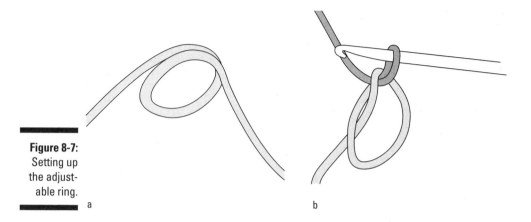

Figure 8-7:
Setting up
the adjust-
able ring.

a   b

6. **Yarn over and draw the yarn through both loops on your hook.**

   One single crochet in the center of the ring is now complete (see Figure 8-8b).

7. **Work 5 more single crochets in the center of the ring and then pull the tail end of the yarn until the center of the ring is closed.**

   Figure 8-8c shows 6 single crochet stitches in an adjustable ring with the tail end pulled tight to close the hole at the center of the ring.

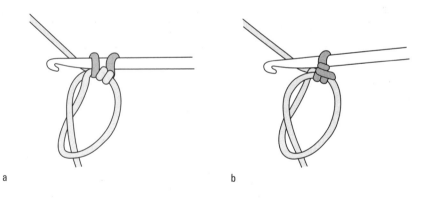

a   b

Figure 8-8:
Making the
first round
of single
crochet
into an
adjustable
ring.

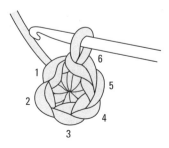

c

Uniting Your Ring

After you complete the number of stitches you need for your first round, you must join the first and last stitch of the round to complete the circle. The most popular way of doing that is by working a slip stitch in the top of the round's first stitch; doing so puts you in the proper position to begin the next round. You join each successive round in the same place, which creates a slightly visible seam (to make a round without a seam, see the later section "Another Option: Spiraling Up and Up").

You join single crochet rounds a little bit differently than rounds of other stitches, so we show you one example of each in the following sections.

Single crochet

To join a round of single crochet stitches, proceed as follows:

1. **After completing the last single crochet (sc) of the round, insert your hook under the top 2 loops of the first single crochet stitch you made.**

   The chain-1 turning chain at the beginning of a single crochet round doesn't count as a stitch, so skip over it and work the slip stitch in the first single crochet.

2. **Yarn over the hook (yo).**

3. **Draw the yarn through the stitch and the loop on your hook to complete 1 slip stitch (sl st), as shown in Figure 8-9a.**

   Congratulations! You've just joined the first round of single crochet. Figure 8-9b shows a stitch diagram depicting the placement of the joining slip stitch, which is the dot at the top. (See Chapter 4 for help reading stitch diagrams.)

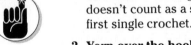

Figure 8-9: Joining a single crochet round with a slip stitch.

a

b

Double crochet and other stitches

To join a round of double crochet (or any other stitch) you must

1. **Insert your hook in the top of the turning chain after completing the last double crochet (dc) of the round.**

   Note that the turning chain counts as the first stitch of the round.

2. **Yarn over the hook (yo).**

3. **Draw the yarn through the turning chain and the loop on your hook to complete 1 slip stitch (sl st), as shown in Figure 8-10a.**

   You've just joined the first round of double crochet. Figure 8-10b is a stitch diagram depicting the placement of the joining slip stitch, which is the dot at the top, by the turning chain. (Not sure how to read stitch diagrams? Refer to Chapter 4.)

Figure 8-10:
Joining a
double
crochet
round with a
slip stitch.

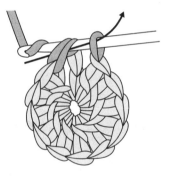
a

b

Adding Rounds

Adding rounds to your work is similar to adding rows, except that you usually don't turn your work and you increase the number of stitches you work in each round so that the piece lies flat. (See Chapter 7 for how to work an increase.)

The method of working subsequent rounds of stitches is the same for all stitches except the single crochet, as you discover in the following sections. However, the number of stitches you start with changes depending on the height of the stitch you're working with. Taller stitches, such as double and triple crochet, require more stitches in each round because the circumference of the circle they create is larger than a circle created with shorter stitches. The pattern you're working with should tell you how many stitches to work for your project.

The slip stitch that joins each round doesn't count as a stitch (regardless of whether you're working in single crochet or a taller stitch). When you join the last stitch to the first stitch, make sure you're working the slip stitch into the first stitch of the round and not the slip stitch from the previous round. So that you don't accidentally work stitches into the slip stitch, be sure to count your stitches at the end of each round to ensure you have the correct amount.

The second round of single crochet

Working rounds of single crochet is different than most other stitches because the turning chain doesn't count as a stitch. To work a second round of single crochet, follow these steps:

1. **After joining the first round, chain 1 (ch 1) for the turning chain.**
2. **Without turning your piece, work 2 single crochet stitches (sc) under the top 2 loops of the first stitch.**

   The first stitch is the one directly below the turning chain; it's the same stitch you worked the joining slip stitch into.

3. **Work 2 single crochet stitches in each stitch around.**
4. **Join the first and last stitch of the round with a slip stitch (sl st).**

The second round of double crochet

When working rounds of taller stitches, remember that the turning chain does in fact count as the first stitch. To work the second round of double crochet stitches, follow the instructions in the preceding section, but omit the chain 1 in Step 1 and substitute a chain 3 turning chain for the first stitch (see Chapter 5 for a refresher on turning chains). And, of course, use double crochet stitches in place of single crochet stitches.

For your piece to lie flat, the number of stitches in each round should increase by the number of stitches worked in the first round. (If you don't increase enough stitches, your piece will begin to turn up in a cuplike shape.) For example, if your first round has a total of 6 stitches, then your second round should increase by 6 stitches for a total of 12 stitches. The third round should again increase by 6 stitches, giving you a total of 18 stitches at the end of the round.

Table 8-1 presents three different examples of round increases, as well how to work them.

Table 8-1	Increasing Stitches in Rounds			
Round Number	*Number of Stitches in the Round*			*How to Work the Increase*
Round 1	6	8	12	N/A
Round 2	12	16	24	Increase 1 stitch in each stitch around
Round 3	18	24	36	Increase 1 stitch in every other stitch around
Round 4	24	32	48	Increase 1 stitch in every third stitch around
Round 5	30	40	60	Increase 1 stitch in every fourth stitch around
Round 6	36	48	72	Increase 1 stitch in every fifth stitch around

These guidelines apply to one specific form of increasing in rounds. You can increase in rounds many different ways, although the principle of increasing in a regular sequence remains the same. Always follow whatever increasing instructions are provided in your pattern.

Because you don't turn your work at the end of each round, you get a definite front and back to your piece. Figure 8-11a shows the *right* (front) side of a round. Notice how the stitches lean toward you? Figure 8-11b shows the *wrong* (back) side. It's a little smoother, and the stitches angle away from you somewhat.

Figure 8-11:
Two definite sides:
(a) the right/front side and (b) the wrong/back side.

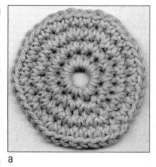 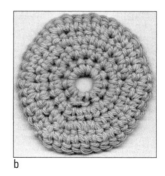

a   b

Sometimes, though, you want to avoid this front-and-back business and create a reversible fabric — especially for projects such as an afghan that you want to look good on both sides. To create a reversible fabric, just turn your piece after you've joined each round. (If you happen to forget this tip while working a pattern that requires a reversible fabric, don't worry. The directions will show you how to turn and where to work the stitches.) When you turn at the end of each joined round, be sure to skip the slip stitch and work your first stitch of the next round into the last stitch worked on the last round.

Another Option: Spiraling Up and Up

Working in a spiral is a way to crochet in rounds when you prefer not to have a visible seam. The usual reasons for working in a spiral are to make hats, mittens, bags, and toys with a three-dimensional shape. Another advantage of working in a spiral is that you don't need to join the end of each round or make a turning chain; this perk makes crocheting items faster and neater. In the following sections, we introduce spiral basics and show you how to work one from a stitch diagram, such as you may find in a pattern you want to try.

Working tall stitches (like triple crochet) in a spiral gives your work an uneven edge. We recommend you use this technique *only* for single crochet stitches.

Working in a spiral

The first round of a spiral design begins the same way as any other round. You create a center ring by using one of the three methods described earlier in this chapter and then work the required number of stitches in the first round. The stitch diagram in Figure 8-12 shows a center ring of 6 chain stitches and a first round of 12 single crochet stitches. (Chapter 4 has more on how to read a stitch diagram.) The twist comes in at the end of the round.

Figure 8-12:
Single
crochet
stitch
diagram for
working in a
spiral.

Instead of joining the round, you work the first stitch of the next round into the first stitch of the last round, and so on for each successive round. The only time you should slip stitch to complete the round is when you've finished the required number of rounds for the design. Reading the diagram in

Figure 8-12 counterclockwise, that means you work the 13th stitch in the first single crochet stitch of Round 1, skipping the turning chain from the first round. This now becomes the first stitch of the second round.

Before continuing on with Round 2, mark the first stitch of the second round with a stitch marker or a safety pin because losing your place or miscounting the stitches in each round is easy to do. (Stitch markers are handy gadgets that we mention in Chapter 2.) When you work your way back around, you work the first stitch of Round 3 into the marked stitch. Remove the marker from Round 2 and place it in the first stitch of Round 3. Continue spiraling until you're too dizzy to go any further or until your design is the size you want.

Ending the spiral

The last stitch in the last round of a spiral design is raised above the level of the previous round. To finish the round and make the edge smooth, you need to slip stitch in the next stitch (the first stitch of the previous round) before fastening off. (We explain how to fasten off in Chapter 5.)

Adding Another Dimension

Not all designs that you work in the round have to be flat. A perfect example is the Bucket Hat project at the end of this chapter. It's a flat round at the top, but then it takes on a tubular shape to fit over your head. If you're worried that transforming a round shape into a tubular one is a difficult technique, don't be — it's actually easier than getting the darn round to lie flat in the first place! We explain what you need to know in the following sections.

You can make some fun three-dimensional projects with this shaping technique (think crocheted dolls and animals). You crochet the pieces into the proper shape and then stuff them with filling to make them soft and plump. (Why not try the Amigurumi Pup project at the end of this chapter? We describe this Japanese craft in a later sidebar.) Christmas ornaments, mittens, slippers, and leg warmers are just a few of the other multidimensional designs that you shape by working in rounds.

Starting to add dimension

In the earlier "Adding Rounds" section, you find out how to keep a round flat by increasing the number of stitches in each successive round. To get the round to start curving up, you simply stop adding new stitches in each round. Here's how:

1. **Make a center ring of 6 chain stitches (ch) and work a complete round of 12 single crochet (sc). Join with a slip stitch (sl st).**

   See the sections "Joining chain stitches into a ring" and "Uniting Your Ring," earlier in this chapter, to find out how to perform this step.

2. **Work 2 more rounds, increasing 12 stitches for Round 2 and 12 more stitches for Round 3, joining after each round.**

   See the earlier "Adding Rounds" section for how to make the turning chain and add new rounds.

   You don't have to stop after 3 rounds. Add more rounds to make a larger design, but keep increasing the stitches by 12 for each round.

3. **To start adding depth, don't add any extra stitches to Round 4. Instead, work 1 single crochet stitch in each stitch of the previous round and join with a slip stitch.**

   Working 1 stitch in each stitch like this causes the edges of your work to turn in. Repeat Step 3 until the piece is as deep as you want.

If you want your piece to start curving in more gradually, don't add as many increase stitches to the rounds in Step 2. Add a few so that the circumference grows, but not enough to keep it lying flat. Try adding just eight stitches to each round. Play around with the number of increases: The fewer you add, the more dramatic the curve; the more you add, the shallower the curve.

Deciding how to wrap up your work

After your work is as deep (or as long) as you want, you have three choices:

- ✔ **Fasten off your work.** You now have something that looks like a cap or a tube sock, depending on how big you made the initial flat round and how many rounds you added for depth.

- ✔ **Begin increasing stitches in each round.** This makes your piece begin to widen and flatten out, kind of like the brim on a hat.

- ✔ **Begin decreasing stitches in each round.** Decreasing the number of stitches starts to close up the edges of your piece, creating a spherical design. You decrease rounds the same way you decrease rows, by combining two stitches into one. (Refer to Chapter 7 for more on decreasing.)

Decreasing evenly in each successive round creates a smooth, even curve, but if you work a large number of decreases in one round, the work will pull in sharply. If you want your design to be symmetrical, decrease at the same rate as you increased on the first half of your piece.

Amigurumi: The art of Japanese toy-making

Amigurumi is the popular Japanese craft of crocheting (or knitting) cute stuffed dolls. Most *amigurumi* projects tend to be animals (such as bears, cats, dogs, birds, or monkeys), but the craft is often seen giving other objects (such as cupcakes, milk cartons, eggs, and mushrooms) *anthropomorphic* features. In other words, the craft bestows human features upon animals and inanimate objects. No matter the subject, the main aesthetic goal of any *amigurumi* project is to be sweet and cute.

Amigurumi is very simple in design and only a little more challenging in construction. The dolls are usually created with tight single crochet stitches (in order to keep any stuffing bits from coming through) that are worked in a spiral method to avoid a seam. The pieces and parts of the toys are worked separately and then sewn together at the end. Embellishments and facial features are added before the pieces are stuffed and finished.

Amigurumi patterns usually let you know exactly what you need to make the project, but here are a few basics you can expect to find in a typical pattern:

- ✔ **Yarn:** You can use any type of yarn, but *amigurumi* projects are usually made with worsted-weight acrylic, wool, or wool-blend yarns. Scraps of various colors may be used to add embroidery for the mouth or nose. *Remember:* The dolls are small, so you don't need a ton of yarn; check your stash first before buying anything new.

- ✔ **Hooks:** Your stitches need to be tight so the stuffing doesn't fall out, so the recommended hook may be at least two sizes smaller than the one normally recommended for the yarn.

- ✔ **Notions:** You'll probably want a stitch marker to help you keep track of your rounds as well as a yarn needle to sew up the pieces and parts.

- ✔ **Facial features:** Many craft stores sell plastic safety eyes and noses, which are great for toys that are given to children because they don't pull off very easily. You can also use beads, buttons, crocheted circles, or embroidery.

- ✔ **Stuffing:** The most commonly used stuffing is fiberfill, found at most craft stores, but you can also use fabric or yarn scraps. Plastic pellets or pony beads are sometimes added to give the toy weight. Whatever you opt for, don't use rice or beans (which can attract bugs).

Bucket Hat Project

The pattern for this versatile hat uses simple single crochet stitches and allows you to practice increasing in rounds. The yarn in this design, shown in the color section, is a cotton-wool blend that's both soft and resilient, allowing you to create a pretty accessory that can be worn throughout the year.

Materials and vital statistics

- **Yarn:** Brown Sheep Company, Inc. "Cotton Fleece" DK-weight yarn (80% cotton/20% wool), (3.5 oz. [100 g], 215 yds [197 m] each skein): 1 skein of #CW400 New Age Teal

- **Hook:** Crochet hook size G-6 U.S. (4 mm) or size needed to obtain gauge

- **Large-eyed yarn needle**

- **Measurements:** 21 in. in circumference; one size fits most adults

- **Gauge:** First 7 rnds = 2½ in. in diameter

- **Stitches used:** Chain stitch (ch), slip stitch (sl st), single crochet (sc), adjustable ring

Directions

The instructions for this project are just as you'd see them in any regular crochet publication, complete with abbreviations. Figure 8-13 gives you a stitch diagram for extra guidance. If you need more info on how to read Crochetese or stitch diagrams, head to Chapter 4 for the scoop on what each abbreviation means and how to work with asterisks. For complete instructions on how to increase and decrease stitches, refer to Chapter 7.

Crown

Center ring: Make an adjustable ring, ch 1.

Rnd 1: Work 6 sc into center of ring, sl st in first sc to join (6 sc).

Rnd 2: Ch 1, work 2 sc in each sc around, sl st in first sc to join (12 sc).

Rnd 3: Ch 1, sc in first sc, 2 sc in next sc, * sc in next sc, 2 sc in next sc; rep from * around, sl st in first sc to join (18 sc).

Rnd 4: Ch 1, sc in first 2 sc, 2 sc in next sc, * sc in next 2 sc, 2 sc in next sc; rep from * around, sl st in first sc to join (24 sc).

Rnd 5: Ch 1, sc in first 3 sc, 2 sc in next sc, * sc in next 3 sc, 2 sc in next sc; rep from * around, sl st in first sc to join (30 sc).

Rnd 6: Ch 1, sc in first 4 sc, 2 sc in next sc, * sc in next 4 sc, 2 sc in next sc; rep from * around, sl st in first sc to join (36 sc).

Rnd 7: Ch 1, sc in first 5 sc, 2 sc in next sc, * sc in next 5 sc, 2 sc in next sc; rep from * around, sl st in first sc to join (42 sc).

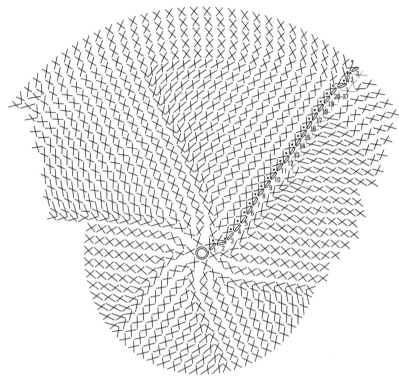

Figure 8-13:
The stitch
diagram for
the Bucket
Hat project.

Rnd 8: Ch 1, sc in first 6 sc, 2 sc in next sc, * sc in next 6 sc, 2 sc in next sc; rep from * around, sl st in first sc to join (48 sc).

Rnd 9: Ch 1, sc in first 7 sc, 2 sc in next sc, * sc in next 7 sc, 2 sc in next sc; rep from * around, sl st in first sc to join (54 sc).

Rnd 10: Ch 1, sc in first 8 sc, 2 sc in next sc, * sc in next 8 sc, 2 sc in next sc; rep from * around, sl st in first sc to join (60 sc).

Rnd 11: Ch 1, sc in first 9 sc, 2 sc in next sc, * sc in next 9 sc, 2 sc in next sc; rep from * around, sl st in first sc to join (66 sc).

Rnd 12: Ch 1, sc in first 10 sc, 2 sc in next sc, * sc in next 10 sc, 2 sc in next sc; rep from * around, sl st in first sc to join (72 sc).

Rnd 13: Ch 1, sc in first 11 sc, 2 sc in next sc, * sc in next 11 sc, 2 sc in next sc; rep from * around, sl st in first sc to join (78 sc).

Rnd 14: Ch 1, sc in first 12 sc, 2 sc in next sc, * sc in next 12 sc, 2 sc in next sc; rep from * around, sl st in first sc to join (84 sc).

Rnd 15: Ch 1, sc in first 13 sc, 2 sc in next sc, * sc in next 13 sc, 2 sc in next sc; rep from * around, sl st in first sc to join (90 sc).

Rnd 16: Ch 1, sc in first 14 sc, 2 sc in next sc, * sc in next 14 sc, 2 sc in next sc; rep from * around, sl st in first sc to join (96 sc).

Rnd 17: Ch 1, sc in first 15 sc, 2 sc in next sc, * sc in next 15 sc, 2 sc in next sc; rep from * around, sl st in first sc to join (102 sc).

Rnd 18: Ch 1, sc in first 16 sc, 2 sc in next sc, * sc in next 16 sc, 2 sc in next sc; rep from * around, sl st in first sc to join (108 sc).

Rnd 19: Ch 1, sc in each sc around, sl st in first sc to join (108 sc).

Rnds 20–37: Rep Rnd 19 for 18 more rnds or 7 in. from beg of hat.

Brim

Rnd 1: Ch 1, 2 sc in first sc, sc in next 26 sc, * 2 sc in next sc, sc in next 26 sc; rep from * around, sl st in first sc to join (112 sc).

Rnd 2: Ch 1, sc in first 27 sc, 2 sc in first sc, * sc in next 27 sc, 2 sc in next sc; rep from * around, sl st in first sc to join (116 sc).

Rnd 3: Ch 1, 2 sc in first sc, sc in next 28 sc, * 2 sc in next sc, sc in next 28 sc; rep from * around, sl st in first sc to join (120 sc).

Rnd 4: Ch 1, sc in first 29 sc, 2 sc in first sc, * sc in next 29 sc, 2 sc in next sc; rep from * around, sl st in first sc to join (124 sc).

Rnd 5: Ch 1, 2 sc in first sc, sc in next 30 sc, * 2 sc in next sc, sc in next 30 sc; rep from * around, sl st in first sc to join (128 sc).

Rnd 6: Ch 1, sc in first 31 sc, 2 sc in first sc, * sc in next 31 sc, 2 sc in next sc; rep from * around, sl st in first sc to join (132 sc).

Rnd 7: Sl st in the front loop of each sc around, sl st in first sl st to join.

Fasten off and weave in loose ends with the yarn needle.

Optional flower

Make a flower by working the Flower Power project in Chapter 14 with the same yarn and hook as you used for the hat. With a yarn needle, sew the flower to the hat by stitching around the center of the flower.

Amigurumi Pup Project

The pieces for this cute puppy (shown in the color section) are made using basic *amigurumi* skills — single crochet stitches worked in a spiral round — that allow you to practice increasing and decreasing to see how shaping occurs (check out the earlier section "Another Option: Spiraling Up and Up" for more info on working in a spiral). The yarn is a basic acrylic with a satin finish, but you can substitute almost any worsted-weight yarn.

The colors in this pattern were inspired by the Pug dog breed. However, if you substitute a furry white yarn for the tan color, you can easily transform this pup into a lamb! Flip to Chapter 9 to find out how to work with a main color (MC) and a contrasting color (CC).

Materials and vital statistics

- **Yarn:** Bernat "Satin" worsted-weight yarn (100% acrylic), Article #164104 (3.5 oz. [100 g], 163 yds [149 m] each skein): 1 skein each of
  - #04011 Sable (MC)
  - #04040 Ebony (CC)
- **Hook:** Crochet hook size F-5 U.S. (3.75 mm) or size needed to obtain gauge
- **Stitch marker**
- **Two 12-mm solid black safety eyes**
- **Fiberfill**
- **Yarn needle**
- **Measurements:** 5 in. tall
- **Gauge:** First 6 rnds of body = 2¼ in. in diameter
- **Stitches used:** Adjustable ring, chain stitch (ch), single crochet (sc), slip stitch (sl st). **Dec 1 sc:** * (insert hook in next st, yo, draw yarn through st) twice, yo, draw yarn through 3 loops on hook *.

Directions

Here's another chance to test your skills at deciphering Crochetese. The following instructions appear just as they would in your average crochet publication, complete with abbreviations. Refer to Figures 8-14, 8-15, 8-16, and 8-17 for extra guidance. If you're not sure what each abbreviation means or how to work with asterisks, see Chapter 4. Refer to Chapter 7 for complete instructions on how to increase and decrease stitches.

Body

See Figure 8-14 for a partial stitch diagram of the pup's body.

Center ring: With MC, make adjustable ring, ch 1.

Rnd 1: Work 6 sc into center of ring, don't join or turn, continue to work in a spiral, place a stitch marker in the first st to keep track of your rnds, move the marker up to the first st with each rnd (6 sc).

Rnd 2: Work 2 sc in each sc around (12 sc).

Rnd 3: * Sc in next sc, 2 sc in next sc; rep from * around (18 sc).

Rnd 4: * Sc in next 2 sc, 2 sc in next sc; rep from * around (24 sc).

Rnd 5: * Sc in next 3 sc, 2 sc in next sc; rep from * around (30 sc).

Rnd 6: * Sc in next 4 sc, 2 sc in next sc; rep from * around (36 sc).

Rnds 7–13: Sc in each sc around.

Rnd 14: * Dec 1 sc in next 2 sc, sc in next 4 sc; rep from * around (30 sc).

Rnd 15: Sc in each sc around.

Rnd 16: * Dec 1 sc in next 2 sc, sc in next 3 sc; rep from * around (24 sc).

Rnd 17: Sc in each sc around.

Rnd 18: * Dec 1 sc in next 2 sc, sc in next 2 sc; rep from * around (18 sc).

Rnd 19: Sc in each sc around. Sl st in next sc to join. Fasten off, leaving 6 in. of tail for sewing.

Arms

Make two arms the same; see Figure 8-15 for the stitch diagram.

Center ring: With MC, make adjustable ring, ch 1.

Rnd 1: Work 6 sc into center of ring without joining or turning, continue to work in a spiral (6 sc).

Figure 8-14:
A partial
stitch dia-
gram of the
Amigurumi
Pup's body.

Rnd 2: Work 2 sc in each sc around (12 sc).

Rnd 3: * Sc in next sc, 2 sc in next sc; rep from * around (18 sc).

Rnds 4–6: Sc in each sc around.

Rnd 7: * Dec 1 sc in next 2 sc, sc in next 4 sc; rep from * around (15 sc).

Rnd 8: Sc in each sc around.

Rnd 9: * Dec 1 sc in next 2 sc, sc in next 3 sc; rep from * around (12 sc).

Rnd 10: Sc in each sc around. Sl st in next sc to join. Fasten off, leaving 6 in. of tail for sewing.

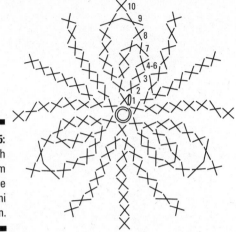

Figure 8-15:
The stitch
diagram
of the
Amigurumi
Pup's arm.

Ears

Make two ears the same; refer to Figure 8-16 for the stitch diagram.

With CC, make adjustable ring, ch 1.

Rnd 1: Work 6 sc into center of ring, *turn* (6 sc).

Rnd 2: Work 2 sc in each sc around (12 sc).

Rnds 3–7: Sc in each sc around.

Rnd 8: [Dec 1 sc in next 2 sc] 6 times around (6 sc). Sl st in next sc. Fasten off, leaving 3 in. of tail for sewing.

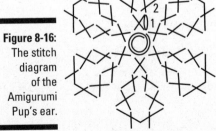

Figure 8-16:
The stitch
diagram
of the
Amigurumi
Pup's ear.

Head

Check out Figure 8-17 for the stitch diagram of the pup's head.

Center ring: With CC, make adjustable ring, ch 1.

Rnd 1: Work 6 sc into center of ring, don't join or turn, continue to work in a spiral (6 sc).

Rnd 2: Work 2 sc in each sc around (12 sc).

Rnd 3: * Sc in next sc, 2 sc in next sc; rep from * around (18 sc).

Rnd 4: Sc in each sc around.

Rnd 5: * Sc in next 2 sc, 2 sc in next sc; rep from * around, change to MC (24 sc).

Rnd 6: * Sc in next 3 sc, 2 sc in next sc; rep from * around (30 sc).

Rnd 7: * Sc in next 4 sc, 2 sc in next sc; rep from * around (36 sc).

Rnd 8: * Sc in next 8 sc, 2 sc in next sc; rep from * around (40 sc).

Rnds 9–13: Sc in each sc around.

Rnd 14: * Dec 1 sc in next 2 sc, sc in next 8 sc; rep from * around (36 sc).

Rnd 15: * Dec 1 sc in next 2 sc, sc in next 4 sc; rep from * around (30 sc).

Rnd 16: * Dec 1 sc in next 2 sc, sc in next 3 sc; rep from * around (24 sc).

Insert safety eyes, making sure they're positioned in a desirable spot before putting the backs on. Pinch the ears flat and thread the long tail onto the yarn needle. Using the yarn needle, whipstitch the ears to each side of the head just above the eyes (see Chapter 15 for pointers on whipstitching). Stuff the head with fiberfill until full.

Rnd 17: * Dec 1 sc in next 2 sc, sc in next 2 sc; rep from * around (18 sc).

Rnd 18: * Dec 1 sc in next 2 sc, sc in next sc; rep from * around (12 sc).

Rnd 19: [Dec 1 sc in next 2 sc] 6 times around (6 sc). Sl st in next sc. Fasten off, leaving 4 in. of tail.

Thread the yarn needle with the tail end and weave the tail through the remaining 6 stitches, inserting the needle under both loops of each stitch and then pulling the tail to close the end. Weave in all loose ends.

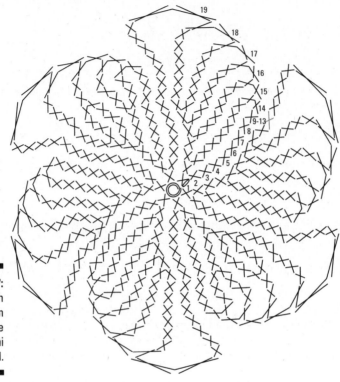

Figure 8-17:
The stitch
diagram
of the
Amigurumi
Pup's head.

Assembly

Follow these steps to put your Amigurumi Pup together:

1. **Stuff the body with fiberfill until firm.**

2. **Stuff each arm half full of fiberfill.**

3. **Pinch the opening of each arm together and line up the flattened edge to one side of the body opening.**

4. **Whipstitch the arms to each side of the body, inserting your needle under the top loops of the body and the top loops of the stitches on each side of the flattened edge of the arm.**

5. **Center the head on the opening of the body so that the puppy is facing you from a seated position and then thread the long tail of the body onto the yarn needle.**

6. **Whipstitch the body to the head, inserting the needle under the top loops of the body stitches and around the nearest single crochet stitch on the head.**

7. **Weave in the loose ends with the yarn needle.**

Chapter 9

Crocheting in Technicolor

In This Chapter

▶ Changing from one color to another

▶ Avoiding the snipping and rejoining part by carrying your yarn

▶ Deciphering color codes and color charts

▶ Getting crafty with the Fibonacci sequence (not as scary as it sounds!)

▶ Decorating with a colorful pillow

*H*ave you ever stopped to imagine what the world would be like without color? Everywhere you look, from outside your windows to inside your home to the clothes on your body, color shapes your life and the way you view things. Well, the same holds true for the designs you crochet. Take, for example, an afghan. Worked in a single color, it provides warmth but not much else. Add one or more colors, though, and not only do you have a warm blanket to snuggle up with but you also have a work of art to display.

Whether you want to create a simple stripe pattern or a complex mosaic design in many colors, this chapter explains the various techniques for working with color and reading color charts. If you work the fun Mod Pillow project at the end of this chapter, you can practice your newfound techniques.

Bringing Designs to Life: Joining Colors

Working color changes properly gives your finished project a smooth, clean appearance with no unsightly bumps and knots. You usually switch colors at one of two different places within your design:

   ✔ **At the beginning (or end) of a row or round:** You typically change colors at the beginning of a row when working a striped pattern. Of course, you can also look at this as changing color at the end of a row or round because the end of one is the beginning of another.

   ✔ **In the middle of a row or round:** For *charted patterns,* which have a picture in the middle of the design, you need to change colors in the middle of a row. (See the later section "Charting color change" for more details.)

The next sections show you how to create a smooth, clean transition between colors regardless of whether you need to switch in the beginning, middle, or end of a row or round.

Changing color at the beginning (or end)

If you're going for stripes, master changing colors at the beginning (or end) of a row because you'll be doing this a lot. Fortunately, you change colors at the beginning (or end) of a row or round the same way you join a new strand of yarn of the same color — by making the change while working the last stitch of the previous row or round. (Need a refresher on joining yarn? See Chapter 6.)

Practice this technique by crocheting a swatch of double crochet several rows long with your first color; then follow these steps to join the new color:

1. **Using the first color, double crochet (dc) in each stitch across to the next-to-last stitch of the row.**

2. **Work the last double crochet to the point where only 2 loops are left on the hook.**

3. **Drop the first yarn color and pick up the second color.**

4. **Wrap the end of the second yarn color around the hook.**

5. **Draw the second yarn color through the 2 loops of the first yarn color that are on your hook, as in Figure 9-1.**

   At this point, you should have 2 strands of yarn hanging down.

6. **Tug on the end of the first color at the base of the double crochet to tighten up the stitch.**

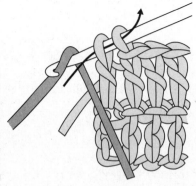

Figure 9-1:
Joining a
new color at
the begin-
ning (or end)
of a row.

If you plan to pick up the first color in a later row, leave the first color of yarn hanging and continue on with the second color. (See the section "Hitching a Ride: Carrying the Yarn," later in this chapter, to find out what to do with the unused first color strand of yarn.) If you don't plan to pick up the first color in a nearby row, cut the yarn (after joining the second color as explained in Step 5 of the preceding list). Be sure to leave a 6-inch tail for weaving in later.

To hide the tail end of the first yarn color, lay it across the tops of the stitches in the previous row and work over it or weave it in with a yarn needle when you finish crocheting.

When you join a new yarn color, always finish the last stitch of the first color with the second color, regardless of the type of stitch you're working. Doing so gets you ready to start the first stitch of the second color with the correct color loop on your hook, thereby preventing _color drag,_ which happens when part of a stitch is one color and the rest of the stitch is another color. This holds true regardless of where the color change is made — at the beginning, end, or middle of a row or round.

Changing color midstream

If you're making a design with a picture in the middle (a _charted pattern_), you change colors in the middle of a row. As when changing colors at the beginning of a row, correctly switching to a new color is important in order to prevent color drag.

Practice this technique by crocheting a swatch of double crochet several rows long with your first color. To add a new color within a row, follow these steps:

1. **Work the last stitch prior to the stitch where you're going to make the color change up to the point where only 2 loops are left on the hook.**

2. **Drop the first yarn color to the wrong (back) side and pick up the second color.**

3. **Wrap the end of the second yarn color around the hook.**

4. **Draw the second yarn color through the 2 loops (of the first yarn color) on your hook, thus completing the stitch with the second yarn color.**

   Figure 9-2a illustrates what this step looks like. If you don't plan to use the first color of yarn in the next few rows, cut the yarn, leaving a tail. Fasten off the first color by drawing the tail end through the current stitch as described in the preceding section. Then work over this tail with the new color or weave it in later with a yarn needle.

5. **Continue working with the new color of yarn, as in Figure 9-2b.**

Figure 9-2:
Changing
to a new
color of yarn
within a
row, wrong
side facing.

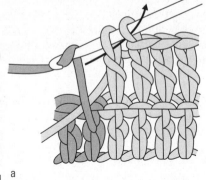
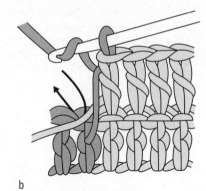

a   b

You can change color with either the right side or the wrong side of the work facing you. Just remember to drop the tail end of the first color of yarn to the wrong side, even if it's the side of the work that's facing you.

Hitching a Ride: Carrying the Yarn

When you're crocheting with two or more colors, you often carry the yarn that you're not presently working with to avoid having to fasten it off and rejoin a new strand each time you make a color change. As you find out in the following sections, you have several different options for carrying the yarn, each of which produces a different result.

If you're carrying several different colors, you can end up with a tangled mess in seconds. The simple act of turning your work at the end of each row becomes a nightmare if you have many different balls of yarn attached to your work at the same time. For small areas of color, cutting off a few yards of the required color and winding it around a bobbin alleviates this mess. (See Chapter 2 for more on yarn bobbins.) For the most prominent colors, however, leave the whole skein intact.

Carrying on the wrong side

Carrying the yarn across the row on the wrong side of the fabric is probably the easiest method to use when working with different colors. When you're working a design that changes colors fairly frequently, such as vertical stripes or multicolored charted designs, fastening off each color each time you have to change is too much of a hassle. It also produces an incredibly sloppy finished product.

To carry a strand on the wrong side of the fabric, work over the strand every few stitches with the second color, as shown in Figure 9-3. (Please note that Figure 9-3 shows the wrong side of the fabric.) To do this, lay the strand horizontally across the tops of the stitches along the wrong side of the fabric. When you complete the next stitch, make sure to encase the yarn as you draw it through the first two loops.

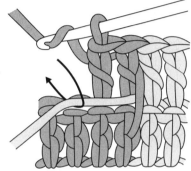

Figure 9-3: Carrying a strand across the wrong side.

The *wrong* (back) side of your piece is facing you as you work every other row, so make sure you're always carrying the yarn on the same side. If you're changing color on a *right* (front) side row, you carry the first color on the wrong side of your work.

If you'll be switching back to the carried color several times across the row, then carry the yarn all the way across. If the design is only in a particular section of the work, such as a picture in the middle of a sweater back, carry the yarn only in the part of the row where the design is featured and then let it drop while you finish the row. When you work back across the row, the color will be available for you to pick up in the spot dictated by the design.

Keep the carried strand tight enough so that it lies flat against the wrong side of the fabric and doesn't catch on anything, but don't pull the strand too taut, or else the fabric can pucker.

Working over a carried strand

Working over the carried strand produces a neater appearance on the wrong side of the fabric, which is especially important in a design where the backside is visible, such as an afghan or a scarf.

The technique for working over a carried strand is basically the same as working over the end of the yarn when joining a new ball in the middle of a row (refer to Chapter 6). Just lay the unused strand of yarn across the tops of the stitches of the previous row. Then, using the new color, work the stitches in the current row and encase the strand, as in Figure 9-4.

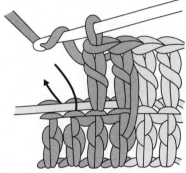

Figure 9-4:
Working over a carried strand.

The carried color is sometimes slightly visible, depending on the type and color of the yarn and stitches you're using. Don't worry, though; more often than not this visibility adds depth and contrast to the design.

Carrying on the right side

The only reason you ever carry the yarn on the right side of the fabric is if the carried strand is an integral part of your design. For example, carrying a thin strand studded with sequins or mirrors across the right side can add fancy flash to a project made with otherwise simple yarn.

You carry the yarn across the right side the same way you carry it across the wrong side (as explained in the earlier "Carrying on the wrong side" section). However, you may want to catch the strand every other stitch or even every stitch, depending on the pattern, to make sure that no long, loose loops are hanging around. If your pattern calls for this carrying method, the instructions will indicate how often to catch the yarn.

Carrying up the side

Carrying the yarn up the side comes in handy when you're working a horizontal stripe pattern. However, this technique only works when you're crocheting stripes in even numbers of rows. If you're working a stripe pattern that changes color every row, the carried yarn won't be on the side you need it to be when you want to pick it up in the next row.

To carry a strand of yarn up the side edge of your work:

1. **Work 2 rows in the first color, switching colors of yarn in the last stitch of the second row.**

   To switch colors of yarn, follow the first set of steps in the earlier "Changing color at the beginning (or end)" section.

2. **Work 2 rows with the second color.**

3. **Draw up the first color from 2 rows below to complete the last stitch of the second row (see Figure 9-5) and drop the second color, which you'll pick up later.**

   If you pull the strand too tightly up the side, your design will pucker.

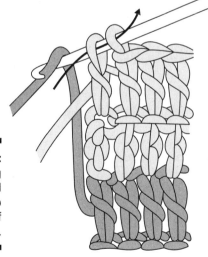

Figure 9-5:
Carrying
the unused
strand up
the side of
your work.

Careful coloration

Choosing different colors for a design may turn into a more daunting process than you originally bargained for. Here are some tips to make combining colors well a tad easier:

✔ **Use a color wheel.** This handy little gadget is available in most craft and yarn stores. Choose colors within the same segment to get several tones that work well together, or for a more vibrant look, choose colors that are exactly opposite each other on the color wheel.

✔ **Pick a multicolored yarn and a solid color yarn.** Many yarn companies create variegated or multicolored yarns to coordinate with their solid colors. Choose a multicolored yarn that appeals to you and then match it up with a solid color yarn. Doing so gives the appearance of using many different yarns, when you actually use only two or three.

✔ **Rely on basic white or off-white to add contrast.** White and off-white work well with almost any other color. If you're looking for a stark contrast, go with a dark secondary color. A lighter color works fine if you want something subtler.

✔ **Use dark and light tones of the same color.** If you favor a particular color, why not use its many shades?

Demystifying Color Codes and Charts

Working with color has its own special language. To make the instructions more compact and concise, most instruction writers use abbreviations when referring to colorful designs. That's why the sections that follow give you the skinny on deciphering color codes and reading color charts.

Abbreviating color names in patterns

When you first look at the instructions for a particular pattern, you obviously check to see what materials you need, including how many different colors of yarn the pattern uses. If the pattern involves two or more colors, you may see some funny letter designations after each color name.

Pairing up: Main color and contrasting color

If a pattern requires only two colors, the *main color* (abbreviated MC) is usually the first and most prominent color within the pattern. The *contrasting color* (CC) is the secondary color.

If the materials call for three skeins of white as the main color (MC) and two skeins of red as the contrasting color (CC) and the instruction is for a striped pattern, you may see something like this:

1. **Row 2: With MC, ch 1, sc in each sc across, complete last st with CC, *turn*. Fasten off MC.**

   Here's what that gobbledygook means: Working with the main color (white), chain 1 and then work 1 single crochet stitch in each single crochet stitch across until you reach the next-to-last stitch. Then work the last stitch, completing it with the contrasting color (red). Fasten off the main color (white). Then turn your work.

2. **Row 3: With CC, ch 1, sc in each sc across, *turn*.**

   Again, an English translation: Working now with the contrasting color (red), chain 1, work 1 single crochet in each single crochet stitch across the row, and then turn your work.

Three's a crowd: Letter abbreviations

When a design calls for three or more colors, patterns use letters of the alphabet to designate the colors. For example, a materials list that calls for six different colors may appear like this:

> 4 balls of Yellow (A); 3 balls each of White (B), Green (C), and Blue (D); 1 ball each of Pink (E) and Lilac (F)

Some patterns may use the initials of color names to abbreviate, such as G for green, W for white, and so on. Then again, sometimes a pattern has a main color (MC) along with several other colors designated A, B, C, and so on. Whichever abbreviation style they use, patterns usually list the yarns needed in order of appearance in the pattern or by the quantity required.

Be sure to read through the materials list at the beginning of each project so you're familiar with the color abbreviations. You may want to write out a separate list of the abbreviations and the color names to help keep things straight.

Charting color change

Many patterns use a color chart rather than written instructions to show designs that have frequent color changes or use several different colors. A *color chart* is a grid, with each square representing one stitch (see Figure 9-6a). Because most crochet publications are in black and white, symbols in each square indicate the different colors. Always refer to the chart key (which looks like Figure 9-6b) to determine which symbol stands for which color.

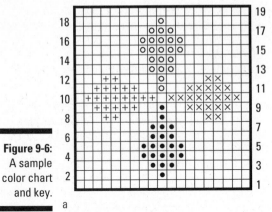

CHART KEY

☐ = White sc
● = Red sc
+ = Yellow sc
✕ = Aqua sc
○ = Green sc

Figure 9-6:
A sample
color chart
and key.

a   b

When reading a color chart, you generally read the odd-numbered rows from right to left and the even-numbered rows from left to right, unless otherwise specified. This is simply because you work your first row after the foundation chain from right to left and the second row from left to right. Figure 9-7 shows a swatch made from the chart in Figure 9-6a.

Figure 9-7:
Sample
swatch
worked
from a
color chart.

Crafty Math: Understanding the Fibonacci Sequence

Like it or not, math and crochet go hand in hand. From calculating gauge (explained in Chapter 3) to determining how to work increases to make a flat or curved circle (described in Chapters 7 and 8), you use math whenever you pick up your hook. One important math concept, the Fibonacci sequence, actually allows you to add balance and interest in crochet patterns involving multiple colors.

The *Fibonacci sequence* is a simple series of numbers that follows a predictable pattern. Here's the beginning of the basic sequence:

0, 1, 1, 2, 3, 5, 8, 13, 21, 34, 55, 89, 144, 233, 377 . . .

To break the pattern down, begin with the first two numbers and add them together to get the third number: 0 + 1 = 1. Next, add the previous two numbers in the sequence to get the fourth number: 1 + 1 = 2. Now the sequence reads 0, 1, 1, 2. Find the fifth number by adding the third and fourth numbers together: 1 + 2 = 3. As you can see, the Fibonacci sequence can go on indefinitely as you continue to add the previous two numbers to find the next number in the series.

Many eye-pleasing objects in nature follow the Fibonacci sequence. Picture the number of petals on your favorite flower. Now count them. We bet you count three, five, or eight petals. Sequences can also occur in the arrangement of petals on a pine cone or the spiraling rings of seeds at the center of a sunflower. If these sequences produce such an orderly appearance in nature, why not apply the same concepts to crochet?

To create an interesting color pattern in your piece, simply apply the basic Fibonacci sequence using two or more colors, as shown in the Mod Pillow project at the end of this chapter. You can apply part of the sequence to the number of rows or stitches in a pattern. For example, you can use a 1-1-2 pattern or a 2-3-5-8-13 pattern. (***Note:*** You can also create texture patterns using the same concept and a variety of basic stitches.)

All patterns involving multiple colors will instruct you on how to create the color patterns for the piece, but you can make a project your own by choosing the colors that reflect your style or by substituting your own Fibonacci sequence.

Mod Pillow Project

One side of this contemporary pillow allows you to master the technique of changing color; the other side uses a Fibonacci sequence to determine the number of rows for each stripe in the following order: 1, 1, 2, 3, 5, 8. The recommended worsted-weight yarn is easy to work with and comes in a bountiful array of colors. Use those shown in the color section, or choose colors that suit your décor and let the Fibonacci sequence do all the work of coordinating them for you.

Materials and vital statistics

- **Yarn:** Brown Sheep Company, Inc. "Lamb's Pride" worsted-weight yarn (85% wool/15% mohair), (4 oz. [113 g], 190 yds [173 m] each skein):
  - 2 skeins of #M28 Chianti (MC)
  - 1 skein of #M83 Raspberry (A)
  - 1 skein of #M89 Roasted Coffee (B)
  - 1 skein of #M105 RPM Pink (C)
  - 1 skein of #M191 Kiwi (D)
- **Hook:** Crochet hook size I-9 U.S. (5.5 mm) or size needed to obtain gauge
- **Large-eyed yarn needle**
- **Pillow form:** 14 in. x 14 in. square
- **Measurements:** 14 in. wide x 14 in. long
- **Gauge:** 13 sts and 12 rows sc = 4 in. in Esc
- **Stitches used:** Chain stitch (ch), extended single crochet (Esc), single crochet (sc), slip stitch (sl st)

Directions

Work the pillow front using the Fibonacci striping sequence. Work the pillow back following the color chart in Figure 9-8a; the chart key is in Figure 9-8b. Read all the odd-numbered rows from right to left and all the even-numbered rows from left to right. To change colors, complete the last single crochet of the first color with the next color. Drop the first color to the wrong side to be picked up later. Attach separate balls of color as needed and fasten off colors when they're not needed in the following row.

To help you keep track of which side is the right side and which side is the wrong side, use a safety pin, stitch marker, or scrap of yarn to mark the right side for both the front and the back of the pillow.

Pillow front

With MC, ch 48.

Row 1 (RS): Esc in second ch from hook, Esc in each ch across changing to A with last Esc (47 Esc), *turn*.

Row 2: Ch 1, Esc in each sc across changing to B with last Esc (47 Esc), *turn*.

Rows 3–4: Rep Row 2 with B.

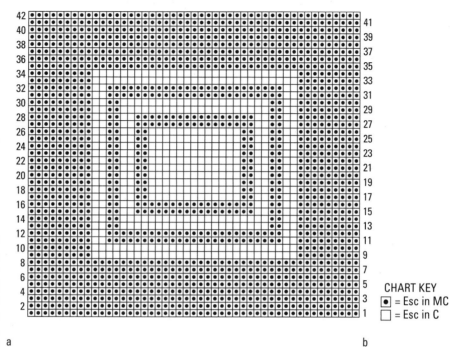

CHART KEY
● = Esc in MC
□ = Esc in C

Figure 9-8:
The color chart and key for the back of the Mod Pillow.

Rows 5–7: Rep Row 2 with C.

Rows 8–12: Rep Row 2 with D.

Rows 13–20: Rep Row 2 with MC.

Row 21: Rep Row 2 with A.

Row 22: Rep Row 2 with B.

Rows 23–24: Rep Row 2 with C.

Rows 25–27: Rep Row 2 with D.

Rows 28–32: Rep Row 2 with MC.

Rows 33–40: Rep Row 2 with A.

Row 41: Rep Row 2 with B.

Row 42: Rep Row 2 with C. Fasten off and weave in the loose ends.

Pillow back

With MC, ch 48.

Row 1 (RS): Esc in second ch from hook, Esc in each ch across (47 Esc), *turn*.

Row 2: Ch 1, Esc in each Esc across (47 Esc), *turn*.

Rows 3–42: Work in Esc foll chart. *Do not* fasten off.

Finishing

With the WS of the front and back facing each other, align the top edges so the sts are lined up together. Working through the sts of the front panel and the back panel at the same time, ch 1, * sc in each set of front and back sc across to the next corner, work 3 sc in the next corner *; rep from * to * around, working sts into each row end on the side edges of the panels. Insert the pillow form into the cover before joining the last side and sl st in first sc to join. Fasten off.

Part III
Advanced Stitches and Techniques

The 5th Wave   By Rich Tennant

"I don't work with a pattern, man. I just make
it up as I go along."

In this part . . .

If you want to delve into more advanced crochet techniques, then you're in the right spot. This part introduces you to a number of more complex stitches to broaden your crochet expertise. To demonstrate the diversity you can achieve with a crochet hook, we take a look at two completely different variations on the craft: Tunisian crochet and filet crochet. You also become well versed in the subject of motifs featuring their star celebrity, the granny square. We demonstrate each new stitch and technique through fun and practical projects that we hope pique your interest.

Chapter 10

Fancy Stitches That Steal the Show

In This Chapter

▶ Combining basic stitches to make fancy ones that add variety to your patterns

▶ Adding texture to your stitches for a three-dimensional effect

▶ Creating an elegant wrap to keep you looking stylish year-round

*O*ne of the qualities of crochet that makes it so unique is its flexibility — you can fashion an almost endless array of patterns and textures based on a few simple stitches (Chapters 5 and 6 show you how to create these basic stitches). In this chapter, we show you how to combine them to make pattern stitches, such as shells and clusters, and textured stitches, such as bobbles, popcorns, and loops. Along with illustrations of the completed stitches, we give you the International Crochet Symbol for each stitch so you're prepared to read stitch diagrams whenever you encounter them (see Chapter 4 for the basics of stitch diagrams). The Elegant All-Season Wrap project at the end of this chapter incorporates many of the fancy stitches we show you in the following pages so you can practice them while creating a beautiful accessory.

Spicing Things Up with Pattern Stitches

The versatile V-stitch, crossed double crochet, shell, cluster, picot, and reverse single crochet stitches can create stitch designs that are open and lacy or tight and compact. As you become familiar with these stitches, you'll recognize them in numerous patterns that span the range from home décor to fashion.

As you branch out in the crocheting world, you'll probably come across variations of the pattern stitches in this section. So don't assume that you always work a cluster stitch exactly as we define it here. Trust your pattern instructions; they usually tell you exactly how to work a pattern stitch, so be sure to carefully read the notes at the beginning.

Showing the V: The V-stitch

The *V-stitch* (abbreviated *V-st*) combination got its name because it resembles (guess what?) a *V*. To create a V-stitch, work one double crochet stitch, chain one, and then work another double crochet stitch all in the same stitch (check out Figure 10-1a to see a completed V-stitch). In Crochetese, that's (Dc, ch 1, dc) in the same stitch. Figure 10-1b shows the International Crochet Symbol for the V-stitch.

Figure 10-1:
The
common
V-stitch,
with its
symbol.

a   b

Seeing XXX's: The crossed double crochet stitch

For the *crossed double crochet stitch* (abbreviated *crossed dc*), you work two double crochet stitches on an angle, producing a pattern that looks like an *X*. To make a crossed double crochet stitch, follow these steps:

1. **Skip the next stitch in the row.**

2. **Work 1 double crochet (dc) in the next stitch.**

3. **Working behind the double crochet you just made, work 1 double crochet in the stitch that you skipped, as shown in Figure 10-2a.**

   Keeping the double crochet stitch you just made in front of your hook, insert your hook from front to back in the specified skipped stitch. Figure 10-2b illustrates the completed stitch, and Figure 10-2c denotes the symbol for the crossed double crochet stitch.

To continue working crossed double crochet stitches across the row, repeat Steps 1 through 3.

Some patterns using the crossed double crochet stitch may specify that you work the second double crochet in front of the first, or even wrapped around the first (having the second double crochet enclose the first). That's all the more reason to read your pattern's instructions so you can crochet the way it wants you to from the start.

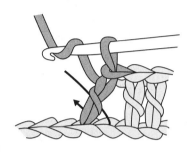 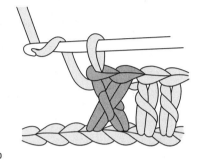

a   b

Figure 10-2:
Working
a crossed
double
crochet
stitch.

c

Spreading out: The shell stitch

The *shell stitch* (abbreviated *shell*) is very versatile, and you can find it just about anywhere. The variation we describe here is one common version of this adaptable stitch. To make a shell stitch, work four double crochet stitches in the same stitch (see Figure 10-3a for the completed stitch and Figure 10-3b for the stitch symbol).

Figure 10-3:
A completed
shell stitch
and its
symbol.

a   b

Usually the base of a shell stitch is surrounded by unworked stitches. However, most shell stitch patterns make sure that the total number of stitches is either the same or close to the same as the number of stitches in the previous row.

Grouping multiple like stitches: The cluster stitch

A *cluster* (no abbreviation) is a set of stitches that you work across an equal number of stitches and join together at the top, forming a triangle shape that resembles an upside-down shell stitch. (In fact, many crocheters use this stitch combination in conjunction with shells.) To make a cluster of four double crochet stitches, work through the following steps:

1. **Yarn over (yo), insert the hook into the next stitch, yarn over, draw the yarn through the stitch, yarn over, and draw the yarn through 2 loops on the hook (2 loops should remain on the hook, as shown in Figure 10-4a).**

   One half-closed double crochet is now complete. A *half-closed stitch* is one that's only worked partway and then finished at the end of the combination.

2. **Repeat Step 1 three times (see Figure 10-4a).**

   You should end up with 5 loops on your hook, like in Figure 10-4b.

3. **Yarn over and draw the yarn through all 5 loops on the hook (refer to Figure 10-4b).**

   Well done. You've just completed one 4-double-crochet (4-dc) cluster. See Figure 10-5a for a visual of what the completed cluster should look like and Figure 10-5b for its symbol.

Figure 10-4: Working a 4-double-crochet cluster.

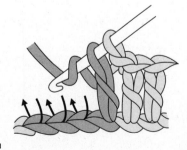

a

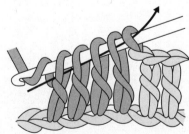

b

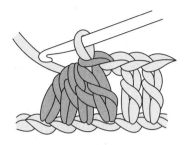

Figure 10-5:
A completed
4-double-
crochet
cluster
stitch, with
symbol.

a   b

Getting decorative: The picot stitch

Picots (no abbreviation) are pretty little round-shaped stitches that add a decorative touch to an edging or fill an empty space in a mesh design. You see them quite often in thread crochet, but you can also make them with yarn. To make a picot, follow these steps:

1. **Chain 3 (ch 3).**

2. **Insert your hook into the third chain from the hook, as shown in Figure 10-6a.**

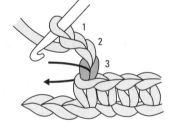
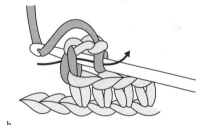

Figure 10-6:
Making a
picot stitch.

a   b

3. **Yarn over (yo).**

4. **Draw the yarn through the stitch and through the loop on the hook, like in Figure 10-6b.**

    Figure 10-7a depicts a completed picot. Check out this stitch's symbol in Figure 10-7b.

Figure 10-7:
A finished picot stitch and its symbol.

a

b

Working backward: The reverse single crochet stitch

The *reverse single crochet stitch* (abbreviated *reverse sc*) is sometimes called the *crab stitch*. The mechanics are the same as for a regular single crochet — except in reverse. Instead of working from right to left, you work from left to right. This stitch creates a somewhat twisted, rounded edge that's good for making a simple finished edge for your work. ***Note:*** You usually don't work stitches into the tops of the reverse single crochet, so you won't find this stitch in the middle of a project.

To work reverse single crochet, follow these steps:

1. **With the right side of your work facing you, insert the hook from front to back in the next stitch to the right, as shown in Figure 10-8a.**

2. **Yarn over (yo) and draw the yarn through the stitch, as in Figure 10-8b.**

Figure 10-8:
Working a reverse single crochet.

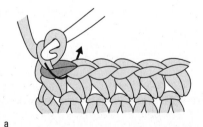

a

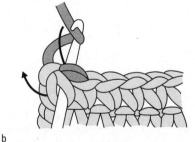

b

3. **Yarn over and draw the yarn through the 2 loops on your hook (see Figure 10-9a).**

One reverse single crochet is now complete.

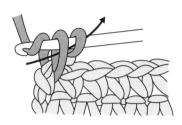
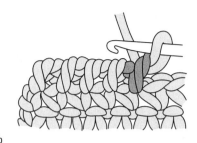

a   b

Figure 10-9:
Finishing
the reverse
single
crochet.

c

4. **Repeat Steps 1 through 3 in each stitch across the row.**

Figure 10-9b shows several completed reverse single crochet stitches, and Figure 10-9c denotes the stitch symbol.

Moving into the Third Dimension with Texture Stitches

If you want to add even more pizzazz to your crocheting, the three-dimensional stitch combinations in the following sections create great textures in your crocheted fabric. You can interchange the first three stitches because they all look like different versions of a bumpy oval. The last one, the loop stitch, creates long, fun loops that come in handy when making toys, sweaters, slippers, and wall hangings.

Because stitches aren't standardized in any way, you may come across many different names for them. For example, *puff stitches* are sometimes referred to as *bobbles,* even though they're created in completely different ways. So always read the specifics for each stitch before beginning your work.

Gently bumping along: The bobble stitch

The *bobble stitch* (no abbreviation) creates a smooth, oval bump and works well with a heavier-weight yarn. Making a bobble stitch is similar to making a cluster (which we describe earlier in this chapter) in that you half-close several stitches worked in the same stitch and then join them together to finish the stitch. To make a 3-double-crochet bobble stitch, follow these simple steps:

1. **Yarn over (yo), insert your hook into the stitch, yarn over, draw the yarn through the stitch, yarn over, and draw the yarn through the 2 loops on your hook.**

   One half-closed double crochet is now complete. You should still have 2 loops on your hook, like in Figure 10-10a.

Figure 10-10:
Creating
a bobble
stitch.

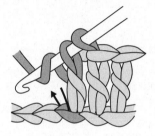
a

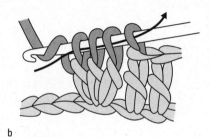
b

2. **In the same stitch, repeat Step 1 twice.**

   You should now have 4 loops on your hook, as in Figure 10-10b.

3. **Yarn over and draw the yarn through all 4 loops on the hook (refer to Figure 10-10b).**

   One 3-double-crochet bobble stitch is now complete. Take a look at Figure 10-11a for the completed stitch and Figure 10-11b for the stitch symbol.

Figure 10-11:
A completed
bobble
stitch and
its symbol.

a

b

In some instances, the bobble stitch may be made with more than three double crochet stitches, as in the Elegant All-Season Wrap project (featured later in this chapter), which uses four double crochet stitches to form the bobble stitch. To increase a 3-double-crochet bobble stitch to a 4-double-crochet bobble stitch, simply work one more partial double crochet into the stitch and finish as you normally would. (Don't worry that you'll have to figure this type of thing out on your own. A good pattern always instructs you on exactly how to make specialized stitches such as the bobble stitch.)

Not a magic dragon: The puff stitch

A *puff stitch* (abbreviated *puff st*) is aptly named because it gently puffs up into an oval shape. The puff stitch differs slightly from other raised stitches because you make it with a series of loops rather than stitches. Follow these few steps to create a puff stitch:

1. **Yarn over (yo) and insert your hook into the stitch (refer to Figure 10-12a).**

Figure 10-12:
Fashioning a puff stitch.

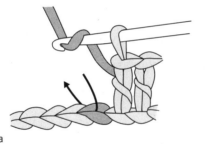
a

b

2. **Yarn over and draw the yarn through the stitch, bringing the loop up to the height of the previous stitch.**

   You should have 3 loops on your hook, as shown in Figure 10-12b.

3. **Working in the same stitch, repeat Steps 1 through 2 four times.**

   At the end of this step, you should have 11 loops on your hook.

4. **Yarn over and draw the yarn through all 11 loops on your hook, as in Figure 10-13a.**

   Tada! You've just completed your first puff stitch. Check out Figure 10-13b to see the completed stitch and Figure 10-13c for its symbol.

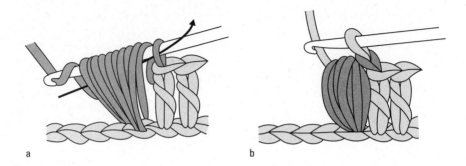

Figure 10-13:
Finishing the
puff stitch.

c

Puff stitches, clusters, bobbles, and popcorn stitches (see the next section), sometimes need an extra chain stitch at the top of the stitch to close them securely. If this is the case, your pattern should tell you so.

Forget the butter: The popcorn stitch

This stitch really pops! The *popcorn stitch* (abbreviated *pop* or *pc*) is a nicely rounded, compact oval that stands out from the fabric. It takes a bit more time to make than other raised stitches, but it's well worth the effort. For even more fun, you can work popcorn stitches so that they "pop" to the front or the back of a fabric, depending on where you want them to stand out. The following steps show you how to work a 5-double-crochet popcorn stitch both ways.

To pop to the front of your design:

1. **Work 5 double crochet stitches (dc) in the same stitch.**

2. **Drop the loop from your hook.**

3. **Insert your hook from front to back under the top 2 loops of the first double crochet of the group.**

4. **Grab the dropped loop with your hook and pull it through the stitch, as shown in Figure 10-14a.**

   One front-popping popcorn stitch is now complete; it should look like the stitch in Figure 10-14b. Note that the stitch symbol shown in Figure 10-14c is the same for a back or front popcorn.

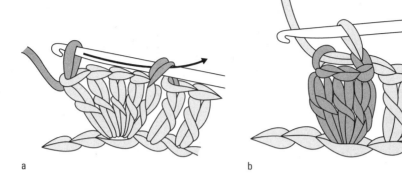

a   b

Figure 10-14:
Completing
a front
popcorn
stitch.

c

To pop to the back of your piece:

1. **Work 5 double crochet stitches (dc) in the same stitch.**

2. **Drop the loop from your hook.**

3. **Insert your hook from back to front under the top 2 loops of the first double crochet of the group.**

4. **Grab the dropped loop with your hook and pull it through the stitch, like in Figure 10-15a.**

   Figure 10-15b illustrates how a completed back-popping popcorn should look.

Figure 10-15:
Completing
a back
popcorn
stitch.

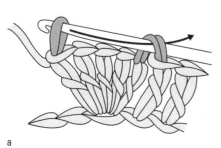

a

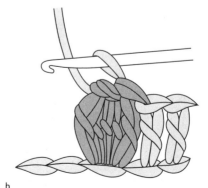

b

Feeling loopy: The loop stitch

The *loop stitch* (no abbreviation) gets its name from the long, loose loops it leaves behind. Getting the loops to be all the same length takes some practice, but when you get the hang of it, the loop stitch adds a lot of interest to garments. It also works great to make a beard for Santa when worked in several consecutive rows.

To create a loop stitch, work through the following steps:

1. **Wrap the yarn from front to back over the index finger of your yarn hand.**

   The length of the loop depends on how loosely or tightly you wrap the yarn in this step.

2. **Insert your hook into the next stitch.**

3. **With your hook, grab the strand of yarn from behind your index finger.**

4. **Draw the yarn through the stitch, as shown in Figure 10-16a.**

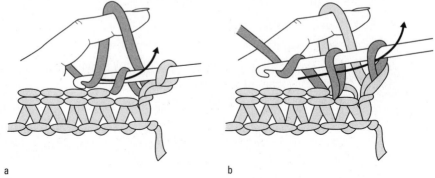

Figure 10-16: Making a loop stitch.

a   b

5. **With the yarn loop still on your index finger, yarn over the hook (yo) and draw the yarn through the 2 loops on your hook (refer to Figure 10-16b).**

   One loop stitch is now complete. Figure 10-17a shows the completed stitch, and Figure 10-17b shows its symbol.

Make sure that all the loops you create are the same length in order to achieve a finished look.

After working an area of loop stitch, you can cut all the loops to create a shaggy dog look.

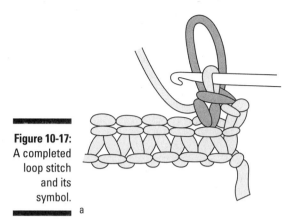

Figure 10-17:
A completed
loop stitch
and its
symbol.

a   b

Elegant All-Season Wrap Project

This stylish project (which you can see in all its glory in the color section)
lets you practice most of the stitches described in this chapter while creating
a beautiful wrap that you can drape over your best dress for a night on the
town or pair with your most comfortable jeans for a stroll on the beach. The
suggested materials call for a cotton-blend yarn for the warmer seasons, but
you can easily substitute a worsted-weight wool or a wool blend for the cooler
months. As always, feel free to experiment with your own color preferences.

Materials and vital statistics

✔ **Yarn:** Coats & Clark "TLC Cotton Plus" worsted-weight yarn (51%
cotton/49% acrylic), Article #E516 (3.52 oz. [100 g], 153 yds [139 m] each
ball): 4 balls of #3590 Lavender

✔ **Hook:** Crochet hook size I-9 U.S. (5.5 mm) or size needed to obtain gauge

✔ **Large-eyed yarn needle**

✔ **Measurements:** 12 in. wide x 60 in. long

✔ **Gauge:** 14 sts and 8 rows in dc = 4 in.

✔ **Stitches used:** Foundation double crochet (fdc), chain stitch (ch), single
crochet (sc), double crochet (dc), triple crochet (tr). **Popcorn (pop):** *
Work 4 dc in same st, drop loop from hook, insert hook from back to front
in top of first dc of group, pull dropped loop through st *. **V-st:** * (Dc, ch 1,
dc) in same st or space *. **Bobble:** * 4 dc (half closed and joined tog)
worked in same st *. **Shell:** * 5 dc in same st or space *. **Picot:** * Ch 3, sl st
in third ch from hook *.

Directions

Work this project in three parts so that the stitches run outward from the center in opposite directions. Begin with the center strip, which consists of only two rows, and then work the first half of the pattern off of the center. Next, simply turn the crocheted piece so the foundation row is facing up. Then complete the second half (which is nearly identical to the first half) by working off of the foundation row. Crocheters use this method quite frequently to create a symmetrical design.

Figure 10-18 presents you with the stitch diagram for the Elegant All-Season Wrap. The steps for this project follow, and they look just as you'd see them in a regular crochet publication. If you need to refresh your memory a bit of what all the abbreviations mean, flip to Chapter 4.

Figure 10-18:
Stitch
diagram for
the Elegant
All-Season
Wrap.

Center strip

Fdc 212.

Row 1 (WS): Ch 4 (counts as the first dc and 1 ch), skip the first 2 dc, * pop in next dc, ch 1, skip 2 dc, V-st in next dc, ch 1, skip next 2 dc *; rep from * to * across until 6 dc remain, pop in next dc, ch 1, skip 2 dc, V-st in next dc, skip next dc, dc in last dc (35 pop sts and 35 V-sts), *turn.*

Row 2: Ch 3 (first dc), dc in each dc, chain space (ch sp) and pop across to turning chain (tch), dc in top of tch (212 dc), *turn.*

First half

Row 1: Ch 3 (first dc), * skip next dc, dc in next dc, working behind dc just made, dc in skipped dc (crossed dc made) *; rep from * to * across to tch, dc in top of tch (105 crossed dc), *turn.*

Row 2: Ch 3 (first dc), dc in each dc across to tch, dc in top of tch (212 dc), *turn.*

Row 3: Ch 3 (first dc), ch 1, skip next dc, * bobble in next dc, ch 1, skip next 2 dc, V-st in next dc, ch 1, skip next 2 dc *; rep from * to * across until 6 dc remain, bobble in next dc, ch 1, skip next 2 dc, V-st in next dc, skip next dc, dc in top of tch (35 bobble sts and 35 V-sts), *turn.*

Row 4: Ch 3 (first dc), work 1 dc in each dc, ch sp and bobble st across to tch, dc in top of tch (212 dc), *turn.*

Row 5: Ch 3 (first dc), skip next 2 dc, * shell in next dc, skip next 4 dc *; rep from * to * across until 4 dc remain, shell in next dc, skip next 2 dc, dc in top of tch (42 shell sts), *turn.*

Fasten off.

Second half

Row 1: With the WS facing and working across the opposite side of the fdc row, join yarn in first fdc, ch 3 (first dc), * skip next fdc, dc in next fdc, working behind dc just made, dc in skipped fdc (crossed dc made) *; rep from * to * across to last fdc, dc in last fdc (105 crossed dc), *turn.*

Rows 2–5: Rep Rows 2–5 of "First half," *turn.* Don't fasten off.

Border

Row 1: Ch 6 (counts as tr and ch 2), * (tr, ch 1, tr) in center dc of next shell in the previous row, ch 2 *; rep from * to * across to last shell, (tr, ch 1, tr) in center dc of last shell, ch 2, (tr, ch 3, tr) in top of tch in previous row, rotate piece to continue work across row ends of short edge, ch 2, skip 1 row end (the shell row), ** (tr, ch 1, tr) in space at end of next row (the dc row), ch 2, skip next row end **; rep from ** to ** 5 times across short end, (tr, ch 3, tr) in first dc of last row of first half; rep from * to * across to last shell, (tr, ch 1, tr) in center dc of last shell, ch 2, (tr, ch 3, tr) in top of last dc, rotate piece to continue work across row ends of second short edge, ch 2, skip 1 row end (the shell row); rep from ** to ** 6 times across short end, (tr, ch 3) in top of dc from previous row (at the base of the tch from the beg of the rnd), sl st in fourth ch of beg ch-6 to join.

Row 2: Ch 1, sc in first ch-2 sp, * ch 1, work ([2 tr, picot] twice, tr) all in ch-1 sp of V-st from previous row, ch 1, sc in next ch-2 sp (between V-sts) *; rep from * to * across to corner ch-3 sp, ch 1, ([2 tr, picot] 3 times, tr) all in corner ch-3 sp **; rep from * to ** for each side of the wrap, ch 1, sl st in first sc to join.

Fasten off. Weave in loose ends with the yarn needle.

Finishing

Block your wrap by washing it in cool water with a mild soap and then rolling it in a towel to remove any excess water. Pull and shape the wrap to the finished measurements and leave it to dry. (See Chapter 19 for the full details on blocking.)

Chapter 11

Creating Texture in Unexpected Ways

. . . .

In This Chapter

▶ Working into different parts of a stitch

▶ Hooking outside the stitch

▶ Felting to create unique crocheted pieces

▶ Creating cool scarves and a fun bag

. . . .

*U*ntil now, you've been content making crochet stitches by inserting your hook through the top loops of the stitches in the previous row, over and over again. But now's your chance to get a little crazy — instead of working a stitch in the top loops, insert your hook in the bottom loops, around the middle loops, or even in loops on the fronts or backs of stitches! This deviant behavior creates a variety of new textures and designs in your fabric.

This chapter shows you a few of the numerous ways you can create new textures in your crocheted pieces. To give your project a whole new look and feel, try shrinking it in the washing machine — a process called *felting*. Felting a crocheted item transforms your work from something that's big, loose, and unstructured into a solid, durable, and functional original. The scarf and bag projects at the end of this chapter offer you a chance to practice all of these new techniques (and then some!).

As you get funky with your hook placement, keep in mind that a stitch is a stitch is a stitch. Regardless of where you insert your hook, you always work a particular stitch in the same way.

Switching Up Your Stitch Placement

Depending on the type of look you're trying to achieve, you can work a stitch pretty much anywhere you can fit your hook — nothing is off-limits. Normally you work a new stitch into both top loops of a stitch you've already made, but to switch things up, you can also work a new stitch into a single top loop, into the base, or into other loops on the front or back of your piece. In Chapter 5, we give you the lowdown on all the parts of a stitch; the next sections show you what you can do with them.

Working into the top and other loops

You can work one stitch into another in a few different ways, regardless of whether you're working in rows or rounds, and each method creates a unique effect in your finished fabric. The resulting look can be either smooth or textured, depending on which loop you choose to use (see what we mean in Figure 11-1a; Figure 11-1b notes the symbols):

- **Crocheting under both top loops:** Working under both top loops is the typical way to crochet a stitch; it creates a smooth, flat fabric. We present this method in earlier chapters.

- **Crocheting in the front loop only:** Working under the front loop only creates a ridge on the opposite side of the fabric. This approach is great for making a rib at the bottom edge and cuffs of a sweater. Another reason to leave the back loop free is so you can work a stitch from a later row into it.

- **Crocheting in the back loop only:** Like front-loop-only stitching, working new stitches in the back loop creates a rib, except it's on the opposite side of the fabric. You may also work in just the back loops when joining two pieces of crocheted fabric together (see Chapter 15 for the scoop on this technique). Leaving the front loops free when joining pieces together creates a decorative raised seam on the front of your work.

- **Crocheting in a loop found on the front or back side of the stitch:** Usually, you look at the stitch from the top to see the front and back loops; however, look at a stitch from the front (right) or back (wrong) side of the fabric, and you'll find additional loops available for your use.

  - Working stitches into a loop on the front side of the stitch pushes the top 2 loops outward to the back of the fabric and is referred to as the *front-most loop* (see Chapter 5).

  - Working stitches into a loop on the back side of the stitch pushes the top 2 loops outward to the front of the fabric, creating a faux knit-like rib, and is called the *back-most loop* (see Chapter 5).

Working in just one loop at the top of a stitch adds a bit of stretch to your piece that working in both top loops just doesn't offer. This flexibility comes in handy when you're working with a yarn that doesn't offer much elasticity, such as cotton, or when you're making a rib around the bottom or cuff edges of a sweater where you want the fabric to have some stretch.

Working in the front or back loop of a stitch doesn't necessarily designate the design's front or back side. After you turn your work at the end of a row (see Chapter 5), the front loop on the previous row becomes the back loop on the current row.

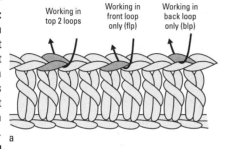

Figure 11-1: Working in the different loops at the top of a stitch, plus the relevant stitch symbols.

⌒ = worked in back loop only

⌣ = worked in front loop only

⌣ = worked in front-most loop

⌒ = worked in back-most loop

Stitching up the sides

You often work around the side of a stitch when you're adding a border to a crocheted item, smoothing out an edge, or joining two pieces of fabric. Only the stitches that are at the end of a row come into play, which is why most pattern instructions refer to working in the side of a stitch as working in *row-end stitches*.

Figure 11-2 shows the proper placement for your hook in a row-end stitch. To avoid gaping holes across the edges, insert your hook where two stitches join together, whether at the base or the top of the stitches or both. You work the new stitch in the same way whether you're working into a complete row-end stitch or a turning chain.

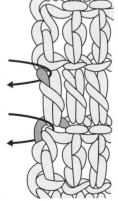

Figure 11-2: Proper hook placement for crocheting into the side of a stitch.

Bucking Tradition and Working Stitches in Spaces and Other Interesting Places

Who says you have to work in a stitch at all? You can create some nice stitch effects by working outside the box — or shall we say stitch? The following sections introduce you to working stitches into the spaces *between* stitches or those created by chain loops and working a stitch in and around the middle of another one.

Squeezing into spaces

Unlike the tight weave of knitted fabric, crocheted fabric has spaces between the stitches because they're not linked on the sides, which unlocks a whole new world of opportunity in which to create new stitches. Even though the spaces between stitches aren't always obvious, trust us, they're there. In the sections that follow, we show you how to work in spaces between stitches and in chain spaces and loops.

Working in the spaces between stitches

Because crocheted stitches aren't linked at the sides, you can work your stitches in between other stitches by inserting your hook into the space between two stitches rather than the loop(s) at the top of a stitch (see Figure 11-3). When you work in between stitches, you lower the base of the new stitch, altering the alignment of the row. You can use this technique to create a zigzag effect: Just work one stitch in between stitches and the next one in the top of the row. Or create a brick pattern by alternating every four stitches, for example, rather than every other one.

Working in between stitches is a great help when you're using novelty yarns (see Chapter 2 for a description of these). Because highly textured yarns can make individual stitches hard to see, working between them keeps your design untangled and you out of the loony bin. You can make a whole design this way without ever working into the top of another stitch.

Figure 11-3: Crocheting in the space between stitches.

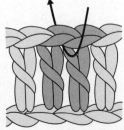

Working in chain spaces and loops

Many lacy patterns, such as filet crochet (see Chapter 13), use chain loops and spaces in their designs in order to achieve a loose, airy look. Although these loops and spaces may appear fancy and complicated, working a stitch into them is a piece of cake because you don't have to be too particular about where you stick your hook. As long as it lands somewhere within the loop or space, you're good to go. Figure 11-4 shows you where to put your hook.

Patterns identify the space or loop you're supposed to work into by how many chain stitches were used to create it. For example, if you need to work into a space created by one chain, the pattern tells you to work into the *chain-1 space,* which may be abbreviated as *ch-1 sp.* If you need to work into a loop created by five chain stitches, the pattern directs you to the *chain-5 loop* (or *ch-5 lp* for short).

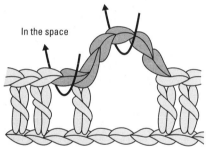

In the loop

In the space

Figure 11-4:
Working
stitches
into a chain
space or
loop.

Going around the middle with post stitches

You can insert your hook around the *post* (body) of a stitch that's one or more rows below the current row to make — you guessed it — a *post stitch.* Post stitches create raised patterns, such as ribbing and cables. The way you insert your hook around the post determines whether you're creating a front post or a back post. The following sections show you how to make both.

Front post stitches

Front post stitches are raised on the surface of the fabric facing you and have a ridge on the opposite side of the fabric. To create a front post double crochet (abbreviated *FPdc*), follow these steps:

1. **Work a row of normal double crochet (dc) for the first row and turn.**

2. **Chain 2 (ch 2) for your first double crochet.**

Because a post stitch is shorter than a normal stitch, you make the turning chain with 1 chain stitch less than the normal turning chain requires. (Chapter 5 covers the basics of turning chains.) In addition, the last stitch in the row may be a shorter stitch to keep the whole row level. For example, if you're working a row of double crochet stitches in the front post of the stitches from the previous row, you make a turning chain with 2 chains rather than 3, and your final stitch is a half double crochet (hdc).

3. **Yarn over (yo) and insert your hook from front to back between the posts of the first and second double crochet of the row below and then from back to front again between the posts of the second and third stitches (see Figure 11-5a).**

   The hook should now be positioned horizontally behind the double crochet that you're working around, as shown in Figure 11-5b.

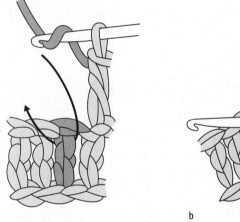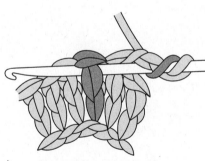

Figure 11-5: Inserting the hook for the front post double crochet.

a   b

4. **Yarn over and draw the yarn around the post of the stitch.**

   You should now have 3 loops on your hook.

5. **Yarn over and draw the yarn through the first 2 loops closest to the hook end twice, like in Figure 11-6a.**

   One front post double crochet is now complete. Refer to Figure 11-6b for the completed stitch and Figure 11-6c for the stitch's symbol.

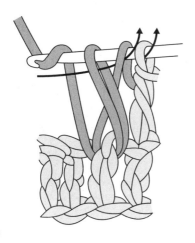

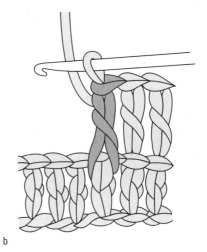

Figure 11-6:
Finishing a
front post
double
crochet and
noting its
symbol.

a

b

c

$$\int = FPdc$$

Back post stitches

Back post stitches appear to recede on the side of the fabric facing you,
creating a ridge. To form a back post double crochet (abbreviated *BPdc*),
follow these steps:

1. **Work a row of normal double crochet (dc) for the first row and turn.**

2. **Chain 2 (ch 2) for the first double crochet.**

    Because a post stitch is shorter than a normal stitch, you make the
    turning chain with 1 chain stitch less than the turning chain normally
    requires. (Flip to Chapter 5 for the basics of turning chains.)

3. **Yarn over (yo) and insert your hook from back to front between the
   posts of the first and second double crochets in the row below and
   then from front to back again between the posts of the second and
   third stitches (see Figure 11-7a).**

    Your hook should now be positioned horizontally in front of the double
    crochet that you're working around, as in Figure 11-7b.

4. **Yarn over and draw the yarn around the post of the stitch.**

    You now have 3 loops on your hook.

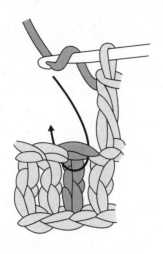
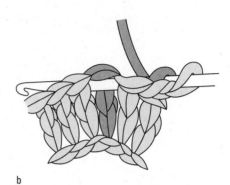

Figure 11-7:
Inserting
your hook
for the back
post double
crochet.

a

b

5. **Yarn over and draw the yarn through the first 2 loops closest to the hook end twice, as shown in Figure 11-8a.**

Figure 11-8b shows 1 complete back post double crochet, and Figure 11-8c denotes the stitch symbol.

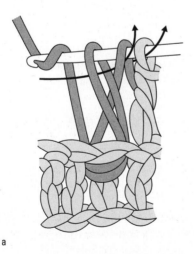
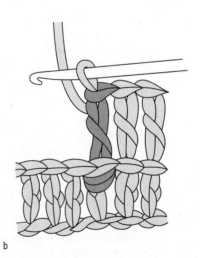

a

b

Figure 11-8:
Completing
a back post
double
crochet and
noting its
stitch
symbol.

$\textint$ = BPdc

c

Solidifying fabric with linked stitches

If you work a swatch of almost any basic stitch, you'll notice that by working each stitch independently of each other, the fabric results in gaps, or spaces, between stitches. You can create a more solid fabric with *linked stitches,* stitches that you link to one another as you work.

Linked stitches are worked with taller stitches such as double and triple crochet (see Chapter 6), where yarn overs are replaced by inserting the hook into the post of the previous stitch and drawing up a loop. In the sections that follow, we describe how to make rows of specific linked stitches called linked triple crochets (abbreviated *Ltr*).

Making your first row of linked stitches

To create your first linked triple crochet:

1. **Chain any number of chains (ch) plus 4 at the end.**

   The 4 stitches at the end create the triple crochet turning chain.

2. **Insert your hook into the second chain away from the hook, yarn over (yo), and draw up a loop.**

   There are 2 loops on the hook (see Figure 11-9a).

3. **Insert your hook into the third chain away from the hook, yarn over, and draw up a loop.**

   Now you have 3 loops on the hook (refer to Figure 11-9b).

4. **Insert your hook into the fifth chain away from the hook, yarn over, and draw up a loop.**

   The reason you skip the fourth chain is so that the first linked triple stitch looks just like the other stitches in the row. There are 4 loops on the hook (see Figure 11-9c).

5. **Yarn over and draw through the first 2 loops on your hook.**

   Now you have 3 loops on the hook (see Figure 11-10a).

6. **Yarn over and draw through the first 2 loops on your hook.**

   You're left with 2 loops on the hook (see Figure 11-10b).

7. **Yarn over and draw through the last 2 loops on your hook.**

   Nice work! You've just finished 1 linked triple crochet (see how yours matches up with Figure 11-10c). Want to know the symbol for this particular stitch? Check out Figure 11-10d.

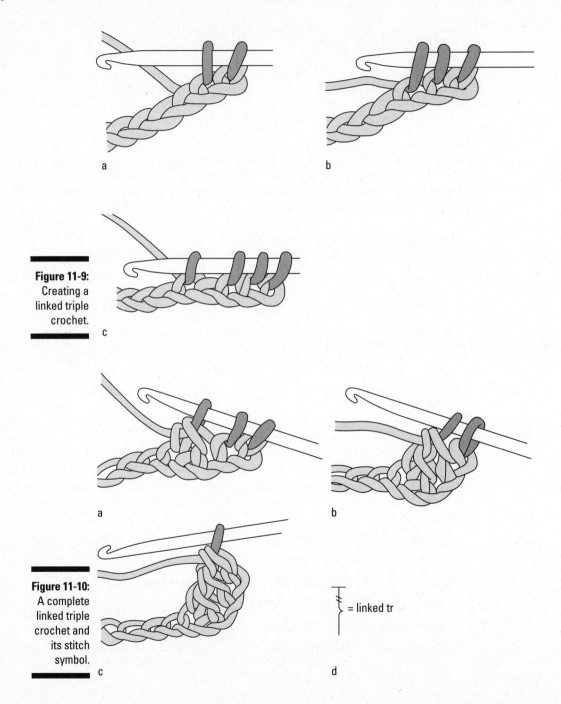

Figure 11-9:
Creating a
linked triple
crochet.

a

b

c

Figure 11-10:
A complete
linked triple
crochet and
its stitch
symbol.

a

b

c

d

= linked tr

To create the second linked triple crochet in the first row:

1. **Insert your hook into the upper horizontal bar found at the side of the last linked triple crochet (ltr) you made, yarn over (yo), and draw up a loop.**

   There are 2 loops on the hook (see Figure 11-11a).

2. **Insert your hook into the lower bar found at the side of the last linked triple crochet you made, yarn over, and draw up a loop.**

   Now you have 3 loops on the hook (refer to Figure 11-11b).

3. **Insert your hook into the next chain of the foundation chain, yarn over, and draw up a loop.**

   There are 4 loops on the hook (see Figure 11-11c).

4. **Yarn over and draw through the first 2 loops on your hook, 3 times.**

   You're left with 1 loop on the hook (see Figure 11-11d).

Repeat the preceding four steps for each linked triple crochet across to the end of the row.

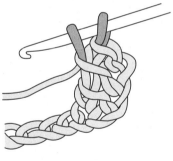

a

b

Figure 11-11:
Working
subsequent
linked triple
crochets.

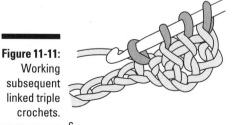

c

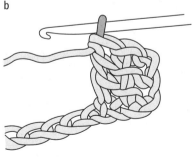

d

Creating your second row of linked stitches

After you've made your first row of linked stitches, follow these steps to transition to the first linked stitch of the second row (and all subsequent rows):

1. **Chain 4 (ch 4) for the turning chain.**

2. **Insert your hook into the second chain away from the hook, yarn over (yo), and draw up a loop.**

   You now have 2 loops on your hook.

3. **Insert your hook into the third chain away from the hook, yarn over, and draw up a loop.**

   A total of 3 loops are now on your hook.

4. **Insert your hook into the top 2 loops of the next stitch, yarn over, and draw up a loop (refer to Figure 11-12a).**

   You now have 4 loops on your hook.

5. **Yarn over and draw through the first 2 loops on your hook, 3 times.**

   Figure 11-12b shows the first linked triple crochet (ltr) in the second row.

To complete additional linked stitches in your second row and all additional rows, just follow the guidelines for adding more stitches to a row (which we describe in the preceding section).

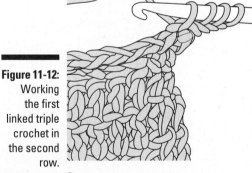 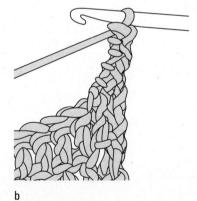

Figure 11-12: Working the first linked triple crochet in the second row.

a   b

Spiking into previous rows

Long stitches (also known as *spikes*) are usually single crochet stitches that you work into either the tops of stitches or the spaces between stitches one or more rows below the current row to create a vertical spike of yarn that extends over several rows of stitches.

Long stitches produce a spike on both sides of the fabric, so they're well suited for a design that's reversible, such as an afghan. They're also particularly striking in a contrasting color.

To create a long single crochet stitch:

1. **Insert your hook from front to back under the top 2 loops of the designated stitch 1 or more rows below the row you're currently working in, as shown in Figure 11-13.**

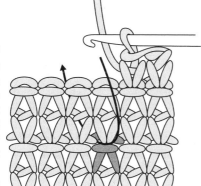

Figure 11-13: Working a long single crochet stitch 3 rows below the current row.

2. **Draw the yarn through the stitch and up to the current level of work.**

   You should now have 2 loops on your hook.

3. **Yarn over (yo) and draw the yarn through the 2 loops on your hook.**

   Figure 11-14a shows you a complete long single crochet stitch (although the length varies depending on where you stick your hook, of course). Figure 11-14b shows a few long-single-crochet stitch symbols.

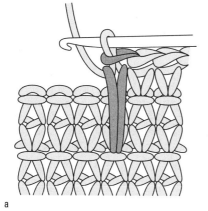

Figure 11-14: A completed long stitch in single crochet.

a

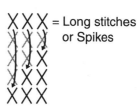

= Long stitches or Spikes

b

To make other types of long stitches, such as a long double crochet, you follow the same steps as for the long single crochet. Just remember to yarn over first as necessary and then make the stitch the same way you always do. The only variation is that you're sticking the hook in a different spot.

When Shrinking Is A-Okay: Felting Your Crocheted Projects

Have you ever tossed your favorite wool sweater into the washing machine and found that it came out a lot smaller than when it went in? Your sweater went through a process known as felting. *Felting* is a method used to shrink a piece of fabric that has been crocheted, knit, or woven by using a combination of hot, soapy water and agitation. The hot, soapy water opens the scales found along the yarn fibers, and the agitation, caused by a washing machine or by rubbing the fabric together by hand, causes the scales to tangle and lock. As the fibers interlock, your project gets smaller and creates a solid, sturdy fabric. The longer you wash your project, the denser it becomes.

Although shrinking crocheted garments may once have been considered an accident, felting is a great way to create a sturdy, dense fabric that's perfect for bags, rugs, garments, and accessories. You can felt your projects by machine or by hand, as you find out in the following sections, but the process usually goes quicker in the washing machine. Felting by hand works best for smaller items and edges that have been cut.

You can only felt yarns that are made of animal fibers, such as sheep, alpaca, rabbit, or goat. Wool yarns that say *superwash* don't felt because they've been treated to create a machine-washable fiber. Look for yarns that say *hand wash in cold water only.*

For both felting methods, you need

- ✓ A washing machine or wash bucket filled with hot water
- ✓ Baking soda or laundry soap
- ✓ A towel

If you don't want to wait for your project to air-dry, you can place it in the dryer, but keep in mind that it may shrink a little more. After your felted project is dry, you can embellish it in ways you may not be able to with regular crocheted fabric. Felted fabric is just like felt; you can embroider, bead, dye, paint, and even cut it. Check out Chapter 18 for fun ideas for embellishing crocheted pieces.

Felting by machine

Here's your step-by-step guide to felting a project by machine:

1. **Set your washing machine for the smallest load on hot water/cold rinse and toss in 3 to 4 tablespoons of baking soda or laundry soap.**

   The water should be very hot. If you find the shrinking process is going too slowly, add a pot of boiling water to turn the heat up.

2. **Place your project into a secured bag (like a zippered laundry bag or pillowcase) and drop it into the machine.**

   Adding a pair of jeans or tennis shoes at this point may speed up the felting process. Their presence in the washing machine increases the agitation on the wool fibers in order to bind them together.

3. **Start the wash cycle and continue resetting it until your project reaches the desired size.**

   Your project will take a few wash cycles to shrink to the desired size, and you want to keep the water hot. When your project has reached its desired size, let the machine move into the rinse cycle to get rid of the soap and most of the excess water. (Check the machine often to keep it from going into the rinse cycle before you're ready.)

4. **Take your project out of the bag, roll it in a towel to remove any remaining water, and then shape it by pulling it to the desired size and smoothing out any warps or wrinkles.**

   Insert a form, if necessary, to help the piece keep its shape and then allow it to dry. (See Chapter 19 for more on blocking three-dimensional projects with forms.)

Felting by hand

To felt your project by hand, follow these steps:

1. **Put 3 to 4 tablespoons of baking soda or laundry soap in a wash bucket and fill the bucket with hot water.**

   If the water is too hot to touch, use heavy-duty cleaning gloves to protect your hands.

2. **Submerge your crochet project completely, allowing it to become thoroughly wet.**

3. **Using both hands, vigorously rub the fabric together, rotating it regularly in order to felt the project evenly, until it has been felted to the desired size.**

To increase the agitation, you can also scrub the project against a washboard or bamboo sushi mat. Be sure to add more hot water and soap as needed.

4. **Rinse out the soap, roll the project in a towel to remove any remaining water, and then shape it by pulling it to the desired size and smoothing out any warps or wrinkles.**

If necessary, insert a form into the project to help it keep its shape. Then give it some time to dry.

Textured Scarf Project

The textured fabric in this scarf comes from alternating between working stitches in the back top loop and the front top loop. Worked in single crochet with a slightly larger hook than you normally use for a worsted-weight yarn, the back loop/front loop pattern creates a nubby effect, and the fringe at each end finishes the design off nicely. The scarf (which you can see in the color section) is a perfect accessory for a cool fall afternoon, and you can find the recommended yarn (which by the way is pretty reasonably priced) in a wide variety of colors to match your wardrobe. If you do change your yarn, be sure to check your gauge; Chapter 3 explains how gauge affects your projects.

Materials and vital statistics

- **Yarn:** Coats & Clark Red Heart "Fiesta" 4-ply worsted-weight yarn (73% acrylic/27% nylon), Article #E704 (6 oz. [170 g], 330 yds [289 m] each skein): 2 skeins of #6013 Wheat
- **Hook:** Crochet hook size I-9 U.S. (5.5 mm) or size needed to obtain gauge
- **Scissors**
- **Measurements:** 6½ in. wide x 60 in. long
- **Gauge:** 6 sts and 6 rows sc = 2 in.
- **Stitches used:** Chain stitch (ch), single crochet (sc)

Directions

If the directions in this project look a little foreign to you, flip to Chapter 4 for a little Reading Crochetese 101. The stitch diagram for this project is shown in Figure 11-15.

Figure 11-15:
Stitch
diagram
for the
Textured
Scarf
project.

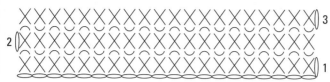

Ch 21 for the foundation chain.

Row 1: Sc in second ch from hook, sc in each ch across (20 sc), *turn.*

Row 2: Ch 1, sc in blp of first sc, sc in flp of next sc, * sc in blp of next sc, sc in flp of next sc *; rep from * to * across (20 sc), *turn.*

Row 3: Ch 1, sc in flp of first sc, sc in blp of next sc, * sc in flp of next sc, sc in blp of next sc *; rep from * to * across (20 sc), *turn.*

Rep Rows 2–3 for patt until scarf measures 60 in. long, or to desired length.

Last Row: Ch 1, sc in both loops of each sc across (20 sc). Fasten off.

Finishing

Cut the yarn into 11-in. lengths. Using 2 lengths for each fringe, single knot 1 fringe in each st across each short edge of the scarf. Trim the ends even. (For tips on making fringe, see Chapter 18.)

Basketweave Scarf Project

Crocheting the Basketweave Scarf provides an opportunity to work with post stitches and see the texture that they create. Take your time on the first couple rows, and you'll breeze right through the rest of 'em.

The reasonably priced yarn used in this design is a wonderfully soft, flexible acrylic that's available in most craft stores. If the beige yarn shown in the color section isn't your style, go ahead and get another color. This stitch pattern shows up beautifully in any solid color. (Of course, if you make a change, you should be sure to check your gauge, as we explain in Chapter 3.)

Materials and vital statistics

- **Yarn:** Lion Brand Yarn "Microspun" sport-weight yarn (100% microfiber acrylic), Article #910 (2.5 oz. [70 g], 168 yds [154 m] each skein): 4 skeins of #910-124 Mocha

- **Hook:** Crochet hook size H-8 U.S. (5.5 mm) or size needed to obtain gauge

- **Large-eyed yarn needle**

- **Measurements:** 8 in. wide x 60 in. long

- **Gauge:** 8 sts in patt = 2 in.; 8 rows in patt = 2¾ in.

- **Stitches used:** Chain stitch (ch), double crochet (dc), front post double crochet (FPdc), back post double crochet (BPdc)

Directions

We give you the following steps as you'd see them in a regular crochet publication. If you need to refresh your memory a bit on how to read 'em, flip to Chapter 4. Figure 11-16 shows a reduced sample of this stitch pattern.

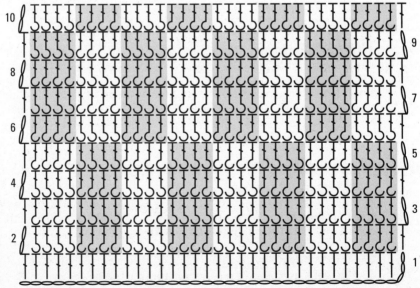

Figure 11-16: Reduced sample of basketweave stitch pattern.

Ch 33 + 3 (first dc).

Row 1: Dc in fourth ch from hook, dc in each ch across (34 dc counting the turning chain as 1 dc), *turn.*

Rows 2–5: Ch 2 (first post dc), * FPdc around the post of each of next 4 dc, BPdc around the post of each of next 4 dc *; rep from * to * across to within last dc, dc in last dc (34 sts), *turn.*

Rows 6–9: Ch 2 (first post dc), * BPdc around the post of each of next 4 dc, FPdc around the post of each of next 4 dc *; rep from * to * across to within last dc, dc in last dc (34 sts), *turn.*

Rep Rows 2–9 for patt until the scarf measures 60 in. long (or desired length), ending with Row 5 or Row 9 of patt. Fasten off and weave in loose ends using the yarn needle.

Felted Shoulder Bag Project

Make the simple felted bag in this section, and you'll have a basic everyday accessory that's sturdy enough to carry your belongings without the need for a lining. This project allows you to explore the felting technique described earlier in this chapter while working with basic stitches and techniques. This moderately priced yarn is readily available in most yarn stores, comes in a variety of colors, and felts easily. ***Remember:*** A felted project needs room to shrink, so don't worry if the bag looks big, loose, and unattractive before you felt it.

Materials and vital statistics

- **Yarn:** Cascade 220 "Heathers" worsted-weight wool yarn (100% wool), (3.5 oz. [100 g], 220 yds [201 m] each skein): 4 skeins of #2431 Brown (MC)

  Cascade 220 "Wool" worsted-weight wool yarn (100% wool), (3.5 oz. [100 g], 220 yds [201 m] each skein): 1 skein of #8892 Blue (CC)

- **Hook:** Crochet hook size I-9 U.S. (5.5 mm) or size needed to obtain gauge

- **Large-eyed yarn needle**

- **Washing machine**

- **Zippered laundry bag or pillowcase**

- **½ cup baking soda or laundry soap**

- **Old pair of jeans or tennis shoes (optional)**

- **Towel**

- **Plastic grocery bags**

- **Scissors**

- **Final Measurements:** 11 in. wide x 11 in. tall x 2 in. deep, after felting

✔ **Gauge:** 15 sts and 12 rows hdc = 4 in.

✔ **Stitches used:** Chain stitch (ch), half double crochet (hdc), slip stitch (sl st). **Dec 1 hdc (commonly referred to as hdc2tog):** yo, insert hook in next st, yo and pull up loop, yo, insert hook in next st, yo and pull up loop, yo and draw through all 5 loops on hook.

Directions

The following sections break down the directions for crocheting each piece of the Felted Shoulder Bag; check out Chapter 4 for the lowdown on reading Crochetese if you're unfamiliar with it and flip to Chapter 8 for tips on crocheting in rounds. The stitch diagram for this pattern is shown in Figure 11-17.

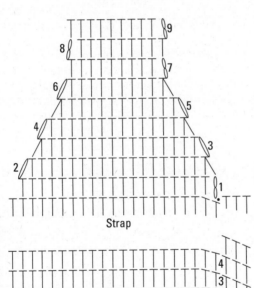

Strap

Figure 11-17:
The stitch diagram for the Felted Shoulder Bag.

Body

Body

With MC, ch 141.

Rnd 1: Hdc in third ch from hook, hdc in each ch across, sl st in top of beg ch-2 to join into a ring, (140 hdc) *don't turn*.

Rnd 2: Ch 2 (counts as first hdc), skip first hdc, hdc in each hdc around, don't join to first hdc, continue to work in a spiral going in the same direction until the bag measures 13 in. tall from the beg.

First end of strap

Row 1: Ch 2 (counts as first hdc), skip first hdc, hdc in next 19 hdc, (20 hdc), *turn.*

Row 2: Ch 1, skip first hdc, hdc in each hdc across until only 2 hdc remain, dec 1 hdc over last 2 hdc, (18 hdc), *turn.*

Row 3: Ch 1, skip first hdc, hdc in each hdc across until only 2 hdc remain (don't include the ch-1 at the beg of the last row), dec 1 hdc over last 2 hdc, (16 hdc), *turn.*

Rep Row 3 until 10 sts remain. Work back and forth in hdc on the remaining 10 sts until the strap measures 15 in. Fasten off. Weave in the loose ends.

Second end of strap

Skip the next 50 hdc after the last hdc worked on Row 1 of the first end of the strap. Insert hook in next hdc and draw up a loop of MC. Work as for first strap until 10 sts remain and the strap measures 15 in. Don't fasten off.

Holding the last row of the first strap end together with the last row of the second strap end, sl st across working through both layers at the same time. Fasten off. Weave in the loose ends.

Flap

Skip the next 4 hdc from the last hdc worked on Row 1 of the second strap end. Insert hook in next hdc and draw up a loop of MC.

Row 1: Ch 2 (counts as first hdc), skip first hdc, hdc in next 41 hdc, (42 hdc), *turn.*

Row 2: Ch 2, skip first hdc, hdc in each hdc across, *turn.*

Rep Row 2 until the flap measures 5 in. long.

To shape the flap:

Row 1: Ch 2, dec 1 hdc over next 2 sts, hdc in each hdc across until 3 hdc remain, dec 1 hdc over next 2 sts, hdc in last st, (40 hdc), *turn.*

Rows 2–4: Rep Row 1 of flap shaping. You should have 34 hdc at the end of the last row. Fasten off. Weave in the loose ends.

Finishing

With RS facing and CC, insert hook in the space at the end of the first row of 1 of the straps. Ch 2, working across the long edge of the strap, * work 2 hdc in the next row-end, 1 hdc in the next row-end *; rep from * to * across to opposite side of the bag. Continue around open edge of bag by working 1 hdc in each st until you reach the beg ch-2. Sl st in the top of the ch-2 to join. Fasten off. Rep for second side of the strap. When you reach the flap, rep from * to * for each side edge of the flap and work 1 hdc in each st across the bottom edge of the flap. Fasten off and weave in any loose ends with the yarn needle.

Turn the bag inside out. Using the yarn needle and yarn, whipstitch the bottom opening together so the straps are positioned at the center of each side of the bag (see Chapter 15 for more on sewing pieces together).

Take 1 point at the end of the bottom seam and fold it in 2 in. so the point lines up with the seam. Whipstitch the point down with a few stitches. Rep for the point at the opposite end of the bottom seam. By folding these corner points inward, you create a box bottom for the bag (see Figure 11-18).

Figure 11-18: Creating a box bottom for your Felted Shoulder Bag.

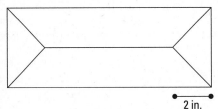

2 in.

Place your shoulder bag in a zippered laundry bag or pillowcase and felt it by machine with baking soda or laundry soap until it measures 11 in. wide by 11 in. tall. When the bag is felted to size, roll it in a towel to remove the excess moisture. Then stuff it with plastic grocery bags to help it keep its shape as it air-dries.

Chapter 12

Like Knitting with a Hook: Tunisian Crochet

. . . .

In This Chapter

▶ Gathering the tools you need to get started with Tunisian crochet

▶ Figuring out how to make and shape the Tunisian simple stitch

▶ Adding variety with the Tunisian knit and purl stitches

▶ Working with color and design

▶ Making an absorbent hand towel to match your décor

. . . .

*T*unisian crochet is a special kind of stitch that you can use to make any-thing from home décor items, such as afghans, place mats, and rugs, to sweaters, coats, and accessories. This type of crochet is different from standard crochet stitches in that each row is worked in two separate halves: The first half adds the loops to your hook, and the second half takes them off. Tunisian crochet produces a rather solid fabric that closely resembles knitted fabric, although it uses much more yarn and therefore produces a heavier fabric than knitting does. (When making clothing using Tunisian cro-chet, use a lighter-weight yarn, such as a sport weight. Worsted-weight yarn is more suitable for afghans, and rugs work up beautifully using bulky-weight yarn.) The stitches themselves are squarish, which makes the fabric perfect for working multicolored designs or as a base for cross-stitch designs.

Tunisian crochet stitches have many variations that look quite different from each other, but in this chapter we tell you how to work three of the most common ones: the basic Tunisian stitch and the knit and purl variations. We also show you what special hooks you need, how to increase and decrease stitches, and how to work from a chart for designs with color changes as well as for cross-stitch designs. After you master the Tunisian crochet technique, try out the Absorbent Hand Towel project at the end of this chapter.

Note: Tunisian crochet has many names attached to it. So if you come across any of the following names, know that they're referring to Tunisian crochet: *afghan stitch, tricot crochet, shepherd's knitting, hook knitting,* and *railroad knitting.*

Taking a Look at Tunisian Crochet Tools

Tunisian crochet is a unique form of crochet that calls for a unique hook. Unlike standard crochet, where you work each stitch off to one loop before going on to the next stitch, Tunisian crochet requires you to pick up a whole row of stitches on the hook before you work off the loops on a second pass. To accommodate all of these stitches, you need a hook with a cap or a stopper on the end to hold the stitches. Standard Tunisian hooks are long and straight with a cap, but you can also find hooks with longer cable attachments and even double-ended hooks that give you more flexibility when working wider projects.

Tunisian hooks are longer than standard hooks, too, coming in a variety of lengths and sizes; the most popular Tunisian hooks are 10 to 14 inches long and range in size from size G to size K. The longest hooks, like those with cable-cord attachments, are ideal for making large afghans. You can see a sampling of Tunisian crochet hooks in Figure 12-1.

Longer hooks can be cumbersome if you don't need the extra length. The best way to determine what hook length suits your purpose is to refer to the beginning of your pattern's instructions. If the materials list doesn't mention a specific length, take a look at the measurements of the pieces you'll be working and use a hook that fits the size of each piece. For example, if each piece is 13 inches wide, use a 14-inch hook. If you work an afghan in one piece that measures 40 inches wide, then the 22-inch flexible hook or the 40-inch double-ended hook is appropriate.

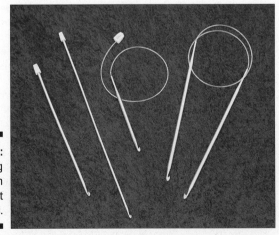

Figure 12-1:
A sampling of Tunisian crochet hooks.

When you want to crochet small pieces in Tunisian crochet (or when you just want to try out the technique), you can actually use a standard crochet hook rather than a Tunisian crochet hook. Simply wrap a rubber band several times around the base of the standard hook to keep the stitches from falling off the end. If you want to try Tunisian crochet with finer yarn or cotton thread, use a smaller crochet hook.

Creating the Tunisian Simple Stitch

If a pattern calls for Tunisian crochet, it's usually referring to the *Tunisian simple stitch,* abbreviated *Tss.* Tunisian simple stitches are shaped like little squares with two horizontal strands of yarn and a vertical bar on top of them. (You can see a sample in Figure 12-2.)

Each row of Tunisian simple stitch is worked in two halves:

- ✔ **Forward (first) half:** Picking up the loops. (The forward half is sometimes called the *forward pass* or *forward row.*)

- ✔ **Return (second) half:** Working off the loops, without turning your work between rows. (The return half is sometimes called the *return pass* or *return row.*)

Figure 12-2:
A swatch of Tunisian simple stitch.

As you discover in the next sections, you start out with a foundation row that you work the same way for all variations of Tunisian crochet. The forward half of the second row, and beyond, establishes the pattern — in this case the Tunisian simple stitch. (Check out the section "Varying Your Tunisian Crochet" for instructions on the knit stitch and purl stitch variations.) You usually work the return half of each row (from the second row on) in the same way for all variations of Tunisian crochet.

To practice working the Tunisian simple stitch, use a worsted-weight yarn and a 10-inch size H-8 U.S. (5 mm) Tunisian crochet hook.

Starting with a foundation row

Because Tunisian stitches require you to pull loops up through existing stitches, you need to start with a foundation row, which is actually the first row of the design. Chain 16 stitches for your foundation chain, and you're ready to begin the forward half of your foundation row of Tunisian crochet.

Working the forward half of your foundation row

Follow these steps to work the forward half of the foundation row, drawing up the loops of each stitch onto your hook:

1. **Insert your hook into the second chain stitch (ch) from the hook.**

   See Chapter 5 for more on counting chain stitches.

2. **Yarn over the hook (yo).**

3. **Draw your yarn through the chain stitch, as shown in Figure 12-3a.**

   You should have 2 loops on your hook.

Figure 12-3:
Working the forward half of the foundation row.

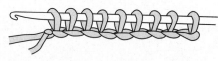

a   b

4. **Insert your hook into the next chain stitch and repeat Steps 2 and 3 in each chain stitch across the foundation chain until your hook is loaded with loops (like in Figure 12-3b).**

   This technique is known as *drawing up the loops.* If you have 16 loops on your hook — 1 for each chain stitch in your foundation chain — then the forward half of your foundation row of Tunisian crochet is complete.

Working the return half of your foundation row

To work the return half of the foundation row, work the loops off the hook by doing the following:

1. **Yarn over the hook (yo).**

2. **Draw your yarn through the first loop on the hook, as shown in Figure 12-4a.**

3. **Yarn over the hook.**

4. **Draw your yarn through the next 2 loops on the hook (see Figure 12-4b).**

5. **Repeat Steps 3 and 4 across the row until 1 loop remains on the hook.**

   You've just successfully worked Tunisian crochet across your foundation row. Well done! One loop remains on your hook (see Figure 12-5), and it counts as the first stitch of the next row.

Figure 12-4: Working off the loops on the return half.

a

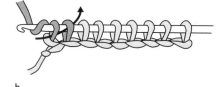
b

Figure 12-5: A completed foundation row of Tunisian crochet.

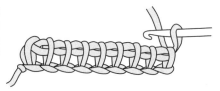

Continuing to the second row and beyond

You place your hook differently for the stitches in the second row of Tunisian crochet, but otherwise, you work them across the row in the same manner as for the foundation row. You then work each successive row the same way as the second row.

GARY PUBLIC LIBRARY

Working the forward half of the second row

To begin the forward half of your next row of Tunisian simple stitch:

1. **Insert your hook behind the next vertical bar in the row below.**

   Don't work into the vertical bar directly below the loop on your hook; if you do, you'll end up adding a stitch to the row.

2. **Yarn over the hook (yo).**

3. **Draw the yarn through the stitch, as shown in Figure 12-6a.**

4. **Repeat Steps 1 through 3 in each vertical bar across the row until you reach the next-to-last stitch.**

5. **Insert your hook under the last 2 vertical bars at the end of the row (refer to Figure 12-6b).**

6. **Yarn over the hook.**

7. **Draw your yarn through both vertical bars.**

   You should now have 16 loops on your hook. If you do, then the forward half of this row is complete.

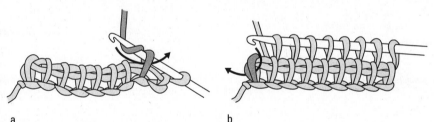

Figure 12-6: Working the forward half of your second row.

a   b

Working the return half of the second row

To work the return half of the second row, repeat Steps 1 through 5 from the earlier section "Working the return half of your foundation row." Continue working rows of Tunisian simple stitch until you feel comfortable with this technique (a good length for a practice swatch is 4 inches).

Binding off

When you finish your last row of Tunisian simple stitch, you can't just fasten off your yarn like you do with other standard crochet stitches. Instead, you need to *bind off* the top edge of your last row of Tunisian crochet with a row of slip stitches. If you don't bind off the last row, the stitches will have gaps

GARY PUBLIC LIBRARY

in them and won't look like the rest of the piece. So, using the same hook, work a slip stitch under each vertical bar across the last row. (See Chapter 5 for instructions on making slip stitches.)

The different variations of Tunisian crochet may call for a different binding-off stitch (like a row of single crochet, for example). The specific pattern you're following indicates what stitch to use when binding off, so make sure you check for this info before you automatically start binding off with slip stitches.

Shaping the Tunisian Simple Stitch

When working in Tunisian crochet, you may occasionally need to shape your work, particularly when you're making sweaters. The great thing about Tunisian crochet stitches is that you increase and decrease in the same way whether you do it at the beginning, middle, or end of a row. And the same general technique applies to all variations of Tunisian crochet — you do all of your increasing and decreasing on the forward half of a row. In the following sections, we explain how to increase and decrease in Tunisian simple stitch.

Increasing in Tunisian simple stitch

You always make increases in the forward half of a row of Tunisian simple stitch, creating the extra loops on your hook; then you work off all the loops in the return half, as usual.

To practice making increases, grab the swatch you made in the earlier "Creating the Tunisian Simple Stitch" section or head there to make one. To increase by one stitch, work the forward half of the row as follows:

1. **With 1 loop on your hook from the previous row, insert your hook into the space between the first and second stitch (not under the vertical bar). (Refer to Figure 12-7a.)**

2. **Yarn over (yo).**

3. **Draw the yarn through the stitch.**

   One increase at the beginning of the row is now complete.

4. **Work in Tunisian simple stitch (Tss) across the rest of the row, starting in the next vertical bar.**

   You should have 17 loops on your hook because you added 1. (The extra loop is highlighted in Figure 12-7b.)

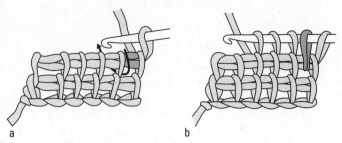

Figure 12-7:
Increasing
at the begin-
ning of the
forward half
of a row.

a   b

Working the return half of a row is pretty standard, whether you're working the foundation row or Row 12 of Tunisian crochet. To work the return half of the increase row, repeat Steps 1 through 5 from the earlier "Working the return half of your foundation row" section.

Decreasing in Tunisian simple stitch

Making a decrease in the Tunisian simple stitch is pretty similar to making an increase: You decrease in the forward half of a row of Tunisian simple stitch, subtracting loops from your hook; then you work off all the loops in the return half, just like you always do.

To practice making decreases, use the swatch you just made the increase on (if you're following this chapter in order), or head to the earlier "Creating the Tunisian Simple Stitch" section to make a swatch. To decrease one stitch, work the forward half of the row as follows:

1. **With 1 loop on your hook from the previous row, insert your hook behind the second and third vertical bars in the row below. (See Figure 12-8a.)**

2. **Yarn over (yo).**

3. **Draw the yarn through both stitches.**

   One decrease at the beginning of the row is now complete.

4. **Work in Tunisian simple stitch (Tss) across the rest of the row.**

   You should have 15 loops on your hook because you decreased by 1 stitch. (Refer to Figure 12-8b.)

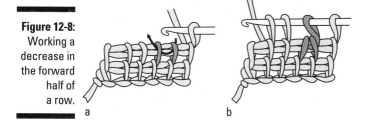

Figure 12-8:
Working a
decrease in
the forward
half of
a row.

a   b

To work the return half of the decrease row, repeat Steps 1 through 5 of the "Working the return half of your foundation row" section, found earlier in this chapter.

Varying Your Tunisian Crochet

Two of the most common variations of the Tunisian simple stitch are the *Tunisian knit stitch* and the *Tunisian purl stitch,* which, not surprisingly, resemble the knitting stitches they're named after — *knit* and *purl.* The crocheted fabric is thicker than the knitted, however, and you can see a noticeable ridge on the back of it.

When working any variation of Tunisian crochet, begin the pattern on the second row of your piece, after the foundation row of Tunisian simple stitch (which you always work the same way).

Tunisian knit stitch

Tunisian knit stitch, abbreviated *Tks,* is also known as *stockinette stitch.* It looks like rows of *V*s nesting in the row below (see for yourself in Figure 12-9). You can use the Tunisian knit stitch for afghans, as well as for home décor and fashion items. Like working with any kind of Tunisian crochet, you begin with a foundation row made up of Tunisian simple stitch. For the purposes of this exercise, work a foundation row of 16 stitches. (Refer to the section "Starting with a foundation row," earlier in this chapter, to find out how.)

Figure 12-9:
A swatch of
Tunisian knit
stitch.

To begin the forward half of the first row of Tunisian knit stitch:

1. **Insert your hook, from front to back, between the front and back strands of the next vertical stitch.**

2. **Yarn over (yo).**

3. **Draw the yarn through the stitch, as in Figure 12-10a.**

Figure 12-10:
Working
the forward
half of the
Tunisian knit
stitch row.

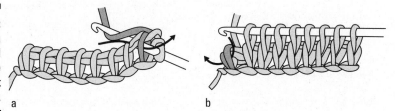

a   b

4. **Repeat Steps 1 through 3 across the row until you reach the next-to-last stitch.**

5. **Insert your hook under the last 2 vertical bars at the end of the row, like in Figure 12-10b.**

6. **Yarn over.**

7. **Draw the yarn through the stitch.**

   You should now have 16 loops on your hook.

To work the return half of the first row, repeat Steps 1 through 5 of the earlier "Working the return half of your foundation row" section across the row. The first row of Tunisian knit stitch is now complete; yours should look like the example in Figure 12-11.

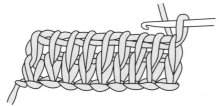

Figure 12-11:
A completed
first row
of Tunisian
knit stitch.

For each additional row of Tunisian knit stitch, repeat the preceding steps. Work this stitch until you feel comfortable with it.

Tunisian purl stitch

Tunisian purl stitch, abbreviated *Tps,* is also known as *purl stitch* and looks like rows of rounded bumps (see Figure 12-12). Tunisian purl stitch is useful by itself or in combination with other Tunisian stitches to produce textured patterns. Like working any other type of Tunisian crochet, you need to build from a foundation row. To get started, work a 16-stitch foundation row (follow the instructions in the earlier "Starting with a foundation row" section).

Figure 12-12:
A swatch
of Tunisian
purl stitch.

People tend to tighten up their stitches when working in Tunisian purl stitch. Be very conscious of tension and be sure to double-check your gauge when working this stitch. If you feel that you can't loosen up with the hook that a pattern suggests, change to a larger hook in order to get the desired gauge. (For more on gauge, refer to Chapter 3.)

Here's how to begin the forward half of your first row of Tunisian purl stitch:

1. **With the index finger of your yarn hand, bring the working yarn to the front of your work and insert your hook under the vertical bar of the next stitch (but behind the strand of working yarn).**

   Figure 12-13a shows this action, as well as how to work Steps 2 and 3 that follow.

Figure 12-13:
Working the forward half of the Tunisian purl stitch.

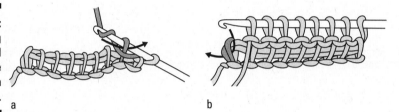

a   b

2. **Yarn over (yo).**

3. **Draw the yarn through the stitch.**

4. **Repeat Steps 1 through 3 across the row until you reach the next-to-last stitch.**

5. **Insert your hook under the last 2 vertical bars at the end of the row, as shown in Figure 12-13b.**

6. **Yarn over.**

7. **Draw the yarn through the stitch.**

   You should have 16 loops on your hook.

To work the return half of the row, repeat Steps 1 through 5 of the "Working the return half of your foundation row" section, found earlier in this chapter. For each additional row of Tunisian purl stitch, repeat the preceding steps; keep practicing until you feel comfortable performing this technique. Figure 12-14 shows a finished row of Tunisian purl stitch for your reference.

Figure 12-14:
A completed row of Tunisian purl stitch.

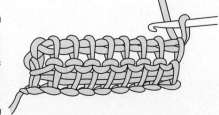

Addressing the curling problem

Fabric made of Tunisian crochet tends to curl up along the bottom edge. This is normal and happens because more yarn is on the back of the work than on the front. If you're having problems with curling, try working your Tunisian crochet in one of the following ways:

✔ Work the foundation row in just the *top loop* (the one at the top when the right side is facing you) of the foundation chain. (Refer to Chapter 5 for more on foundation chains.)

✔ Work the foundation row in the top 2 loops (the part of each chain stitch that forms a *V*) of the foundation chain.

✔ Work the foundation row in the back loop of the foundation chain. To do so, turn your foundation chain over. Notice one little raised-up loop on the backside of each stitch? Work your foundation row in these loops.

✔ After working the foundation row, purl the first row or two. Because Tunisian purl stitch tends to have just as much yarn on the front of the work as it does on the back, it doesn't curl much. Working a few rows of Tunisian purl stitch before beginning the pattern may solve your curling problem. (See the section "Tunisian purl stitch," earlier in this chapter, for more on this particular stitch.)

If your work still curls after trying these methods, don't despair. You can remedy the curling problem by

✔ Blocking your design while working on it or after you finish it. (See Chapter 19 for blocking directions.)

✔ Placing a heavy object (such as a large book) on the edge of your work for a few days to flatten it out.

✔ Working a border around the design, especially a heavy border with lots of stitches.

Coloring Your Tunisian Crochet

Because Tunisian crochet produces a gridlike stitch pattern, it's an excellent medium for creating colored designs. You can work color into the design while you're crocheting, or you can cross-stitch a colored design onto the surface after you've finished crocheting. Either of these techniques works great for afghans, wall hangings, rugs, place mats, potholders, and even sweaters. The sections that follow delve into the ins and outs of adding color to your Tunisian crochet pieces.

Crocheting with more than one color

Most patterns that call for color changes in Tunisian crochet provide a chart to show where you switch colors. If you're going to use a color again in the same row with no more than three stitches in between, you can carry the color loosely on the wrong side of the work and pick it up later, as Chapter 9 shows you how to do. However, be aware that the carried strand is visible on the back of your work. If you have more than three stitches in between, we suggest you fasten off and rejoin the yarn when you need it.

When working with several different colors and different balls of yarn, alleviate the inevitable tangle on the back of your work by joining small balls of yarn rather than whole skeins of each color. If you're going to work just a few stitches of a certain color, estimate the amount of yarn that you need for a patch of color by counting the number of stitches in the patch and allowing 2 inches for each stitch plus 4 more inches at each end. Wind the allotted amount of yarn into a small ball or wrap it around a yarn bobbin (Chapter 2 fills you in on this cool crocheting tool).

Figure 12-15 shows you an example of a color chart, a chart key, and the end product. To use the color chart, read all the rows from right to left when working the forward half of the rows. After you work the return half of the row, you're back at the right side to begin the next row. Each square counts as one complete stitch.

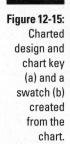

Figure 12-15: Charted design and chart key (a) and a swatch (b) created from the chart.

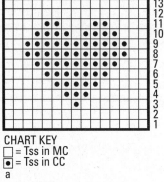

CHART KEY
□ = Tss in MC
⊡ = Tss in CC

a

b

Note that the following steps for using a color chart for Tunisian simple stitch changes are general and don't correspond with the chart in Figure 12-15:

1. **Draw up the designated number of loops of the first color according to the squares on the chart.**

   The first loop on the hook counts as the first stitch of the row.

2. **When you need to switch to a new color, drop the first color to the wrong side so you can pick it up in the return half of the row.**

3. **With the new color behind your work, insert your hook into the next stitch, yarn over (yo) with the new color, and draw that yarn through the stitch.**

Everyone deserves a little pampering in life. These luxurious washcloths are generously plush and absorbent, making them the perfect project for developing your basic stitch skills (see Chapter 5 for the patterns).

The stitch combinations used in this sassy scarf allow you to get plenty of practice working basic stitches, but the results are far from ordinary. You can crochet this scarf in the royal purple color shown, or you can choose a color to match your wardrobe (see Chapter 6 for the pattern).

© MATT BOWEN

© MATT BOWEN

Crocheted blankets are timeless treasures. This sweet blanket makes the perfect gift for a new baby, or you can use it as a throw for your lap while you're stitching on the couch (see Chapter 7 for the pattern).

Stylish and fun, this simple bucket hat will have you crocheting in circles in no time (see Chapter 8 for the pattern).

© MATT BOWEN

© MATT BOWEN

Man's best friend? We don't think so! This cute little pup is sure to be *anyone's* best friend. Check out Chapter 8 to find out what you need to know about *amigurumi* and how to make this *amigurumi* pup yourself.

Crochet isn't just for scarves and hats; you can crochet for your home as well. Whether you like your accessories bright and bold or subdued and neutral, this striped pillow is a great way to give your home a fresh burst of color (see Chapter 9 for the pattern).

© MATT BOWEN

© MATT BOWER

Crochet is a versatile craft; it can be casual or elegant. This all-season wrap pairs well with jeans and a T-shirt, or you can dress it up for a night on the town (see Chapter 10 for the pattern).

Scarves are some of the most popular projects to crochet. Take your stitches to the next level with this textured scarf (left) and this basketweave scarf (right), and you're sure to be warm and cozy (see Chapter 11 for the patterns).

You'll be amazed by the transformation your project undergoes when you run it through the wash. Felting is a popular technique that works great for bags and other projects requiring a sturdy fabric. Give felting a whirl with this shoulder bag (see Chapter 11 for the pattern).

© MATT BOWEN

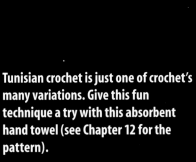

© MATT BOWEN

Tunisian crochet is just one of crochet's many variations. Give this fun technique a try with this absorbent hand towel (see Chapter 12 for the pattern).

© MATT BOWEN

Work this beautiful table runner using filet crochet to create an elegant accent for any room in your house (see Chapter 13 for the pattern). Display it by itself, sew it to a pillow front, or frame it on a solid-color background; the choice is yours!

Make your life a little greener by replacing disposable bags with bags you can wash and use over and over. This mesh market bag is a quick and simple introduction to working with lacy mesh stitch patterns (see Chapter 13 for the pattern).

© MATT BOWEN

© MATT BOWER

You can whip up a pair of stylish earrings in a raindrop motif by using basic crochet stitches (see Chapter 14 for the pattern).

Crocheted flowers are all the rage! These flowers are a stylish way to top a package, embellish an Afghan, or adorn a hat. You can work the pattern in bulky-weight yarn, fine crochet cotton, or anything in between, making the applications for its use unlimited (see Chapter 14 for the pattern).

Granny squares are anything but "square" with this simple yet elegant cuff. It's the perfect gift for your friends and family — just don't forget to make one for yourself! (See Chapter 15 for the pattern.)

© MATT BOWER

Minimal shaping and simple stitch patterns make this sweater a breeze to crochet. The vibrant red-orange yarn is heavyweight in size, yet deceptively light. This casual sweater is perfect to throw on for those cool fall and colder winter days (see Chapter 16 for the pattern).

Handmade gifts make anyone feel special. This camisole will please your favorite girl with a dainty drawstring and a pocket that can hold her little treasures (see Chapter 17 for the pattern).

4. **Continue by drawing up the designated number of loops of the new color.**

   Figure 12-16 shows 4 loops of the old color and 1 loop of the new color being drawn up.

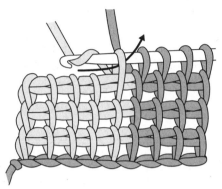

Figure 12-16:
Drawing up the designated number of loops of the next color.

5. **Repeat Steps 2 through 4 for each section of a new color across the row of the chart.**

6. **For the return half of the row, work off the loops with the matching color until 1 loop of the current color remains on the hook.**

7. **Pick up the next color in sequence from the wrong side of the work, drawing it under the working end of the first color (thereby twisting the yarn to prevent holes in the work), and yarn over.**

8. **Draw the new color through 1 loop of the previous color and 1 loop of the matching color, as shown in Figure 12-17.**

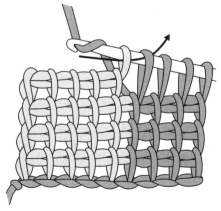

Figure 12-17:
Working off the next color.

9. **Repeat Steps 6 through 8 as needed across the row until 1 loop remains on the hook.**

   One row of the chart is now complete. Each time you finish changing colors, continue working off the loops as you normally would. Then repeat Steps 6 through 8 as necessary to change colors.

10. **Repeat Steps 1 through 9 for each row of the chart.**

Cross-stitching on top of Tunisian crochet

Tunisian crochet, especially Tunisian simple stitch, makes an ideal base for working cross-stitch designs and is often used for just that. You can produce a more delicate color pattern, as well as a more elaborate one, when cross-stitching on Tunisian crochet fabric rather than working color changes within the crochet. Plus you don't have to deal with changing colors in the middle of a row while crocheting. In the sections that follow, we provide a few pointers on cross-stitching on top of Tunisian crochet and explain how to make a complete cross-stitch row.

A few handy tips before you begin

You work cross-stitch designs by following a chart (see Figure 12-18) so you can see where to place the stitches. Each square on the chart represents one stitch in Tunisian crochet and one cross-stitch. If you're working a small design on a large piece of crocheted fabric, the instructions tell you where to position the design on your piece. A chart key accompanies the chart, indicating what color the symbols on the chart stand for.

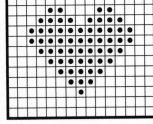

Figure 12-18: Cross-stitch chart and key.

CHART KEY
☐ = Background Tss
⬛ = Cross st

Cross-stitch in one color at a time, following the chart from left to right in rows. If you're going to work several stitches in a row with the same color, work the first half of each stitch across the row and then come back from right to left to work the second half of each stitch.

Standard cross-stitch technique, where the needle goes through the fabric to the back and then up through the fabric to the front, produces a rather sloppy back on your item. To avoid the yarn showing on the back, be careful to slide your needle under the two horizontal strands of the Tunisian stitch near the surface of your work. Check the back of your work frequently to make sure nothing is showing.

If you make your cross-stitches too tight, you can ruin your design. The cross-stitches should lay over the Tunisian crochet without causing the background to pucker.

The first part of a cross-stitch row

To work cross-stitch on Tunisian simple stitch, follow these steps (which reference Figure 12-19) to make the first half of a row:

1. **Thread a length of the designated color yarn onto a yarn needle.**

   Use a length of yarn that's comfortable to work with. An 18-inch length is about average.

2. **Insert the needle from back to front at Position A (the bottom left-hand corner of the designated stitch) and draw the needle up, leaving a 4-inch length of yarn on the back (which you'll later weave in).**

3. **Insert the needle at Position B (the top right-hand corner of the same stitch), angled vertically down, behind the 2 horizontal threads.**

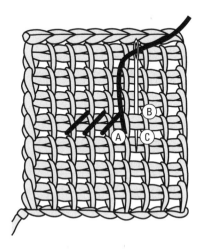

Figure 12-19:
Working the first half of a row of cross-stitch on Tunisian simple stitch.

4. **Bring the needle out at Position C (the bottom right-hand corner of the same stitch) and draw the yarn through until it stretches neatly across the stitch.**

5. **Position C now becomes Position A of the next stitch.**

6. **Repeat Steps 3 through 5 across the row in the stitches where the chart calls for cross-stitching.**

The second part of a cross-stitch row

To make the second half of a cross-stitch row, follow these steps (which refer to Figure 12-20):

1. **Insert your needle at Position D (the top left-hand corner of the same stitch you ended the first half with), angled vertically down, behind the 2 horizontal threads.**

   The thread should form an *X* with the already-completed first half of the stitch.

2. **Bring the needle out at Position E (the bottom left-hand corner of the same stitch) and draw the yarn through until it stretches neatly across the stitch.**

3. **Repeat Steps 1 and 2 across the row, completing each cross-stitch.**

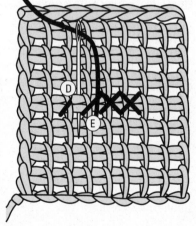

Figure 12-20: Working the second half of a row of cross-stitch on Tunisian simple stitch.

When you're finished working cross-stitches with a particular color, weave the ends through the Tunisian background for several inches to hide the strands. Then clip off the excess yarn (see Chapter 5 for more information on weaving in ends). Figure 12-21 shows a finished cross-stitch design.

Figure 12-21:
A swatch of
cross-stitch
on Tunisian
simple
stitch.

Always work cross-stitches with the thread crossing on top in the same direction. And don't tie knots in the yarn at the beginning or the end of your work. Simply weave in the ends to secure them and snip off the excess.

Absorbent Hand Towel Project

This project uses Tunisian simple stitch and Tunisian purl stitch to make a thick and thirsty hand towel. The yarn is made of absorbent cotton and comes in a nice selection of colors so you can put together colors that complement your bathroom or kitchen. The project is finished with simple cross-stitches on bands of Tunisian simple stitch to add classic contrast and design.

Materials and vital statistics

- **Yarn:** Elmore-Pisgah "Peaches & Crème" 4-ply worsted-weight yarn (100% cotton), Article #930 (2.5 oz. [70.8 g], 122 yds [112 m] each ball): 2 balls of #1 White (MC) and 1 ball of #10 Yellow (CC)

- **Hooks:**
  - 10-in. Tunisian crochet hook size J-9 U.S. (6 mm) or size needed to obtain gauge
  - Standard crochet hook size J-9 U.S. (6 mm) or size needed to obtain gauge

- **Large-eyed yarn needle**

- **Measurements:** 27 in. long x 17 in. wide

✔ **Gauge:** 14 sts and 12 rows = 4 in. in alternating Tunisian simple stitch (Tss) and Tunisian purl stitch (Tps) pattern

✔ **Stitches used:** Chain stitch (ch), Tunisian simple stitch (Tss), Tunisian purl stitch (Tps), single crochet (sc), slip stitch (sl st)

Directions

The Absorbent Hand Towel is worked lengthwise in five sections using two different stitch patterns. The first, third, and fifth sections are created by alternating one stitch of Tunisian simple stitch with one stitch of Tunisian purl stitch to create a honeycomb pattern. The second and fourth sections are worked in plain Tunisian simple stitch, which creates the background for cross-stitching embellishment at the end. Follow the chart in Figure 12-22.

Figure 12-22:
Absorbent
Hand Towel
chart and
chart key.

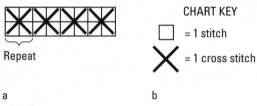

Repeat

CHART KEY

☐ = 1 stitch

✕ = 1 cross stitch

a   b

Making the foundation row

With the Tunisian crochet hook and MC, ch 95.

The following steps explain in detail how to work your foundation row for this project: Insert hook in second ch from hook, yo, draw yarn through ch, * insert hook in next ch, yo, draw yarn through ch *; rep from * to * across, keeping all loops on the hook (95 loops — forward half of foundation row complete), beg return half of row, yo, draw yarn through 1 loop on hook, ** yo, draw yarn through 2 loops on hook **; rep from ** to ** across (1 loop remains and counts as first st of next row).

Working the rest of the pattern

Row 1: Skip first st, * Tps in next st, Tss in next st; rep from * across; work return half.

Row 2: Skip first st, * Tss in next st, Tps in next st; rep from * across; work return half.

Rows 3–4: Rep Rows 1–2.

Row 5: Rep Row 1.

Row 6: Skip first st, Tps in next st and each st across; work return half, change to CC with last st.

Rows 7–12: Skip first st, Tss in next st and each st across; work return half, changing to MC with last st.

Row 13: Skip first st, Tps in next st and each st across; work return half.

Rows 14–35: Rep Rows 1–2 eleven times.

Row 36: Rep Row 1.

Rows 37–44: Rep Rows 6–13 once.

Rows 45–49: Rep Rows 1–2 twice, then rep Row 1.

Row 50: Skip first st, Tss in next st and each st across; work return half.

Bind off: Skip first st, sl st under each vertical bar across the last row.

Finishing

With a standard crochet hook, ch 1, working across side edge * sc in each row-end st across side edge to next corner, work 3 sc in next corner st, sc in each st across bottom edge to next corner, work 3 sc in next corner st *; rep from * to * around, sl st in first sc to join. Fasten off. Weave in loose ends with yarn needle.

With MC and yarn needle, cross-stitch across center 2 rows of each Tss stitch section (Rows 10 and 11 and Rows 41 and 42), making each cross-stitch 2 stitches (Tss "boxes") wide by 2 rows tall (as shown in Figure 12-22).

Chapter 13

Filet and Mesh Crochet: Creating a New Style

In This Chapter

▶ Presenting Filet Crochet 101 (it's easier than you think)

▶ Giving your filet crocheted pieces shape with increases and decreases

▶ Using fancy-schmancy filet stitches to add interest to your designs

▶ Exploring variations in basic mesh patterns

▶ Enjoying the beauty and usefulness of a butterfly table runner and a mesh market bag

*N*ot to be confused with filet mignon or filet of sole, *filet crochet* (also known as *net stitch*) is a technique that imitates a 17th-century form of lace worked on mesh netting stretched across a frame. Over the years, the technique evolved into what it is today — a series of blocks and spaces that form a design. Because of the uniformity of the designs, the directions are shown in a chart, with each square of the chart representing specific stitches.

Mesh patterns, which are related to filet crochet, use a combination of chain stitches and basic stitches, like single crochet and double crochet, to create light, open, lacy projects. Quick to work up and simple to master, mesh patterns can be used on their own or to form the background for embellishment. With simple changes to stitch height, number of chains, and placement of stitches, creating many new mesh stitch patterns is easy.

This chapter gives you the lowdown on both filet and mesh crochet. You find out how to create filet crochet using blocks and spaces, how to read filet crochet charts, and how to shape your filet crochet designs, as well as a few variations of basic mesh patterns. Even better than that? At the end of this chapter, you can practice your skills with a butterfly table runner and an environmentally friendly mesh market bag.

Filet Crochet for Newbies

You've probably seen filet crochet many times, but you may not have known it. Its distinct meshlike designs, usually worked in white cotton thread, are often used for tablecloths, table runners, curtains, and wall hangings; they're especially elegant against a dark wood surface or brightly colored cloth background. Filet crochet is much simpler than it looks, so it's great for beginners. In the sections that follow, we introduce you to the basics of making filet crochet; one project at the end of this chapter, the Butterfly Runner that you can see in the color section, is a typical example of the filet crochet technique.

Breaking down filet crochet stitches

Perhaps you've seen a drawing or painting made of small dots or squares. Looking at the drawing from a distance, you see only the design or picture, but as you come closer, you can see the tiny dots/squares that make up the larger picture. Similar to the tiny dots/squares in the drawing, filet crochet is a grid of blocks and spaces that make up a design. The spaces form the background, and the blocks create the design. Patterns for these designs are given as charts (see the next section). Because of its detail, filet crochet is commonly used for lettering. (Here's an interesting tidbit for you: The earliest-known text depicted with filet crochet is *The Lord's Prayer*.)

Each space and block is made up of three stitches:

- ✔ **Spaces** begin with two chain stitches, followed by a double crochet stitch.
- ✔ **Blocks** are made up of three double crochet stitches, which you can work in the stitches or spaces of the previous row.

To make sure your design is clear, work filet crochet patterns with cotton thread. Start with size 10 thread and a size 7 steel (1.50 mm) hook. After you have some experience with this technique, move on to a smaller size 20 or size 30 thread and a size 12 (0.75 mm) or 14 (0.60 mm) steel hook to create a much more delicate and elegant design. (Flip to Chapter 2 for the basics on different types of threads and hooks.)

Following a chart

Because of the repetitive nature of filet crochet, the instructions are usually depicted in chart form. (Not only would written instructions be really lengthy, but you'd probably lose your place and become cross-eyed in no time at all.) After you understand how to read a chart, you'll find it's much easier to follow than written instructions.

Filet crochet charts look somewhat like graph paper. They're made up of tons of squares, some of which are empty (spaces), and some of which are filled in (blocks). Each pattern also provides you with a chart key that explains what each square means and whether you work each space or block with three stitches or with another number of stitches that the designer may have chosen. Long empty spaces are bars, and the small, curved lines — the ones that look kind of like *Vs* — are the lacets (see the later section "Spacin' Out with Lacets and Bars" for the scoop on these two stitches). Figure 13-1a shows a sample filet crochet chart, and Figure 13-1b shows a sample chart key. *Note:* The first double crochet in each of the groups of stitches in the chart key represents the last stitch of the previous space or block.

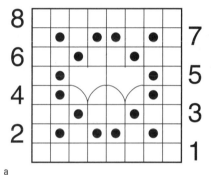
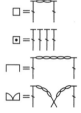

Figure 13-1: A sample filet crochet chart and key.

a   b

Each row of the chart has a number, beginning with Row 1 at the bottom and ending with the last row at the top. The instructions normally tell you the number of chains you need to make for the foundation chain, and they may or may not write out the first row's instructions. Read all the odd-numbered rows from right to left and all the even-numbered rows from left to right (because you actually work the second row from the left-hand side of the piece to the right-hand side).

Sometimes large patterns that repeat a series of rows over and over again show you the repeated rows only once in the chart. The instructions tell you to work the chart from Row 1 to the last row and then repeat the chart, beginning at Row 1 again, a designated number of times to complete the project. This is often the case when you're making a table runner, tablecloth, or curtains.

If the filet crochet chart is for a large piece, the squares may be small and hard to read. Make a copy of the chart and enlarge it for easier reading instead of working directly from the original instructions. With a copy, you can also mark up the chart without destroying the original. You can highlight the row you're working on or place a mark next to the last row that you worked when you have to put your project down for a while.

Chaining the foundation

You need to do a little bit of math in order to make your foundation chain of filet crochet (but we promise it's not hard). Each block or space in a filet crochet chart is actually three stitches. This means that each row of filet crochet has a multiple of three stitches plus one double crochet at the end to complete the last space or block.

Here's how to create a foundation chain for a sample design that calls for five spaces across the first row:

1. **Multiply the number of spaces (or blocks) in the row by 3.**

   $5 \times 3 = 15$ chain stitches (ch).

2. **Add 3 more chain stitches for the turning chain of the next row's first double crochet stitch (dc).**

   $15 + 3$ (first double crochet) = 18 chain stitches. (Refer to Chapter 5 for more on turning chains.)

Getting the tension just right for your foundation chain is important. If your foundation chain is too tight, your design can pucker or be misshapen. If it's too loose, you'll have a lot of droopy loops hanging off the edge. The stitches in your foundation chain should be the same size and just big enough to fit your hook into comfortably. Most people have a tendency to chain too tightly. If you fall into this category, go to the next-largest hook size to work the foundation chain. If you chain too loosely, try the next size down.

Nothing is more frustrating than getting to the end of your first row in a large design and finding out that you don't have enough stitches. If you're working on a large filet crochet design, chances are your foundation chain is several hundred stitches long. To avoid miscounting, crochet your foundation chain with a separate ball of thread. When you think you have the right number of chain stitches, attach a new ball of thread in the first chain stitch that you created, working your first row from there. If you miscounted, you can easily add (or subtract) chain stitches at the end of the foundation row with the first ball of thread that you used. Fasten off the first ball of thread when you complete the first row and weave in the end to keep it from unraveling.

Creating spaces

If you're armed with the foundation chain you created in the preceding section, you're ready to start working your first row of filet crochet. To work a first row of spaces, proceed as follows:

1. **Chain 2 (ch 2) to create the top of the first space.**

You already chained the turning chain for the first stitch when you crocheted your foundation chain.

2. **Double crochet (dc) in the eighth chain from your hook to make the first space.**

   Not sure how to make a double crochet stitch? See Chapter 6.

3. **Chain 2.**

4. **Skip the next 2 chain stitches.**

5. **Double crochet in the next chain to make the second space.**

6. **Repeat Steps 3 through 5 across the row.**

   You work your last double crochet in the last chain of the foundation chain, and you should have 5 spaces at the end of the row, as in Figure 13-2.

Figure 13-2:
The first
row of filet
crochet
spaces.

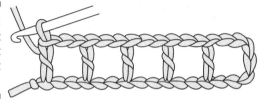

To work a second row of spaces

1. **Turn your work.**

   Refer to Chapter 5 for the how-to on turning your work.

2. **Chain 3 (ch 3) for the turning chain for your first double crochet (dc).**

3. **Chain 2 to make the first space.**

4. **Skip the next 2 chain stitches.**

5. **Double crochet in the next double crochet stitch to make the first space of the second row.**

6. **Repeat Steps 3 through 5 across the row.**

   You should wind up with 5 spaces at the end of the second row.

Work each successive row the same way as the second row until you're comfortable with the technique.

Take care to notice the way that the spaces form squares and that they line up one on top of another. Filet crochet is a symmetrical design technique, and if the squares are skewed, then your whole piece will look out of kilter. If you find that you've made a mistake, tear out your work to that spot and rework your design from there. You can't hide mistakes in filet crochet.

Building blocks

Blocks are what create the actual substance of a filet crochet design. Some designs also start with a row of blocks for the first row to create a border. Using the foundation chain of 15 chain stitches plus 3 for the turning chain (see the earlier "Chaining the foundation" section), work a first row of blocks.

1. **Double crochet (dc) in the fourth chain (ch) from the hook.**

   Flip to Chapter 6 to see how to make a double crochet stitch.

2. **Double crochet in each of the next 2 chain stitches to complete the first block.**

3. **Double crochet in each of the next 3 chain stitches to complete the second block.**

4. **Repeat Step 3 across the row.**

   You should have 5 blocks at the end of the row (or 15 double crochet stitches plus the turning chain), as shown in Figure 13-3. *Remember:* You always have 1 more stitch than the multiple of 3.

Figure 13-3: The first row of filet crochet blocks.

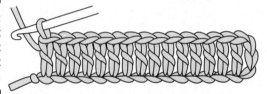

To work the second row of blocks, follow these steps:

1. **Turn your work.**

   See Chapter 5 for pointers on turning your work.

2. **Chain 3 (ch 3) for the turning chain for your first double crochet (dc).**

3. **Double crochet in each of the next 3 double crochet stitches to make the first block.**

4. **Double crochet in each of the next 3 double crochet stitches to complete the second block.**

5. **Repeat Step 4 across the row.**

   You should have 5 blocks at the end of the second row.

Combining spaces and blocks

To create the design you're going for, you must combine spaces and blocks, which is easy to do because both techniques are based on three stitches.

As you're crocheting, make sure your blocks and spaces line up with all the vertical and horizontal lines lying at right angles. The double crochet stitches that form the beginning and end of each block or space must line up one on top of the other to create the gridlike appearance.

To work a space in the next row over a block:

1. **Work the first double crochet (dc).**

2. **Chain 2 (ch 2).**

3. **Skip the next 2 double crochet stitches.**

   The double crochet that closes the space is actually considered the first stitch of the next space or block in the row.

To work a block over a space:

1. **Double crochet (dc) in the first double crochet stitch of the space below.**

2. **Work 2 double crochet stitches in the chain-2 space (ch-2 sp) or in the 2 chain stitches (ch) in the row below.**

   You can either work your stitches in the chain space or you can work them directly into the chain stitches — try it both ways to see which one you prefer. Most crocheters find working in the space easier and neater. (Flip to Chapter 11 for the lowdown on working in the spaces between stitches.)

Don't worry if the stitches look a bit skewed as you're crocheting. After you finish the design, you can pin it out and starch it (see Chapter 19 for more on this process, which is commonly referred to as blocking) to straighten out the stitches.

Figure 13-4 shows a swatch of filet crochet that combines spaces and blocks. In this figure, the stitches are worked in the chain space.

Figure 13-4:
A swatch
of filet
crochet
that
combines
spaces and
blocks.

Diving into Deeper Waters: Shaping Your Filet Crochet Design

You're not limited to straight-edged, rectangular pieces in filet crochet. Instead, you can add interest to corners and edges by increasing or decreasing the number of spaces and blocks in a row to make inset corners and step-like edges, as explained in the following sections.

Increasing spaces and blocks

Increasing the number of spaces and blocks at the end of a row shapes the edges of the design. Because most filet crochet designs are symmetrical, if you increase at the beginning of a row, you need to increase at the end of the row, too. However, the process is a little different for each end.

Increasing one space at the beginning of a row

In order to increase one space at the beginning of a row, you must chain enough stitches to make up a space. Here's how to work a one-space increase at the beginning of a row:

1. **At the end of the row that precedes the row you're going to increase, turn your work and then chain 2 (ch 2) to create the base of the first increase space.**

2. **Chain 3 more for the turning chain of the space's first double crochet (dc).**

3. **Chain 2 more to complete the top of the first space.**

4. **Double crochet in the last double crochet stitch of the previous row, as shown in Figure 13-5a.**

   One increase is now complete, which you can see in Figure 13-5b. Continue across the row with blocks or spaces, as detailed earlier in this chapter.

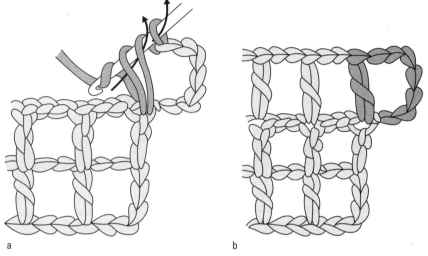

Figure 13-5:
Increasing one filet crochet space at the beginning of a row.

a   b

Increasing more than one space at the beginning of a row

Increasing more than one space at the beginning of a row works the same way as increasing one space; you just have to know how many additional chain stitches to make for each additional space.

When increasing spaces, chain 2 for the first space increase and then chain 3 more for each additional space required. The first double crochet of a row is always a chain 3.

Follow these steps to increase more than one space:

1. **When you reach the end of the row that precedes the row you're going to increase, turn your work and then chain 2 (ch 2) for the base of the first increase space.**

2. **Chain 3 more for each additional space required.**

   The example in these steps adds 1 more space for a total of 2 increases. Therefore, you're chaining a total of 5 stitches for the 2 increases.

3. **Chain 3 more for the turning chain of the row's first double crochet stitch (dc).**

4. **Chain 2 more for the top of the first space.**

5. **Double crochet in the eighth chain from the hook, as shown in Figure 13-6a.**

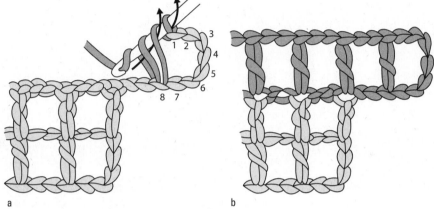

Figure 13-6:
Increasing
two spaces
at the
start of a
row.

a   b

6. **Chain 2 for the top of the second increase space.**

7. **Skip the next 2 chain stitches.**

8. **Double crochet in the next chain stitch.**

   You've now increased the row by 2 spaces.

9. **Chain 2 to make the top of the next space.**

10. **Skip the next 2 stitches.**

11. **Double crochet in the next double crochet stitch to make the next space of the row.**

12. **Repeat Steps 9 through 11 across the row to complete a row of spaces.**

   Your completed row should look similar to Figure 13-6b.

Increasing one or more blocks at the beginning of a row

Increasing one block at the beginning of a row is similar to increasing one space. The big difference is that you replace the two chain stitches you make for the top of the space with two double crochet stitches. To increase one block at the beginning of a row, proceed as follows:

1. **At the end of the row that precedes the row you're going to increase, turn your work and then chain 2 (ch 2) to make the base of the first increase block.**

2. **Chain 3 more to complete the turning chain of the block's first double crochet stitch (dc).**

3. **Double crochet in the fourth chain from the hook to complete the second double crochet stitch of the block. (See Figure 13-7a.)**

4. **Double crochet in each of the next 2 chain stitches to complete the block.**

   The first block increase is now complete; yours should look like the one in Figure 13-7b. From here, continue making blocks or spaces across the row.

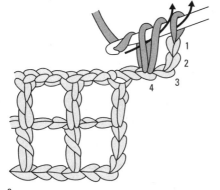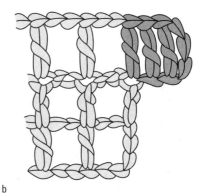

Figure 13-7: Increasing one block at the start of a row.

a

b

 To increase additional blocks, follow the same steps for increasing one block, but remember the additional chain stitches you need to make for the additional blocks. Here's the simple math: Chain 2 for your first increase block, chain 3 more for each additional block, and then chain 3 for the turning chain of the row's first double crochet. So if you want to increase 2 blocks at the beginning of a row, you chain 2 for the first block, 3 for the second block, and 3 more for the turning chain, which is 11 chain stitches total.

After you chain the required number of stitches, follow Steps 3 and 4 in the previous list to make the first block; then work another set of three double crochet stitches for the other increase block (see Figure 13-8).

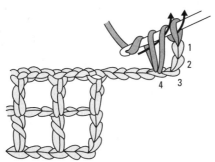

Figure 13-8: The beginning of a two-block increase at the start of a row.

Increasing one or more spaces at the end of a row

When you need to increase a space at the end of a row, you start at the *top* of the last double crochet in the row just prior to the increase. In order to create the extra space(s), you work a chain-2 space followed by a stitch called a *triple triple crochet* (abbreviated *trtr*), which is one step taller than a double triple crochet stitch (presented in Chapter 6). By working a triple triple crochet stitch, you create a length equivalent to five chain stitches, which is what you need to make one filet space — two chain stitches for the width of the space plus three chain stitches for the height of one double crochet.

To increase one space at the end of a row, follow these instructions:

1. **Chain 2 (ch 2) to create the top of the first space.**
2. **Yarn over the hook (yo) 4 times.**
3. **Insert your hook into the same stitch as the last double crochet stitch (dc) that you worked, like in Figure 13-9a.**
4. **Yarn over and draw the yarn through the stitch.**
5. **Yarn over and draw the yarn through the first 2 loops on the hook.**
6. **Repeat Step 5 three times until you have 1 loop on the hook, completing 1 triple triple crochet (trtr).**

   Figure 13-9b shows 1 completed space increase at the end of a row.

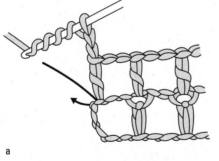

Figure 13-9: Working an increase space at the end of a row.

a   b

To increase more than one space at the end of a row, you just repeat the steps for increasing one space. The only difference is that in Step 3, you insert the hook in the middle of the post of the triple triple crochet that you made for the first space increase. Refer to Figure 13-10 to see what we mean, and flip to Chapter 5 if you need a refresher on stitch parts.

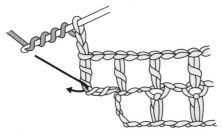

Figure 13-10:
Working
additional
spaces at
the end
of a row.

Increasing one or more blocks at the end of a row

Increasing a block at the end of a row is a bit tricky but still relatively simple. The key is to make sure you don't tighten up too much on your stitches.

When increasing blocks, you use a triple crochet stitch rather than a double crochet. The extra length compensates for not having a row of chain stitches to serve as the base.

Here's how to increase one block at the end of a row:

1. **Yarn over (yo) twice.**

2. **Insert your hook into the top of the last stitch of the previous row, which is where you just worked the last double crochet (dc) of the current row. (Refer to Figure 13-11a.)**

3. **Yarn over and draw the yarn through the stitch.**

4. **Yarn over and draw the yarn through the first 2 loops on the hook.**

5. **Repeat Step 4 twice.**

   You now have 1 loop remaining on your hook and have completed 1 triple crochet (tr) as well as the second stitch of the block.

6. **Yarn over twice.**

7. **Insert your hook near the bottom of the post of the last triple crochet that you made, as shown in Figure 13-11b.**

8. **Yarn over and draw the yarn through the first 2 loops on the hook.**

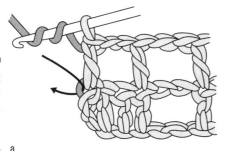
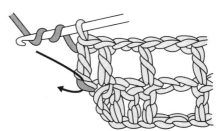

Figure 13-11:
Working an
extra block
at the end
of a row.

a   b

9. **Repeat Step 8 twice until you have just 1 loop on the hook (completing 1 triple crochet).**

10. **Repeat Steps 7 through 9 (completing the third stitch of the block).**

   See Figure 13-12 for the visual.

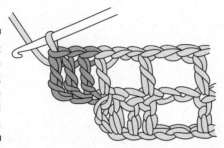

Figure 13-12:
A complete
block
increase
at the end
of a row.

After you master increasing one block, increasing more than one is easy. You just repeat Steps 7 through 9 three times for each additional block that you want.

Decreasing spaces and blocks

The method for decreasing both spaces and blocks is the same. It's simply a matter of counting.

Decreasing spaces or blocks at the beginning of a row

To decrease one space or block at the beginning of a row, simply slip stitch across to where you want to begin the first space or block.

1. **At the end of the row immediately before the row you're decreasing, turn your work.**

2. **Slip stitch (sl st) across 3 stitches for each space or block that you're decreasing.**

   If you're decreasing 1 space or block, then slip stitch across 3 stitches; if you're decreasing 2 spaces or blocks, slip stitch across 6 stitches. (Check out Chapter 5 for the scoop on making slip stitches.)

3. **Slip stitch in the next stitch.**

   Doing so brings your hook into the correct stitch to begin your first space or block of the row.

4. **Chain 3 (ch 3) for the turning chain of the row's first double crochet (dc). (See Figure 13-13.)**

5. **Work across the row with either blocks or spaces.**

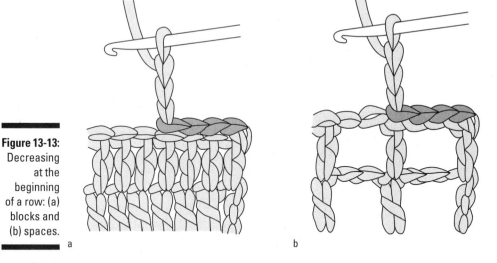

Figure 13-13:
Decreasing
at the
beginning
of a row: (a)
blocks and
(b) spaces.

a

b

Decreasing spaces or blocks at the end of a row

The method for decreasing spaces or blocks at the end of a row is the same
regardless of how many you need to decrease. You work across the row following the chart, stop crocheting at the point where you want to make the
decrease, and then turn your work to begin the next row. Keep in mind that
the decrease must end with a double crochet stitch or a complete space
or block. Figure 13-14 shows the decrease at the end of a row after you've
turned and are ready to begin the next row.

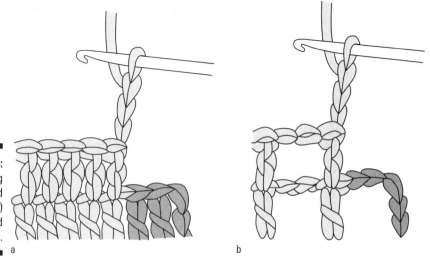

Figure 13-14:
Decreasing
at the end
of a row: (a)
blocks and
(b) spaces.

a

b

Spacin' Out with Lacets and Bars

Lacets and bars are two more filet crochet stitches that create an elegant, lacy look. Despite their fancy names, you work them with just double crochet, chain, and single crochet stitches, but the spacing is different. Instead of working them across three stitches, you work them in six stitches or two spaces. (***Remember:*** The last stitch that completes the block is really the first stitch of the next space or block.) Not all filet crochet designs incorporate these fancy-schmancy stitches, but they can add interest to a design. See how to make them in the next sections.

Getting fancy with lacets

A *lacet,* which is sometimes called a *fancy stitch,* looks somewhat like a *V* and is worked across five stitches or the interior width of two spaces. To make a lacet, proceed as follows:

1. **Work the first double crochet (dc) as you would to begin a regular block or space.**

   See the sections "Building blocks" or "Creating spaces," earlier in this chapter, for guidance.

2. **Chain 3 (ch 3).**

3. **Skip the next 2 stitches.**

4. **Single crochet (sc) in the next stitch.**

   See Chapter 5 for the basics on working single crochet.

   If you're working the lacet over a *bar* (a double space), you can work the single crochet in the center chain stitch or in the chain loop, whichever you prefer. If you're working it over 2 separate spaces or blocks, then work the single crochet in the center double crochet between the first and second space or block.

5. **Chain 3.**

6. **Skip the next 2 stitches.**

7. **Double crochet in the next double crochet to complete 1 lacet.**

   Figure 13-15 depicts a completed lacet over 2 spaces.

Figure 13-15:
A finished lacet over two spaces.

Bridging the gap with bars

Bars, sometimes referred to as *double spaces,* are long spaces that cross over the two blocks or spaces or the one lacet below them. They're generally worked over a lacet. To make a bar:

1. **Work the first double crochet (dc) as you would to begin a regular block or space.**

   Refer to the sections "Building blocks" or "Creating spaces," earlier in this chapter, for help with this step.

2. **Chain 5 (ch 5).**

3. **Skip the next 5 stitches or 2 spaces.**

4. **Double crochet in the next double crochet stitch to complete 1 bar.**

   To see what a completed bar looks like, check out Figure 13-16.

Figure 13-16:
A bar worked over a lacet.

Figure 13-17 shows a swatch of filet crochet worked with all four stitches: blocks, spaces, lacets, and bars. Pretty cool, huh?

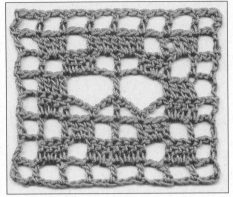

Figure 13-17:
A finished swatch of filet crochet featuring all four stitches.

Making Mesh, the Simplest Lace

By crocheting mesh stitch patterns, also called *net* or *trellis* patterns, you can quickly work up simple lace that you can use for many types of projects. When paired with delicate yarns, mesh is great for crocheting elegant scarves and summer camisoles. Worked up in a sturdier yarn, such as cotton, mesh helps you create lace curtains and bags.

For the basic mesh stitch pattern, use the instructions for making spaces in filet crochet (see the earlier "Creating spaces" section for the how-to) to create a simple gridlike pattern of open squares that are neatly stacked on top of each other. To vary up your basic mesh stitch pattern, try the brick stitch. When worked with a sturdy cotton yarn, the brick stitch is perfect for making bags (like the later String Market Bag project). You can also use this mesh stitch variation to create a light, airy scarf for fall out of warm, worsted merino wool.

Follow these steps to work the brick stitch:

1. **Chain 32 (ch 32).**

2. **Double crochet (dc) in the 12th chain from the hook.**

   The 11 skipped stitches make up 4 skipped chains, 1 double crochet (3 chains), and a chain-4 space (ch-4 sp).

3. **Chain 4, skip 4 chain stitches, and work 1 double crochet in the next chain stitch.**

4. **Repeat Step 3 across to the end of the row and then turn.**

   You should have 5 brick-shaped spaces.

Here's how to work the second row of brick stitch:

1. **Chain 5 (ch 5).**

   These chains count as 1 triple crochet (tr) and 2 chains.

2. **Double crochet (dc) in the first chain-4 space (ch-4 sp).**

   Flip to Chapter 11 for help working into spaces and loops.

3. **Chain 4 and work 1 double crochet in the next chain-4 space.**

4. **Repeat Step 2 across to the chain-4 space before the space made by the turning chain in the previous row.**

5. **Chain 4, work 1 double crochet in the turning chain space, chain 2, double crochet in the seventh chain of the turning chain, and turn.**

To work the third row of the brick stitch pattern:

1. **Chain 7 (ch 7).**

   These chains count as 1 double crochet (dc) and 4 chain stitches.

2. **Work 1 double crochet in the next chain-4 space (ch-4 sp); then chain 4.**

3. **Repeat Step 2 across to the turning chain; work 1 double crochet in the third chain of the turning chain and then turn.**

Keep repeating Rows 2 and 3, and you'll see an alternating block pattern form that resembles a brick pattern. Check out a finished swatch of brick stitch in Figure 13-18.

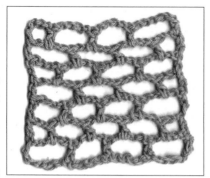

Figure 13-18:
A swatch of the brick stitch pattern.

By changing the number of chains in a basic mesh pattern, you can create a space that's wider or narrower. By changing the stitch height, substituting the double crochet for the single crochet or triple crochet, you can make the space shorter or taller.

Butterfly Runner Project

This beautiful filet crochet runner is a simple rectangle that uses spaces, blocks, bars, and lacets. We made the sample in the color section by using size 20 thread with a size 12 (0.75 mm) steel hook, but if you'd feel more comfortable using the larger size 10 thread with a size 7 (1.50 mm) steel hook, go right ahead. Your finished design will be larger but just as pretty.

If you're feeling pretty confident and want to spice up the runner a tad, you can shape the corners of it by using the increasing and decreasing technique. The runner shown in the color section of this book features this corner variation. (Don't worry. We include another chart and directions to help you with this change.)

Materials and vital statistics

- **Cotton thread:** DMC "Cebelia" size 20 crochet cotton (100% mercerized cotton), Article #167 (1.76 oz. [50 g], 405 yds [370 m] each ball): 1 ball of White

- **Hook:** Steel crochet hook size 12 U.S. (0.75 mm) or size needed to obtain gauge

- **Measurements:** 10 in. wide x 12½ in. long

- **Gauge:** 7 spaces = 2 in.; 9 rows dc = 2 in.

- **Stitches used:** Chain stitch (ch), slip stitch (sl st), single crochet (sc), double crochet (dc). **Filet st:** * Dc in dc, ch 2, skip next 2 sts *, 1 space made. * Dc in dc, dc in each of next 2 sts *, 1 block made. * Dc in dc, ch 3, skip next 2 sts, sc in next st, ch 3, skip next 2 sts *, 1 lacet made. * Dc in dc, ch 5, skip next 5 sts, or 2 spaces *, 1 bar made.

- **Additional stitches for corner option:** To dec 1 space at beg of row: Sl st to designated dc, ch 3 (first dc) to beg row. **To dec 1 space at end of row:** Work to designated dc, *turn* to beg next row.

Directions

For complete information on reading crochet instructions, refer to Chapter 4. With that said, have fun creating your first filet crochet masterpiece!

Ch 180 + 3 (first dc) + 2 (first space).

Row 1: Dc in eighth ch from hook, (ch 2, skip next 2 ch, dc in next ch) 4 times, * dc in each of next 6 ch, (ch 2, skip next 2 ch, dc in next ch) 4 times, * rep from * to * across until 3 ch remains, ch 2, skip next 2 ch, dc in last ch (first row of chart complete — 60 spaces and blocks), *turn.*

Rows 2–48: Work in blocks, spaces, bars, and lacets following chart (see Figure 13-19). Read all odd-numbered rows from right to left and all even-numbered rows from left to right. Fasten off at end of last row.

Figure 13-19: Chart and chart key for the Butterfly Runner project.

Optional directions for corner variation

Ch 150 + 3 (first dc).

Row 1: Dc in fourth ch from hook, dc in each of next 5 ch, * (ch 2, skip next 2 ch, dc in next ch) 4 times, dc in each of next 6 ch *; rep from * to * across (first row of chart complete — 50 spaces and blocks), *turn.*

Rows 2–48: Work in blocks, spaces, bars, and lacets following chart (see Figure 13-20). Read all odd-numbered rows from right to left and all even-numbered rows from left to right. Fasten off at end of last row.

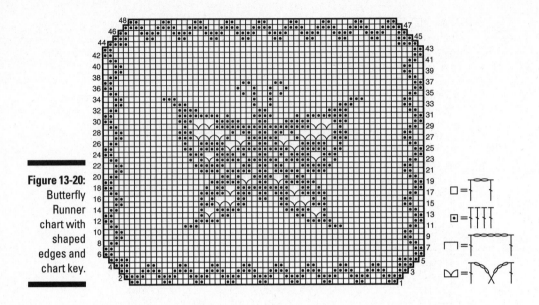

Figure 13-20:
Butterfly
Runner
chart with
shaped
edges and
chart key.

Finishing

Using liquid starch, block the finished piece (see Chapter 19 for instructions).

String Market Bag Project

The String Market Bag (which you can see in the color section) is the perfect accessory for a trip to the local farmers' market. The open mesh stitch pattern is stretchy and expands to fit almost anything you want to carry. When you're not using it, scrunch up the bag and toss it into your purse or car for unexpected shopping trips.

Easy-to-find, 100-percent cotton yarn makes this bag strong and sturdy. However, if you want or need to make a substitution for the yarn, suitable options are kitchen string and nylon twine.

Materials and vital statistics

✔ **Yarn:** Elmore-Pisgah "Peaches and Crème" worsted-weight soft cotton (100% cotton), Article #930 (2.5 oz. [71 g], 122 yds [111.5 m] each ball): 2 balls of #4 Ecru

- ✔ **Hook:** Crochet hook size H-8 U.S. (5 mm) or size needed to obtain gauge
- ✔ **4 stitch markers**
- ✔ **Large-eyed yarn needle**
- ✔ **Measurements:** 12 in. wide x 14 in. tall
- ✔ **Gauge:** 7 spaces = 2 in.; 9 rows dc = 2 in.
- ✔ **Stitches used:** Chain stitch (ch), slip stitch (sl st), single crochet (sc), double crochet (dc)

Directions

The following directions appear as you'd see them in a standard crochet publication, including the stitch diagram (see Figure 13-21). If you're having trouble deciphering the abbreviations, head to Chapter 4 for a refresher on Crochetese. Also, because the String Market Bag is worked in the round, you may want to visit Chapter 8 to brush up on this technique.

Top edging

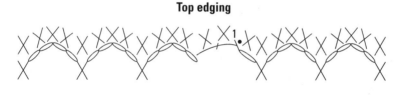

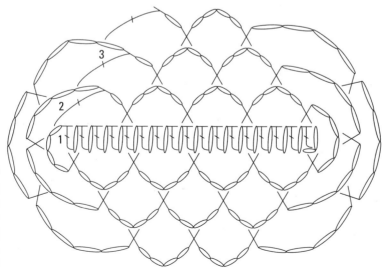

Figure 13-21:
The stitch
diagram for
the String
Market Bag.

Body

Fdc 53.

Rnd 1: Ch 4, working across bottom of foundation stitches, sc in chain at the bottom of the fdc just worked, * ch 4, skip next 3 ch, sc in next ch *; rep from * to * across to last ch, sc in last ch, ch 4, working across top of foundation stitches, sc in top of same fdc, ** ch 4, skip next 3 dc, sc in next dc **; rep from ** to ** across until 5 dc remain, sc in next dc, ch 1, dc in first ch-4 sp of rnd, place a marker in the dc just worked to help keep track of the rnds, *don't turn* — 28 loops.

Rnd 2: Ch 4, sc in same ch-4 sp you worked the dc into, * ch 4, sc in next ch-4 sp *; rep from * to * around to last ch-4 sp of the rnd, ch 4, sc in last ch-4 sp, ch 1, dc in first ch-4 sp of the rnd, move the marker up to dc just worked, *don't turn*.

Rep Rnd 2 until the bag measures 10 in. tall, or desired size.

Top edge

Rnd 1: 2 sc around the post of the dc just worked, * 3 sc in next ch-4 sp, sc in next sc *; rep from * to * around, work 1 sc in ch-1 sp at the end of last rnd, sl st in dc — 111 sc.

Rnds 2–3: Ch 1, sc in each st around, sl st in first sc to join — 111 sc.

Lay the bag down so that it's flat. Find the center st on one side of the bag that marks the separation between the front and back of the bag. Count 8 sts from the marker across the front of the bag and * place a marker in the next st, count 38 sts in the same direction, and place a marker in the next st * — these are the front markers. Count 16 sts around to the back, rep from * to * across the back. You should have 2 markers on the front and 2 markers on the back.

Bag handles

Rnd 1: Ch 1, sc in each st across to first front marker, ch 55, skip next 38 sc, sc into next front marker stitch, sc around to first back marker, ch 55, skip next 38 sc, sc into next back marker stitch, sc around to first sc, sl st in first sc to join.

Rnd 2: Sl st in each st around, sl st in first sl st to join. Fasten off. Weave in loose ends with the yarn needle.

Chapter 14

Building on Your Skills with Motifs

In This Chapter

▶ Making squares out of circles

▶ Playing with motifs of varying shapes and sizes

▶ Adorning yourself with a pair of classic earrings

▶ Creating blossoming flowers

*A*fter you know a few basic stitches and techniques, you're ready to crochet motifs. Considered the building blocks of crochet, *motifs* are small pieces that can be used on their own as doilies, jewelry, or appliqués. You can also join them together to create larger projects such as scarves, bags, or afghans. Because they're small and quick to stitch, motifs are great for using up bits and pieces of leftover yarn. If you like to take your projects with you, motifs are the perfect project for the crocheter on the go, fitting easily into your purse or bag.

Often using a foundation of simple geometric or nature-inspired patterns, motifs can be a variety of shapes, sizes, and colors. The possibilities are endless. This chapter shows you how to morph rounds (which we introduce in Chapter 8) into granny squares, which are the foundation of many square motifs. We also show you examples of a few playful motifs that you can use as decorative accents for your home or wardrobe, or as inspiration for your own designs. Motifs are a great way to get used to looking at stitch diagrams, so we give you the text instructions along with a stitch diagram for each motif.

At the end of this chapter, you can practice your new skills with a supersimple project that'll have you in a pair of pretty raindrop earrings in less than an hour. Or you can try out the Flower Power project, which leaves you with a three-dimensional appliqué flower you can use to garnish gifts and accessories.

Granny's a Square: Cornering Your Rounds

Just because you can work in rounds doesn't mean you can only make circles. Turning a circle into a square is very simple to do; just add four corners to your round. The *granny square* is an extremely common circle-turned-square that has been the foundation of crochet fashion for decades. In the following sections, we explain how to work a few rounds of the granny square motif; see Chapter 8 for an introduction to crocheting in the round.

The first round

Figure 14-1 is the stitch diagram for the granny square; it shows you how the rounds square off with the addition of four short chain loops for the corners. To start a typical granny square, follow these steps:

1. **Chain 4 (ch 4).**
2. **Close into a ring with 1 slip stitch (sl st) in the first chain.**

   This is your center ring.

Next, follow these instructions to complete the first round of your granny square:

1. **Chain 3 (ch 3) for your first double crochet (dc) and then work 2 more double crochet stitches into the ring. Chain 2.**

   Here's your first corner.

2. **Work 3 more double crochet stitches into the ring and chain 2.**
3. **Repeat Step 2 twice.**

   Tada! You now have your 4 corners, and each one is made of a chain-2 space between the sets of 3 double crochets.

4. **Join the round by working 1 slip stitch in the top of the turning chain (without turning your work).**

The second round

To go on to the second round of the granny square, proceed as follows:

1. **Slip stitch (sl st) across to the first chain-2 space (ch-2 sp) and then chain 3 (ch 3) for the first double crochet (dc).**

   Refer to Chapter 5 for info on traveling across stitches with the slip stitch.

2. **Work 2 double crochet stitches in the first chain-2 space, chain 2, and then work 3 more double crochet stitches in the same chain-2 space. Chain 1.**
3. **Work 3 double crochet stitches, chain 2, and then work 3 more double crochet stitches all in the next chain-2 space. Chain 1.**
4. **Repeat Step 3 twice to get to the last side of the motif; work 1 slip stitch in the top of the turning chain to join.**

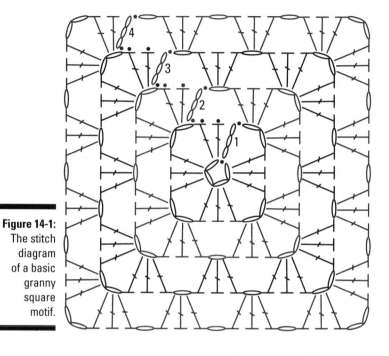

Figure 14-1:
The stitch diagram of a basic granny square motif.

The third round and beyond

1. **Slip stitch (sl st) across to the first chain-2 space (ch-2 sp) and then chain 3 (ch 3) for the first double crochet (dc).**

2. **Work 2 double crochet stitches in the first chain-2 space, chain 2, and then work 3 more double crochet stitches in the same chain-2 space. Chain 1.**

3. **Work 3 double crochet stitches in the next chain-1 space. Chain 1.**

4. **Work 3 double crochet stitches, chain 2, and then work 3 more double crochet stitches all in the next chain-2 space. Chain 1.**

5. **Repeat Steps 3 and 4 twice to get to the last side of the motif; repeat Step 3 once more; work 1 slip stitch in the top of the turning chain to join.**

You can add as many rounds as you want to the granny square. Heck, you can make it as big as an entire afghan if you want to. Just remember that each successive round has additional chain-1 spaces across the sides. Simply work three double crochet stitches, followed by a chain 1, in each space across the sides and work your corners the same way. (To see a completed granny square with four rounds, check out Figure 14-2.)

Figure 14-2:
A granny
square
swatch.

Don't Be Square: Motifs of Different Shapes

Squares and circles aren't the only ways to create motifs. They can have other geometric angles, such as stars and hexagons, or they can be fun shapes like hearts, raindrops, or flowers. Start with the motifs in the next sections and then use your newfound skills to try out motifs on your own.

The lacy hexagon motif

Commonly worked in the round, polygons such as triangles (which have three sides) and hexagons (which have six sides) follow the same concept as the granny square described earlier in this chapter; to shape them, you just need a different number of corners. Figure 14-3 shows the stitch diagram for a lacy hexagon motif with four rounds. Follow these simple instructions to start the motif:

1. **Chain 4 (ch 4).**

2. **Close into a ring with 1 slip stitch (sl st) in the first chain.**

    This is the center ring.

Work the first round as follows:

1. **Chain 3 (ch 3) to create the first double crochet (dc); then work 1 double crochet into the ring and chain 2.**

2. **Work 2 double crochet stitches and 2 chains into the ring 5 times; slip stitch (sl st) into the top of the turning chain to join.**

   You should have 6 chain-2 spaces (ch-2 sp) and 6 pairs of double crochet stitches.

To make the second round:

1. **Slip stitch (sl st) across to the next chain-2 space (ch-2 sp); then chain 3 (ch 3) for the first double crochet (dc).**

2. **Work 1 double crochet, 2 chains, and 2 double crochet in the same chain-2 space. Chain 1.**

3. **Work 2 double crochet, 2 chains, and 2 double crochet in the next chain-2 space. Chain 1.**

4. **Repeat Step 3 in each chain-2 space (the corner spaces) around; then slip stitch in the top of the beginning turning chain to join.**

If you want to make the lacy hexagon motif larger, simply continue adding rounds (refer to Figure 14-3, which shows four rounds). With each round you'll have one more chain-1 space, across the sides. Work two double crochet stitches in each chain-1 space, followed by a chain 1, across the sides and work your corners the same as you did on the first two rounds. Figure 14-4 shows a sample of a completed lacy hexagon motif.

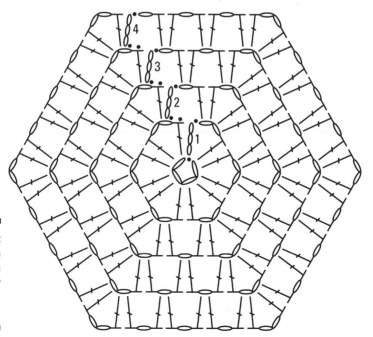

Figure 14-3:
The stitch
diagram
for the lacy
hexagon
motif.

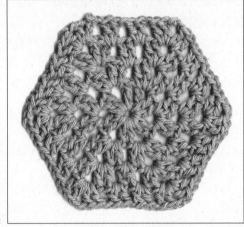

Figure 14-4:
A finished
sample of
the lacy
hexagon
motif.

You can also form many geometric shapes (such as hexagons and triangles) by working in rows and using the increasing and decreasing techniques found in Chapter 7.

The flat flower motif

Motif shapes don't have to be found in the geometry classroom; you may be inspired to make them from objects you find in nature or around your home. For example, attach a chain of green yarn to a circle crocheted in red yarn, and you have a delicious cherry. This section features instructions for creating a wonderful flat flower motif. Treat it as a topper for gifts and hats, or use it to add a little beauty to everyday items such as barrettes, bags, and even jeans.

Figure 14-5 shows the stitch diagram for three rounds of the flat flower motif. To start creating the motif, follow these steps:

1. **Chain 6 (ch 6).**

2. **Close into a ring with 1 slip stitch (sl st) in the first ch.**

   This is the center ring.

Now, follow these instructions to complete the first three rounds:

1. **Chain 1 (ch 1) and work 15 single crochet stitches (sc) into the ring; slip stitch (sl st) in the first single crochet to join.**

   The first round is complete.

2. **Chain 1 and single crochet in the first single crochet.**

3. **Chain 3, skip the next 2 single crochet, and then single crochet in the next single crochet.**

4. **Repeat Step 3 three more times.**

5. **Chain 3, skip the next 2 single crochet, and slip stitch in the first single crochet to join.**

   You've just made 5 chain-3 loops for the second round. (See Chapter 11 for more about spaces and loops.)

6. **Slip stitch into the first chain-3 loop (ch-3 lp) and then chain 1.**

7. **Work the following in each chain-3 loop: 1 single crochet, 1 half double crochet (hdc), 3 double crochet, 1 half double crochet, and 1 single crochet. Slip stitch in the first single crochet to join.**

   Your final round should leave you with 5 petals.

8. **Fasten off.**

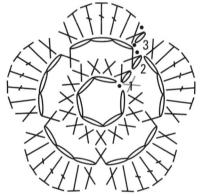

Figure 14-5:
The stitch diagram for the flat flower motif.

Figure 14-6 depicts a completed flower motif that you can use on its own or as the foundation for multiple layers, as shown in the next section.

The layered flower motif

Some motifs have multiple layers for a pleasing three-dimensional appearance. These types of motifs are good decorative accents for your wardrobe all on their own, but if you want, you can join them together to make a larger piece. In the preceding section, we show you how to make a flat flower motif (a flower with only one layer). In this section, you find out how to add layers to create a blossoming flower.

Figure 14-6:
A completed sample of the flat flower motif.

Figure 14-7 shows the stitch diagram for the layered flower motif. Begin with the flat flower motif described in the preceding section, but don't fasten off. To work the second layer of petals (which consists of two rounds), follow these steps:

1. **Chain 4 (ch 4), skip the next 6 stitches, and then slip stitch (sl st) in the next single crochet (sc).**

2. **Repeat Step 1 around the motif 4 times to make a total of 5 chain-4 loops (ch-4 lps).**

3. **Slip stitch in the first chain-4 loop. Chain 1.**

4. **Work 1 single crochet, 1 half double crochet (hdc), 2 double crochet (dc), 1 triple crochet (tr), 2 double crochet, 1 half double crochet, and 1 single crochet in each chain-4 loop around.**

5. **Slip stitch in the first single crochet to join.**

You've worked two rounds of a multilayered flower with these instructions, so now you're ready to compare your work to the sample in Figure 14-8. Continue adding layers with the Flower Power project at the end of this chapter to make a bigger blossoming flower.

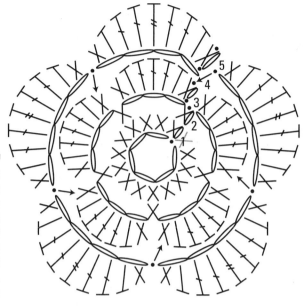

Figure 14-7:
The stitch diagram for the layered flower motif with two layers of petals.

Figure 14-8:
A finished sample of the layered flower motif.

Joining flower motifs is pretty easy if you sew petals at the tips or join them on the last round as you go (refer to Chapter 15 for joining methods). To join the flower petals on the last round, begin the last round of the flower as usual until you've made the first triple crochet stitch. Work one slip stitch in the triple crochet stitch on an already completed flower motif; then continue working the petals as before. Repeat the slip stitch method of joining stitches on the next petal so the flowers are connected at two petals. Make several flower motifs, using a variety of colors, and then join them together in a single row for a colorful scarf. Or try joining multiple rows together to make a garden-inspired shawl, bag, or blanket.

Raindrop Earrings Project

Using basic crochet stitches, you can fashion a pair of elegant earrings in a raindrop motif in just under an hour. These earrings are crocheted with mercerized crochet thread and a steel hook and then slightly stiffened to hold their shape. The color shown in the color section matches the cuff bracelet in Chapter 15, but if it doesn't appeal to you, go ahead and change it. Whatever color you choose, this project will make a wonderful accessory for you, your friends, and your family members.

You can make jewelry out of almost any crochet motif just by using crochet thread and a steel hook. Some motifs can be quite large, so feel free to experiment, working just two or three rounds to keep your project small and light.

Materials and vital statistics

- **Yarn:** Coats & Clark Aunt Lydia's "Fashion Crochet Thread" size 3 crochet thread (100% mercerized cotton), Article #182 (1.3 oz. [37 g], 150 yds [137 m] each ball): 1 ball of #65 Warm Teal

- **Hook:** Steel crochet hook size 1 U.S. (2.75 mm) or size needed to obtain gauge

- **Yarn needle**

- **Bowl or plastic baggie**

- **Aleene's Fabric and Draping Liquid (or any other type of fabric stiffener)**

- **Paper towels**

- **Parchment paper**

- **2 gold (or silver) jump rings**

- **2 gold (or silver) earring hooks**

- **Measurements:** 1 in. long

- **Gauge:** Motif = 1 in. long

- **Stitches used:** Chain stitch (ch), slip stitch (sl st), single crochet (sc), half double crochet (hdc), double crochet (dc), triple crochet (tr)

Directions

The directions here tell you how to make a raindrop motif and then assemble the earrings with common jewelry findings. We give them to you in standard crochet language, but if they seem like a bunch of gibberish, refer to Chapter 4 for help reading patterns. The stitch diagram in Figure 14-9 also shows you where to make your stitches.

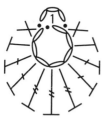

Figure 14-9: The stitch diagram of the raindrop earring motif.

Motif (make 2): Ch 7 and close into a ring with 1 sl st in first ch.

Rnd 1 (RS): Ch 1, work (1 sl st, 1 sc, 1 hdc, 2 dc, 3 tr, 2 dc, 1 hdc, 1 sc, and 1 sl st) into the ring, ch 3, sl st in first sl st to join.

Fasten off and weave in the ends using the yarn needle.

Finishing

Place the motifs into a bowl or a plastic baggie. Pour in equal parts water and fabric stiffener; there should be just enough to cover the motifs completely. Allow the motifs to become completely saturated; this should take 2 or 3 minutes. Remove the motifs from the mixture and dab with paper towels to remove excess stiffener. Lay the motifs out on a piece of parchment paper, shape them to the desired size, and allow them to dry completely.

Assembly

Using your fingers, open 1 jump ring and place it in the ch-3 space at the top of the motif. Join the earring hook to the jump ring and press the jump ring closed. Repeat for the second motif.

Flower Power Project

The three-dimensional flowers in this project (shown in the color section) are quick and easy to make — plus they let you show off your new motif skills. They make great package toppers, or you can eliminate the ties and sew them onto a hat.

This project gives you two different color options: Use one color of yarn for the whole flower or two different solid colors to create different-colored petals. You can also make the flowers smaller by using a lighter-weight yarn such as sport-weight with a size F-5 (3.75 mm) hook. To make them even smaller and more delicate, use cotton thread and a size 7 steel (1.5 mm) hook.

Materials and vital statistics

- **For solid and two-color flowers:** Coats & Clark Red Heart "Classic" worsted-weight yarn (100% acrylic), Article #E267 (3.5 oz. [100 g], 190 yds [174 m] each skein): 1 skein each of

  - #1 White

  - #230 Yellow

  - #912 Cherry Red

- **Hook:** Crochet hook size F-5 U.S. (3.75 mm) or size needed to obtain gauge

- **Yarn needle**

- **Measurements:** Approximately 3 in. in diameter

- **Gauge:** First 3 rnds = 1¾ in. in diameter

- **Stitches used:** Chain stitch (ch), slip stitch (sl st), single crochet (sc), half double crochet (hdc), double crochet (dc), triple crochet (tr)

Directions

The following instructions use Crochetese to explain how to make a flower motif with three layers. If you need to refresh your memory of crochet abbreviations, head to Chapter 4. Refer to the stitch diagram in Figure 14-10 as a another way to see where to make your stitches.

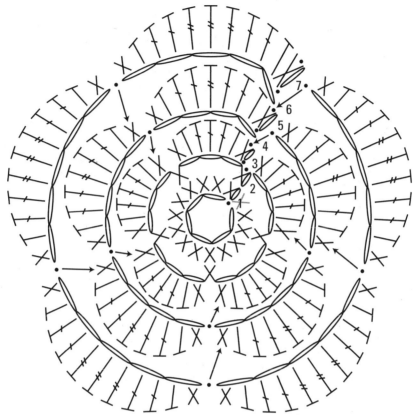

Figure 14-10:
The stitch
diagram for
the Flower
Power
project.

One-color flower

Work the layered flower motif described earlier in this chapter. Then work an additional layer of petals as follows:

Rnd 1: * Ch 5, skip next 8 sts, sl st in next sc *; rep from * to * around (5 chain-5 loops [ch-5 lps] made).

Rnd 2: Sl st in first ch-5 lp, ch 1, (sc, hdc, 2 dc, 3 tr, 2 dc, hdc, sc) in each ch-5 lp around (5 petals made), sl st in first sc to join. Fasten off.

Two-toned flower

For a two-toned flower, you work the stitches the same way as in the one-color flower. Work the center ring and Round 1 in the first color. Fasten off the first color and join the second color. Work Rounds 2–5 in the second color. Fasten off and join the first color to work Rounds 6 and 7.

Ties

If you want to tie the flower to a package, make a tie in your desired color.

Make a chain 2 inches longer than the combined circumference of the package in both directions. Fasten off, leaving a 6-inch sewing length. Wrap the tie around the package in both directions, with the ends meeting at the center top. Tie the ends in a knot at the center top.

Curlicues

Create as many curlicues as desired in colors to match or contrast with your flowers.

Make a chain long enough to reach from the flower to the edge of the package.

Row 1: 3 sc in second ch from hook, 3 sc in each ch across. Fasten off, leaving a 6-in. sewing length. With yarn needle and sewing lengths, sew 1 end to WS of Rnd 1 of flower as desired.

Finishing

Arrange the flower on top of the package as desired. With a yarn needle and the extra sewing lengths, sew the flower to the ties.

Part IV
Putting It All Together

The 5th Wave
By Rich Tennant

"Don't get me wrong, it's beautiful. But you make
a mistake crocheting a hat or a scarf, what's
the worst that can happen? Now, a crocheted
parachute is another thing."

In this part . . .

A crocheted project is rarely complete when you fasten off the last row or round. Certain finishing techniques help to complement and enhance your project.

This part presents several methods for neatly joining projects made in pieces and shows you how to add fun finishing touches and embellishments. You also find out all you need to know about sweater basics and construction so you can make the simple garments featured in Chapters 16 and 17. Finally, we offer tips on caring for your valuable crocheted handiwork so that it always looks its best and can withstand the test of time.

Chapter 15

Connecting the Parts: Joining Seams

In This Chapter

▶ Sewing up parts to create a whole

▶ Joining pieces with a variety of crochet stitches

▶ Fashioning a versatile cuff bracelet

*W*hether you're working with the seams of a garment, the individual motifs of an afghan, or the long panels of a shawl, the techniques for joining crocheted pieces are many and varied. Do you want a visible or an invisible seam? Is the seam an integral part of the overall design, or is it purely functional? Should you crochet the seam, or do you feel more comfortable sewing it?

If you're crocheting a design pattern, the instructions usually tell you how to put the pieces together. However, if you don't care for that method or you just want to try another one, feel free to experiment. This chapter details several joining methods so you can choose the one that's best for you, and the project at the end of this chapter gives you an opportunity to try out joining on the last round. The Simple Sweater project in Chapter 16 and the Girl's Versatile Camisole project in Chapter 17 let you practice other methods for creating seams.

No matter which method you use to join your pieces together, you definitely want to keep them evenly aligned so you don't end up with extra fabric sticking out on one side or the other when you're all done. To make sure you're joining the pieces together evenly, pin them together with a few sewing pins or safety pins. Start by pinning the pieces together at the top, then the middle, and finally the bottom. If you see lots of space between the pins, add a few more to fill in the gaps. Then remove the pins as you work your seam.

Sewing Pieces Together

When the seams of a piece are functional rather than decorative, sewing them together is probably your best bet. A sewn seam is flexible and nearly invisible, plus it doesn't add any additional bulk. You don't need a sewing machine or many special tools to join pieces by sewing; just grab a yarn needle or a tapestry needle, whichever works with the material you're using, and the leftover yarn or cotton that you used to crochet your design. (See Chapter 2 for more information on needles.)

When you want to sew pieces together, you have a variety of stitches to choose from, namely the whipstitch, the blanket stitch, the mattress stitch, and the backstitch. Each of these stitches has its purpose, and your pattern should tell you which one to use in your project. If it doesn't, know that the whipstitch is always a good stitch to lean on. We guide you through the process of creating these stitches in the following sections.

Regardless of whether you're working with the whipstitch, the blanket stitch, the mattress stitch, or the backstitch, take care not to pull the yarn too tight as you sew. If you do, the fabric will pucker. Keep your stitches even and neat, and you're sure to end up with a beautifully finished seam.

If the design you're sewing together has a striped pattern, leave a yarn tail at least 6 inches long at the beginning and end of each stripe. This way you have the correct yarn colors available and positioned right where you need them when you're ready to sew the pieces together. To do just that, slip your yarn needle onto the tail and sew the corresponding color stripes together. (This move saves you a lot of time when you're finishing up your project.)

Whipping up the whipstitch for shorter stitches

The *whipstitch* is best for joining rows made up of the shorter stitches, such as single crochet, half double crochet, and double crochet. When you're sewing the side seams of a garment, you join the pieces by sewing the row-ends together. When you're sewing shoulder seams or motifs, you generally work in the tops of the stitches. The key to joining seams together successfully with the whipstitch is to match up the crocheted stitches on each side of the seam using straight, even stitches and without pulling too tightly. For projects that use the whipstitch, check out the Simple Sweater project in Chapter 16 and the Girl's Versatile Camisole project in Chapter 17.

Whipstitching seams together while holding the right sides of the fabric facing each other is a common technique that allows the seam to be hidden on the inside of your project. The whipstitch can also be used to create a decorative seam, especially when you're sewing motifs together. To do this, put the wrong sides of the motifs facing each other, match their stitches across each edge, and sew the motifs together through the back loops of the stitches only. Doing so creates a raised ridge on the right side of the work.

To make a whipstitch:

1. **Position the pieces with right sides (or wrong sides, depending on the pattern) facing each other, taking care to match the stitches across each side edge.**

2. **Using a yarn needle and matching yarn, weave the yarn back and forth through several stitches on one of the pieces to secure the end.**

   You can tie a small knot at the beginning of the seam if you want to secure it better, but it usually isn't necessary.

3. **Insert the needle and pull the yarn through the inside loops of the first 2 corresponding stitches of the 2 pieces to be joined.**

   Figure 15-1 shows the correct positioning of the needle in the inside loops.

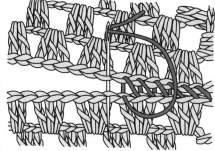

Figure 15-1: Making a whipstitch.

4. **Draw the needle up and over the 2 loops of the first stitch.**

   Pull the yarn tightly enough so the pieces of fabric are fairly snug against each other, but not so tightly that the stitches become distorted.

5. **Repeat Steps 3 and 4 across the edges to be joined.**

6. **At the end of the seam, weave the yarn back through several stitches to secure.**

   If you're not sure how to weave in ends, flip to Chapter 5. Otherwise, check out Figure 15-2 to see a completed whipstitch seam.

Figure 15-2:
A completed
whipstitch
seam.

Saving the blanket stitch for taller stitches

The *blanket stitch* is a good choice when you're joining pieces consisting of taller stitches, such as triple crochet and taller. This stitch adds some stability to the backside of the seam and reduces the seam's tendency to gap.

Always join taller stitches at the top and at the base, which is how the stitches are joined to each other within the fabric.

To make a blanket stitch, follow these steps:

1. **With the correct sides facing each other (right side/wrong side, depending on the pattern), open up the pieces and lay them side by side on a flat, smooth surface, aligning the edges and stitches.**

2. **Using a yarn needle and matching yarn, thread the yarn through the base of the first few corresponding stitches, leaving a yarn length of 6 to 8 inches to weave in later to secure the seam.**

3. **Lay the working end of the yarn against the fabric in the direction of the stitches, as shown in Figure 15-3.**

4. **Thread your yarn through the base of the next 2 corresponding stitches, making sure that the working end of the yarn is underneath the needle (refer to Figure 15-3).**

5. **Repeat Steps 3 and 4 across the edges to be joined.**

6. **At the end of the seam, weave the yarn back through several stitches to secure.**

   Figure 15-4 shows a complete blanket stitch seam, and Chapter 5 explains how to weave in ends if you need a refresher.

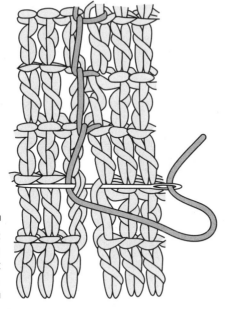

Figure 15-3:
Making
a blanket
stitch.

Figure 15-4:
A completed
blanket
stitch seam.

Creating invisible seams with the mattress stitch

The *mattress stitch,* also known as the *invisible seam* or *invisible weaving,* is a very flexible seam that works best for sewing garment pieces together because it makes for a flat, invisible seam. You always work this stitch with the right sides facing up so you can make sure the seam is invisible on its best side. The key to this stitch is to make small stitches, weaving your needle back and forth between the two pieces while working up the inside of the edges to be joined.

Here's how to use the mattress stitch to sew the row ends of two pieces worked in double crochet:

1. **Place the pieces to be joined on a flat table with the right sides facing you.**

   The pieces should be side by side. Make sure the stitches themselves are aligned and that any stripes or patterns are aligned too. (If you're having trouble keeping everything aligned, you can always use safety pins or sewing pins to keep the 2 pieces together.)

2. **With an 18-inch length of yarn (or the long tail end) threaded onto a yarn needle, insert the needle up through the bottom-most stitch of 1 piece and out the middle of the post, or turning chain, of the same stitch, as shown in Figure 15-5a.**

   If you're not using a tail end, leave a 6-inch tail with your first stitch so you can weave it in later.

3. **Insert your needle up through the corresponding stitch of the second piece and out the middle of the post, or turning chain, of the stitch, like in Figure 15-5b.**

   If you aren't using a secured tail end, weave the needle through the same stitches referenced in Steps 2 and 3 to secure the yarn.

4. **Insert your needle in the same spot where the last stitch came out on the opposite piece and bring it up and out the top of the double crochet stitch (dc), as in Figure 15-6a.**

5. **Insert your needle in the same spot of the corresponding double crochet on the second piece and draw it out of the top of the double crochet. (Refer to Figure 15-6b.)**

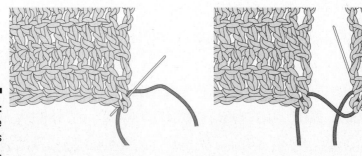

Figure 15-5:
Starting the mattress stitch.

a   b

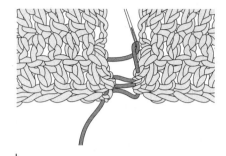

Figure 15-6:
Joining
the sides
through
the next 2
stitches.

a   b

6. **Pull the yarn to draw the 2 pieces together, but not so tight that the fabric puckers.**

7. **Continue weaving your needle back and forth as you move up the inside edges, making 2 stitches along the post of each double crochet on each piece to be joined (see Figure 15-7).**

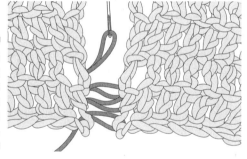

Figure 15-7:
Continuing
to join the
pieces with
the mattress
stitch.

8. **To fasten off, weave the yarn back and forth 1 more time through the last 2 stitches worked and cut the yarn, leaving a 6-inch tail for weaving in.**

Figure 15-8 presents you with two finished pieces joined with the mattress stitch. Figure 15-8a shows the opened mattress stitch; Figure 15-8b shows the complete, closed mattress stitch.

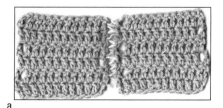

Figure 15-8:
The
completed
mattress
stitch seam.

a   b

You can work the mattress stitch to join pieces of any stitch height. Just make sure you weave the yarn back and forth using evenly spaced stitches. For single crochet stitches, simply insert the needle through the bottom-most stitch and out the top of the same stitch; then do the same for the corresponding stitch on the second piece. For the next row, move up to the next stitch. For the triple crochet, weave the needle back and forth three times for each post before moving on to the next row.

If you're using the mattress stitch along the top loops of a row, simply follow the preceding steps for sewing the row ends; just be sure to keep your stitches short.

Fashioning sturdy seams with the backstitch

The *backstitch* produces a strong, bulky seam that doesn't have a lot of stretch. Use it whenever you need to join two pieces together with a sturdy seam, like for bags or baskets. You work the backstitch on the wrong side of the project because it's visible (and not exactly pretty).

The key to understanding the backstitch is to think of it as two steps forward and one step back. This is because you bring the needle to the front of your fabric two spaces forward and then push it to the back of the fabric one space back.

You can use the backstitch to join pieces along the tops or sides of the parts that need joining. If you're working along the top edges, simply stitch the seam under the top loops of a stitch. If you're working along the side edges, insert your needle under the two threads found along the side of the stitch's post. (See Chapter 5 for a refresher on stitch anatomy.)

To join two pieces along the top edge by using the backstitch:

1. **Pin the 2 pieces together with their right sides facing each other and their edges aligned.**

   If you're seaming the sides of the pieces, make sure the rows are lined up; if you're seaming the top edges of the pieces, make sure their stitches are lined up.

2. **With an 18-inch length of yarn (or the long tail end) threaded onto your yarn needle, insert the needle from front to back under the top loops of the first stitch, pushing the needle through both layers.**

Figure 15-9a illustrates this step, which starts at the upper-right corner and gets worked from right to left if you're right-handed. Lefties do the reverse.

3. **Bring the needle back to the front about a ¼ inch farther along the seam, as shown in Figure 15-9b.**

   You're always working through both layers.

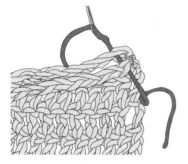

Figure 15-9:
Beginning a
backstitch
seam.

a   b

4. **Bring the needle back to the first spot and insert it from front to back.**

5. **Repeat Steps 3 and 4 twice.**

   You've now secured the yarn to the beginning of the seam, so you're ready to start backstitching.

6. **Bring the needle back to the front a ½ inch farther along the seam.**

   This is about a ¼ inch farther than where you brought it to the front the last time, as you can see in Figure 15-10a — hence the "2 spaces forward" concept.

7. **Insert the needle from front to back a ¼ inch back along the seam. (Refer to Figure 15-10b.)**

   This is the same spot where you brought the yarn to the front on the last stitch, hence the "1 space back" idea.

8. **Repeat Steps 6 and 7 as you work along the seam edge to the end designated by your pattern.**

9. **To secure the yarn, work the last stitch 2 or 3 times in the same spots and then cut the yarn, leaving a 6-inch tail for weaving in later.**

Figure 15-11 shows a finished backstitch seam.

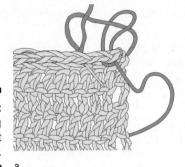
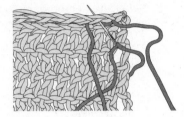

Figure 15-10:
Working
the next
stitches.

a   b

Figure 15-11:
The com-
pleted
backstitch
seam.

Crocheting Pieces Together

Sometimes a pattern asks you to crochet your seams, whether for functional or decorative purposes. A crocheted seam is strong and comes in handy when joining pieces that are going to be put through a lot of wear and tear, such as motifs in an afghan. It can also become a part of your design if you work it on the right side of the fabric.

If the wrong sides of the pieces are facing each other when you join a seam, then the crocheted seam appears on the right side. If the right sides are facing, then the crocheted seam appears on the wrong side. Take a few seconds to make sure your pieces are facing in the correct direction based on where you want your seam to appear before joining them. Trust us, ripping out a seam is pretty frustrating.

In the following sections, we show you different methods for crocheting your pieces together with slip stitches, single crochet stitches, and more.

Joining with a slip stitch seam

A slip stitch seam is secure but a little inflexible. When you work it on the wrong side of the fabric, this seam is great for items that take a beating, like purses and tote bags. If worked on the right side of the fabric, the slip stitch seam looks like an embroidered chain stitch. You can join pieces with the slip stitch to create two different looks: a ridged seam or a flat seam. The Girl's Versatile Camisole project in Chapter 17 is an example of joining pieces with a slip stitch seam.

Creating a ridged seam

If you choose to create a ridge along your seam, you can either hide it (on the wrong side of the fabric) or make it part of the design (on the right side). Ridged seams are sometimes used to create a decorative look, like in an afghan made up of motifs; you can use a contrasting color to add another design element. Here's how to slip stitch a ridged seam:

1. **Position the 2 pieces together with right sides facing (for a wrong side seam) or wrong sides together (for a right side seam).**

   Make sure the stitches across each edge match.

2. **Working through the double thickness of both pieces and using the same size crochet hook that you used in the design, insert your hook through the back 2 loops of the first 2 stitches, leaving a yarn tail about 6 inches long.**

   Figure 15-12 shows the correct positioning of the hook in the back loops.

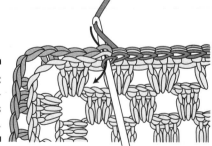

Figure 15-12: Slip stitching pieces together.

3. **Yarn over the hook (yo).**

4. **Pull the yarn through and repeat Steps 2 and 3 in each stitch across; fasten off and weave in the ends.**

Take a look at the completed ridged seam in Figure 15-13 and refer to Chapter 5 for the how-to on weaving in ends.

Figure 15-13:
Two crocheted pieces joined with a ridged slip stitch seam.

Creating a flat seam

You can slip stitch two pieces together to create a flat seam, which crocheters often use when they want the seam to be invisible (think of a side seam joining the front and back of a sweater). To slip stitch a seam in this fashion:

1. **Lay the 2 pieces to be joined side by side on a flat surface, with right sides facing up (for a right side seam) or wrong sides facing up (for a wrong side seam).**

   Check that the stitches across each edge match before moving on.

2. **Working in the top loops of the stitches only and using the same size crochet hook you used in the design, insert your hook through the loops of the first 2 stitches, leaving a yarn tail several inches long.**

   Figure 15-14 shows the correct positioning of the hook in the loops.

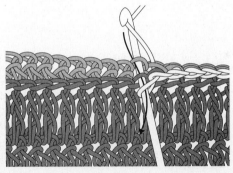

Figure 15-14:
Creating a flat seam by slip stitching.

3. **Yarn over the hook (yo).**

4. **Pull the yarn through the loops and repeat Steps 2 and 3 in each stitch across. Fasten off and weave in the ends as described in Chapter 5.**

   Figure 15-15 shows you what a completed flat seam should look like.

Figure 15-15:
Two pieces joined with a flat slip stitch seam.

Joining with single crochet

When you join two pieces with single crochet stitches, you create a sturdy seam that's more flexible than one created with slip stitches. A seam made with single crochet creates a raised ridge that looks like a decorative chain. If you work it in a matching or contrasting color, it can become an integral part of your design.

Using single crochet stitches to join the seam in a garment has both positive and negative sides. When used for a strictly functional purpose (to join pieces together), the single crochet seam can cause uncomfortable lumpiness if it's on the inside of the finished piece. However, used on the right, or outside of the work, it can add wonderful texture and another design element to your creation.

Follow these steps to work a seam using single crochet stitches:

1. **Position the pieces with the right sides (or wrong sides) together and match the stitches across each side edge.**

2. **Working through the double thickness of both pieces and using the same size crochet hook that you used when creating the design, insert your hook through the top 2 loops of the first 2 corresponding stitches.**

   Figure 15-16 shows the correct positioning of the hook in the top loops.

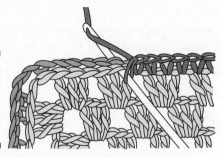

Figure 15-16:
Creating a seam with single crochet.

3. Yarn over the hook (yo).

4. Pull the yarn through both stitches, as shown in Figure 15-16.

5. Yarn over and pull the yarn through the 2 loops on your hook.

6. Insert the hook through the top 2 loops of the next 2 corresponding stitches and then repeat Steps 3 through 5 in each stitch across.

7. Finish by fastening off and weaving in the ends with the yarn needle.

Figure 15-17 depicts a completed single crochet seam.

Figure 15-17:
A decorative single crochet seam on the right side of the work.

Joining with a row of stitches

Joining two pieces with another row of stitches creates a different look from the other seams presented earlier in this chapter. Instead of working through the double thickness of two crocheted pieces, you work back and forth between them, usually on the right side of the piece. The row between the two pieces can be as narrow as a single stitch, or it can be wide and lacy. You can use this joining method to connect motifs when making a shawl, to add interest to the side seams of a garment, or to join panels when crocheting an afghan.

To crochet a joining row that's a chain-2 space wide:

1. **Lay the pieces side by side on a flat surface, matching stitches across the adjacent edges that you're going to join.**

2. **Insert your hook under the top 2 loops in the designated stitch on the first piece, chain 1 (ch 1), single crochet (sc) in the same stitch, and then chain 2 stitches for the joining row.**

3. **Insert your hook under the top 2 loops of the designated corresponding stitch on the second piece, yarn over (yo), and pull the yarn through the stitch. (Refer to Figure 15-18.)**

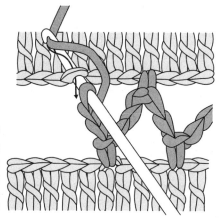

Figure 15-18: Crocheting a joining row.

4. **Yarn over, draw the yarn through the 2 loops on your hook, and single crochet the stitch complete.**

5. **Chain 2, insert your hook under the top 2 loops of the designated stitch on the first piece, yarn over, and pull the yarn through the stitch.**

6. **Yarn over and draw the yarn through the 2 loops on your hook.**

7. **Chain 2; then repeat Steps 3 through 6 across the row to the ending point designated in the pattern.**

8. **Fasten off and weave in the ends with the yarn needle.**

   Check out Figure 15-19 to see a completed seam made with a row of stitches.

Figure 15-19:
A seam
made by
joining with
a row of
stitches.

Joining on the last row or round

Some pieces, like the motifs we cover in Chapter 14, are joined together while working the last row or round. Joining pieces as you go saves you from the daunting task of having to sew or crochet lots (and lots!) of pieces together at the end of a project.

Because motifs use an endless variety of stitch patterns, not all of them are joined in the same spot, but some general guidelines do exist:

Crocheting seamlessly

If you think seams are pretty unappealing looking in sweaters, or if you just hate making them, we bet you'll be delighted to know that there are several interesting and attractive sweater styles you can create with few, if any, seams. Here are some ideas:

✔ Search out a pattern for a raglan-style sweater. You can work this style of sweater without a single seam from the neck down, all in one piece.

✔ Work a cardigan in one piece across the fronts and the back to the armholes; then

work the fronts and backs off of the body. The only sewing you have to do is the shoulder seams.

✔ Work the sleeves of a sweater in rounds and directly off of the armholes, thus eliminating the underarm and shoulder seams.

✔ Trim cuffs and bottom edges in post double crochet ribbing right off of the edges of the sweater (see Chapter 17 for more on ribbing).

✔ Motifs that have side edges, like squares or triangles, are usually joined along one or more sides.

✔ Motifs with points (think flowers and stars) are joined at one or more points.

Note: The pattern you're working should let you know exactly where to place your joining stitches. If for some reason it doesn't, then you're working with a poor pattern.

Following are the general steps for joining on the last round of a granny square motif. (You can get even more practice with this technique by giving the Granny Square Cuff project at the end of this chapter a shot.)

1. **Work the first granny square completely and fasten off.**

   Head to Chapter 14 for instructions on creating the granny square motif.

2. **Work the next square until you reach the point where you want to join the 2 pieces together.**

   This point is usually a corner stitch or chain space.

3. **Work the corner stitch or chain for the square you're currently on, as described in Chapter 14.**

4. **Holding the 2 pieces with wrong sides together, insert your hook from the back of the current square into the same corner stitch or space of the square you completed in Step 1.**

5. **Yarn over and draw your hook through the corner stitch, or space, and the stitch on your hook, as shown in Figure 15-20.**

   You now have a slip stitch seam at the corner.

Figure 15-20:
Joining
pieces on
the last
round.

6. **Continue working the stitches across the side of the square, joining stitches or spaces as directed.**

7. Finish the square you're working on to the end of the round and fasten off; weave in any loose ends using a yarn needle.

Continue working any remaining motifs the same way. To see what 2 pieces joined together on the last round look like, see Figure 15-21.

If you're working a row of squares, like for a scarf, you have to join squares on only one side. If you're working a blanket or a shawl, however, you need to join the pieces together on more than one side. Blanket and shawl designs often consist of several rows containing a number of motifs that must be joined, which is why you join them on more than one side.

Figure 15-21:
A seam created by joining two pieces on the last round.

Granny Square Cuff Project

This simple cuff (shown in the color section) is the perfect project to get you started with joining motifs as you go, which means you don't have to do any seaming at the end. This project uses crochet thread that's easy to find in most yarn and craft stores (see Chapter 2 for more info). Crochet thread is available in a variety of colors and fibers, so you can make a cuff for any occasion. Use a metallic thread to add bling for a night on the town or try a natural-colored cotton for a summer outing. Quick to stitch, you'll want to make one of these cuffs for you and all of your girlfriends.

Materials and vital statistics

- **Yarn:** Coats & Clark Aunt Lydia's "Fashion Crochet Thread" size 3 crochet thread (100% mercerized cotton), Article #182 (1.3 oz. [37 g], 150 yds [137 m] each ball): 1 ball of #65 Warm Teal

- ✔ **Hook:** Steel crochet hook size 1 U.S. (2.75 mm) or size needed to obtain gauge
- ✔ **Bowl or plastic baggie**
- ✔ **Fabric stiffener**
- ✔ **Paper towels**
- ✔ **1-in. plastic shaft button**
- ✔ **Yarn needle**
- ✔ **Measurements:** 7 in. long x 2 in. wide
- ✔ **Gauge:** Motif = 1½ in. square
- ✔ **Stitches used:** Chain stitch (ch), slip stitch (sl st), single crochet (sc), double crochet (dc)

Directions

In a nutshell, here's how you make the Granny Square Cuff: Crochet one granny square motif completely; then make a second motif and join it to the first motif on the last round. Make and join two more motifs in the same manner to form a row of motifs. Easy as pie!

If looking at the following instructions has you thinking aliens took over our bodies and made us write in a strange language, then refer to Chapter 4 for a crash course in reading Crochetese. The stitch diagram in Figure 15-22 also shows you where to join your motifs.

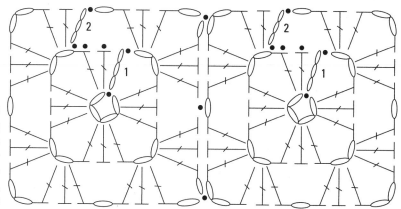

Figure 15-22:
The stitch diagram for the Granny Square Cuff.

First granny square motif

Follow the directions in Chapter 14 to make 2 rounds of a basic granny square. Fasten off.

Remaining granny square motifs

Rnd 1: Work the first round like you did for the first granny square motif.

Rnd 2: Sl st across to first ch-2 sp, ch 3 (counts as first dc), work (2 dc, ch 2, 3 dc) all in same ch-2 sp, ch 1, work (3 dc, ch 2, 3 dc) in next ch-2 sp, ch 1, work 3 dc in next ch-2 sp, ch 1, holding both pieces with WS together sl st in corresponding corner of completed square, work 3 dc in same ch-2 sp of the current square, sl st in next ch-1 sp of completed square, work 3 dc in next ch-2 sp of current square, sl st in next corresponding corner of completed square, ch 1, work 3 dc in same ch-2 sp of current square, ch 1, sl st in top of turning chain to join. Fasten off.

Repeat these steps for a third and fourth motif forming a single row of motifs.

Edging

With RS facing you, join thread to ch-2 sp at the upper-right corner of 1 short end of the cuff, ch 1, work 3 sc in same ch-2 sp, sc in each dc and ch-1 sp across the short end of the cuff, * work 3 sc in next corner ch-2 sp, working across the long end of the cuff to the next corner ch-2 sp, work 1 sc in each (dc, ch-1 sp, and sl st that joins motifs together) *, work 3 sc in next corner ch-2 sp, sc in next 2 dc, ch 6 for button loop, skip next (dc, ch-1 sp, and dc), sc in next 2 dc; rep from * to * once, sl st in first sc to join. Fasten off. Weave in any loose ends using the yarn needle.

Finishing

Place the cuff in a bowl or sandwich baggie. Pour equal parts water and fabric stiffener (just enough to cover the cuff completely) into the bowl or baggie. Allow the cuff to become completely saturated before removing it from the mixture and dabbing it with paper towels to remove any excess stiffener. Lay the cuff on a piece of parchment paper, straighten it, open up the lacy stitches, and allow it to dry completely.

Assembly

Using the button loop as a guide, sew the button to the opposite side of the cuff with the yarn needle.

Chapter 16

Design 101: Crocheting Your First Sweater

. . . .

In This Chapter

▶ Selecting sweater patterns and colors that suit you perfectly

▶ Flattering your unique form with a great style

▶ Making sure your sweater is just the right size

▶ Fleshing out your cool-weather wardrobe with a simple sweater

. . . .

Does the idea of crocheting a sweater make you break out in a sweat? There's really no need to be nervous, we promise. Although crocheting a sweater may seem like a daunting task, it's really quite easy. Many sweater designs are nothing more than squares sewn together. The simple shaping involved in these designs is as easy as increasing or decreasing a few stitches in the designated places. (Chapter 7 gives you step-by-step directions for increasing and decreasing.) Of course, you'll want to take a few points into consideration before you dig in.

First off, you want to choose a design that you like and that suits your physique. And if you're new to the craft, you also need to consider the difficulty of the pattern. You want to choose your materials carefully, too, picking a yarn that's easy to work with so you don't become frustrated and give up before you finish.

This chapter shows you various sweater styles and how to construct them. You also see how sweaters are sized so you can adjust patterns to suit your needs. And at the end of the chapter, we give you instructions for a simple sweater that you can crochet in no time flat.

Choosing Stitches and Yarn for Your Sweater

To guarantee your first sweater attempt isn't your last, choose your stitch pattern and yarn carefully. You can crochet beautiful sweaters with simple stitch patterns and readily available yarns. The sections that follow give you a heads-up on what to keep in mind.

Making the right pattern choice

First and foremost, make sure the pattern you're considering isn't too complicated for your skill level before you buy it or any of the materials. (Refer to Chapter 4 if you need help reading patterns.) Here are some factors to consider:

✔ If you want a sweater design that has an open, lacy pattern, try a pattern that uses yarn (it's easier to work with than the cotton thread many lacy patterns call for) and a simple stitch repeat.

✔ If you want to crochet a sweater with more than one color, choose a pattern that has stripes or many different-colored motifs (see Chapter 14 for more on motifs). Crocheting a pattern with color changes throughout is much more difficult than working a sweater in simple stripes or motifs. Another option is to use a multicolored or variegated yarn, both of which give you color variation without you having to worry about changing yarn colors constantly (see Chapter 2 for info on substituting yarns).

✔ As a newbie, you want to avoid a pattern that calls for crocheting with two strands of yarn held together as one. Working with more than one strand of yarn can be confusing.

✔ For your first sweater, find a pattern that suggests a smooth yarn, such as wool or a wool blend, or a synthetic yarn, such as acrylic. These yarns are easier to work with than highly textured novelty yarns, such as *bouclé* or *eyelash* yarn. (Flip to Chapter 2 for details on the various types of yarn.) The extra tufts on some novelty yarns make for a bumpy crochet experience, and if you happen to make a mistake and have to tear out some stitches, you may end up tearing out your hair as well.

✔ Choose a pattern that you like, or else be prepared to lose interest within the first ten minutes.

If you're brave enough to go ahead and buy a pattern with new stitches, be sure to work a practice swatch to get a feel for them before beginning your sweater.

Finding the right yarn

Choosing the right yarn to work with means more than just picking your favorite color. You also need to select a yarn that complements the pattern and yet won't tie you up in knots while you're crocheting with it. Of course, the pattern usually recommends a yarn so you have a ballpark idea of the yarn weight you need, such as sport weight or worsted weight, and the yarn material, such as acrylic or wool blend. (Head to Chapter 2 for the full details on yarn weights and materials.)

Keep in mind the following factors when you go yarn shopping:

- ✔ **Feel:** For a softer sweater, choose a lighter-weight yarn or a pattern with looser stitches. Although some of the bulky-weight yarns are relatively light, crocheting with the heavier weights of yarn quite often produces a stiff sweater that feels a bit like a cardboard box — definitely not an attractive (or comfortable!) option.

- ✔ **Fiber content:** Generally, natural fibers make for a more attractive and comfortable garment; however, they can be expensive and may require hand washing or dry cleaning. For your first sweater, *blends* (yarns that contain natural fibers along with synthetic fibers) and acrylic yarns may be more practical and easier to work with. Don't forget to check the label to see whether the blend is machine washable.

Mixing materials can lead to disastrous results when you wash your sweater, so if a pattern calls for two or more yarn types or colors, be sure to compare the care instructions on the yarn labels. Always choose yarns with the same laundering requirements.

- ✔ **Twist:** Use yarns with a nice twist to the strand; yarns without much twist have a tendency to split while you're crocheting.

- ✔ **Quantity:** When buying yarn for a project, be sure to purchase enough for the entire project. The materials list at the beginning of the pattern specifies the amount you need in order to complete the design. If you run out, you may not be able to find the color you need in the same *dye lot* (yarn dyed in the same batch), which means you may end up with an unplanned two-tone sweater.

- ✔ **Quality:** Don't skimp on materials. You get what you pay for, and after all your hard work, you want a sweater that retains its beauty for years to come.

Selecting a Super Sweater Style

You work most sweater designs in separate pieces — the back, the front (or fronts for a cardigan), the sleeves, and any desired borders — and sew or crochet them together after you complete them. (See Chapter 15 for how to join pieces of crochet.) How you make these pieces and put them together determines the sweater's style. The simpler styles have little or no shaping to the pieces, but more complicated designs may have shaping or decreasing around the armholes and at the neck. The next sections show you several basic sweater designs you may want to consider.

For your first sweater, choose a pattern with simple shaping. Most sweater patterns include a *schematic* — a diagram of the sweater construction. The schematic includes the important measurements, such as the width of the back and front(s), the *armhole depth* (the size of the opening that you put your arms through), the sleeve length, and the finished back length.

Baring your arms: Sleeveless sweaters

The simplest sleeveless sweater styles have two panels that you join at the center back and center front, producing a V-neck with a small overhang at the shoulders (see Figure 16-1a). You can make a shell, one of the other sleeveless styles, by merely skipping stitches at the side seams to make armholes and skipping across the center to make the neck opening (see Figure 16-1b).

Figure 16-1:
Sleeveless sweater styles: (a) two-panel V-neck and (b) simple shell.

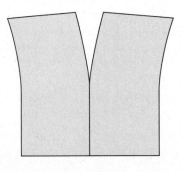
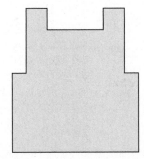

a   b

With only minor shaping at the armholes and around the neck, you can make a simple tank top like the one in Figure 16-2a. The classic sleeveless vest cardigan (shown in Figure 16-2b) usually requires a bit more shaping at the armholes and neck, but you can still make it with relative ease.

Figure 16-2: More sleeveless sweater styles: (a) tank top with shaping and (b) classic vest cardigan.

a

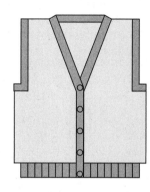

b

Going the classic route: Pullovers

You can make a pullover with almost any combination of sleeve and neck styles. Figure 16-3 shows you one of the simplest combinations. It has drop shoulders, wide cuffs, and a boat neck without borders or ribbing to complicate the design. A long sweater with no ribbing at the bottom is a *tunic* style, and a short sweater is sometimes called a *crop top*.

Figure 16-3: A pullover with no shaping.

Sweaters with tapered sleeves and some shaping at the neck are more common. Both sweaters in Figure 16-4 have tapered sleeves. (Tapered sleeves are easier than they look. You either start at the cuff edge and increase on each side until the sleeves reach the desired circumference or you start at the top edge and decrease until you get to the cuff.) The crew-neck sweater in Figure 16-4a has no armhole shaping and subsequently has dropped shoulders; the V-neck sweater in Figure 16-4b has inset sleeves for a more tailored look.

Frequently, ribbing or borders edge the bottom, cuffs, and neck opening of a pullover-style sweater. (Check out Chapter 17 for more on ribbing and borders.)

Figure 16-4: Pullover styles: (a) drop-shoulder crew-neck and (b) inset sleeves with a V-neck.

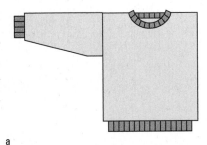
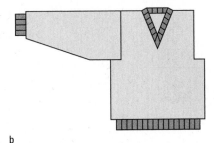

a   b

The cap-sleeve pullover style is fitted to the shape of the body and produces less bulk under the arms. The upper sleeve edge is shaped in a curve to fit into the shaped armholes. The cap-sleeve sweater in Figure 16-5a sports a scoop neck and fold-down collar. You usually work the raglan-sleeve style shown in Figure 16-5b in one piece, starting at the neck and increasing at the "seam" point between the sleeves and the body of the sweater as you work down. This style has the advantage of having few, if any, seams to sew.

Figure 16-5: More pullover styles: (a) cap sleeves with a scoop neck and (b) raglan styling.

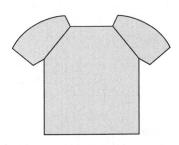

a   b

Buttoning up: Cardigans

Cardigans can have tapered sleeves or straight sleeves, inset sleeves or dropped shoulders, scooped necks, V-necks or boat necks, just like pullovers. The only difference is that cardigans have two fronts, so you sew the front to the back a little differently. Figure 16-6 shows a V-neck cardigan and a hooded cardigan, both with tapered sleeves.

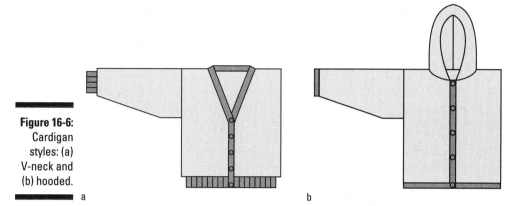

Figure 16-6:
Cardigan styles: (a) V-neck and (b) hooded.

a   b

Getting visually interesting: Motifs and vertical rows

Motifs and vertical rows are two fairly common design methods that can create a sweater with a lot of visual interest without you having to learn a bunch of complex stitch patterns:

- ✔ *Motifs* are small crocheted pieces worked in rounds that you sew or crochet together (see Figure 16-7a). You can use square, hexagonal, round, or triangular motifs of almost any size, providing that all the parts add up to the sweater measurements. Flip to Chapter 14 for more on motifs.

- ✔ You can also crochet a one-piece sweater in vertical rows (see Figure 16-7b) by starting at one cuff edge, working to the shoulder, and then increasing for the length of the body of the sweater in the front and the back. Even though it seems a bit more complex, this technique is great for making a flattering sweater.

Figure 16-7:
Unique construction: (a) motif sweater and (b) vertical-stripe cardigan.

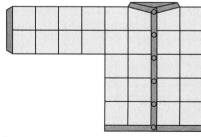
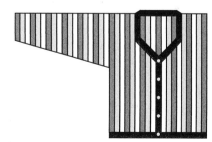

a   b

Think flatter, not fatter

Before you buy a pattern, consider the style of the sweater that you hope to crochet. Does it flatter you, or does it make you look like a pumpkin? Vertical lines can make you look thinner, but the construction of the sweater also affects how it looks on you. For example, dropped shoulders can look rather sloppy, but inset sleeves look tailored.

The length of the sweater is important to consider, too. Not everyone is cut out to wear a crop top. A sweater with ribbing that tends to cut you across the waist may be ideal for a thin, tall shape; a long tunic style, on the other hand, has a streamlining effect on a fuller figure. A boat neck can take away the look of sloped shoulders, and if you have narrow shoulders, wearing a cap sleeve with a slight puff can beef them up.

Sizing Up the Sweater Situation

When is a small not a small? When your sweater pattern lists it as a medium — and it may do just that. So far, no industry sizing standard exists, so you need to look carefully to determine your size when picking out a pattern. As if that weren't enough, each type of sweater (see the several styles covered in the previous sections) will fit your body differently. One size may be right if you want a snug sweater, but that same size may be all wrong if you're setting out to crochet a sweater so baggy it could hold you and a friend. Even if you can't find the perfect pattern, you may be able to alter the next best thing to get what you want. The following sections show you how to read sweater pattern sizes, determine the right size for you, and adjust your pattern accordingly.

Understanding sweater pattern sizes

Most sweater patterns list the size ranges (and one pattern may include several sizes) at the beginning of the instructions. You may find the back length and sleeve length listed as well. In fact, you may even find a schematic diagram showing the measurements of all the different pieces.

Sweater patterns also include the instructions for making all the listed sizes. Typically patterns list the directions for the smallest size first, followed by changes for the larger sizes in parentheses. For example:

Sc in each of next 50 (54, 58) sts.

In this example, you work 50 single crochet stitches if you're making a small sweater, 54 single crochet stitches for a medium one, and 58 single crochet stitches for a large one.

To make a particular sweater pattern easier to follow, highlight all the numbers for your desired size before you begin.

Figuring out fit

Choosing the right sweater size depends on the kind of fit you want. Some sweater styles are specifically designed to be loose fitting, but others are supposed to be snug. So if you normally wear a medium top, don't assume that the medium in the sweater pattern is automatically the fit you want.

The best way to ensure a great-fitting sweater is to first decide what fit you want: body hugging, close fitting, normal fitting, loose fitting, or oversized. Then forget what the pattern labels as small or large, measure your own bust line, and add to or subtract from the resulting measurement to get your desired fit. Table 16-1 tells you how many inches to add to (or subtract from) your own bust measurement to come up with a finished bust measurement that achieves the fit you desire. (The *finished bust measurement* is the total number of inches around the bust of the finished sweater — which isn't necessarily the same as your own bust measurement.) You then take this adjusted bust measurement and find the pattern size that matches it.

Table 16-1	Determining Sweater Fit
Fit You Want	*Number of Inches to Subtract from or Add to Your Bust Measurement*
Body hugging	− 1–2
Close	+ 1–2
Normal	+ 2–4
Loose	+ 4–6
Oversized	+ 6–8

For example, if you have a 36-inch bust and want to make a normal-fitting sweater, add 2 to 4 inches to your bust measurement for a total finished bust measurement of 38 to 40 inches. Now look at the pattern for the finished bust measurement closest to this range. If you don't find an exact measurement, choose the next largest size for a comfortable fit. Usually patterns offer sizes in 4-inch increments. However, that's not always the case. You may have a pattern that offers the bust sizes of 36 inches, 41 inches, and 46 inches. In this case, the 41-inch size is your best choice for a comfortable fit.

Working to the designated gauge is especially important when making sweaters. The gauge determines how many stitches you use for a given finished bust size. If your gauge is off, then your finished garment will be as well. The sweater that's supposed to have a 38-inch finished bust measurement may very well end up being a 34 if your gauge is too tight, or a 42 if it's too loose. (Check out Chapter 3 for gauge basics.)

Customizing your pattern

If you find a sweater that you want to make, but it doesn't have directions for your size, you may be able to alter it on your own. These sections show you how to get the size you need.

Adjusting the finished bust measurement

For sweaters that you work in horizontal rows, adjusting the bust size is fairly simple; you just add inches to (or subtract them from) the front and back pieces evenly. Suppose that the pattern for a cardigan offers finished bust measurements of 36, 40, and 44 inches, but you need a 48-inch finished bust. To get the extra 4 inches you need, adjust the directions for the largest size by adding 2 inches to the back width and 1 inch to each of the two front pieces (or 2 inches to the front width if you're working the front as one piece). You work the armholes and the length in the same manner as in the size-44 pattern.

Now check the gauge (refer to Chapter 3) for the pattern stitch and calculate approximately how many extra stitches you need to add to the back and the front to get your extra 4 inches. For example, if the pattern has just 1 stitch, such as single crochet, and the gauge is 9 stitches = 2 inches, you need to add approximately 9 stitches to the back width and approximately 5 stitches to each front piece of the cardigan.

But if you have a stitch pattern that repeats across the body of the sweater, you need to increase your stitch count in multiples of the stitch repeat. For example, if the pattern for the body of the sweater is * (double crochet, chain 1, double crochet) in next stitch, skip next 2 stitches *, then the multiple (or repeated part of the pattern) is 3 stitches. So any adjusting you do must be in a multiple of 3 stitches. For the back, you can easily add 9 stitches, which is a multiple of 3 stitches. But for the front, 5 stitches isn't divisible by 3, so you need to add the next multiple of 3, which is 6 stitches.

Sometimes you can make a good guesstimate from the existing multisized pattern. For example, if the differences between small and medium and between medium and large are both four stitches, then you can usually assume that the difference between a large and an extra-large is also four stitches. The benefit of this approach is that the pattern designer has (theoretically) already figured out the multiple sizes in relation to the repeats.

For patterns with large repeats, adjusting the size and maintaining the original pattern isn't always possible. Sometimes changing to a larger crochet hook and working the largest size offered creates a sweater that's a size larger. Crochet a gauge swatch (see Chapter 3) with the next largest hook size and calculate how big the sweater would be if you used that hook size. If the result isn't large enough, try the *next* largest hook. Make sure the looser gauge produces a comfortable fabric that isn't too sloppy looking or so holey that you can see through it.

Lengthening the sweater and sleeves

If you want to adjust the sweater or sleeve length, you can usually just increase or reduce the number of rows you work:

- Adjust the length of the sweater by adding or deleting rows at the bottom edge (so you don't mess up the shaping around the arm holes).
- Alter the sleeve length either above or below the shaping, depending on how it's made. Just make sure you've added all the stitches to ensure a comfortable fit around the upper arm and shoulder.

Simple Sweater Project

The pullover design in this simple sweater (pictured in the color section) has minimal shaping and only a few simple stitches, but it creates a beautiful garment that you can wear for years to come. It features drop shoulders and a crew neck finished with simple rounds of single crochet. The yarn for this pattern is a heavy worsted-weight wool blend that allows you to crochet the sweater in a relatively short amount of time.

Materials and vital statistics

- ✔ **Size:** Directions are for size Small (4–6). Changes for Medium (8–10), Large (12–14), and X-Large (16–18) are in parentheses.

- ✔ **Yarn:** Fiesta Yarns "Kokopelli" heavy worsted-weight yarn (60% mohair/40% wool), (4 oz. [113 g], 125 yds [114.3 m] each hank): 8 (9, 9, 10) hanks of #K20 Indian Paint Brush

- ✔ **Hook:** Crochet hook size K-10½ U.S. (6.5 mm) or size needed to obtain gauge

- ✔ **Yarn needle**

- ✔ **Measurements:** Finished bust: 36 (40, 44, 48) in. Back length: 26 (26, 27, 28) in. Sleeve length: 21 in. Use the sweater schematic in Figure 16-8 to determine which size to make.

- ✔ **Gauge:** 8 sts = 3 in.; 10 rows in patt = 5 in.

- ✔ **Stitches used:** Chain stitch (ch), slip stitch (sl st), single crochet (sc), half double crochet (hdc), double crochet (dc), triple crochet (tr). **Crossed dc:** * Skip next st, dc in next st, working behind dc just made, dc in last skipped st *. (For more information on the crossed double crochet stitch in this design, see Chapter 10.) **Dec 1 hdc:** * (Yo, insert hook in next st, yo, draw yarn through st) 2 times, yo, draw yarn through 5 loops on hook *.

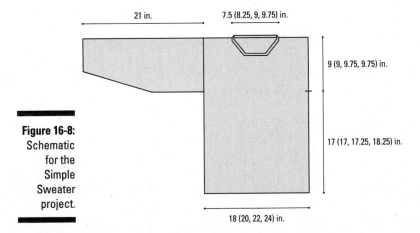

Figure 16-8: Schematic for the Simple Sweater project.

21 in.

7.5 (8.25, 9, 9.75) in.

9 (9, 9.75, 9.75) in.

17 (17, 17.25, 18.25) in.

18 (20, 22, 24) in.

Directions

We give you the row-by-row instructions for this sweater as you'd see them in any crochet publication. Figure 16-9 shows a reduced sample of the stitch-repeat pattern for Rows 1–12. If the instructions there seem like Greek to you, head on over to Chapter 4 for pointers on reading crochet patterns.

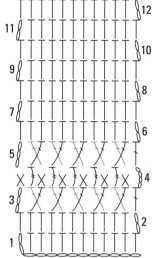

Figure 16-9:
A reduced
sample of
the stitch-
repeat
pattern for
the Simple
Sweater.

Back

Ch 47 (53, 59, 65) + 2 (first hdc).

Row 1 (WS): Hdc in third ch from hook, hdc in each ch across (48 [54, 60, 66] hdc), *turn.*

Row 2 (RS): Ch 2 (first hdc), hdc in each hdc across, hdc in top of turning ch (48 [54, 60, 66] hdc), *turn.*

Row 3: Ch 3 (first dc), * skip next hdc, dc in next hdc, working behind dc just made, dc in skipped hdc (crossed dc made) *; rep from * to * across to within turning ch, dc in top of turning ch (48 [54, 60, 66] dc), *turn.*

Row 4: Ch 4 (first tr), * sc in next dc, tr in next dc *; rep from * to * across to within turning ch, sc in top of turning ch (48 [54, 60, 66] sts), *turn.*

Row 5: Ch 3 (first dc), * skip next tr, dc in next sc, working behind dc just made, dc in last skipped tr (crossed dc made) *; rep from * to * across to within turning ch, dc in turning ch (48 [54, 60, 66] dc), *turn.*

Rows 6–12: Ch 2 (first hdc), hdc in each st across, hdc in turning ch (48 [54, 60, 66] hdc), *turn.*

Rows 13–52: Rep Rows 3–12 (4 times). Fasten off sizes Small and Medium.

For sizes Large and X-Large only:

Rows 53–54 (53–56): Rep Row 2 (2 [4] times). Fasten off.

Front

Work same as back through Row 46 (46, 48, 50).

Shape right neck

Row 47 (47, 49, 51): Ch 2 (first hdc), hdc in each of next 17 (19, 21, 23) hdc (18 [20, 22, 24] hdc), *turn.*

Row 48 (48, 50, 52): Ch 2 (first hdc), dec 1 hdc in next 2 sts, hdc in each hdc across, hdc in top of turning ch (17 [19, 21, 23] hdc), *turn.*

Row 49 (49, 51, 53): Ch 2 (first hdc), hdc in each hdc across to within last 2 sts, dec 1 hdc in last 2 sts (16 [18, 20, 22] hdc), *turn.*

Rows 50–51 (50–51, 52–53, 54–55): Rep Rows 48–49 (48–49, 50–51, 52–53) 1 time (14 [16, 18, 20] hdc at end of last row), *turn.*

Row 52 (52, 54, 56): Ch 2 (first hdc), hdc in each st across (14 [16, 18, 20] hdc). Fasten off.

Shape left neck

Row 47 (47, 49, 51): With WS facing, skip 12 (14, 16, 18) hdc to the left of last hdc made in first row of right neck shaping, join yarn in next st, ch 2 (first hdc), hdc in each hdc across, hdc in top of turning ch (18 [20, 22, 24] hdc), *turn.*

Row 48 (48, 50, 52): Ch 2 (first hdc), hdc in each hdc across to within last 2 sts, dec 1 hdc in last 2 sts (17 [19, 21, 23] hdc), *turn.*

Row 49 (49, 51, 53): Ch 2 (first hdc), dec 1 hdc in next 2 sts, hdc in each hdc across, hdc in top of turning ch (16 [18, 20, 22] hdc), *turn.*

Rows 50–51 (50–51, 52–53, 54–55): Rep Rows 48–49 (48–49, 50–51, 52–53) 1 time (14 [16, 18, 20] hdc at end of last row), *turn.*

Row 52 (52, 54, 56): Ch 2 (first hdc), hdc in each st across (14 [16, 18, 20] hdc). Fasten off.

Sleeves

Make 2: Ch 23 (23, 27, 27) + 2 (first hdc).

Row 1 (WS): Hdc in third ch from hook, hdc in each ch across (24 [24, 28, 28] hdc), *turn.*

Row 2 (RS): Ch 2 (first hdc), hdc in each hdc across, hdc in top of turning ch (24 [24, 28, 28] hdc), *turn.*

Row 3: Ch 3 (first dc), * skip next hdc, dc in next hdc, working behind dc just made, dc in skipped hdc (crossed dc made) *; rep from * to * across to within turning ch, dc in top of turning ch (24 [24, 28, 28] dc), *turn.*

Row 4: Ch 4 (first tr), * sc in next dc, tr in next dc *; rep from * to * across, to within turning ch, sc in top of turning ch (24 [24, 28, 28] sts), *turn.*

Row 5: Ch 3 (first dc), * skip next tr, dc in next sc, working behind dc just made, dc in last skipped tr (crossed dc made) *; rep from * to * across to within turning ch, dc in top of turning ch (24 [24, 28, 28] dc), *turn.*

Row 6: Ch 2 (first hdc), hdc in first dc (inc made), hdc in each st across to within turning ch, 2 hdc in top of turning ch (inc made) (26 [26, 30, 30] hdc), *turn.*

Row 7: Ch 2 (first hdc), hdc in each hdc across, hdc in top of turning ch (26 [26, 30, 30] hdc), *turn.*

Row 8: Ch 2 (first hdc), hdc in first dc (inc made), hdc in each st across to within turning ch, 2 hdc in top of turning ch (inc made) (28 [28, 32, 32] hdc), *turn.*

Row 9: Ch 2 (first hdc), hdc in each hdc across, hdc in top of turning ch (28 [28, 32, 32] hdc), *turn.*

Row 10: Ch 2 (first hdc), hdc in first dc (inc made), hdc in each st across to within turning ch, 2 hdc in top of turning ch (inc made) (30 [30, 34, 34] hdc), *turn.*

Row 11: Ch 2 (first hdc), hdc in each hdc across, hdc in top of turning ch (30 [30, 34, 34] hdc), *turn.*

Row 12: Ch 2 (first hdc), hdc in first dc (inc made), hdc in each st across to within turning ch, 2 hdc in top of turning ch (inc made) (32 [32, 36, 36] hdc), *turn.*

Rows 13–32: Rep Rows 3–12 (twice) (48 [48, 52, 52] sts at end of last row).

Rows 33–35: Rep Rows 3–5 (once).

Rows 36–42: Ch 2 (first hdc), hdc in each st across, hdc in top of turning ch (48 [48, 52, 52] hdc), *turn.* Fasten off.

Assembly

With the right sides of the front and back facing each other, take a yarn needle and yarn and follow these steps:

1. **Using the whipstitch, sew front to back across the shoulders.**

   Check out Chapter 15 for all things sewing related.

2. **With the right side of the fabric facing in, fold the sleeves in half lengthwise.**

3. **Matching the center fold to the shoulder seam, sew each sleeve in place using the whipstitch.**

4. **Beginning at the lower edge of the right side of the sweater, match stitches across the side edges and sew side and underarm seams using the whipstitch.**

5. **Repeat Step 4 on the left side of the sweater.**

Use the schematic in Figure 16-8 to check your finished pieces for accuracy in sizing.

Finishing

The neck edging for this sweater is just your basic single crochet stitch.

Rnd 1: With RS facing, join yarn in 1 shoulder seam, ch 1, sc evenly around entire neck edge, sl st in first sc to join.

Rnds 2–3: Ch 1, sc in each sc around, sl st in first sc to join. Fasten off.

Chapter 17

Finishing Functionally: Borders, Buttons, and Pockets

In This Chapter

▶ Tacking on edgings, borders, and collars to your work for a finishing touch

▶ Buttoning up and tying together a crocheted garment

▶ Fashioning pretty pockets

▶ Giving away a pretty little girl's top

*Y*ou've conquered crochet and completed the body of a great new sweater or cardigan. But something's missing. How are you going to keep those wide-open sleeves from dragging without a cuff? Or how is that cardigan going to keep you warm if you can't fasten it shut? This chapter shows you how to make your new garments functional with important finishing touches such as borders, cuffs, collars, buttonholes, and pockets. And the best part is that creating these finishing touches is easy. Try out the Girl's Versatile Camisole project at the end of this chapter for a beautiful garment you can crochet for your favorite girl — as well as a little practice making ribbing, buttonholes, edgings, and pockets.

If you want to practice your buttonholes or collars before trying them in another pattern, grab a few of the practice swatches that you made when practicing new stitches and add a buttonhole or collar to them.

Adding Trims: Edgings, Borders, and Collars

If you're thinking that you can make only the most basic of sweaters — two squares hung on your shoulders — forget it. The following sections show you how to add simple edgings, ribbed borders, and elegant collars that bring your projects to life without a lot of work.

Outlining your designs with edging

Crocheting a basic edging of one or two rows or rounds on the outer edges of a design can smooth out the rough spots and add a finished, professional look to your crocheted items. You can even add crocheted edgings to other materials. Here are a few options:

- ✔ Crochet a round of single crochet stitches around the bottom edge, neck edge, and cuffs of a sweater, especially one that you worked in a heavier-weight yarn. (Flip to Chapter 5 for a refresher on single crochet.)

- ✔ When making a patchwork afghan or sweater, edge each panel or motif with a row of stitches (typically the slip stitch or single crochet is used to create a smoother edge for joining).

- ✔ Crochet decorative strips of some of the fancier stitches (such as shells, clusters, and chain loops) with cotton thread and sew these edgings on pillowcases, sheets, handkerchiefs, and towels — or down the seam of your jeans! (Chapters 10 and 11 describe a variety of fancy crochet stitches you can use.)

Although knowing how to do a simple edging on your own is helpful, any pattern that includes an edging to finish off the design will tell you in detail how to complete it.

Bordering your masterpieces with ribbing

Borders can be quite elaborate and may consist of a number of rows or rounds that are a design unto themselves. If intricate borders tickle your fancy, check out a few of the many publications available to find dozens of complex border designs. (Head to the appendix for a list of some of the best publications.) In the next sections, however, we show you how to make two of the most common borders used on garments: single crochet ribbing and post stitch ribbing.

Single crochet ribbing

Single crochet ribbing is a long strip of very short vertical single crochet rows. Because these rib rows lay perpendicular to the rows in the body of the finished sweater, you normally make the ribbing first and then work the body of the sweater off the row-end stitches along the long edge of the rib.

Typically, you want the ribbing to cinch in a little around the bottom of the sweater and at the cuffs but still be flexible enough to stretch. You accomplish this by applying two techniques at the same time: 1) making the rib with a hook that's one size smaller than the one you use for the rest of the sweater and 2) working in *only* the back loops of each single crochet stitch across the row. You can make a wider border by increasing the stitches in each row (or you can create a narrower border by simply working fewer stitches). A typical bottom rib is 1 to 3 inches wide, or about 4 to 10 stitches.

To make ribbing that's approximately 2 inches wide using worsted-weight yarn and a size H-8 U.S. (5 mm) hook, follow these steps:

1. **Chain 9 (ch 9).**

2. **Single crochet (sc) in the second chain from the hook and then single crochet in each chain across;** *turn.*

   You now have 8 single crochet stitches.

3. **Chain 1 and then single crochet in the back loop of each single crochet across the row (like in Figure 17-1);** *turn.*

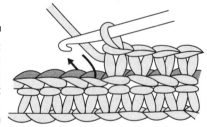

Figure 17-1:
Working
single
crochet
ribbing.

4. **Repeat Step 3 until the rib reaches your desired length.**

Typically, you make the rib an inch or two shorter than the width or diameter of the part of the sweater that you're crocheting. For example, if you have a sweater cuff that's 10 inches in diameter, you make the rib 8 or 9 inches in diameter. The amount of "cinching in" that you want to achieve and the elasticity of the yarn you're working with are determining factors in deciding the length of the rib strip.

Figure 17-2a illustrates how a standard single crochet ribbing should appear, and Figure 17-2b shows the stitch diagram.

You can add single crochet ribbing after you've crocheted the body of a sweater, but doing so takes more time (plus the appearance may not be as neat as if you worked the ribbing first). If the pattern you're working asks you to do this, it'll provide instructions.

Single crochet ribbing works better with some yarns than with others. For example, if the yarn you're using is soft and has little elasticity, it may not be suitable for single crochet ribbing. Yarns with some type of wool in them are the most suitable for ribbing projects.

Figure 17-2:
A swatch
of single
crochet
ribbing with
its stitch
diagram.

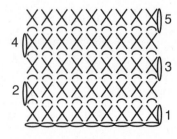

a   b

If your ribbing looks flat, try working with a smaller hook to tighten it up. As a last resort, you can tighten up your flat ribbing by weaving elastic thread in several places around the bottom rib of a sweater to cinch it in. If that doesn't do the trick, you may want to opt for post stitch ribbing (described in the next section).

Post stitch ribbing

Post stitch ribbing (double crochet stitches worked around the posts of previous stitches) isn't as elastic as single crochet ribbing, but it creates a more rounded style of ribbing that always maintains its ribbed appearance. Because you work post stitch ribbing in horizontal rows, you can either make the ribbing first and then work the body across the top edge of the ribbing or you can make the body first and then work the ribbing off the bottom edge of the garment (which is normally how you want to do it).

To fashion a typical post stitch ribbing across a sweater's bottom edge:

1. **Work 1 row of double crochet (dc) across the bottom edge and *turn*.**

2. **Chain 2 (ch 2).**

   This counts as your first post stitch.

3. **Work 1 front post double crochet (FPdc) around the post of the next double crochet, as shown in Figure 17-3a.**

   See Chapter 11 for detailed information on working post stitches.

4. **Work 1 back post double crochet (BPdc) around the post of the next double crochet. (Refer to Figure 17-3b.)**

5. **Repeat Steps 3 and 4 until you reach the last stitch.**

6. **Work 1 half double crochet (hdc) in the last stitch; *turn*.**

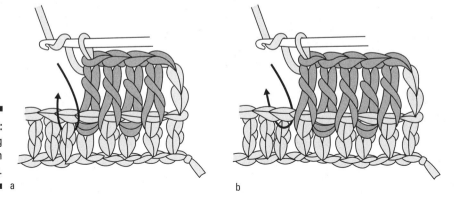

Figure 17-3:
Working
post stitch
ribbing.

a   b

Here's how to work the next row:

1. **Chain 2 (ch 2) for your first post stitch.**

2. **If the next post stitch from the previous row is raised to the front, work 1 front post double crochet (FPdc) around its post. If the next post stitch is raised to the back, work 1 back post double crochet (BPdc) around its post.**

   In Figure 17-4a, the stitches that appear to be raised to the front are front post stitches.

3. **Repeat Step 2 across the row until you reach the last stitch.**

4. **Work 1 half double crochet (hdc) in the last stitch and then *turn*.**

5. **Repeat Steps 1 through 4 until the rib measures the desired depth.**

Figure 17-4a shows a post stitch ribbing swatch, and Figure 17-4b depicts the stitch diagram.

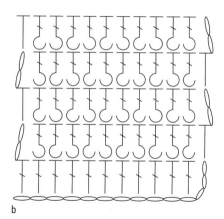

Figure 17-4:
Double
crochet
post stitch
ribbing
swatch
with stitch
diagram.

a   b

When creating post stitch ribbing, always make sure your post stitches are raised to the same side in each successive row or round. Keep an eye on the ribs and remember this: If the stitch you're working is raised to the front, work a front post stitch; if the stitch is raised to the back, work a back post stitch.

Post stitch ribbing is much thicker and tighter than single crochet ribbing. Consequently, it can be pretty stiff and inflexible if you're using a heavier yarn. Using a larger crochet hook gets you a softer, more flexible feel.

Gracing your neck with a common collar

Collars are a broad subject, with variations too numerous to explain in detail. However, if you can work basic crochet stitches (like the ones we describe in Chapters 5 and 6), you can fashion almost any style collar you can think of. Among the myriad collar options are soft, draping shawl collars, stiff mandarin-style collars, turtlenecks, and the traditional flared collar. (If you need to create another type of collar as part of a pattern, the pattern instructions will tell you how.)

A common collar is the traditional flared collar, which features pointed ends like a standard shirt collar. This collar often appears on cardigans, crew neck pullovers, and polo-style sweaters with front openings and plackets. To work a flared collar, follow these steps:

1. **With the right side of the sweater facing you, join the yarn with a slip stitch (sl st) in the top right-hand corner of the right front neck edge. Chain 1 (ch 1).**

2. **Single crochet (sc) evenly from the right front neck edge around to the top left-hand corner stitch of the left front neck edge; *turn*.**

3. **Chain 1 and then work 2 single crochet stitches (sc) in the first single crochet stitch. Single crochet in each stitch across, ending with 2 single crochets in the last stitch; *turn*.**

   Work the extra stitch at both edges of the collar to add the flare to it.

4. **Repeat Step 3 until the collar reaches 3 inches deep, or your desired depth.**

   To figure out how deep your collar should be, try measuring the collar on one of your favorite shirts or sweaters.

5. **Fasten off at the end of the last row.**

Holding Things Together: Buttonholes, Ties, and Drawstrings

When you button up your shirt in the morning, do you ever stop to think about which side the buttons are on and which side the holes are on? Or about how much space is between them? How about the ties on that cute new coverup? Are they flat or round? Do they have tassels or beads at the end, or are they just finished with a knot? The following sections show you all you need to know to keep your new clothes on — with buttons, ties, and drawstrings, that is.

Making room for buttons: Buttonholes

The design of the garment you're crocheting determines whether you work buttonholes horizontally or vertically, although both appear as vertical slits when finished.

- ✔ If the garment has front *plackets* (those narrow bands that run up the inside edges of the front or back of a shirt or sweater opening), you create the buttonhole horizontally, right into the placket.
- ✔ If the design doesn't have front plackets, you work buttonholes vertically into the garment itself.

On a woman's shirt, the buttonholes are on the right side of the shirt when you're wearing it; on a man's shirt, the buttonholes are on the left.

Of course, you can't have buttonholes without buttons. Check out Chapter 18 for info on making your own buttons. But in the meantime, take a look at the next few sections to see just how you can whip up some buttonholes. We also show you how to make button loops, which can be a pretty alternative to buttonholes.

Working buttonholes in front plackets

Making buttonholes in front plackets is easy. All you do is skip enough stitches in the designated row of the placket to accommodate the button size wherever you want a buttonhole. The buttonhole is usually created in a row close to the center of the placket, with a row or two following to add strength. To see how this technique is used, check out the Girl's Versatile Camisole project at the end of this chapter.

Here's how to fashion a standard buttonhole using this method:

1. **Place markers across the front edge of the placket to mark the beginning and end of each desired buttonhole position.**

2. **Crochet across the row in the stitch designated by the pattern to the first marker, chain 2 (ch 2), skip the next 2 stitches, and then continue crocheting across to the next marker. (Refer to Figure 17-5a.)**

   If you have a larger button, chain the required number of stitches for that button size. Then skip the same number of stitches as you made chain stitches.

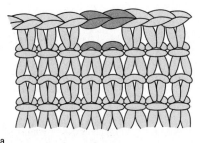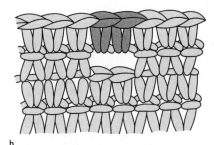

Figure 17-5:
Working a
buttonhole
horizontally.

a   b

3. **Repeat Step 2 for each marker until you reach the end of the row;** *turn.*

4. **Crochet evenly across the previous row, working an equal number of stitches into the chain space as it has chain stitches.**

   In this example, you work 2 stitches into the space because you made 2 chain stitches in the previous row. Refer to Figure 17-5b to see the completed buttonhole.

The number of stitches you skip, and therefore chain, depends on the size of the buttons you're using. Have your buttons on hand before crocheting any buttonholes — that way you can better fit the hole to the button.

Working buttonholes in the garment body

If your sweater design doesn't have front plackets, you work a buttonhole right into the body of the sweater by first working across the row to the point where the buttonhole will appear and then turning your work, leaving several stitches unworked. Next, you fasten off and rejoin the yarn in the stitch on the other side of the buttonhole, skipping a stitch to create the buttonhole.

You then work in the few stitches that you left unworked in previous rows to create the other side of the buttonhole. What all of this means is that you need to plan ahead and determine your buttonhole positions before you work the body of your sweater.

Here's how to crochet a vertical buttonhole (like the one illustrated in Figure 17-6b) on a single crochet sweater:

1. **When you're ready to begin the designated row for the bottom of the buttonhole, chain 1 (ch 1) to start the new row. Single crochet (sc) in each of the first 3 stitches and then turn, leaving the remaining stitches of the row unworked.**

2. **Chain 1 and then single crochet in each stitch across the first half of the buttonhole; *turn.***

3. **Repeat Step 2.**

   Figure 17-6a shows what your buttonhole should look like after you complete this step.

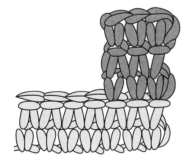 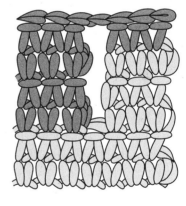

Figure 17-6:
Working a
buttonhole
vertically.

a   b

4. **Fasten off the yarn and, with the right side facing you, skip 1 single crochet and rejoin the yarn on the other side to begin making the second side of the buttonhole.**

Rejoin the yarn so that you work in the same direction as the other side; otherwise you end up with a different stitch pattern. For example, if you work the first row of the buttonhole row with the right side of the project facing you, make sure that when you rejoin your yarn to work the second side, the right side of your work is once again facing you.

5. **Chain 1 and single crochet in each stitch across the remainder of the front; *turn*.**

6. **Work 3 more rows of single crochet across, ending with a wrong side row at the top of the buttonhole.**

7. **Chain 1, skip the space for the buttonhole, and single crochet in each of the next 3 single crochets on the first side of the buttonhole. (Refer to Figure 17-6b.)**

Repeat Steps 1 through 7 for each buttonhole.

Working button loops

Button loops are nice alternatives to buttonholes. You can use them in a lightweight garment where you don't need a tight closure to the front or as a simple one-button closure at the top of a neckline. You work these loops into the final rows of an edging of a garment, and the number of rows depends on the weight of your yarn:

- ✔ If you're using a lightweight yarn, work the loop in the last two rows to give it more strength.

- ✔ If you're using a heavier yarn, a loop worked in the last row is sufficient.

Here's how to make a button loop on the last two rows of an edging:

1. **On the next-to-last row of the edging, mark positions across the front edge where you want the beginning of your loops to be positioned.**

2. **Crochet in the specified pattern stitch across the row until you reach a marked position.**

3. **Make a chain that's just long enough to form a loop that the button can slip through.**

4. **Without skipping any stitches, continue crocheting until you reach the marker for the next loop.**

5. **Repeat Steps 2 through 4 across the row; *turn*.**

6. **For the last row, crochet evenly across, working the same number of stitches as there were chains in the chain space of each loop.**

   Check out Figure 17-7 to see a sample single crochet button loop.

When you're working the button loop stitches, you can also work each stitch into the chain stitch itself. However, most patterns tell you where to place your stitches for the button loop.

Figure 17-7:
A completed button loop worked in the last two rows of edging.

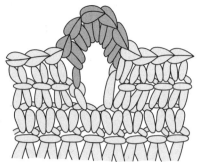

To make a button loop on the last row of an edging, proceed as follows:

1. **Before you begin the last row, mark positions where you want to place your loops across the front edge, marking both the beginning and ending of each loop.**

2. **Crochet in the specified pattern stitch across the row until you reach the second marker for the first loop (as shown in Figure 17-8a);** *turn.*

3. **Make a chain that's large enough to slip the button through.**

4. **Join the chain with a slip stitch (sl st) at the edge of the first marker of the first loop;** *turn.*

   Refer to Figure 17-8b for a visual of this step; note that the work shown hasn't been turned yet.

5. **To complete the button loop, work the same number of stitches as there were chain stitches into the chain space.**

   Figure 17-9 shows a completed button loop. To create additional button loops, repeat Steps 2 through 5 for each loop.

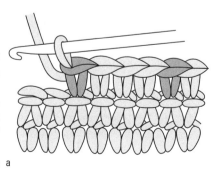
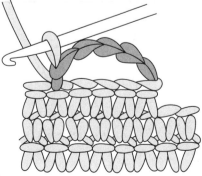

Figure 17-8:
Working a button loop in the last row of edging.

a   b

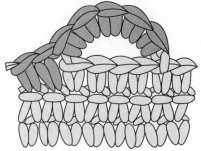

Figure 17-9:
A completed
button loop
on the edge
of a work.

Keeping your clothes on (or just spicing them up): Ties and drawstrings

Ties and drawstrings make fun and easy closures for the front (or back) of a garment. They can be as simple as a single tie attached to each side of a light sweater's front or as elaborate as a threaded drawstring criss-crossing the back of a summer halter top.

You usually attach ties to the top-front portion of a garment, close to the neck opening, or at the beginning of the front neck shaping, centered over the chest. However, you can also place ties in a row down the entire front of a sweater. You attach ties to garments with the excess lengths of yarn left from the beginning of the tie to "tie" them to the correct position on the garment.

Drawstrings, which you weave through a round with *eyelets* (a round created with a pattern of spaces) or post stitches (see Chapter 11) crocheted into the body of a sweater or sleeve, often adorn the neckline, waistline, bottom edges, and cuff edges of some sweaters. You can also place drawstrings in the center-back area of a garment, weaving them back and forth between the open edges of, say, a halter top to draw the sides together. The Girl's Versatile Camisole project, at the end of this chapter, gives you practice creating a drawstring and then weaving it through a round of post stitches that act as belt loops.

The following list gives you a few options for crocheting a tie or drawstring:

- ✔ **Make a simple chain.** Chain the required length for the tie or the drawstring. (You may use one or more strands of yarn.) Note that this is how we made the drawstring in the Girl's Versatile Camisole project.

- ✔ **Make a round cord.** Chain 5 (or the required number for the thickness of the cord) and slip stitch in the first chain to join. Single crochet in each chain around. Then, working in a spiral, continue to single crochet in each single crochet around until the cord reaches your desired length.

✔ **Single crochet or slip stitch a cord.** Chain the required length, turn, and slip stitch or single crochet in the back bump loop of each chain across.

To spice up your ties and drawstrings, add embellishments such as tassels (see Chapter 18) or just tie each end in a simple knot.

Purely Pockets

If you're like most people, you enjoy having a place to stuff everything from pens and lip balm to your hands. Pockets to the rescue! The sections that follow briefly describe three common types of pockets — patch, slashed, and inseam (see Figure 17-10) — and give you the basics on how to add them to a garment.

Figure 17-10:
Three classic pocket styles.

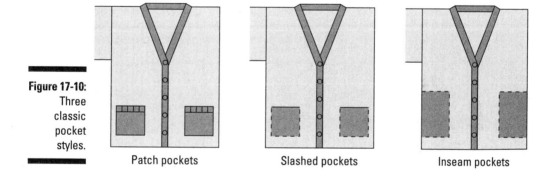

Patch pockets   Slashed pockets   Inseam pockets

Patch pockets: Tacked onto the front

Patch pockets are by far the simplest form of pocket to create. You simply crochet two squares or rectangles, usually in the same stitch pattern as the body of the sweater, and then whipstitch them onto the front of a garment, usually closer to the side seams than to the front edge, as you can see in Figure 17-10. (Chapter 15 has tips on sewing crocheted pieces together.) To see how a patch pocket might be used, check out the Girl's Versatile Camisole project at the end of this chapter.

If your sweater features a contrasting color of yarn for the ribbing, you can outline the tops of your pockets with an edging in the same color for a creative and colorful touch.

Slashed pockets: Slotted in the front

A slashed pocket is similar to a patch pocket in shape and position. However, instead of sewing the pocket to the outside of the garment, you make a lining, generally in single crochet, and then attach the pocket to the wrong side (the inside) of the front.

A little more planning is involved in creating slashed pockets because when you're crocheting the front, you have to allow for the opening. Your pattern will tell you exactly how to form and attach the pocket, but the general idea goes like this: You work the first row above the pocket opening across the top of the pocket lining (which you've already crocheted) and then skip the appropriate number of stitches across the front of the sweater to create the opening. Your lining is now attached to the body of the garment. Using the whipstitch, sew the lining to the wrong side of the garment around three sides directly below the opening (see Figure 17-10). For a decorative touch, crochet the top edge of the pocket opening on the front of the garment in a contrasting color.

Inseam pockets: Positioned at your sides for ultimate convenience

Inseam pockets are openings in the side seams of a garment, as you can see in Figure 17-10. To create inseam pockets, you first need to crochet a solid fabric pocket. That means you have three layers of crochet at the point where you place the pockets, a fact you should keep in mind if you're working with a heavier-weight yarn because crocheted fabric tends to be thick.

Crochet inseam pockets with a lighter-weight yarn that matches your sweater and a smaller hook to reduce bulk.

To create a double-sided pocket to be sewn into an inseam:

1. **Chain (ch) the number of chain stitches needed to create the width of the pocket.**

2. **Single crochet (sc) in the second chain from the hook and then single crochet in each chain across; *turn*.**

3. **Chain 1 and then single crochet in each single crochet across.**

4. **Repeat Step 3 until your pocket reaches the desired depth.**

5. **Fasten off the yarn.**

6. **Repeat Steps 1 through 5 to create the second side of the pocket.**

After you make both sides of a pocket and sew them along three sides using the whipstitch, either sew or crochet the pocket into the side seam of the garment. Join one side of the pocket opening to the front side seam and the other side of the pocket opening to the back side seam. Close the rest of the side seam however the pattern instructs you to.

Girl's Versatile Camisole Project

You don't have to be an expert or be able to crochet numerous fancy stitches to create a garment that you'll love to give as a gift to your favorite little girl. This project lets you create a darling camisole while practicing simple skills, including a patch pocket with a ribbed border, delicate picot edging, buttonholes, and a drawstring tie. The real beauty of this camisole is that it's extremely versatile. Your favorite girl can wear it solo in the summer, or she can layer a T-shirt under it in the winter (as shown in the color section).

The mercerized cotton yarn recommended for this project comes in many vibrant colors and has a beautiful drape that's perfect for crochet. The stitch pattern is a simple alternating repeat of two basic stitches, single crochet and double crochet, that adds a slight texture to the fabric yet keeps the stitches close together to reduce gaps.

Materials and vital statistics

- ✔ **Size:** Directions are for size Small (4). Changes for Medium (6), Large (8), and X-Large (10) are in parentheses.

- ✔ **Yarn:** Patons "Grace" light worsted- or DK-weight mercerized cotton yarn (100% mercerized cotton), (1.75 oz. [50 g], 136 yds [125 m]): 4 (4, 4, 5) balls of #62104 Azure

- ✔ **Hooks:**

    - Crochet hook size G-6 U.S. (4 mm) or size needed to obtain gauge

    - Crochet hook size E-4 U.S. (3.5 mm), for pocket ribbing only

- ✔ **Yarn needle**

- ✔ **Buttons:** 6 (7, 8, 9) ½-in. size buttons

✓ **Measurements:** Finished bust: 25 (27, 29, 30½) in. to fit actual chest size 23 (25, 27, 28½) in. Back length: 12½ (13½, 15½, 16½) in. Figure 17-11 shows the finished measurements.

✓ **Gauge:** With larger hook, 20 sts and 14 rows (while alternating 1 row of sc with 1 row of dc) = 4 in.

✓ **Stitches used:** Foundation single crochet (fsc), chain stitch (ch), slip stitch (sl st), single crochet in the front loop only (sc-flo), single crochet in the back loop only (sc-blo), double crochet in the front loop only (dc-flo). **Dec 1 dc:** * (Yo, insert hook in next st, yo, draw yarn through st, yo, draw yarn through first 2 loops on hook) twice, yo, draw yarn through 3 loops on hook *. **FPtr:** Yo (twice), insert hook from front to back around the post of the fsc 2 rows below, yo, and draw back to the front of the work (yo and draw through first 2 loops on the hook) 3 times. **Picot:** Ch 3, sl st into third ch from hook.

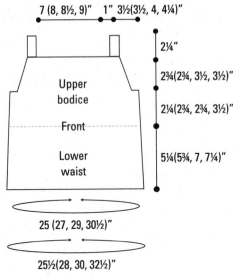

7 (8, 8½, 9)"   1"   3½(3½, 4, 4¼)"

2¼"

2¾(2¾, 3½, 3½)"

Upper
bodice

2¼(2¾, 2¾, 3½)"

Front

Lower
waist

5¼(5¾, 7, 7¼)"

Figure 17-11:
Schematic
for the Girl's
Versatile
Camisole.

25 (27, 29, 30½)"

25½(28, 30, 32½)"

Directions

Begin by crocheting the front and back portions of the upper bodice in one piece from the upper waist to the underarms. Then divide your work into front and back sections by skipping stitches and working stitches together to create the separation between the front and back of the camisole and the armholes. Working off the foundation of the upper bodice, you complete the camisole by working from the top down through the lower waist.

Do you recall seeing two sets of measurements in the Measurements bullet of the earlier "Materials and vital statistics" section? The smaller set of measurements represents the actual chest size of the person wearing the camisole. The bigger set of measurements indicates the finished size of the camisole itself. There's a difference of 2 inches, which allows the wearer a little extra room for comfort or for layering the camisole over a shirt.

To help you keep track of which size you're working on, read through the whole pattern before you begin and circle or highlight the size you're making. Then you'll never have to worry about losing your place.

Upper bodice

With the larger hook, fsc 124 (134, 144, 154).

Row 1 (RS): Ch 3, dc-flo in each st across 124 (134, 144, 154) dc, *turn.*

Row 2: Ch 1, sc-flo in each st across 124 (134, 144, 154) sc, *turn.*

Rows 3–8 (10, 10, 12): Rep Rows 1–2.

Shape back left

Row 1 (RS): Ch 3 (counts as first dc), dc-flo in next 23 (25, 28, 31) sc, dec 1 dc, dc-flo in last st, (26 [28, 31, 34] dc), *turn.*

Row 2: Ch 1, sc-flo in first st and each st across, (26 [28, 31, 34] sc), *turn.*

Row 3: Ch 3 (counts as first dc), dc-flo in each st across until 3 sts remain, dec 1 dc, dc-flo in last st, (25 [27, 30, 33] dc), *turn.*

Rows 4–9: Rep Rows 2–3, (22 [24, 27, 30] dc), *turn.*

Row 10: Ch 1, sc-flo in first st and each st across, (22 [24, 27, 30] sc), *turn.* Fasten off sizes Small and Medium only.

For sizes Large and X-Large only:

Row 11: Ch 3 (counts as first dc), dc-flo in each st across until 3 sts remain, dec 1 dc, dc-flo in last st, (26 [29] dc), *turn.*

Row 12: Ch 1, sc-flo in first st and each st across, (26 [29] sc), *turn.* Fasten off.

Shape front

Row 1: With RS facing, skip 8 sts from first row of back left, join yarn in next st. Ch 3 (counts as first dc), dec 1 dc, dc-flo in next 48 (54, 58, 62) sc, dec 1 dc, dc-flo in last sc, (52 [58, 62, 66] sts), *turn.*

Row 2: Ch 1, sc-flo in first st and each st across, (52 [58, 62, 66] sc).

Row 3: Ch 3 (counts as first dc), dec 1 dc, dc-flo in each st across until 3 sts remain, dec 1 dc, dc-flo in last sc, (50 [56, 60, 64] dc), *turn*.

Rows 4–9: Rep Rows 2–3, (44 [50, 54, 58] dc), *turn*.

Row 10: Ch 1, sc-flo in first st and each st across, (44 [50, 54, 58] sc), *turn*. Fasten off sizes Small and Medium only.

For sizes Large and X-Large only:

Row 11: Ch 3 (counts as first dc), dec 1 dc, dc in each st until 3 sts remain, dec 1 dc, dc-flo in last sc, (52 [56] dc), *turn*.

Row 12: Ch 1, sc-flo in first st and each st across, (52 [56] sc), *turn*. Fasten off.

Shape back right

Row 1: With RS facing, skip 8 sts from first row of front, join yarn in next st. Ch 3 (counts as first dc), dec 1 dc, dc-flo in next 24 (26, 29, 32) sc, (26 [28, 31, 34] dc), *turn*.

Row 2: Ch 1, sc-flo in first st and each st across, (26 [28, 31, 34] sc), *turn*.

Row 3: Ch 3 (counts as first dc), dec 1 dc, dc-flo in each st across, (25 [27, 30, 33] dc), *turn*.

Rows 4–9: Rep Rows 2–3, (22 [24, 27, 30] dc), *turn*.

Row 10: Ch 1, sc-flo in first st and each st across, (22 [24, 27, 30] sc), *turn*. Fasten off sizes Small and Medium only.

For sizes Large and X-Large only:

Row 11: Ch 3 (counts as first dc), dec 1 dc, dc-flo in each st across, (26 [29] dc), *turn*.

Row 12: Ch 1, sc-flo in first st and each st across, (26 [29] sc), *turn*. Fasten off.

Straps

With RS facing, skip first 17 (19, 21, 24) sc of back left, join yarn in next sc with sl st.

Row 1 (RS): Ch 1, sc in same st and next 4 sc, (5 sc), *turn*.

Row 2: Ch 3 (counts as first dc), dc in each st across, (5 dc), *turn*.

Rows 3–8: Rep Rows 1–2. Fasten off.

With RS facing, join yarn to first st of front. Rep Rows 1–8 of Straps instructions. Fasten off. Join yarn 5 sts in from opposite edge of front. Rep Rows 1–8 of Straps instructions. Fasten off. Join yarn to first st of back right. Rep Rows 1–8 of Straps instructions. Fasten off.

Waistband

Row 1: With WS facing, turn camisole over to work into foundation ch, join yarn in first ch, ch 3 (counts as first dc), dc-flo across, 124 (134, 144, 154), *turn*.

Row 2: Ch 1, sc-flo in first 4 dc, * FPtr around the post of fsc 2 rows below, sc-flo in next 4 dc *; rep from * to * across, turn 24 (26, 28, 30) FPtr.

Lower waist

Row 1 (WS): Ch 3 (counts as first dc), dc-flo in each st across, 124 (134, 144, 154), *turn*.

Row 2: Ch 1, sc-flo in each st across, 124 (134, 144, 154), *turn*.

Rows 3–4: Rep Rows 1–2.

Row 5: Rep Row 1.

Row 6: Ch 1, sc-flo in first 45 (49, 53, 57) sts, 2 sc-flo in next st, sc-flo in next 32 (34, 36, 38) sts, 2 sc-flo in next st, sc-flo across to end, 126 (136, 146, 156) sc, *turn*.

Rows 7–11: Rep Rows 1–5.

Row 12: Ch 1, sc-flo in first 23 (25, 27, 29) sts, 2 sc-flo in next st, sc-flo in next 78 (84, 90, 96) sts, 2 sc-flo in next st, sc-flo across to end, 128 (138, 148, 158) sc, *turn*.

For size Small only:

Rows 13–16: Rep Rows 1–4. Fasten off.

For size Medium only:

Rows 13–17: Rep Rows 1–5.

Row 18: Ch 1, sc-flo in first 62 sts, 2 sc-flo in next st, sc-flo in next 12 sts, 2 sc-flo in next st, sc-flo across to end, (140 sc). Fasten off.

For size Large only:

Rows 13–17: Rep Rows 1–5.

Row 18: Ch 1, sc-flo in first 66 sts, 2 sc-flo in next st, sc-flo in next 14 sts, 2 sc-flo in next st, sc-flo across to end, (150 sc), *turn.*

Rows 19–22: Rep Rows 1–4. Fasten off.

For size X-Large only:

Rows 13–17: Rep Rows 1–5.

Row 18: Ch 1, sc-flo in first 70 sts, 2 sc-flo in next st, sc-flo in next 16 sts, 2 sc-flo in next st, sc-flo across to end, (160 sc), *turn.*

Rows 19–23: Rep Rows 1–5.

Row 24: Ch 1, sc-flo in first 5 sts, 2 sc-flo in next st, sc-flo across until 6 sts remain, 2 sc-flo in next st, sc-flo across to end, (162 sc). Fasten off.

Assembly

With the yarn needle and the right sides together, slip stitch the front straps to the back straps across the shoulders. (Refer to Chapter 15 for specific pointers on joining with the slip stitch.) *Note:* The straps are easily adjustable. If the person tries it on and the straps are too long or too short, simply unravel the slip stitch seam and adjust the number of rows until they're perfect.

Finishing

All that's left to do is to add a few rows along the back right and left edges for the buttonholes and buttons, edge the armholes and neck, rib and create a pocket, and add a drawstring.

Buttonhole placket
Row 1: With RS facing, join yarn at lower right-hand corner of back left. Working into the row ends, sc evenly across, placing 1 sc in the end of each sc row and 2 sc in the end of each dc row (54 [60, 69, 75] sc), *turn.*

Row 2: Ch 1, sc in first sc, * ch 2, skip 2 sc, sc in next 6 sc across *; rep from * to * 5 (6, 7, 8) times across, sc in each sc to end, (6 [7, 8, 9] ch-2 sp), *turn.*

Row 3: Ch 1, sc across, working 1 sc in each sc and 2 sc in each ch-2 sp, (54 [60, 69, 75] sc). Fasten off.

Button placket

Row 1: With RS facing, join yarn at upper left-hand corner of back right. Working into the row ends along the back edge, sc evenly across, placing 1 sc in the end of each sc row and 2 sc in the end of each dc row 54 (60, 69, 75) sc, *turn.*

Row 2: Ch 1, sc in each sc across, *turn.*

Row 3: Ch 1, sc in each sc across. Fasten off.

Using 6-in. lengths of yarn threaded onto the yarn needle, secure buttons onto the button placket using the buttonholes as a guide.

Armhole edging

With RS facing, join yarn at center of underarm, working evenly around armhole and placing 1 sc in each st and sc row-end and 2 sc in each dc row-end, * work 2 sc, picot *; rep from * to * around. Sl st in first sc to join. Fasten off.

Rep for second armhole.

Neck edging

With RS facing, join yarn at upper corner of back left panel. Working evenly around neckline, work picot edging as for armhole.

Pocket ribbing

With smaller hook, ch 5.

Row 1: Sc-blo of the second ch and each ch across, (4 sc-blo), *turn.*

Row 2: Ch 1, sc-blo of each sc across, *turn.*

Rows 3–13: Rep Row 2. Don't fasten off.

Pocket body

Row 1: Turn ribbing to work along longest edge. With larger hook, place 1 sc in each row-end st across, (13 sc), *turn.*

Row 2: Ch 3 (counts as dc), dc-flo in first sc (inc made), dc-flo in each sc across to last sc, 2 dc-flo in last sc, (15 dc), *turn*.

Row 3: Ch 1, sc-flo in each dc across, (15 sc), *turn*.

Row 4: Ch 3 (counts as dc), dc-flo in next sc and in each sc across, (15 dc), *turn*.

Rows 5–6: Rep Row 3. Fasten off.

Whipstitch pocket to lower half of right front positioned 2 in. above the bottom edge and 2 in. in from the side fold. (Flip to Chapter 15 for details on sewing.)

Drawstring

With the smaller hook, make a chain that's 40 inches long, unstretched. Weave in the ends and tie a small overhand knot at each end. Weave the drawstring through the front post stitches at the camisole's waistband, allowing the ends to meet at the center front. Weave in any loose ends.

Chapter 18

It's All in the Details: Embellishing Crochet

In This Chapter

▶ Dangling fringe and tassels from your work

▶ Making your creations unique with buttons and embroidery

What is it about your favorite pieces of clothing that strikes your fancy? The color? The style? Perhaps a special finishing touch? This chapter shows you how to create those special touches that can turn a so-so piece into one that everybody raves about — from fringes and tassels to buttons and embroidery. The best part is that creating these finishing touches is very easy. So let your creative side run free!

Hanging Off the Edge: Fringe and Tassels

Fringe and tassels, which are the focus of the following sections, are two of the most common crochet embellishments. Fringe often complements a scarf or afghan, and tassels sometimes finish off drawstrings or ties on a sweater, the top of a hat, or a filet crochet wall hanging. (See Chapter 13 for the scoop on filet crochet.) Simple to make, fringe and tassels don't require any additional materials other than the yarn and hook you use to crochet your piece. We explain how to make them in the next sections.

To spice up your look, you can interchange fringe and tassels (meaning that if a design calls for fringe at the ends of the piece, you can add tassels instead if you prefer the way they look). You can also add beads to individual strands or even fray the yarn by separating the fibers in a strand to create a fuller, fluffier appearance.

Tying a piece together with fringe

Fringe commonly borders the short edges of a scarf or the ends of an afghan. It gives a nice finishing touch and also hides those sometimes unsightly end rows. If your design incorporates several colors, you can tie them all together with fringe. Fringe looks best when it's fluffy and full, so depending on the type of yarn you use, combine several strands for each fringe or just use whatever number's in your pattern instructions. To make fringe, follow these steps:

1. **Cut the yarn into the required number of equal lengths.**

   For example, if each fringe has 3 strands of yarn and you have 20 stitches across the edge that you're attaching the fringe to, then you need 60 lengths of yarn, all equal in length.

   Cut the yarn twice as long as you want the final fringe to be because you're going to fold the yarn in half. In fact, err on the safe side and cut it even a little longer to account for the knot. You can always cut the fringe shorter when you're finished, but you can't make it longer. (Fortunately, patterns usually tell you what the length of each fringe should be.)

2. **Fold the strands of yarn for 1 fringe in half, forming a loop at one end and matching the cut ends of the yarn at the other end.**

3. **Working from the right side of the fabric, take your hook and draw the loop through the stitch that you're attaching the fringe to, as shown in Figure 18-1a.**

4. **Draw the loose ends of the yarn through the loop, as in Figure 18-1b.**

Figure 18-1: Making a single-knot fringe.

5. **Holding the top of the fringe in one hand, pull gently on the fringe ends with your other hand to tighten the knot.**

6. **To finish, trim the ends of the fringe so they're even.**

   Tada! You've just completed 1 single-knot fringe. (It should look like the one in Figure 18-2.)

Figure 18-2:
Finished
fringe
attached to
crochet.

Tacking on tassels

You generally use tassels to embellish spots like the points on a shawl, the back of a hat, the ends of drawstrings or ties, or the lower edges of a wall hanging. Instead of working tassels directly in a stitch, as you do with fringe, you usually make them separately and then tie them to the design. Here's how to make a tassel:

1. **Cut a piece of cardboard the same width as your desired tassel length.**

   If you're following a pattern, refer to the instructions to see what size to cut the cardboard.

2. **Wrap the yarn around the piece of cardboard several times.**

   The more times you wrap, the fuller your tassel will be.

3. **Tie the yarn bundle together at one end with a separate length of yarn (see Figure 18-3).**

   This separate length of yarn should be at least 6 inches in length, long enough to tie the bundle together and then tie the tassel to the piece when complete. (*Note:* Some pattern instructions may give you an exact length to use. If they do, go with that instead.)

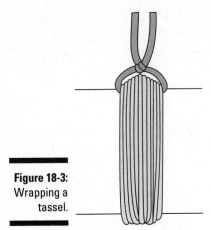

Figure 18-3:
Wrapping a tassel.

4. Slide the bundle of yarn off the cardboard piece.

5. Wrap another length of yarn 2 or 3 times around the bundle, approximately 1 inch below the tied end, and tie in a knot to secure (refer to Figure 18-4).

6. Cut the loops on the opposite end of the bundle from the tied end.

7. Trim the ends of the tassel so they're even.

8. With the top tie's remaining yarn, tie the tassel to the designated spot or stitch and make a knot.

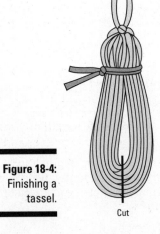

Figure 18-4:
Finishing a tassel.

Cut

Attaching a tassel is the same no matter what you're attaching it to. If it's the back point on a bandana, then the stitch on the very end holds the knot. If you're attaching tassels across the edges of a scarf, then the instructions designate which stitches to tie them to (for example, every other stitch or every third stitch).

Adding Special Touches with Buttons and Embroidery

If you want to embellish your crochet fabric a little bit (and with minimal fuss), you have an endless array of options. For example:

- ✔ Spice up an otherwise plain cardigan with some pretty buttons.
- ✔ Add a splash of embroidery to a piece worked in the square stitches of Tunisian crochet (see Chapter 12 for more on this technique).

The following sections show you how to apply these embellishment techniques to your pieces.

Attaching unique buttons

If you just can't find the perfect buttons, try making your own by working stitches over a plastic ring. Plastic rings are available in a wide variety of sizes, and you can use them to make buttons with the same yarn that you're using for your design.

Crocheting over a ring is similar to working into a center ring or an adjustable ring (refer to Chapter 8 for the how-to on making a center or adjustable ring): Instead of inserting your hook into a stitch, you draw your yarn through the center of the ring, thereby working your stitch around the ring. Single or double crochet stitches are best for this. The yarn may be thick enough to fill in the ring with just one round, but sometimes you need to make additional stitches to fill in the hole, which you then draw together and close at the top.

Easing into elegant embroidery

What's not to love about embroidery? Using a needle and thread (or yarn) on the surface of a crocheted fabric gives you the freedom to create unique designs that embellish your work of art. Many relatively plain pieces of crochet are transformed by this method. You can transfer almost any embroidery design onto a piece of crocheted fabric, whether that's the front of a sweater, the panels of an afghan, or a crocheted background design. *Crewel* (embroidery created with yarn rather than thread) and cross-stitch work especially well on crocheting.

- **Creating crewel work:** Traditionally, crewel requires fine wool yarn, but over the years, it has become a style of embroidery that's worked with any type of yarn rather than thread. The designs are varied and numerous; basically any design you can embroider with thread can be embroidered with yarn. Crewel works especially well on plackets, collars, and cuffs, or for creating a large picture on the front or back of a sweater, pillow, or handbag. You can work free-flowing designs in crewel, so let your imagination go. It's a wonderful way to use up all that scrap yarn you have floating around. Check out your local craft store for some fun crewel designs.

- **Enjoying cross-stitch:** Adding cross-stitch to your crochet design is a perfect way to combine your efforts and show off your multitalented self. A Tunisian crochet design just screams to be cross-stitched on. The small squares that are integral to the design make transferring pretty much any cross-stitch pattern to the right side a snap. For more info on the Tunisian crochet and adding cross-stitch to a project, flip to Chapter 12.

Chapter 19

Neatness Counts: Fixing, Blocking, and Caring for Your Work

. . . .

In This Chapter

▶ Correcting mistakes while you crochet

▶ Shaping your finished project with water, heat, or starch

▶ Using everyday objects to give shape to a three-dimensional design

▶ Keeping your creations clean and storing them properly

. . . .

*I*t's a fact: Even the most experienced crocheters make mistakes as they work. But fret not! In this chapter, we run through a few handy methods for fixing errors while you crochet. Of course, even after you're finished with a piece, you may find that your work is still a little misshapen or that it doesn't quite match the dimensions the pattern gave for the finished item. Don't panic — your project just needs to be *blocked,* or pulled into shape with the help of a little water, heat, or starch. Blocking helps even out uneven stitches, square off corners, and make true circles out of rounds. In this chapter, we also show you how to block your crocheted items and then how to launder and store them so they last forever (well, almost).

Troubleshooting Mistakes as You Crochet

No matter how much experience you have as a crocheter, you *will* make mistakes — and that's perfectly okay! Sure, discovering that you've lost a stitch or made some other typical error can be a frustrating experience, but knowing how to identify the problem and how to fix it will get you back on track in no time. In the sections that follow, we introduce you to a few of the most common crocheting problems. You discover why they happen, how to fix 'em, and how to keep 'em from happening again. Well, what are you waiting for? The key to stress-free crocheting awaits!

You're struggling to fit your hook into the stitches

Trust us. We know how easy it is to get frustrated when you're struggling to slide your hook into stitches. Following are a couple reasons why your stitches may be too tight (along with a couple easy fixes):

- ✔ **You're pulling the working yarn too tight as you work.** Try loosening up your tension by adjusting how you hold the yarn. (Head to Chapter 5 for pointers on how to hold yarn properly.)

- ✔ **The loop is sitting on the skinny end of the hook.** Make sure that when you finish the stitch, the loop on the hook is on the fat portion of the hook, not near the hook part.

- ✔ **The hook's too small for the yarn you're working with.** By switching to a larger hook, you can make bigger stitches that are easier to work with. (Flip to Chapter 2 for the scoop on hook sizes.)

To keep from having too-tight stitches ever again, make sure you're checking your gauge against the pattern before you begin to crochet. Taking the time to make a gauge swatch early on saves you serious time in the long run. Check out Chapter 3 for more on gauge.

The edges of the fabric are shrinking

You're crocheting along when suddenly you realize that your work is getting skinnier — something it's not supposed to do. This problem is a common one for those who are still getting the hang of crocheting. If your project is growing narrower as you work, then you probably lost one or more stitches somewhere along the way.

To fix this problem, count the number of stitches in the last row. If you've lost stitches, hold up the fabric and look for any spots where you may have skipped a stitch. If you can't easily see where you began losing stitches, carefully pull out the last row and count the number of stitches in the next row. (To pull out a row, simply remove the yarn loop from your hook and then gently pull on the tail end of the yarn to unravel the stitches. Be careful not to pull too fast though, because you may end up pulling out more stitches than you need to.) Continue to pull rows out one by one, counting as you go, until you're back to the correct number of stitches and then try, try again.

Alternatively, if you've lost just one or two stitches, you can simply add the same number of stitches to the next row by working two stitches in the same space until you're back to the correct stitch count. When you're done adding stitches, hold up your work to make sure the edges still look even.

Stitches are commonly lost at the beginning or end of a row because it's hard to tell where the first or last stitch of the row is due to the fact that both are typically turning chains and therefore have a different appearance than a regular stitch. To help you distinguish where different rows start and end, place a removable stitch marker in the first and last stitch of a row. When you work your way back to the marker, you'll know exactly where you need to place the stitch. (See Chapter 5 for more on turning chains.)

The edges of the fabric are getting wider

Occasionally you may find that the edges of your work are actually growing. If your work is getting wider and you didn't intend for it to, that means you've unknowingly added stitches somewhere.

To trim your project back down to size, count the stitches in the last row to determine how many extra stitches you have. If you have more stitches than you're supposed to, carefully pull out the last row (as explained in the preceding section) and count the number of stitches in the next row. Continue pulling rows out one by one, counting as you go, until you're back to the correct number of stitches. Then you can start over safely.

What to do if you've only added one or two stitches? Just subtract the same number of stitches in the next row by working two stitches together until you're back to the correct stitch count. After you've decreased the stitches, hold up your work to make sure the decrease isn't noticeable. (See Chapter 7 for the how-to on decreasing stitches.)

To keep from having to redo your work in the future, make sure to count your stitches after every row until you feel more confident in your crochet skills. And don't forget that turning chains count as the first stitch in taller stitches; make sure to work into them at the end of a row. Refer to Chapters 5 and 6 for details on how to work into the turning chain.

The foundation edge is tighter than the rest of the fabric

If after working a few inches of your project you notice that the piece is getting wider and you didn't add any stitches, there's a chance your foundation edge may be too tight. The chain stitch is easy to make narrower than the other, more structured stitches, so accidentally making the foundation chain too tight is quite common. To avoid this issue, try to keep your chain stitches loose as you work the foundation chain. To keep your stitches loose, you can either consciously make loose stitches by keeping your tension looser than you would for regular stitches or you can use a hook that's one size larger than the one the pattern calls for. The resulting chain may look a little messy, but some of the slack will be taken up when you work the following row of stitches. (Keep in mind that your foundation chain should look like a big fat worm!)

The corners are curled

When the corners of your work are starting to curl and just won't lie flat, you may need to try adjusting your tension. Stitches that are worked too tightly together result in a stiff fabric, which often causes the corners to curl in.

To fix this problem, try stretching the fabric. That just might loosen up the stitches and allow the piece to lie flat. If the corners begin to curl again, make sure you're using the appropriately sized hook for the yarn you're working with. Switching to a larger hook size will create bigger stitches and loosen up the fabric, allowing it to lie flat. If all else fails, you may need to adjust your tension by changing the way you hold the yarn. Flip to Chapter 5 for guidance on holding yarn the right way.

Sometimes you won't realize that the corners of a project are curling until you're all done with it. Instead of tossing your work away in a heap of frustration, try blocking it (using one of the processes we describe later in this chapter). With some yarns, such as wool, blocking loosens up the fibers, allowing you to stretch out any curls.

One way to prevent curled corners is by simply loosening up your stitches. If you find that your hands are cramping up, chances are you're holding the hook too tightly and therefore creating stitches that are too tight as well. Relax your grip for looser stitches.

Making a gauge swatch helps you identify and prevent any potential problems early on. If your swatch is curling, then your project will probably curl as well. Always make sure you're working to the gauge specified in your pattern if you want to wind up with a successful project.

Blocking Your Way into Perfect Shape

To get most crocheted garments, such as sweaters, vests, and jackets, to match a pattern's finished measurements, you must block them. *Blocking* is a process used to shape crocheted work. It can be as simple as spraying your design with water or completely immersing it in a tub to get it good and wet. Or you may use some heat by applying steam from your steam iron. Some items, such as cotton doilies or three-dimensional designs, need a little extra shaping help from starch or another stiffening agent.

The final use of your design helps you determine which method of blocking to use. Another consideration is your yarn type. Different types of yarn respond differently to water, steam, and heat, and using the wrong method can have disastrous results. But don't be alarmed; the following sections help you avoid blocking-related pitfalls by giving you the scoop on the various blocking methods and when you use each one. Of course, before you begin any project, you need to make sure you have the right tools on hand, so we give you a quick list of these as well.

If your design has pieces that you join together, such as the sleeves and body of a sweater or the different motifs for an afghan, block each piece separately before joining. Doing so makes joining the pieces easier because each one is the correct size and shape. It also gives you a more accurate finished size.

If the design that you're blocking is a garment and it doesn't fit correctly before blocking (it's too small or too large as is), don't try to stretch it (or squash it) to fit when blocking. Blocking only shapes the garment; it doesn't change its size. If you try to stretch (or squash) your garment during blocking, you may ruin it entirely. If your garment doesn't fit, chalk it up to experience and pass it along to someone who can use it. Don't despair if this happens; it's all part of the experience of becoming a better crocheter.

The essential tools

You probably already have most of the tools you need to correctly block your designs. First, make sure you have the finished design dimensions from the pattern so you know what shape you're shooting for. Second, find a flat, padded surface that's large enough to accommodate your design when you stretch it to its finished measurements. (The surface must be padded so you can pin your piece down.) A bed, the floor, a large piece of sturdy cardboard covered in plastic wrap, an ironing board, or a mesh drying rack all work fine as a padded surface.

Here are some other tools you may need, depending on which blocking method you're using:

- Large tub or sink
- Several large, absorbent towels
- Tape measure or ruler
- Rustproof straight pins (always pin out your crocheted designs with this kind of pin to prevent nasty rust stains)
- Spray bottle
- Thin cotton towels (two or three should suffice) or a pressing cloth (an old sheet or T-shirt works well)

✔ Steam iron

✔ Spray starch, liquid starch, or fabric stiffener (available at most craft stores)

Wet blocking

To *wet block* an item, you submerge the whole thing in water. This method works for just about any yarn, but read the yarn label just to be sure it's not a dry-clean-only fiber. You can also gently wash your crocheted item at this time to rid it of the dirt and oils that the yarn is sure to have picked up from your hands. Use a mild soap made for delicate fabrics (*not* detergent) and rinse well in cool water before blocking. This method is useful for many items, including garments, afghans, and home décor.

If you're not sure whether your yarn is colorfast, be sure to test a swatch before dunking your whole design into a tubful of water. Bleeding colors, especially in a striped design, can ruin your work. If you use a solid color, the effect of bleeding isn't as bad, although you may encounter some fading if you continue to wash the piece over time.

To wet block your work, follow these seven simple steps:

1. **Fill a clean, large tub or sink with cool water and immerse your crocheted design completely, allowing it to become thoroughly wet.**

   If you want to wash your design, now's the time. Add some soap to the water and swish your garment around. Rinse it well with cool, clean water, taking care not to twist or wring out the fabric.

2. **Drain the water from the tub or sink without removing your crochet project.**

3. **Press down on your work in the tub to remove some excess water and then pick it up and gently squeeze it to remove more water, being careful not to let any part of it hang down and stretch.**

Never wring your wet crocheted item. Doing so can cause friction between the fibers and alter the appearance of your design. More importantly, it can stretch the fibers beyond repair, and you could end up with a misshapen piece.

4. **Lay your design flat on top of a large towel and then roll the towel and crocheted design together like a jellyroll to absorb more of the water.**

   You don't want to remove too much of the water — just enough so that the material isn't soaking wet.

5. **Place another large towel on your blocking surface and lay your work flat on it.**

   Your blocking surface needs to be a place where you can leave your design undisturbed for a day or two because it may take that long to dry completely.

6. **Following the schematic (garments) or measurements (afghans or other nonwearables) for the design, use a ruler or tape measure to gently shape and stretch the item to the correct size.**

   If the design has three-dimensional elements to it, such as bobble stitches or popcorn stitches, gently puff them into shape. If the design is lacy, make sure to open up the loops so that the design is evident.

7. **Allow your design to dry thoroughly.**

   If you need to dry your work in a hurry, place a large fan in front of the damp design to speed up the drying process. Don't place it so close that the fan can blow your masterpiece around, though.

   Don't ever use a blow-dryer to dry your design. The heat could shrink your piece or melt the fibers in a synthetic yarn.

Spray blocking

Spray blocking is similar to wet blocking, but instead of immersing the piece completely in water, you spray it with water to dampen the fabric. It's kind of like spritzing your hair to spruce up your 'do when you don't have time to wash it. Use spray blocking when your piece needs only a little bit of help to shape up or when you don't want to take the time to wet block. Here's how to spray block:

1. **Prepare a blocking surface that's suitable for pinning down your design.**

   See the earlier "The essential tools" section for ideas of appropriate blocking surfaces.

2. **Lay out your design on the blocking surface, stretching it to the correct measurements; with rustproof pins, pin it in place along the edges every few inches to make sure it stays put.**

3. **Grab a clean spray bottle filled with lukewarm water and spray the design evenly to a uniform dampness.**

4. **Gently smooth the fabric with your hands to even it out, shaping any three-dimensional stitches as needed.**

5. **Allow the design to dry completely before removing it from the blocking surface.**

Heat blocking

You can *heat block* your design by either ironing it or steaming it. Faster than wet blocking and spray blocking, heat blocking works best on natural fibers, such as wool and cotton, but you must take extra care not to burn the fibers. The next sections fill you in on how to iron and steam your work.

We don't recommend heat blocking for synthetic fibers because they can melt, thereby ruining your design.

Ironing it out

The ironing method of heat blocking works well for flat items, such as doilies, that have no three-dimensional stitches. To block your design with the ironing method:

1. **Set your iron to the correct temperature as indicated on the yarn label.**

   If the label doesn't recommend a temperature, be cautious and set the iron on a medium-low setting (the steam function should be off as well). You can always make the iron warmer, but burns are irreversible.

2. **Lay out your design on a heat-resistant blocking surface and pin it out to the proper dimensions.**

3. **Cover your crocheted design with a clean cotton towel or a pressing cloth. Then, using a spray bottle, spray it with water to slightly dampen the cloth.**

   If you prefer to dry press, cover the crocheted design with the cloth and omit the spraying step.

4. **Iron the item through the cloth by gently pressing and then lifting the iron and moving it to a new section.**

   Running the iron over the design while pressing down flattens your stitches and may harm the yarn fibers.

5. **Allow your design to cool and then remove it from the blocking surface. If necessary, repeat the process on the other side.**

Steaming your fabric's pores

Steaming works especially well for correcting curling edges. It's also quite useful when you have to shape just a small section, such as a cuff or collar that won't behave. All you need to steam press your work is a normal steam iron, which you probably have in your laundry room. To steam block your design:

1. **Set your iron to the correct temperature indicated on the yarn label.**

   If the label doesn't recommend a temperature, be cautious and set the iron on a medium-low setting.

2. **Lay out your design on a heat-resistant blocking surface and pin it out to the proper dimensions.**

3. **Holding your steam iron about an inch above the fabric, steam separate sections of the design, being careful not to let the iron touch the fabric.**

4. **Give your design time to cool and dry before removing it from the blocking surface.**

Blocking with starch

Doilies, collars, ornaments, edgings, and three-dimensional designs often require a little extra help when blocking in order to show off the stitches and, in some cases, to create the proper shape. When your design calls for a stiffer finish, it's time to call in the starch. ***Note:*** You use starch and stiffening agents almost exclusively with cotton thread.

For designs such as pillowcases or towel edgings, you want a lightly starched finish, or else your piece may become too scratchy to actually use. Doilies and filet crochet designs require a heavier finish, so use heavy spray starch or liquid starch in order to show off the stitch detail and maintain the proper shape. To permanently stiffen your works of art, such as ornamental snowflakes and other three-dimensional designs, a commercial fabric stiffener, which you can find at most craft stores, is in order.

The following sections cover the how-tos of working with spray starch, liquid starch, and fabric stiffeners.

Achieving targeted stiffness with spray starch

Spray starch is your ticket for a light- to medium-crisp finish. To block a crocheted item with spray starch, proceed as follows:

1. **Hand wash the crocheted design with a mild soap and cool water, rinsing several times to remove all the soap residue.**

   Make sure not to twist or wring out the design while rinsing it.

2. **With a clean towel (or several, if you need them), blot out any excess moisture until the design is just damp.**

3. **Prepare a blocking surface suitable for pinning down your design.**

   Not sure what constitutes a good blocking surface? See our recommendations in the earlier "The essential tools" section.

4. **Spray one side of your design with starch and place the starched side down on your blocking surface.**

5. **With rustproof pins, pin out your design to the required dimensions, taking extra care to shape stitch patterns as shown in the photo that accompanies your pattern.**

   This could mean opening up the spaces in lace patterns or straightening out picot stitches.

   Work quickly so that you get the design pinned down before the starch dries.

6. **Spray the other side of the design, making sure the fabric is lightly saturated.**

7. **Blot excess starch from the design with a clean, dry towel and allow it to dry completely.**

Immersing your piece in liquid starch or fabric stiffener

Blocking a crocheted design with liquid starch allows you a bit more range when determining the desired crispness. Follow the manufacturer's advice on the bottle of starch for the amount of starch you need and whether you need to dilute or not.

If your final design has a permanent shape, such as snowflake ornaments, baskets, or other three-dimensional designs, use a commercial fabric stiffener rather than liquid starch. Liquid starch loses its hold over time, whereas a commercial stiffener is meant to last. A design blocked with a commercial fabric stiffener should hold up for years to come with the proper care.

To block with liquid starch or fabric stiffener, follow these steps:

1. **Using cool water, gently hand wash your design with a mild soap, rinsing several times to remove all the soap residue.**

   Avoiding wringing out or twisting the fabric as you rinse it.

2. **In a clean tub or sink, prepare the solution as directed on the container.**

3. **Immerse your crocheted item in the solution and allow it to penetrate the fabric.**

   Your fabric should be soaked through with the solution in a couple minutes.

4. **Prepare a blocking surface suitable for pinning down your design.**

5. **Remove the item from the solution and, with a clean, dry towel, blot your crocheted item to remove any extra solution.**

6. **With rustproof pins, pin out the design to the required dimensions on your blocking surface, taking extra care to shape stitch patterns as shown in the photos accompanying your pattern.**

7. **After pinning, blot the design again to remove any remaining excess solution.**

If you're using commercial fabric stiffener, be extra careful to remove as much excess solution from the stitches and between the stitches as possible. When dry, the solution can leave a hard residue that obscures the design.

8. **Allow your masterpiece to dry completely before removing the pins.**

Shaping Three-Dimensional Designs with Household Items

Not all crochet is designed to be flat. One of the beautiful aspects of this craft is that with it you can create three-dimensional designs, whether your creation is as simple as a hat or as complex as a decorative, three-dimensional Lilliputian village that you work in many pieces.

Many three-dimensional designs need to be coaxed and shaped after you finish the actual crocheting, however. Most patterns include detailed instructions on how to finish and shape your work. If yours doesn't, you can follow the wet-blocking instructions presented earlier in this chapter. (***Note:*** The one change to the standard wet-blocking procedure in this case is that instead of pinning your design out flat, you mold it over the appropriate shape and pin down the edges so it can dry that way.)

Some of the supplies to have on hand when you're shaping a three-dimensional design are

- ✔ **A kitchen bowl:** Pick one in an appropriate size (comparable to the finished design measurements) for wet blocking a hat or shaping a doily into a decorative bowl.

- ✔ **Paper cups:** Shape cotton-thread Christmas ornaments, such as bells, with paper cups.

- ✔ **Plastic wrap:** Probably the most useful tool, plastic wrap can stuff, prop up, and shape many three-dimensional designs.

- ✔ **Preformed foam shapes:** Available in most craft stores, foam shapes, such as cones, can shape the bodies for objects such as crocheted Christmas tree toppers.

As you can see, you don't need any fancy supplies. Just look around your house, and you'll find that you already have many of the items you might need on hand.

From This Day Forward: Caring for Your Work

Most crocheters take great pride in their creations, but when all is said and done, caring for the finished design is often an afterthought. Considering the many hours you inevitably invest in making a crocheted design just right, taking the time to find out how best to care for your piece is worth your while. The following sections outline different methods for washing your finished work as well as the best way to store it afterward to avoid stretching and discoloring.

Scrub-a-dub-dub: Washing your work

As with all types of fabrics, you want to follow certain guidelines when washing your work. Different yarns have different needs, so be sure to check the yarn label for specific care instructions. You don't want to throw a wool sweater into the washer and dryer, for example, unless you want to end up with a sweater for a doll. Hand washing, dry cleaning, and machine washing (all of which we cover in the next sections) all work well to get your clothes clean, but beware the fiber content of your yarn. As with tags on store-bought items, the yarn label tells you how to take care of your piece.

Most yarn labels use the International Fabric Care Symbols shown in Figure 19-1 to tell you how to care for the yarn. Look for them and pay attention to them.

Figure 19-1: The International Fabric Care Symbols for yarn care.

Normal wash   Hand wash   Do not wash

Dry clean   Do not dry clean   Machine washable

Cool iron   Warm iron   Hot iron   Do not iron

Hand washing

If your yarn of choice is washable, hand washing the item with gentle soap made for delicates (*not* detergent) is by far the best way to go because it preserves the integrity of the piece. Machine washing can be tough on fabric, and you don't want to lose all of your hard work to modern conveniences.

Depending on the size of the item you're washing, fill a clean sink or tub with cool to lukewarm water and add a small amount of soap. Wash your piece gently and then rinse it thoroughly. Squeeze it gently to remove excess water; blot it with soft, absorbent towels; and then lay it flat to dry, blocking it into shape using the original method you used to block it when you first completed it. (***Remember:*** Any time your piece gets wet, it must be reshaped.)

If it's practical, place your creation in a colander when rinsing it to avoid stretching the fibers.

Dry cleaning

If the yarn label says *dry clean only,* then dry clean your design. You can be sure that the manufacturers have a good reason for labeling the yarn dry clean only, the most likely one being that water damages the fibers. Take the item to your favorite dry cleaner along with the yarn label, if possible. Most dry cleaners are willing to take extra special care of an object if they know it's handmade.

Machine washing and drying

Some yarns, especially acrylics, are suitable for machine washing and drying, although hand washing is always the safer route. Before dumping your piece in the washing machine, though, read the label for the correct temperature for both washing and drying and be sure to set the speed to the gentle cycle. The agitation in washing machines doesn't make for happy yarn and can cause irreparable damage if it's too rough.

Drying your item by laying it flat is always preferable but not always practical. If you must put your design in the dryer, make sure you dry it on the lowest heat setting.

Rest in peace, dear sweater: Storing your work

The most important rule to remember when putting your crocheted designs away is to never, never, never hang them. Hanging crocheted pieces stretches the stitches all out of shape. The design may even become unusable if it's left hanging for any length of time.

Keep all of your work — whether that's clothes, home décor items, or a mix of the two — in a cool, dry place, away from direct light. Ultraviolet light, excessive humidity, and extreme temperature changes all have adverse effects on yarn. Find a nice, quiet place and let your creations rest in peace until you're ready for them again.

Store crocheted garments neatly folded in a drawer or on your closet shelf — likewise with tablecloths, bedspreads, and blankets. Smaller items that don't need to be folded should be stored flat.

If your crocheted designs (such as holiday items) are going into storage for any length of time, invest in some acid-free tissue paper. Placing the paper between the folds and around items keeps the dust and dirt off and preserves the fibers. And always put your work away clean. Time allows stains to set in, and they may not come out a year later.

Part V
The Part of Tens

The 5th Wave

By Rich Tennant

BERNICE AND HER CROCHET CLUB VISIT THE GREAT SHAWL OF CHINA.

©RICHTENNANT

"Wait—don't take the picture yet. My watch is snagged."

In this part . . .

This part leads you to more adventures in the art of crochet and offers advice on how to make the most of your crochet experience. With our list of ten ways you can do good with crochet, you discover how to help others in your community through crochet and how crochet can help you reduce your impact on the environment. Our list of ten interesting crochet variations may inspire you to try something new, too.

Chapter 20

Ten Ways to Do Good with Crochet

In This Chapter
- ▶ Giving the gift of crochet to your friends
- ▶ Crocheting for important causes
- ▶ Making green choices and repurposing your junk

You don't have to be an expert in crochet to make a difference with it. The moment you found out how to guide your hook through the stitches you became empowered to make positive changes in the world. In this chapter, we highlight ten ways that you can do good things with crochet — for your friends, your community, and your planet.

Share Your Passion with a Crochet Basket

Give the gift of crochet by putting together a "Learn to Crochet" basket for a friend. Be sure to include all of the tools someone would need to start crocheting right away: a book on how to crochet (why not this one?), an H-8 U.S. (5 mm) hook, some worsted-weight yarn, and a yarn needle. Make your basket extraspecial by including a coupon for a free one-on-one lesson with you.

Host a Stash Swap Party for Friends

Instead of buying new yarn, host a stash swap party with some of your fellow knitters and crocheters. Maybe you've bought some delicious yarn on sale but had no pattern in mind to go with it, or perhaps you just have a couple balls left over from a different project. A stash swap party allows you to go through your *stash* (a collection of yarn) and sort out the yarns that you haven't been able to use. Everyone brings his or her contribution to the party, and you get to have fun trading yarn while bonding with your fellow stitchers.

Teach Someone How to Crochet

Now that you know how to crochet, why keep it to yourself? Share your new hobby by teaching someone else. Even children as young as 6 years old can easily pick up on the basics of crochet. Start by showing your pupil how to make a chain that she can use as a hair tie, bracelet, or necklace, and then move on to basic squares that can be used as doll blankets or donated to a charity that makes blankets for the homeless (see the next section for more information).

For a complete manual on teaching children (and grown-ups) how to crochet, check out the Crochet Guild of America's Web site at www.crochet.org.

Donate Crochet Supplies to Community Groups

If you find you have too much yarn or too many hooks, or if you just feel like sharing the crochet wealth, you can donate yarn, hooks, and other crochet supplies to one of many organizations (including schools and senior centers) looking for craft supplies. To find a group that will be happy to take your dona- tion, check with your local crochet guild (see the appendix for details on find- ing yours), senior center, or school district. You can also contact the Helping Hands Needle Arts Mentoring Program (www.needleartsmentoring.org), which creates community partnerships to promote and encourage the shar- ing of needle arts with children.

Crochet for a Cause

You only need to know a few simple stitches to make a difference in the lives of others. Hundreds of nonprofit organizations have been created by caring people to collect handmade items in support of a good cause. From crocheted hats for hospitalized infants to blankets for homeless pets, there's an organi- zation for almost any project, and many of them provide simple patterns for you to follow.

To find an organization that interests you, contact your local crochet guild, hospital, shelter, or senior center, or try getting in touch with any of these established resources:

- ✔ **Bev's Country Cottage:** This Web site (www.bevscountrycottage. com) is a great resource for patterns, and it has links to charities from around the world.

- ✔ **Stitches from the Heart:** This charity organization collects hats, blankets, and booties for premature infants born in hospitals across the United States. Check its Web site (www.stitchesfromtheheart.org) for patterns and tips on choosing appropriate yarn.

- ✔ **Warm Up America!:** This charity collects handmade blankets to give to shelters, children's hospitals, nursing homes, and anyone in need. Its Web site (www.warmupamerica.org) has patterns and tips for making and joining squares. (***Note:*** A similar organization exists in Canada. Check out the Blankets for Canada Society at www.blankets4canada.ca.)

Buy Local Yarn

You can lighten your impact on the planet by supporting the fiber-producing farms in your area. Some local farms even have community-supported agriculture (CSA) programs where you can invest directly in the farm and get lots of yarn or wool for spinning at the end of the season. For many city folks, investing in a yarn CSA is the next best thing to owning their own sheep. To find a fiber-producing farm in your area, check with your local yarn shop and farmers' markets.

Use Eco-Friendly Fibers and Natural-Colored Yarn

Don't be swayed by the first pretty color or texture of yarn that meets your eye. Instead, think about the planet as you make your yarn purchases and keep these important considerations in mind while you shop:

- ✔ **Seek out yarns that are organically produced, environmentally friendly, or have companies behind them that support fair trade practices.** By supporting eco-friendly companies you're helping to promote a greener earth one stitch at a time. To find out which yarn brands are eco-friendly, check the label, ask your local yarn shop, search the Internet, or join eco-friendly groups on social networking sites such as Ravelry (www.ravelry.com).

✔ **Purchase yarns that are naturally colored or made with low-impact dyes.** Yarns come in a wide rainbow of colors. However, many of the dyes used to create those colors include harmful chemicals that are toxic to the environment. Using yarns that are naturally colored or made with low-impact dyes helps reduce mankind's toll on the earth. Many yarn companies offer a range of natural-colored yarns; in fact, we bet you'll be surprised at how many shades there are. Check the label or ask your local yarn shop to help you find out which yarns are naturally colored.

Crochet Green Items for Your Home

Make your home a little greener by trading in your disposable goods for reusable items. Here are just a couple ideas:

✔ **Replace your paper towels with washable, crocheted towels.** The Absorbent Hand Towel project in Chapter 12, made with Tunisian stitches, produces large, absorbent towels, but you can also use any of the stitches and stitch patterns found in this book to whip up your own towel designs. Just be sure to use a cotton yarn, because cotton tends to be the most absorbent fiber.

✔ **Skip the paper and plastic bags for your own crocheted bag when shopping.** The String Market Bag project in Chapter 13 leaves you with a handy bag to replace those plastic grocery bags that usually end up in the trash. Be sure to make a few bags to keep in your car or purse for those unexpected trips to the yarn shop.

Recycle Old Fabric with a Crocheted Rag Rug

Instead of tossing or donating old sheets and clothes, consider giving them a new purpose. *Rag crochet* involves tearing or cutting fabric into long strips and working with them in the same way you would with yarn. The only difference is that the fabric tends to be a little thicker, so there's a bit of prep work involved. To find suitable rag material, check your closet for worn clothes and linens, or hit the secondhand store.

To get you started, here's a pattern for a simple, small, round rag rug that's suitable for a bathroom, child's room, or entryway. To make this rug larger, just keep increasing each round by six stitches in the same pattern until the rug reaches the desired size. Check out a finished rag rug in Figure 20-1.

Turning rags into rugs is an age-old tradition, but why stop at rugs? Take rag crochet in a whole new direction by making bags, pillows, or baskets.

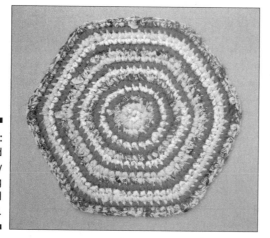

Figure 20-1:
Recycle old
fabric by
making
a round
rag rug.

Materials and vital statistics

- ✔ **4 clean and dry twin-size sheets, or 1 clean and dry twin-size sheet per color**
- ✔ **Hook:** Crochet hook size P-15 U.S. (11.5 mm) or size needed to obtain gauge
- ✔ **Scissors**
- ✔ **Ruler**
- ✔ **Measurements:** 20 in. in diameter
- ✔ **Gauge:** First 5 rounds = 6½ in. in diameter
- ✔ **Stitches used:** Chain stitch (ch), slip stitch (sl st), single crochet (sc)

Directions

The directions here are suitable for light- to medium-weight fabrics, like the kind you'd find with most shirts and sheets. If you use a heavier-weight fabric, such as denim, wool, or terrycloth, you may need to switch up to a larger hook size. In any case, feel free to adjust the hook size so you can crochet the fabric strips comfortably.

Preparing the strips

You can cut fabric into strips for crochet in several ways. The most basic way is to simply cut the fabric into equal-sized strips and then knot, sew, or loop them together into one long, continuous strand. If you'd prefer not to join the fabric strips, follow this method:

1. **Beginning with the short end of a twin-size sheet facing you, make a cut 1 inch in from the longest edge of the sheet.**

2. **Cut or tear the fabric, maintaining about a 1-inch width down the length of the sheet until 1 inch of fabric remains at the end; then stop.**

3. **Working in the opposite direction, make a cut 1 inch over from the last cut edge. Cut or tear the fabric in about a 1-inch width back across the length of the sheet until 1 inch remains; stop.**

4. **Repeat Step 3 until you've made a zigzag cut of 1-inch wide strips across the width of the sheet (see Figure 20-2).**

5. **Starting at either the beginning or the end of your cut, wind the fabric strip in the same way you would a ball of yarn.**

   Head to Chapter 2 for an explanation of how to wind a ball of yarn. And don't worry about the corners at the end of each fabric strip. With rag rugs, corners and knots add character.

Repeat the preceding directions and wind each sheet into separate balls.

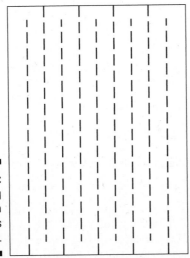

Figure 20-2:
Cutting
fabric into a
continuous
strip.

Making the rug

The directions for this rug are identical to the first 16 rounds of the Bucket Hat project at the end of Chapter 8 (see how the same stitch patterns can be used for a variety of designs?). *Note:* If you're using different colors to make the rug, join a new color at the beginning of each round. (And if you're having trouble reading the Crochetese, flip to Chapter 4 for help reading patterns.)

Center ring: Make an adjustable ring, ch 1.

Rnds 1–16: Follow the first 16 rnds of the Bucket Hat project at the end of Chapter 8.

Fasten off and weave in the loose ends with your hook.

Save the Planet One Crocheted Bag at a Time

In recent years, plastic bags have become a sort of environmental conundrum. Research has shown that although producing plastic grocery bags is more efficient than producing paper ones, the plastic bags are slower to degrade, filling landfills and posing a threat to wildlife and marine life. So, as more and more plastic grocery bags are being replaced by cloth totes, why not turn your leftover plastic bags into a reusable crocheted bag? Plastic bags can be crocheted like yarn; they just need a little bit of prep work to become plastic yarn, or *plarn*.

If you don't have enough plastic bags to make the bag shown in Figure 20-3, ask around and help relieve your neighbors of their unwanted bags.

Materials and vital statistics

- **50 to 60 plastic grocery bags, cleaned and dried thoroughly**
- **Hook:** Crochet hook size N-13 U.S. (9 mm) or size needed to crochet comfortably
- **Scissors**
- **Ruler**
- **4 stitch markers**

✔ **Measurements:** 12 in. wide x 10 in. long

✔ **Gauge:** 9 sc and 10 rows = 4 in.

✔ **Stitches used:** Chain stitch (ch), slip stitch (sl st), single crochet (sc)

Figure 20-3:
You can
create a
reusable
tote made
with loops
of plastic.

Directions

The directions here are written in Crochetese. Refer to Chapter 4 for a refresher on how to read crochet patterns if you get stuck. Gauge isn't crucial with this project, so feel free to adjust the hook size so you're crocheting comfortably with the plastic yarn.

Preparing the strips

All you need to prepare your plastic grocery bag strips is a pair of long, sharp scissors and a trash bag for unwanted ends. Be warned, though, that cutting so many bags is a little time consuming. Why not alleviate the tediousness by cutting bags and getting caught up with your favorite TV shows at the same time?

Follow these steps for cutting loops from plastic grocery bags:

1. **Lay a plastic bag flat, fold it in half lengthwise so that the handles are at one end, and fold it in half lengthwise again.**

2. **Cut off the top and bottom of the bag, removing the handles and bottom seam.**

3. **Cut the remainder of the bag in 1½- to 2-inch pieces widthwise for the loops.**

4. **Repeat for the remaining plastic bags.**

Joining the strips

Joining the plarn loops together may seem a little awkward at first, but you'll have the rhythm down in no time. Just follow these simple steps to achieve the result shown in Figure 20-4:

1. **Holding two loops, pull the end of one loop halfway through the open center of the other loop.**

2. **Continue to pull the end of the first loop through the opposite end of its own loop and pull to make a knot.**

   At this point, the end of the second loop should be secured inside the knot.

3. **Take another free loop and pull it halfway through the open center of one of the joined loops; continue to pull the end through the opposite end of its own loop and pull to make a knot.**

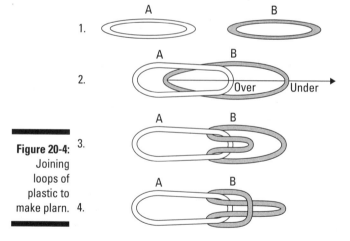

Figure 20-4: Joining loops of plastic to make plarn.

Repeat Step 3 for all plastic bag loops to make one long, double-thick strand of plarn. Wind the plarn into a ball.

Making the bag

Ch 28.

Rnd 1: 3 sc in second ch from hook, sc in each ch across to last ch, 3 sc in last ch. Working across opposite side of foundation chain, sc in each ch across to first sc, sl st in first sc to join (56 sc).

Rnd 2: Ch 1, sc in each st around, don't join to first sc.

Continue to work in sc around the bag in a spiral fashion without joining or turning at the end of a rnd. Work in sc until the bag is 10 in. long.

Lay the bag flat. Find the center front of the bag and place a stitch marker on either side of the center 12 sts. Mark the center 12 sts on the back to coincide with the front. There should be 16 sts between each center group of 12 sts.

Continue to work around in sc to the first stitch marker. Ch 12, skip 10 sts, sc in next marked stitch, sc in each st around to the next marker, ch 12, skip 10 sts, sc in the next marked stitch. * Continue to sc in each st around to first ch-12. Work 20 sc in ch-12 sp; * rep from * to * around. Sc in next 8 sts, sl st in next st. Fasten off and weave in the loose ends with your hook.

Chapter 21

Ten Variations on Crochet

In This Chapter

▶ Looking at variations in stitch technique
▶ Playing with tools to create special pieces
▶ Crocheting on fabric and other oddities

People have experimented quite a bit with the art of crochet over the years. They've taken the basic stitches and found unique ways of manipulating them to create variations on the original art form. They've also combined the use of the crochet hook with other tools to produce totally new techniques. They've even experimented with a variety of materials to broaden the scope of the craft.

This chapter shows you ten of the many possibilities out there in the world of crochet, starting with four special stitch techniques, moving on to three techniques requiring special tools, and closing with three diverse materials you can use. Each of these variations demonstrates the versatility of a craft that has been evolving for centuries and will surely continue to grow and change as long as people have the drive to create. You may not want to tackle any of these crochet variations right now, but hey, it's always good to have something to shoot for, right? If you do want to try your hand at any of these crochet variations, the resources in the appendix can point you to instructions.

Irish Crochet

Developed in the mid-19th century, *Irish crochet* (inspired by the popular Venetian laces of the time) is a stitch technique that combines floral and leaf motifs arranged on a board and then joined together with a network of mesh. It's usually worked in fine cottons to produce the traditional delicate look, and often the pieces are padded by working over a cotton strand called a *foundation cord*.

You can use Irish crochet (shown in Figure 21-1) to produce beautiful home décor items such as pillow toppers, bedspreads, curtains, and tablecloths — basically anything you'd normally crochet with cotton. Though not often worked these days, you can still find examples of gorgeous blouses, dresses, collars, and evening gowns worked in Irish crochet.

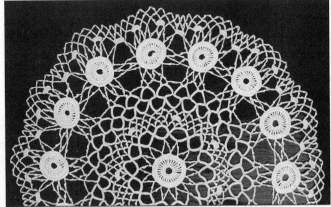

Figure 21-1:
Sample
of Irish
crochet.

Free-Form Crochet

Free-form crochet, also known as *scrumbling,* is kind of like coloring outside the lines. Whereas most crochet patterns have you work a regular, symmetrical pattern in rows of uniform stitches or in neat, concentric circles, free-form crochet opens the door to a more random and artistic approach to the craft. Although patterns can be written for such pieces, the beauty of this technique is that you can use your own imagination and instincts to produce truly unique creations.

This stitch technique supports irregular stitch heights, curves, and zigzags; a mixture of highly textured areas with lightly textured ones; a combination of rounds with rows; and randomly shaped areas to create a patchwork look like that of the sample in Figure 21-2. Combining different colors and textures of yarns helps enhance the effect of free-form crochet.

Free-form crochet lends itself to unique fashions and accessories, abstract and pictorial wall hangings, and three-dimensional sculptures.

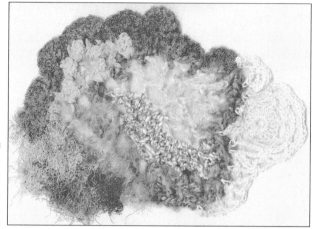

Figure 21-2:
Free-form
crochet
sample.

Surface Crochet

Surface crochet, which resembles embroidery, is crocheting (generally with yarn) onto a crocheted fabric background (see Figure 21-3). You work surface crochet just like a slip stitch (presented in Chapter 5) over the surface of the background. You can surface crochet in a straight line to add stripes to an otherwise solid piece or create pictures on your background. It's frequently used to turn a horizontally striped piece into a plaid by adding the vertical lines afterward.

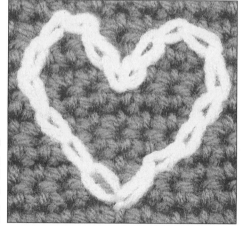

Figure 21-3:
Sample of
surface
crochet.

Tapestry Crochet

Popular in Africa and South America, *tapestry crochet* is a technique that's gaining momentum throughout the crochet community. It's generally worked in single crochet in charted, repetitive patterns that resemble woven tapestries (see Figure 21-4). You can work tapestry crochet in rows to produce flat pieces or in rounds to produce three-dimensional objects.

Figure 21-4: Tapestry crochet sample.

What makes tapestry crochet different from standard single crochet is the practice of working in more than one color at a time, carrying the unused color under the current color, and working your stitches very tightly. You usually work tapestry crochet with a stiffer material, such as a sport-weight cotton, to produce the characteristic of a stiff tapestry.

This stitch technique is ideal for producing baskets, handbags, wall hangings, place mats, and hats. To make beautiful garments (such as scarves, shawls, and even sweaters) with tapestry crochet, work your stitches more loosely and with a soft yarn.

Broomstick Lace

Broomstick lace is a crochet technique that uses a large dowel or needle to form clusters of loops within a fabric. The loops form circles of yarn that produce a unique texture (see Figure 21-5) that's suitable for afghans, shawls, and sweaters. This technique can also work with fine cotton to produce unusual lacy home décor items.

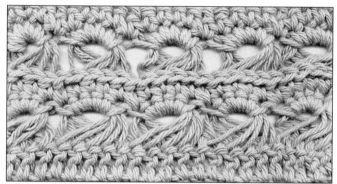

Figure 21-5:
Sample of broomstick lace.

Hairpin Lace

Hairpin lace (see Figure 21-6 for a sample) is worked on a hairpin lace loom to produce long strips of lacy loops. The technique was originally worked on actual hairpins, which are much smaller, but has since evolved into a larger version that's good for making lacy shawls and afghans.

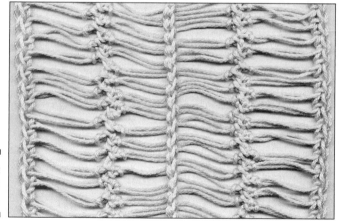

Figure 21-6:
Hairpin lace sample.

Hairpin lace looms are adjustable to different widths, so you can vary the laciness of your strips. You can also vary how the loops are joined together, allowing for a myriad of designs.

Double-Ended Crochet

Double-ended crochet (also known as *cro-hooking*) is similar to working Tunisian crochet (refer to Chapter 12 for more on this). The difference between the two techniques is the hook. Double-ended crochet uses a long, double-ended hook that allows you to work stitches on or off from either end.

This technique is usually used with two alternating colors, working loops onto the hook with one color and then turning the work around and working the stitches off with the second color. Double-ended crochet produces a fabric that's reversible because it has a different color pattern on either side (as you can see in Figure 21-7). The fabric is softer and more elastic than the basic Tunisian stitch, making it ideal for afghans, scarves, and stoles.

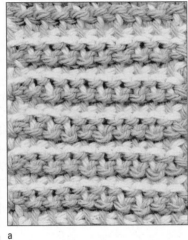
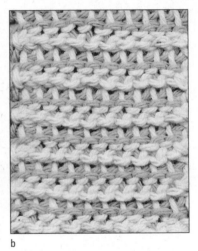

Figure 21-7: Both sides of a double-ended crochet sample.

a   b

Crocheting on Fabric

If you have a fabric whose edges won't unravel, you can actually crochet an edging onto it with cotton thread. You can crochet edgings on pillowcases, tablecloths, or on a piece of linen to create a simple place mat. Working with heavier cotton or sport-weight yarn, you can also produce fashions and accessories with suede pieces, felt, or fleece. You can even use crochet to join pieces of fabric together to create jackets, bathrobes, totes, purses, vests, and skirts.

With lightweight fabrics, you can usually just poke through using a tiny hook. In fact, you may find linen pieces hemmed and equipped with small holes around the edges for the purpose of crocheting onto the fabric. With suede or heavier fabrics, you must poke or punch holes into the fabric at evenly spaced intervals and work the stitches into them.

Bead Crochet

Bead crochet has grown in popularity, perhaps thanks to the ever-expanding selection of beads available in craft stores. You can add beads to crochet in two basic ways:

- ✔ **Sew them on after you finish crocheting.** If you want only a few beads to highlight certain areas, sew them on after you're done crocheting. If you're using smaller beads, you can sew them on with a regular sewing needle and matching sewing thread (or clear nylon thread). However, if your beads are fairly large, you must use a yarn or tapestry needle and the yarn you used to crochet the piece.

- ✔ **Crochet them right into the fabric.** If the beads are an integral part of the design, you can easily crochet them in as you work. String the beads onto the yarn or thread with a needle and begin to crochet according to the pattern until you reach the first stitch or row where you want to add a bead. Then insert your hook into the next stitch, draw a bead up close to the hook, yarn over, draw the thread through the stitch, and then complete the stitch as you normally would. Figure 21-8 shows beaded double crochet stitches, with a row of regular (nonbeaded) single crochet in between.

Figure 21-8:
Beaded
double
crochet
stitches.

 Make sure that the weight of the yarn is compatible with the weight of the beads. If you're using a lightweight yarn, don't use heavy, oversized beads. The weight of the beads can cause the stitches to droop and pull, creating an unsightly mess. On the flip side, if you're working with a heavier-weight yarn, choose beads that won't get lost in the stitches.

Wire Crochet

Crocheting with wire is a technique that goes hand-in-hand with free-form crochet (which we describe earlier in this chapter) to produce unique crocheted art. Using soft wire and a relatively large hook, you can create beautiful crocheted sculptures. Soft, colored wire is now readily available in most craft stores. With the addition of some fun and funky beads, you can crochet yourself a choker and matching bracelet.

Any of the basic crochet stitches will work for wire crochet except the Tunisian stitch. Whichever stitch you decide on, keep it simple because the materials used for wire crochet pose enough challenges on their own.

Sources and Resources

· ·

*W*arning: After you're hooked into crocheting, you can never get enough. You'll soon be browsing around for new kinds of yarn, fresh patterns, and more challenging techniques. In this appendix, we give you the best of the best crochet information that's available.

No matter how experienced you become, reference materials never go to waste. The Internet is also a wonderful way to search for new materials and ideas. We list a few of our favorite sites in the next few pages, but look around because you may find some you like better.

Yarn Sources

You can find most of the yarns used for the projects in this book online or at your local craft or yarn shop. If you're unable to find them, or if they're unavailable in your area, you can contact the following manufacturers directly.

Bernat
320 Livingstone Ave. South
Listowel, ON
Canada N4W 3H3
Phone 888-368-8401
E-mail inquire@bernat.com
Web site www.bernat.com

Berroco, Inc.
14 Elmdale Rd.
P.O. Box 367
Uxbridge, MA 01569
Phone 508-278-2527
E-mail info@berroco.com
Web site www.berroco.com

Blue Sky Alpacas, Inc.
P.O. Box 88
Cedar, MN 55011
Phone 888-460-8862 or 763-753-5815
E-mail info@blueskyalpacas.com
Web site www.blueskyalpacas.com

Brown Sheep Company, Inc.
100662 County Rd. 16
Mitchell, NE 69357
Phone 800-826-9136
Web site www.brownsheep.com

Caron International
P.O. Box 222
Washington, NC 27889
Phone 866-336-9185
E-mail public_relations@
        caron.com
Web site www.caron.com

Cascade Yarns
1224 Andover Park E
Tukwila, WA 98188
Phone 206-574-0440
Web site www.cascadeyarns.com

Coats & Clark
Consumer Services
P.O. Box 12229
Greenville, SC 29612
Phone 800-648-1479
Web site www.coatsandclark.com

The DMC Corporation
77 South Hackensack Ave.
Building 10F
South Kearny, NJ 07032
Phone 973-589-0606
Web site www.dmc-usa.com

Elmore-Pisgah
550 Orchard St.
Old Fort, NC 28762
Phone 800-633-7829 or 828-668-7667
E-mail peaches-creme@
        verizon.net
Web site www.elmore-pisgah.com

Fiesta Yarns
5401 San Diego Ave. NE
Albuquerque, NM 87113
Phone 505-892-5008
E-mail customerservice@
        FiestaYarns.com
Web site www.fiestayarns.com

Lion Brand Yarn
135 Kero Rd.
Carlstadt, NJ 07072
Phone 800-258-9276
Web site www.lionbrand.com

Patons Yarns
320 Livingstone Ave. South
Listowel, ON
Canada N4W 3H3
Phone 888-368-8401
E-mail inquire@patonsyarns.com
Web site www.patonsyarns.com

Crochet Magazines

Magazines are a great source of information about what's going on in the crochet world. They tend to feature lots of patterns along with techniques and where to find the newest yarns. Following are two of our favorite crochet magazines:

✔ **Crochet!:** *Crochet!* is the official bimonthly magazine of the Crochet Guild of America and is filled with patterns for both fashion and home décor. Regular features include book reviews, what's new in crochet, and charitable crochet in your community and beyond. The magazine is available in print at your local yarn or bookstore, or you can buy and download a digital copy online (www.crochetmagazine.com). To order a subscription for about $20 a year, call 800-449-0440.

> ✔ **Interweave Crochet:** *Interweave Crochet* (www.interweavecrochet.com) is a quarterly publication that features contemporary crochet patterns in fashion and home décor for all levels of experience. It also contains stitch charts and in-depth articles about crochet, yarn, and tools. You can find this magazine at most craft and yarn stores as well as your local bookstore. To order an annual subscription for $22, visit the Web site or call 800-272-2193.

Online Crochet Communities

Seeking fellow crocheters to share your excitement over coming up with a new pattern or your frustrations at mastering a tough technique? Become a member of one (or more!) of the many *online crochet communities,* social networking sites with forums that allow you to discuss your favorite subject — crochet! We recommend these three (all of which are free to join):

> ✔ **CrochetMe:** This site (www.crochetme.com) gives crocheters a place to offer crochet patterns, tips, and advice to one another. Membership is free, and registering is easy (you can do it right from the Web site's home page).

> ✔ **Crochetville:** This site (www.crochetville.com) is a crochet-only community. Members can discuss all things crochet and show off their current projects in a variety of forums. To become a member, simply log on and register for free at the site.

> ✔ **Ravelry:** This site (www.ravelry.com) is a sophisticated knit and crochet community that allows you to share photos of your projects along with your yarn stash. There are lots of groups you can join that are interest specific, so if you're a Trekkie, for example, you can find other Trekkies who share your passion for crochet, Spock, and Tribbles. To join this community, simply log on to the Web site and create your free account.

The Crochet Guild of America

The Crochet Guild of America (CGOA; www.crochet.org) is the largest organization dedicated to crochet. Its members span the United States and are continually working to introduce people to the craft of crochet. In addition to sponsoring crochet events in various cities around the country, the CGOA operates a Web site featuring up-to-date information about new projects and gadgets, as well as a chat room where you can always find someone to help with a question. Membership is about $35 per year and includes a subscription to *Crochet!,* the CGOA's magazine. To see whether belonging to the CGOA is right for you, search for your local chapter/guild on the Web site and attend one of its meetings.

Index

Symbols

asterisk (*), 48
bullet (•), 48
cross (†), 48
plus sign (+), 48

• A •

abbreviations
  of color names in patterns, 162–163
  described, 9
  in written instructions, 43–44
Absorbent Hand Towel project, 227–229, 354
Afghan stitch. *See* Tunisian crochet
American terms, British terms compared
    to, 13, 45
amigurumi, 145
Amigurumi Pup project, 149–154
anatomy of a stitch
  back loop, 82, 83
  back-most loop, 82, 83
  base, 82, 83
  front loop, 82, 83
  front-most loop, 82, 83
  overview, 82
  post, 82, 83
  top 2 loops, 82, 83
article number on yarn labels, 25
assembly section in crochet patterns, 43
asterisk (*), 48

• B •

Baby Washcloth project, 88
baby weight, 20
back loop
  described, 82, 83
  stitch placement in, 188

back post stitches, 193–194
back-most loop
  described, 82, 83
  stitch placement in, 188
backstitch, sewing pieces together with,
    278–280
ball of yarn, 24
bars, 247–248
base, described, 82, 83
basic stitches, 66–74. *See also specific
    stitches*
Basketweave Scarf project, 203–205
bead crochet, 367
beginners, yarn for, 8
Bernat, 369
Berroco, Inc., 369
Bev's Country Cottage, 353
binding off, 214–215
blanket stitch, sewing pieces together with,
    274–275
Blankets for Canada Society, 353
blends, yarn, 293
blocking
  described, 335
  gauge swatch (sample), 36
  heat, 342–343
  overview, 338–339
  spray, 341
  with starch, 343–345
  tools for, 339–340
  wet, 340–341
blocks
  combining spaces and, 237–238
  creating, 236
Blue Sky Alpacas, Inc., 369
bobble stitch
  International Crochet Symbol for, 178
  overview, 178–179

brackets in written instructions, 47
brand name on yarn labels, 25
brands of crochet hooks, differences in, 16
brick stitch, 248–249
broomstick lace, 364–365
Brown Sheep Company, Inc., 369
Bucket Hat project, 145–148
bulky weight, 20
bullet (•), 48
Butterfly Runner project, 250–252
button loops, 316–318
buttonholes
    button loops as alternative to, 316–318
    in front plackets, 313–314
    in garment body, 314–316
    overview, 313
buttons, 333

• C •

cardigans, 296–297
care instructions on yarn labels, 25
Caron International, 370
carrying yarn
    overview, 158
    on right side, 160
    up the side, 161
    working over a carried strand, 159–160
    on wrong side, 158–159
Cascade Yarns, 370
CC (contrasting color), 162
center ring
    adjustable ring used to create, 136–137
    chain stitch used to create, 134–136
    chain stitches joined into, 132–134
    creating, 132–133
    overview, 131–132
CGOA (Crochet Guild of America), 352, 372
chain loops, stitch placement in, 191
chain spaces, stitch placement in, 191
chain stitch (ch)
    counting, 69
    creating your first, 66–67
    foundation chain, 66

joined into center ring, 132–134
loose chain stitches, fixing, 67
overview, 66
right side, determining, 68–69
tight chain stitches, fixing, 67
turning chain, 79–80
working a round of stitches into one
    chain stitch to create center ring,
    134–136
working other stitches into chain
    stitches, 69–70
wrong side, determining, 68–69
yarn tension, controlling, 67–68
charted patterns, changing color in,
    157–158
charts for filet crochet, following, 232–233
chunky weight, 20
circles. See rounds
cluster stitch
    International Crochet Symbol for, 175
    overview, 174–175
Coats & Clark, 370
collars, 312–313
color
    abbreviating color names in patterns,
        162–163
    carrying yarn to keep colors separate,
        158–161
    changing, 10
    charted patterns, changing color in,
        157–158
    choosing, 162
    combining, 162
    contrasting color (CC), 162
    Fibonacci sequence used to create color
        pattern, 165
    joining new colors, 155–158
    main color (MC), 162
    multiple colors, use of letters in patterns
        to designate, 163
    rows, changing color at beginning or
        end of, 156–157
    rows, changing color in middle of, 157–158
    in Tunisian crochet, 221–224
    working with, 27

color chart, 163–164
color name and number on yarn labels, 25
color wheel, 162
combination stitches, 70
combinations, creating yarn, 28–29
combining color, 162
company name and logo on yarn labels, 25
continental (metric) system for sizing
    crochet hooks, 17–19
contrasting color (CC), 162
conversion chart for sizing
  of standard crochet hooks, 19
  of steel crochet hooks, 18
correct hand for hooking, determining, 59–60
cotton yarn, 22
counting chain stitches, 69
Craft Yarn Council of America, 21
crewel work, 334
Crochet!, 370, 372
Crochet Guild of America (CGOA), 352, 372
crochet hook
  brands, differences in, 16
  changing hook size to compensate for
    tight/loose style of crocheting, 39
  continental (metric) system for
    sizing, 17–19
  conversion chart for sizes of, 18–19
  handle, 16
  household uses for, 19
  how to hold, 60–61
  overview, 8, 15–16
  parts of, 15–16
  point, 16
  shaft, 16
  size of, 17–19
  standard, 17
  steel, 17
  struggling to fit your hook into
    stitches, 336
  throat, 16
  thumb rest, 16
  in Tunisian crochet, 210–211
UK (English) system for sizing, 17–19
U.S. (American) system for sizing, 17–19

crochet patterns
  assembly section, 43
  crocheting directions section, 42
  finishing section, 43
  gauge recommendation, 34
  gauge section, 42
  level of experience section, 42
  materials section, 42
  overview, 41–43
  sections of, 41–43
  size information section, 42
  stitch diagrams, 50–55
  stitches section, 42
  using, 9
  written instructions, 43–50
crochet terminology, 13, 45
crochet thread, 20
crochet variations
  bead crochet, 367
  broomstick lace, 364–365
  crocheting on fabric, 366–367
  cro-hooking, 366
  double-ended crochet, 366
  free-form crochet, 362–363
  hairpin lace, 365
  Irish crochet, 361–362
  overview, 361
  surface crochet, 363
  tapestry crochet, 364
  wire crochet, 368
Crocheted Bag project, 357–360
crocheted fabric, slip stitch used for
    embellishing, 70
crocheted towels, 354
crocheting
  directions section in crochet patterns, 42
  on fabric, 366–367
  joining seams by, 280–288
  reasons for, 7
crocheting pieces together
  flat seam creating, 282–283
  on last row or round, 286–288
  overview, 280–281
  with a ridged seam, 281–282

crocheting pieces together *(continued)*
  with a row of stitches, 284–286
  with single crochet, 283–284
  with a slip stitch seam, 281–283
CrochetMe, 371
Crochetville, 371
cro-hooking, 366
crop tops, 295
crossed double crochet stitch (crossed dc)
  International Crochet Symbol for, 173
  overview, 172–173
cross (†), 48
cross-stitching
  as embellishment, 334
  on top of Tunisian crochet, 224–227
curling corners, 338
curling problem with Tunisian crochet, 221
customizing sweater patterns, 300–301

• *D* •

decreasing spaces and blocks in filet
    crochet, 244–245
decreasing stitches (dec)
  with double crochet, 123–125
  overview, 121
  with single crochet, 121–122
  by skipping stitches, 126
  with slip stitches at start of row, 125–126
  by stopping and turning before you reach
    end of row, 126–127
  in Tunisian simple stitch (Tss), 216–217
details, adding final, 12
distractions, picking a place to work
    without, 13
DK (double knitting) weight, 20
DMC Corporation, 370
dominant hand, 59
donating crochet supplies to community
    groups, 352
double crochet (dc)
  decreasing stitches with, 123–125
  first row of, 90–92

increasing stitches with double crochet
    at beginning of row, 119–120
increasing stitches with double crochet
    in middle or end of row, 120–121
  length of stitch, 100
  overview, 13, 90
  procedure for, 90–94
  second row of, 92–93
  setup for, 90
double knitting (DK) weight, 20
double triple crochet (dtr)
  first row of, 97–99
  length of stitch, 100
  overview, 97
  procedure for, 97–100
  second row of, 99
  setup for, 97–98
double triple triple crochet (dtrtr), 100
double-ended crochet, 366
drawstrings, 318–319
dry cleaning, 347
dye lot number on yarn labels, 26

• *E* •

eco-friendly fibers, using, 353–354
edges
  shrinking, 336–337
  slip stitch used for finishing, 70
  tightening of, 337–338
  widening of, 337
edging, 308
Elegant All-Season Wrap project, 183–186
Elmore-Pisgah, 370
embellishment
  buttons, 333
  cross-stitch as, 334
  embroidery, 334
  fringe, 329–331
  tassels, 329, 331–333
embroidery, 334
experienced crocheter to help explain new
    techniques, finding, 14

extended crochet stitches, 104–109
extended double crochet (Edc), 107–109
extended single crochet (Esc), 104–106
extending stitches, 104–109
eyelets, 318

● *F* ●

fabric stiffener, 344–345
fabrics, 11
fair trade fibers, 23
fancy stitch, 246
fastening off
    overview, 83
    weaving in end, 84
    yarn, cutting, 83
feel of yarn, 293
Felted Shoulder Bag project, 205–208
felting
    described, 187
    by hand, 201–202
    by machine, 201
    overview, 200
fiber content of yarn, 27, 293
Fibonacci sequence, 164–165
Fiesta Yarns, 370
filet crochet
    bars, 247–248
    blocks, 236–238
    charts for, 232–233
    decreasing spaces and blocks, 244–245
    foundation chain, 234
    increasing spaces and blocks, 238–244
    lacets, 246–247
    overview, 231–232
    shaping, 238–245
    spaces, combining blocks and, 237–238
    spaces in, creating, 234–235
    stitches in, 232
fingering weight, 20
finished bust measurement
    adjusting, 300–301
    described, 299
finishing section in crochet patterns, 43

finishing touches
    button loops, 316–318
    buttonholes, 313–318
    buttons, 333
    collars, 312–313
    drawstrings, 318–319
    edging, 308
    embellishments, 329–334
    embroidery, 334
    fringe, 329–331
    pockets, 319–321
    ribbing, 308–312
    tassels, 329, 331–333
    ties, 318–319
finishing your work
    caring for your creations, 13
    details, adding final, 12
    overview, 12
    pieces, putting together all your, 12
first round in granny squares, 256
first row
    of double crochet (dc), 90–92
    of double triple crochet (dtr), 97–99
    of half double crochet (hdc), 101–102
    of linked stitches of single crochet (sc),
        73–74, 195–197
    of triple crochet (tr), 94–96
fit of sweater, determining, 299–300
flat flower motif, 260–261
flat seam, creating a, 282–283
Flower Power project, 266–268
following stitch diagrams, 52–55
foundation chain
    filet crochet, 234
    overview, 66
foundation cord, 361
foundation singe crochet (fsc)
    creating your first, 75–76
    creating your second, 76–78
foundation stitches
    advantages of, 74
    overview, 74–75
free-form crochet, 362–363
fringe, 329–331
front loop
    described, 82, 83
    stitch placement in, 188

front plackets
  buttonholes in, 313–314
  described, 313
front post stitches, 191–193
front-most loop
  described, 82, 83
  stitch placement in, 188
frustration with new stitch, dealing
      with, 13
fundamentals of crochet
  overview, 8
  pattern, crocheting from, 9
  tension, adjusting, 9
  tools, 8
fundamentals of stitch diagrams, 52

• **G** •

garment body, buttonholes in, 314–316
gauge
  creating your own, 39–40
  defined, 33
  importance of, 33
  overview, 33–34
  pattern recommendation for, 34
  for sweaters, 34
  on yarn labels, 26
gauge section in crochet patterns, 42
gauge swatch
  blocking, 36
  correcting gauges with measurements
      from, 38–39
  overview, 34
  practicing new stitch of technique by
      working on a, 13, 82
  repeating pattern, measuring a swatch
      made with a, 37
  single crochet stitches, measuring, 36
  sizing, 35
  stitches and rounds, measuring, 37–38
  stitches and rows, measuring, 36–37
  uses for, 35
Girl's Versatile Camisole project, 321–328
Granny Square Cuff project, 288–290
granny squares
  first round in, 256
  joining, 287–288
  overview, 255–256
  rounds, adding, 256–257
  second round in, 256
  technique for, 256–258
green items for your home, 354

• **H** •

H-8 U.S. (5 mm) crochet hook, 8
hairpin lace, 365
half double crochet (hdc)
  first row of, 101–102
  overview, 100–101
  procedure for, 101–103
  second row of, 102–103
  setup for, 101
half-closed stitch, 174
hand, felting by, 201–202
hand for hooking, determining correct,
      59–60
hand washing, 347
handle of crochet hook, 16
hank of yarn, 24
heat blocking
  by ironing, 342
  overview, 342
  by steaming, 342–343
heavy worsted weight, 20
Helping Hands Needle Arts Mentoring
      Program, 352
hooks
  brands, differences in, 16
  changing hook size to compensate for
      tight/loose style of crocheting, 39
  continental (metric) system for sizing,
      17–19
  conversion chart for sizes of, 18–19
  handle, 16
  household uses for, 19
  how to hold, 60–61
  overview, 15–16
  parts of, 15–16
  point, 16
  shaft, 16
  size of, 17–19
  standard, 17
  steel, 17

struggling to fit into stitches, 336
throat, 16
thumb rest, 16
in Tunisian crochet, 210–211
UK (English) system for sizing, 17–19
U.S. (American) system for sizing, 17–19
hook knitting. *See* Tunisian crochet
hook roll, 31
household uses for crochet hooks, 19
hyphens in written instructions, 44

• I •

icons explained, 4
increasing spaces and blocks in filet
    crochet, 238–244
increasing stitches (inc)
    with double crochet at beginning of row,
        119–120
    with double crochet in middle or end of
        row, 120–121
    overview, 118
    in rounds, 141–142
    with single crochet, 118–119
    in Tunisian simple stitch (Tss), 215–216
inseam pockets, 320–321
International Crochet Symbols
    bobble stitch, 178
    cluster stitch, 175
    crossed double crochet stitch
        (crossed dc), 173
    described, 50
    loop stitch, 183
    overview, 51
    picot stitch, 176
    popcorn stitch (pop), 181
    puff stitch (puff st), 180
    reverse single crochet stitch
        (reverse sc), 177
    shell stitch (shell), 173
    stitch diagrams, 50–51
    V-stitch (V-st), 172
International Fabric Care Symbols for
    yarn care, 346
Interweave Crochet, 371
Irish crochet, 361–362
ironing, heat blocking by, 342

• J •

jargon in written instructions, 46
joining granny squares, 287–288
joining new colors, 155–158
joining rounds
    of double crochet stitches, 139
    of single crochet stitches, 138
joining seams
    by crocheting, 280–288
    overview, 271
    by sewing, 272–280
joining yarn at end of row, 110
    in middle of row, 111–112
    overview, 109

• K •

kitchen bowl, for shaping three-
    dimensional designs, 345

• L •

lace, mesh crochet used to make, 248–249
lace weight, 20
lacets, 246–247
lacy hexagon motif, 258–260
last row or round, crocheting pieces
    together on the, 286–288
layered flower motif, 261–264
"Learn to Crochet" basket, making and
    giving away, 351
left-handers
    over-the-hook position, 60, 64
    overview, 10
    skipknot, working a, 63–64
    tips for, 62
    translating instructions for, 62
    under-the-hook position, 60–61, 64
    yarn, how to hold, 61–63
length of stitch
    double crochet (dc), 100
    double triple crochet (dtr), 100
    double triple triple crochet (dtrtr), 100
    long stitches, 198–200
    quadruple triple triple crochet (quad), 100
    single crochet (sc), 100
    triple crochet (tr), 100
    triple triple crochet (trtr), 100

lengthening sweater patterns, 301
level of experience section in
    crochet patterns, 42
light worsted weight, 20
linked stitches
    first row of, 195–197
    overview, 195
    second row of, 198
Lion Brand Yarn, 370
liquid starch, 344–345
local yarn, buying, 353
long stitches
    creating, 199
    overview, 198–200
loop, described, 46
loop stitch
    International Crochet Symbol for, 183
    overview, 182–183
loose chain stitches, fixing, 67
loose style of crocheting, changing hook
    size to compensate for, 39
Luxurious Washcloth projects
    Baby Washcloth project, 88
    Luxurious Washcloth with Border
        project, 85–88
    Simple Luxurious Washcloth project,
        84–85

• M •

machine, felting by, 201
machine washing and drying, 347
magazines
    Crochet!, 370, 372
    Interweave Crochet, 371
main color (MC), 162
man-made fiber
    natural fiber compared to, 27–28
    overview, 27–28
manufacturer's address on yarn labels, 26
materials section in crochet patterns, 42
mattress stitch, sewing pieces together
    with, 275–278
mesh crochet
    brick stitch, 248–249
    overview, 248
Mod Pillow project, 165–168

motifs
    crocheting pieces together in, 286–288
    flat flower, 260–261
    Flower Power project, 266–268
    Granny Square Cuff project, 288–290
    granny squares, 255–258
    lacy hexagon, 258–260
    layered flower, 261–264
    overview, 255
    Raindrop Earrings project, 264–265
    sweater created with, 297
multiple colors, use of letters in patterns to
    designate, 163

• N •

natural fiber
    man-made fiber compared to, 27–28
    overview, 27–28
natural-colored yarn, using, 353–354
net patterns. *See* mesh crochet
net stitch. *See* filet crochet
nonprofit organizations, donating your
    crocheted goods to, 352–353
novelty yarn, 23

• O •

online crochet communities
    CrochetMe, 371
    Crochetville, 371
    Ravelry, 353, 371
organic yarn, 23
over-the-hook position, 60, 64

• P •

paper cups, for shaping three-dimensional
    designs, 345
parentheses in written instructions, 46–47
patch pockets, 319–320
Patons Yarns, 370
pattern stitches
    cluster stitch, 174–175
    crossed double crochet stitch
        (crossed dc), 172–173

overview, 171
picot stitch, 175–176
reverse single crochet stitch (reverse
    sc), 176–177
shell stitch (shell), 173–174
V-stitch (V-st), 172
patterns
    assembly section, 43
    crocheting directions section, 42
    finishing section, 43
    gauge recommendation, 34
    gauge section, 42
    level of experience section, 42
    materials section, 42
    overview, 41–43
    sections of, 41–43
    size information section, 42
    stitch diagrams, 50–55
    stitches section, 42
    using, 9
    written instructions, 43–50
picot stitch
    International Crochet Symbol for, 176
    overview, 175–176
pieces, putting together all your, 12
plastic wrap, for shaping three-dimensional
    designs, 345
plastic yarn (plarn), converting plastic
    bags into, 357–360
plus sign (+), 48
ply, 26
ply on yarn labels, 26
pockets
    inseam, 320–321
    patch, 319–320
    slashed, 320
    types of, 319
point of crochet hook, 16
popcorn stitch (pop)
    International Crochet Symbol for, 181
    overview, 180–181
positive acts with crochet
    converting plastic bags to plastic yarn
        (plarn), 357–360
    donating crochet supplies to community
        groups, 352

eco-friendly fibers, using, 353–354
green items for your home, crocheting, 354
"Learn to Crochet" basket, making and
    giving away, 351
local yarn, buying, 353
natural-colored yarn, using, 353–354
nonprofit organizations, donating your
    crocheted goods to, 352–353
recycling old fabric with a crocheted rag
    rug, 354–357
stash swap party, hosting, 351
teaching someone how to crochet, 352
post, 82, 83
post stitches
    back, 193–194
    front, 191–193
    overview, 191
    ribbing, 310–312
practice, importance of, 10
preformed foam shapes, for shaping three-
    dimensional designs, 345
preparation for crocheting
    correct hand for hooking, determining,
        59–60
    hook, how to hold, 60–61
    skipknot, working a, 63–64
    wrapping yarn over the hook, 65–66
    yarn, how to hold, 61–63
    yarn over (yo), 65–66
projects
    Absorbent Hand Towel, 227–229, 354
    Amigurumi Pup, 149–154
    Basketweave Scarf, 203–205
    Bucket Hat, 145–148
    Butterfly Runner, 250–252
    Crocheted Bag, 357–360
    Elegant All-season Wrap, 183–186
    Felted Shoulder Bag, 205–208
    Flower Power, 266–268
    Girl's Versatile Camisole, 321–328
    Granny Square Cuff, 288–290
    Luxurious Washcloth, 84–88
    Mod Pillow, 165–168
    Rag Rug, 354–357
    Raindrop Earrings, 264–265
    Sassy Scarf, 112–115

projects *(continued)*
  Simple Ripple Blanket, 127–130
  Simple Sweater, 301–306
  String Market Bag, 252–254, 354
  Textured Scarf, 202–203
puff stitch (puff st)
  International Crochet Symbol for, 180
  overview, 179–180
pullovers, 295–296

• *Q* •

quadruple triple triple crochet (quad), 100
quality of yarn, 293
quantity of yarn to purchase, 293

• *R* •

rag crochet, 354–357
Rag Rug project, 354–357
railroad knitting. *See* Tunisian crochet
Raindrop Earrings project, 264–265
Ravelry, 353, 371
reasons for crocheting, 7
recommended hook size on yarn labels, 26
recycling old fabric with crocheted rag rug, 354–357
Remember icon, explained, 4
removable stitch markers, 30
repeating pattern, measuring swatch made with a, 37
resources
  Crochet Guild of America (CGOA), 372
  crochet magazines, 370–371
  online crochet communities, 371
  for yarn, 369–370
reverse single crochet stitch (reverse sc)
  International Crochet Symbol for, 177
  overview, 176–177
ribbing
  overview, 308
  post stitch, 310–312
  single crochet, 308–310
ridged seam, crocheting pieces together with a, 281–282
right side
  carrying yarn on, 160
  determining, 68–69

ring, slip stitch used for creating, 70
rounds
  adding, 139–142
  center rings for, 131–137
  in granny squares, 256–257
  increasing stitches in, 141–142
  joining a round of double crochet stitches, 139
  joining a round of single crochet stitches, 138
  overview, 131
  repeating, 49–50
  second round of double crochet, 140
  second round of single crochet, 140
  spiral, 142–143
  three-dimensional, 143–144
  working in, 10
row-end stitches, stitch placement in, 189
rows. *See also* first row; second row
  changing color at beginning or end of, 156–157
  changing color in middle of, 157–158
  crocheting pieces together with a row of stitches, 284–286
  joining yarn at end of row, 110
  joining yarn in middle of row, 111–112
  new row of single crochet, creating, 80–82
  repeating, 49–50
  stitch placement in previous rows, 198–200
ruler, 29
rustproof straight pins, 29

• *S* •

safety pins, 29
Sassy Scarf project, 112–115
schematic, 42
schematic for sweater patterns, 294
scissors, 29
seamless crocheting, 286
seams, slip stitch used for, 70
second round
  of double crochet, 140
  in granny squares, 256
  of single crochet, 140
second row
  of double crochet (dc), 92–93
  of double triple crochet (dtr), 99

of half double crochet (hdc), 102–103
of linked stitches, 198
of triple crochet (tr), 96–97
of Tunisian simple stitch (Tss), 213–214
sections of crochet patterns, 41–43
setup
　for double crochet (dc), 90
　for double triple crochet (dtr), 97–98
　for half double crochet (hdc), 101
　for triple crochet (tr), 94
sewing pieces together
　with backstitch, 278–280
　with blanket stitch, 274–275
　with mattress stitch, 275–278
　overview, 272
　with whipstitch, 272–274
shaft of crochet hook, 16
shapes, 12
shaping
　filet crochet, 238–245
　projects, 10
　slip stitch used for, 70
　three-dimensional designs, 345
　Tunisian crochet, 215–217
　Tunisian simple stitch (Tss), 215–217
shell, 45
shell stitch (shell)
　International Crochet Symbol for, 173
　overview, 173–174
shepherd's knitting. *See* Tunisian crochet
shrinking, edges of fabric are, 336–337
side of stitch, stitch placement in, 189
silk yarn, 22
Simple Luxurious Washcloth project, 84–85
Simple Ripple Blanket project, 127–130
Simple Sweater project, 301–306
single crochet ribbing, 308–310
single crochet (sc)
　creating your first, 72–73
　crocheting pieces together with, 283–284
　decreasing stitches with, 121–122
　first row of, 73–74
　increasing stitches with, 118–119
　length of stitch, 100
　measuring stitches, 36
　overview, 72

size information section in crochet
　patterns, 42
size of crochet hooks, 17–19
sizing
　gauge swatch, 35
　sweater patterns, 298–299
　sweaters, 298–301
skein of yarn, 24
skipknot, working a, 63–64
skipping stitches, decreasing stitches
　by, 126
slashed pockets, 320
sleeveless sweater, 294–295
sleeves, lengthening, 301
slip stitch seam, crocheting pieces
　together with a, 281–283
slip stitch (sl st)
　decreasing stitches with, 125–126
　for embellishing, 70
　for finishing edges, 70
　for forming combination stitches, 70
　overview, 70
　ring, steps for making slip stitch that
　　forms a, 70–72
　uses for, 70
sock weight, 20
spaces
　combining blocks and, 237–238
　creating, 234–235
　described, 46
　between stitches, stitch placement in, 190
special stitches in written instructions, 45
special symbols in written
　instructions, 48–49
spiral
　ending a, 143
　overview, 142
　working in a, 142–143
split stitch markers, 30
sport weight, 20
spray blocking, 341
spray starch, 343–344
standard crochet hooks
　conversion chart for sizes of, 19
　described, 17
Standard Yarn Weight System, 21

starch for blocking
  fabric stiffener, 344–345
  liquid starch, 344–345
  overview, 343
  spray starch, 343–344
stash, 351
stash swap party, hosting, 351
steaming, heat blocking by, 342–343
steel crochet hooks
  conversion chart for sizes of, 18
  described, 17
stem. *See* post
stitch descriptions at beginning of each
    pattern, always read, 13
stitch diagrams
  advantages of, 50
  crochet patterns, 50–55
  following, 52–55
  fundamentals of, 52
  International Crochet Symbols, 50–51
  overview, 50–51
  written instruction, translating a stitch
    diagram into, 52–55
stitch placement
  in back loop, 188
  in back-most loop, 188
  under both top loops, 188
  in chain loops, 191
  in chain spaces, 191
  in front loop, 188
  in front-most loop, 188
  linked stitches, 195–198
  long stitches, 198–200
  overview, 187–188
  post stitches, 191–194
  in previous rows, 198–200
  in row-end stitches, 189
  in side of stitch, 189
  in spaces between stitches, 190
stitches. *See also specific stitches*
  extending, 104–109
  length of, 100
  overview, 11
  UK terminology for, 13, 45

  U.S. terminology for, 13, 45
  width of, 109
stitches and rounds, measuring, 37–38
stitches and rows, measuring, 36–37
stitches (basic)
  chain stitch (ch), 66–70
  single crochet (sc), 72–74
  slip stitch (sl st), 70–72
stitches (foundation)
  advantages of, 74
  foundation single crochet (fsc), creating
    your first, 75–76
  foundation single crochet (fsc), creating
    your second, 76–78
  overview, 74–75
Stitches from the Heart, 353
stitches section in crochet patterns, 42
stopping and turning before you reach end
    of row, decreasing stitches by, 126–127
storing your work, 347–348
String Market Bag project, 252–254, 354
style for sweater, choosing, 294–298
substituting yarn, 28
super bulky weight, 20
surface crochet, 363
sustainably sourced yarn, 23
swatch
  blocking, 36
  correcting gauge with measurements
    from, 38–39
  overview, 34
  practicing new stitch or technique by
    working on a, 13, 82
  repeating pattern, measuring a swatch
    made with a, 37
  single crochet stitches, measuring, 36
  sizing, 35
  stitches and rounds, measuring, 37–38
  stitches and rows, measuring, 36–37
  uses for, 35
sweaters
  cardigans, 296–297
  crop tops, 295
  finished bust measurement, 299

fit, determining, 299–300
gauge for, 34
with motifs, 297
pullovers, 295–296
Simple Sweater project, 301–306
sizing, 298–301
sleeveless, 294–295
style, choosing, 294–298
tunics, 295
with vertical rows, 297
yarn for, choosing, 293
sweater patterns
choosing, 292–293
customizing, 300–301
finished bust measurement, adjusting,
    300–301
lengthening, 301
schematic, 294
sizing, 298–299
sleeves, lengthening, 301
swift, 31
symbols for yarn weight, 21
synthetic yarn, 23

• T •

tape measure, 29
tapestry crochet, 364
tapestry needles, 30
tassels, 329, 331–333
teaching someone how to crochet, 352
techniques
experienced crocheter to help explain,
    finding, 14
for granny squares, 256–258
swatch, practicing by working
    on a, 13, 82
for Tunisian crochet, 211–215
techniques (basic)
colors, changing, 10
overview, 10
practice, importance of, 10
rounds, working in, 10
shaping projects, 10
tension, adjusting, 9
terminology, 13, 45

texture stitches
bobble stitch, 178–179
loop stitch, 182–183
overview, 177
popcorn stitch (pop), 180–181
puff stitch (puff st), 179–180
Textured Scarf project, 202–203
three-dimensional designs, shaping, 345
three-dimensional rounds, 143–144
throat of crochet hook, 16
thumb rest of crochet hook, 16
ties, 318–319
tight, edges of fabric are getting too, 337–338
tight chain stitches, fixing, 67
tight style of crocheting, changing hook
    size to compensate for, 39
Tips icon, explained, 4
tips
dealing with frustration over new
    stitch, 13
finding experienced crocheter to help
    explain new techniques, 14
holding the hook and yarn in a
    way that's comfortable, 13
marking pages of books that are
    important or helpful, 14
picking a place to work without
    distractions, 13
practicing a new stitch or technique
    by working on a gauge swatch, 13
reading the stitch descriptions at the
    beginning of each pattern, 13
tools
for blocking, 339–340
crochet hook, 8
hook roll, 31
overview, 8, 29–31
removable stitch markers, 30
ruler, 29
rustproof straight pins, 29
safety pins, 29
scissors, 29
split stitch markers, 30
swift, 31
tape measure, 29
tapestry needles, 30
yarn, 8

tools *(continued)*
  yarn ball winder, 31
  yarn bobbins, 30
  yarn needles, 30
top 2 loops, 82, 83
top loops, stitch placement under both, 188
treble crochet. *See* triple crochet
trellis patterns. *See* mesh crochet
tricot crochet. *See* Tunisian crochet
triple crochet (tr)
  first row of, 94–96
  length of stitch, 100
  overview, 13, 94
  procedure for, 94–97
  second row of, 96–97
  setup for, 94
triple triple crochet (trtr), 100
troubleshooting
  curling corners, 338
  overview, 335
  for shrinking edges of fabric, 336–337
  struggling to fit your hook into stitches,
    336
  for tight edges of fabric, 337–338
  for widening edges of fabric, 337
tunics, 295
Tunisian crochet
  basic technique for, 211–215
  colors, using multiple, 221–224
  cross-stitching on top of, 224–227
  curling problem with, 221
  hooks used in, 210–211
  overview, 209
  shaping, 215–217
Tunisian knit stitch (Tks), 217–219
Tunisian purl stitch (Tps), 219–220
Tunisian simple stitch (Tss)
  binding off, 214–215
  decreasing, 216–217
  as embellishment, 334
  forward (first) half, 211
  foundation row, 212–213
  increasing, 215–216
  overview, 211–212
  return (second) half, 211
  second row, 213–214
  shaping, 215–217
turning chain, 79–80

turning your work, 78–79
twist, 293
types of yarn, 22–23

• U •

UK (English) system for sizing crochet
    hooks, 17–19
UK terminology for stitches, 13, 45
under-the-hook position, 60–61, 64
up the side, carrying yarn, 161
U.S. (American) system for sizing crochet
    hooks, 17–19
U.S. terminology for stitches, 13, 45

• V •

variations
  bead crochet, 367
  broomstick lace, 364–365
  crocheting on fabric, 366–367
  cro-hooking, 366
  double-ended crochet, 366
  free-form crochet, 362–363
  hairpin lace, 365
  Irish crochet, 361–362
  overview, 361
  surface crochet, 363
  tapestry crochet, 364
  wire crochet, 368
vertical rows, sweater created with, 297
V-stitch (V-st)
  International Crochet Symbol for, 172
  overview, 172

• W •

Warm Up America!, 353
Warning icon, explained, 4
washing your work
  dry cleaning, 347
  hand washing, 347
  International Fabric Care Symbols for
    yarn care, 346
  machine washing and drying, 347
  overview, 346
weaving in ends, 84

weight on yarn labels, 26
wet blocking, 340–341
whipstitch, sewing pieces together with, 272–274
wider, edges of fabric are getting, 337
width of stitches, 109
wire crochet, 368
wool yarn, 22
work across, 46
work around, 46
working over a carried strand, 159–160
working other stitches into chain stitches, 69–70
worsted weight, 20
wrapping yarn over the hook, 65–66
written instructions
  abbreviations in, 43–44
  asterisk (*), 48
  brackets in, 47
  bullet (•), 48
  crochet patterns, 43–50
  cross (†), 48
  hyphens in, 44
  jargon in, 46
  overview, 43
  parentheses in, 46–47
  plus sign (+), 48
  rounds, repeating, 49–50
  rows, repeating, 49–50
  special stitches in, 45
  special symbols in, 48–49
  translating a stitch diagram into, 52–55
wrong side
  carrying yarn on, 158–159
  determining, 68–69

• Y •

yardage on yarn labels, 27
yarn
  for beginners, 8
  blends, 293
  combinations, creating, 28–29
  cotton, 22
  cutting, 83
  dye lot, 293
  fair trade fibers, 23
  feel, 293
  fiber content of, 293
  fibers, choosing, 27
  how to hold, 61–63
  local yarn, buying, 353
  natural-colored yarn, using, 353–354
  novelty, 23
  organic, 23
  overview, 20
  plastic, 357–360
  project, matching yarn to your, 27–29
  quality of, 293
  quantity to purchase, 293
  silk, 22
  slip stitch used for joining new ball of, 70
  substituting, 28
  sustainably sourced, 23
  for sweater, choosing, 293
  synthetic, 23
  texture, working with, 27
  twist, 293
  types of, 22–23
  wool, 22
yarn, joining
  at end of row, 110
  in middle of row, 111–112
  overview, 109
yarn ball winder, 31
yarn bobbins, 30
yarn color. See color
yarn content on yarn labels, 27
yarn hand, 61
yarn labels
  article number on, 25
  brand name on, 25
  care instructions on, 25
  color name and number on, 25
  company name and logo on, 25
  dye lot number on, 26
  gauge on, 26
  manufacturer's address on, 26
  ply on, 26

yarn labels *(continued)*
recommended hook size on, 26
weight on, 26
yardage on, 27
yarn content on, 27
yarn needles, 30
yarn over (yo), 65–66
yarn packaging, 24
yarn size. *See* yarn weight
yarn sources
Bernat, 369
Berroco, Inc., 369
Blue Sky Alpacas, Inc., 369
Brown Sheep Company, Inc., 369
Caron International, 370
Cascade Yarns, 370
Coats & Clark, 370
DMC Corporation, 370
Elmore-Pisgah, 370
Fiesta Yarns, 370

Lion Brand Yarn, 370
Patons Yarns, 370
yarn tension, controlling, 67–68
yarn weight
baby weight, 20
bulky weight, 20
chunky weight, 20
comparison of, 21
double knitting (DK) weight, 20
fingering weight, 20
heavy worsted weight, 20
lace weight, 20
light worsted weight, 20
overview, 20–21
sock weight, 20
sport weight, 20
Standard Yarn Weight System, 21
super bulky weight, 20
symbols for, 21
worsted weight, 20

Business/Accounting & Bookkeeping

Bookkeeping For Dummies
978-0-7645-9848-7

eBay Business
All-in-One For Dummies,
2nd Edition
978-0-470-38536-4

Job Interviews
For Dummies,
3rd Edition
978-0-470-17748-8

Resumes For Dummies,
5th Edition
978-0-470-08037-5

Stock Investing
For Dummies,
3rd Edition
978-0-470-40114-9

Successful Time
Management
For Dummies
978-0-470-29034-7

Computer Hardware

BlackBerry For Dummies,
3rd Edition
978-0-470-45762-7

Computers For Seniors
For Dummies
978-0-470-24055-7

iPhone For Dummies,
2nd Edition
978-0-470-42342-4

Laptops For Dummies,
3rd Edition
978-0-470-27759-1

Macs For Dummies,
10th Edition
978-0-470-27817-8

Cooking & Entertaining

Cooking Basics
For Dummies,
3rd Edition
978-0-7645-7206-7

Wine For Dummies,
4th Edition
978-0-470-04579-4

Diet & Nutrition

Dieting For Dummies,
2nd Edition
978-0-7645-4149-0

Nutrition For Dummies,
4th Edition
978-0-471-79868-2

Weight Training
For Dummies,
3rd Edition
978-0-471-76845-6

Digital Photography

Digital Photography
For Dummies,
6th Edition
978-0-470-25074-7

Photoshop Elements 7
For Dummies
978-0-470-39700-8

Gardening

Gardening Basics
For Dummies
978-0-470-03749-2

Organic Gardening
For Dummies,
2nd Edition
978-0-470-43067-5

Green/Sustainable

Green Building
& Remodeling
For Dummies
978-0-470-17559-0

Green Cleaning
For Dummies
978-0-470-39106-8

Green IT For Dummies
978-0-470-38688-0

Health

Diabetes For Dummies,
3rd Edition
978-0-470-27086-8

Food Allergies
For Dummies
978-0-470-09584-3

Living Gluten-Free
For Dummies
978-0-471-77383-2

Hobbies/General

Chess For Dummies,
2nd Edition
978-0-7645-8404-6

Drawing For Dummies
978-0-7645-5476-6

Knitting For Dummies,
2nd Edition
978-0-470-28747-7

Organizing For Dummies
978-0-7645-5300-4

SuDoku For Dummies
978-0-470-01892-7

Home Improvement

Energy Efficient Homes
For Dummies
978-0-470-37602-7

Home Theater
For Dummies,
3rd Edition
978-0-470-41189-6

Living the Country Lifestyle
All-in-One For Dummies
978-0-470-43061-3

Solar Power Your Home
For Dummies
978-0-470-17569-9

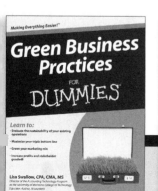

Available wherever books are sold. For more information or to order direct: U.S. customers visit www.dummies.com or call 1-877-762-2974.
U.K. customers visit www.wileyeurope.com or call (0) 1243 843291. Canadian customers visit www.wiley.ca or call 1-800-567-4797.

Internet

Blogging For Dummies,
2nd Edition
978-0-470-23017-6

eBay For Dummies,
6th Edition
978-0-470-49741-8

Facebook For Dummies
978-0-470-26273-3

Google Blogger
For Dummies
978-0-470-40742-4

Web Marketing
For Dummies,
2nd Edition
978-0-470-37181-7

WordPress For Dummies,
2nd Edition
978-0-470-40296-2

Language & Foreign Language

French For Dummies
978-0-7645-5193-2

Italian Phrases
For Dummies
978-0-7645-7203-6

Spanish For Dummies
978-0-7645-5194-9

Spanish For Dummies,
Audio Set
978-0-470-09585-0

Macintosh

Mac OS X Snow Leopard
For Dummies
978-0-470-43543-4

Math & Science

Algebra I For Dummies
978-0-7645-5325-7

Biology For Dummies
978-0-7645-5326-4

Calculus For Dummies
978-0-7645-2498-1

Chemistry For Dummies
978-0-7645-5430-8

Microsoft Office

Excel 2007 For Dummies
978-0-470-03737-9

Office 2007 All-in-One
Desk Reference
For Dummies
978-0-471-78279-7

Music

Guitar For Dummies,
2nd Edition
978-0-7645-9904-0

iPod & iTunes
For Dummies,
6th Edition
978-0-470-39062-7

Piano Exercises
For Dummies
978-0-470-38765-8

Parenting & Education

Parenting For Dummies,
2nd Edition
978-0-7645-5418-6

Type 1 Diabetes
For Dummies
978-0-470-17811-9

Pets

Cats For Dummies,
2nd Edition
978-0-7645-5275-5

Dog Training For Dummies,
2nd Edition
978-0-7645-8418-3

Puppies For Dummies,
2nd Edition
978-0-470-03717-1

Religion & Inspiration

The Bible For Dummies
978-0-7645-5296-0

Catholicism For Dummies
978-0-7645-5391-2

Women in the Bible
For Dummies
978-0-7645-8475-6

Self-Help & Relationship

Anger Management
For Dummies
978-0-470-03715-7

Overcoming Anxiety
For Dummies
978-0-7645-5447-6

Sports

Baseball For Dummies,
3rd Edition
978-0-7645-7537-2

Basketball For Dummies,
2nd Edition
978-0-7645-5248-9

Golf For Dummies,
3rd Edition
978-0-471-76871-5

Web Development

Web Design All-in-One
For Dummies
978-0-470-41796-6

Windows Vista

Windows Vista
For Dummies
978-0-471-75421-3

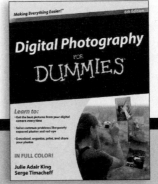

Available wherever books are sold. For more information or to order direct: U.S. customers visit www.dummies.com or call 1-877-762-2974.
U.K. customers visit www.wileyeurope.com or call (0) 1243 843291. Canadian customers visit www.wiley.ca or call 1-800-567-4797.